PACIFIC GROWTH AND FINANCIAL INTERDEPENDENCE

PACIFIC GROWTH AND FINANCIAL INTERDEPENDENCE

Edited by
Augustine H.H. Tan and Basant Kapur

ALLEN and UNWIN Sydney London Boston
In association with
The Pacific Trade and Development Conference Secretariat
The Australian National University

First published in 1986 by
Allen & Unwin Australia Pty Ltd
8 Napier Street, North Sydney NSW 2060 Australia

George Allen & Unwin (Publishers) Ltd
Park Lane, Hemel Hempstead, Herts HP2 4TE England

Allen & Unwin Inc.
8 Winchester Place, Winchester, Mass 01890 USA

National Library of Australia
Cataloguing-in-Publication entry:

Pacific Trade and Development Conference (14th: 1984: Singapore).
  Pacific growth and financial interdependence.

  Bibliography.
  Includes index.
  ISBN 0 86861 904 3.
  ISBN 0 86861 912 4 (pbk.).

  1. Intergovernmental fiscal relations—Pacific Area—Congresses.
  2. Intergovernmental fiscal relations—Asia, Southeastern—
  Congresses. 3. Pacific Area cooperation—Congresses. 4. Asian
  cooperation—Congresses. I. Tan, Augustine H.H. II. Kapur,
  Basant. III. Title.

332′.042′099

Library of Congress Catalog Card Number: 85 73060

Set in 10/11.5 pt Plantin by Graphicraft Typesetters Ltd, Hong Kong
Printed by Singapore National Printers, Singapore

Contents

Tables

FIGURES

Abbreviations

ABM	Asian Bond Market
ACU	Asian Currency Units
ADB	Asian Development Bank
ADCs	Asian Developing Countries
ADM	Asian Dollar Market
AFC	ASEAN Finance Corporation
ALP	Australian Labor Party
ASEAN	Association of Southeast Asian Nations
BA	Bankers' Acceptance
BAAC	Bank for Agriculture and Agricultural Cooperatives (Thailand)
BAPEPAM	Capital Market Executive Agency (Indonesia)
CD	Certificates of Deposit
CIC	Capital Issues Committee (Malaysia)
CIR	Critical Interest Rate
CPF	Central Provident Fund (Singapore)
DACs	Development Assisting Countries
DBU	Domestic Banking Unit
DM	Deutsch Mark
DMB	Deposit Money Banks
DRS	Depository Receipts of Singapore
DTC	Deposit Taking Company
EBM	Euro-Bond Market
EC	European Community
EEC	European Economic Community
EER	Effective Exchange Rate
EPA	Economic Planning Agency
EPF	Employees Provident Fund (Singapore)
EXIMB	Korea Export-Import Bank
FC	Foreign Currency
FCDU	Foreign Currency Deposit Unit
FIR	Finance, Insurance and Real Estate
FS	Financial Statistics
GDP	Gross Domestic Product

GHB	Government Housing Bank (Thailand)
GNP	Gross National Product
GSB	Government Savings Bank (Thailand)
GSIC	Government Securities Investment Corporation (Singapore)
IBF	International Banking Facility
ICOR	Incremental Capital Output Ratio
IFC	International Financial Statistics
IFCT	Industrial Finance Corporation of Thailand
IMF	International Monetary Fund
IMM	International Monetary Market
IWT	Interest Withholding Tax
KDB	Korea Development Bank
KLSE	Kuala Lumpur Stock Exchange
LDCs	Less Developed Countries
LIBOR	London Interbank Offer Rate
MAS	Monetary Authority of Singapore
MMC	Money Market Certificate
MSR	Marginal Savings Rate
NBFI	Non-Bank Financial Institution
NCSC	National Companies and Securities Commission (Australia)
NICs	Newly Industrialising Countries
NOW	Interest-bearing cheque accounts issued by non-bank institutions (USA)
OBU	Offshore Banking Unit
ODA	Official Development Assistance
OECD	Organisation for Economic Cooperation and Development
OIDC	Oil-Importing Developing Country
OOF	Other Official Flows
OPEC	Organisation of Petroleum Exporting Countries
PB5	Pacific Basin (Developed) Five
PB8	Pacific Basin (Less-developed) Eight
PRC	People's Republic of China
SEC	Securities and Exchange Commission
SES	Stock Exchange of Singapore
SET	Securities Exchange of Thailand
SIBOR	Singapore Interbank Offer Rate
SIFO	Small Industrial Finance Office (Thailand)
SIMEX	Singapore International Monetary Exchange
S$NCD	Singapore Dollar Negotiable Certificate of Deposit
TBs	Treasury Bills
US$NCD	United States Dollar Negotiable Certificate of Deposit

Contributors

The Editors: Professor Augustine Tan gained his doctorate from Stanford University. He is an Associate Professor in the Economics Faculty of the National University of Singapore, specialising in international finance and trade. Concurrently, Professor Tan is a Member of Singapore's National Parliament. *Dr Basant Kapur* also obtained his doctorate at Stanford University. Specialising in the theory of international finance, he is a senior lecturer in the Economics Faculty of the National University of Singapore.

Dr Supote Chunanuntathum is an Associate Professor in the Economics Faculty of Thammasat University in Thailand, specialising in international trade.

Dr David Cole of the Development Advisory Service, Harvard University is the co-author of *Financial Development in Korea, 1945–1978* (1983).

Dr Peter Drake is Professor of Economics at the University of New England. Specialising in Asian and Pacific economic development, his publications include *Money, Finance and Development* (1980).

Professor Herbert Grubel is Professor of Economics at Simon Fraser University in Vancouver, Canada. International banking has been the subject of his recent publications.

Professor John Hewson of the Department of Economics, University of New South Wales is currently a consultant for a major Australian bank. He has also acted as a consultant for the Australian Government. Professor Hewson specialises in international banking.

Professor Wontack Hong of the International Economics Faculty of Seoul National University specialises in international trade and economic development. His publications include *Trade Distortions and Employment Growth in Korea* (1979).

Dr William James is a Research Associate in the Resources Systems Institute of the East-West Centre, Hawaii.

Dr Lee Sheng-Yi is an Associate Professor at the National University of Singapore, specialising in international financial cooperation. He is the co-author of *Financial Structures and Monetary Policies in Southeast Asia* (1982).

Dr Lin See-Yan is the Deputy Governor of the Bank Negara Malaysia.

Professor Chesada Loohawenchit works concurrently at Thammasat University and with the Industrial Finance Corporation of Thailand. He specialises in finance and industry.

Dr Jorge Braga de Macedo is an Associate Professor of Economics at Princeton University. His areas of specialisation is international macro-economics.

Professor Ronald McKinnon of the Department of Economics and the Hoover Institution, Stanford University is the author of the influential work *Money and Capital in Economic Development* (1973). He specialises in the role of finance in economic development.

Professor Seiji Naya is the Director of the Resource Systems Institute, East-West Centre and Professor of Economics at the University of Hawaii.

Professor Yung Chul Park is with the Economics Faculty of Korea University. He co-authored *Financial Development in Korea, 1945–1978* (1983). Professor Park's area of specialisation is international macro-economics and development.

Professor Hugh Patrick, now at Columbia University, specialises in, and has published extensively on, financial development in Asian nations.

Professor Eisuke Sakakibara is the Director of the General Administration and Planning Department of the Japan Centre for International Finance.

Dr Masaru Yoshitomi is the Deputy Director-General of the Economic Research Institute in the Economic Planning Agency of Japan. He is presently attached to the OECD, Paris.

Dr Tsao Yuan is a lecturer in the Economics and Statistics Department of the National University of Singapore. She specialises in industrial economics and international capital movements.

Preface

This volume presents the papers written for the Fourteenth Pacific Trade and Development (PAFTAD) Conference, held in Singapore during June 18–21 1984.

The theme of the Conference was 'Pacific Growth and Financial Interdependence'. As such, it represented branching out from the themes of previous Conferences which have tended to focus primarily on trade in goods. Trade in services has in recent years come to attract a good deal of attention, and among services, those of financial intermediaries have obviously been of rapidly growing importance throughout the world economy, and not least in the Pacific area.

Partly by way of background, but also for its intrinsic interest, the first part of the Conference examined issues of 'financial development' in the less developed countries of the Pacific Basin. Financial development, in the sense of deepening of financial structure, the emergence and increasing sophistication of money, banks, non-bank financial intermediaries and security markets, has come to be recognised as an important aspect of economic development. There has been much discussion of the role of government in the financial system, some advocating deregulation, others emphasising the need for positive intervention to promote financial development. Recent events have also led to second thoughts about the desirability of prudential aspects of bank management and regulation. The considerable diversity of experience and viewpoints among the countries of the Pacific region provides rich material for examination of these issues. Such examination takes up most of Parts I and II of this volume.

Parts III and IV focus on financial interdependence among the countries of the Pacific Basin, and especially the problems that have arisen in the relationship between the Japanese and the US economies, the yen and the dollar. The papers and discussion of this set of issues have brought out clearly the benefits and costs on financial interdependence and the main policy options available to handle these complex problems in the best interests of the countries and people of the region.

The Conference was jointly organised by the Department of Economics and Statistics of the National University of Singapore, and the Economic Society of Singapore. It was assisted by advice from the international steering committee of the conference series, comprising Kiyoshi Kojima and Saburo Okita in Japan, Lawrence B. Krause and Hugh Patrick in the United States, Narongchai Akrasanee in Thailand, Romeo Bautista in the Philippines, H. Edward English in Canada and Sir John Crawford and Peter Drysdale in Australia. H.W. Arndt was instrumental in the initial stages of choosing a topic for the Conference. We are also grateful for financial support from the following organisations: Asian Development Bank, Ford and Asia Foundations, the Rockefeller Brothers Fund, Monetary Authority of Singapore and National Institute for Research Advancement, Japan and the Australian National University.

For the convenience of readers, and especially busy readers, the editors have prepared a summary of the papers and discussion which constitutes chapter 1 of this volume.

A.H.H.T. and B.K.
September 1984

1 Introduction: summary of chapters and discussion

AUGUSTINE H.H. TAN AND BASANT KAPUR

The title and theme of this book, 'Pacific Growth and Financial Interdependence', might appear to carry the implicit presumption that the promotion of financial interdependence among the countries of the Pacific Basin is considered to be a desideratum. Deeper reflection will, however, reveal that this presumption has to be carefully qualified. 'Financial interdependence' is a multi-faceted phenomenon, and the kinds of financial relationship that any particular country might wish to enter into with other countries are to a large extend dependent upon the level of domestic, real and financial development that it has attained.

Accordingly, there is a natural tendency to examine the interplay between domestic and international financial structures. As a background, the second chapter by Cole and Patrick documents the broad patterns of domestic financial development of the Pacific Basin economies, especially the developing ones. Over the 1960–81 period, the latter have on the whole undergone substantial 'financial deepening', as measured by trends in the ratios of various financial aggregates to GNP; although as Sir Frank Holmes suggests,[1] data constraints generally preclude the construction of completely accurate measures of financial development. Generally, the authors find that 'commercial banks play a major, indeed frequently dominant, role in the financial growth of all countries'; and that 'economic and financial growth have gone together'.[2]

There is, however, considerable diversity in the features of an individual country's financial landscape, primarily on account of different governmental financial regulations and national inflation rates. Financial repression, while not as extreme as in certain Latin American countries, continues to prevail to varying degrees, because of governmental controls on interest rates and credit allocations. As a consequence, informal 'kerb markets' continue to flourish, and it is not uncommon for privileged borrowers in certain countries to onlend credit received by them at preferential rates to less favoured enterprises. Another characteristic 'had been the emergence of large, family-owned, financial and industrial conglomerates'.[3]

While informal credit markets play a valuable role in complementing formal credit institutions where the latter are repressed, the two sets of institutions taken together are not as efficient in mobilising and allocating funds economy-wide as a liberalised financial system would be. (Although, as Augustine Tan pointed out in discussion, this is not to deny that even in the latter informal markets are likely to continue to have some residual role to play, especially in channelling credit to small borrowers, in both the urban and the rural sectors.) Consideration of that fact has induced many governments to initiate attempts at liberalisation or 'deregulation'. These attempts have generally been successful to varying degres, although a number of problems have been encountered. For example, 'vested interests enjoying market-niche rents strongly resist financial liberalisation of their markets'.[4] Inadvertent exchange-rate policy can also frustrate domestic liberalisation attempts. Moreover, deregulation itself should be effected with considerable caution: there is a need to ensure that, in conjunction with privatisation, it does not lead to a concentration of financial resources 'in the hands of a few wealthy families or industrial groups who take on undue risks or allocate funds to their own purposes in expectation of a government bail-out in emergency'.[5] More generally, prudential standards designed to protect the interest of depositors, shareholders, and others, have to be judiciously formulated and enforced. On the whole, the authors are of the view that further—though possibly uneven—progress will be made on the liberalisation front.

The third chapter, by Tsao Yuan, provides a useful overview of the pattern and evolution of financial flows among the Pacific Basin countries. In particular, the chapter focuses on an aspect which has not been adequately covered in the literature, that of the geographical distribution of financial flows among the Pacific Basin countries, as a first step towards examining financial interdependence within the Pacific Basin.

The main findings of the chapter are that flows from the Pacific Basin Industrialised Five (PB5), comprising Australia, Canada, Japan, New Zealand and the United States, to the Pacific Basin Industrialising Eight (PB8), comprising the five ASEAN countries together with Hong Kong, South Korea and Taiwan, have been relatively more important than flows from the PB5 to other developing countries or flows from other sources to the PB8 in the 1970s and early 1980s. Comparing 1970–72 and 1980–82, the flows of net ODA and net total flows from the PB5 have also increased in relative importance. Since most of the PB8 countries have an investment–savings gap, the PB5 countries have therefore helped in their developmental efforts by being their most important source of foreign funds.

Where foreign investment is concerned the two largest investors in the PB8 countries are the US and Japan, with the US taking the lead in the People's Republic of China as well. From the investor countries' point of view, the PB8 as a region is not as important to the US as it is to Japan; more than a quarter of all Japanese investments abroad were in the PB8 countries in 1982. A relatively newer phenomenon is the overseas investment undertaken by the Asian NICs. Hong Kong has sizeable investments in the other PB8 countries such as textiles in Indonesia. Singapore's investments in Malaysia are substantial. Korean and Taiwanese overseas investments have grown significantly in recent years with a shift of emphasis away from Southeast Asia towards the US partly as a defensive measure and partly to acquire new technology.

The PB5 countries have also been a more important source of medium- and long-term loans to the PB8 countries (excluding Taiwan) than the European countries. This is more evident for official bilateral public debt, but is true for privately sourced public debt as well. Among the PB8 countries Indonesia is the largest recipient of net ODA, private-sector and total flows. Both Japan and the US are the largest sources of flows among the PB5 countries, with Japan playing a leading role in total flows because of the importance of the PB8 countries to her.

The roles of Singapore and Hong Kong, the two offshore centres in the region, are examined. Broadly speaking the data for both show that Asia as a region has been a net borrower with positive inflows to the region over time, implying that offshore centres do perform the function of the geographical distribution of funds. Other types of flows, for which data are not available, are also discussed. The chapter concludes with a discussion of the possible determinants of the financial flows described above.

In chapter 4, Drake explores the state of development of equity and bond markets in the developing countries of the Pacific region and in Australia. On the whole, these are in a fairly rudimentary state, primarily on account of supply, rather than demand inhibitions. The small size of many establishments in LDCs militates against security flotation on their part, on account of the high costs involved, such as those entailed by the need to fulfil various accounting standards. Such costs would only be worth incurring for a particular small company if it were contemplating a rather large share issue, which prospective shareholders might consider to be a risky proposition. As far as the larger enterprises are concerned, they frequently enjoy access to long-term bank financing at preferential rates of interest, either on account of government policy, or of their membership in financial-cum-industrial conglomerates. Finally, the close-knit, familial character of many enterprises has created a predispositon on their part to rely on the gradual accumulation of internal funds or on bank financing, rather than on security issue, on account of the disclosure requirements entailed by the latter.

The issue of the appropriate extent and form of regulation of stock-market activities is, as Phillip Anisan pointed out in discussion, a delicate one. On the one hand, there is a need to prevent fraudulent practices such as insider trading, share issues by 'fly-by-night' companies, and the like. On the other hand, excessive regulation might inhibit the stock market from efficiently.performing its basic capital-mobilisation and risk-sharing functions, especially in view of the aversion to disclosure mentioned above. The thinness of many stock markets further accentuates the problem; it becomes difficult, for example, to draw the line between 'excessive speculative manipulation' of the stock market, and the efficient assumption of risk-taking activities by 'genuine' speculators. One might even wish to argue that a stock market must attain a 'critical minimum size' before it is able to function with an adequate degree of effectiveness, and that the achievement of this would depend upon the extent of industrial development and on governmental policy measures, many of which, such as various kinds of tax incentives and reductions in the extent of preferential access to bank credit, are discussed in the chapter. Finally, one should point out that Malaysia, Singapore, and the Philippines tend to have more active stock markets than the other countries: the former two on account of the extensive involvement of foreign and joint-venture enterprises in their national economies and the fact that their banking systems are geared primarily towards the provision of short-term finance. In the latter it is primarily because of the share-flotation proclivities of resource-related enterprises, which derive in part from the Philippines' exposure to American institutions.

Indeed, the issue of governmental regulation, and the manner in which its consequences ramify throughout the financial system, emerges as one of the major themes of this volume. In chapter 7, a fascinating case study is provided by the Hong and Park discussion of the Korean experience. The Korean government has consistently sought to ensure that export-oriented enterprises receive preferential treatment in terms of loan allocations, both short- and long-term, and interest rates charged. At the same time, Hong and Park's econometric investigations suggest that a considerable amount of 'credit fungibility,' or 'credit diversion' has occurred, whereby these enterprises relend fairly substantial amounts of credit received to other, less favoured, sectors in the thriving informal credit markets. That industrial and financial enterprises frequently operate under the same conglomerate umbrella, and that banks have access to a central bank rediscounting facility for export-related bills at favourable discount rates, are factors that might well facilitate these activities.

The issue therefore arises, and was posed by both Mohammad Ariff and Peter Drysdale in discussion, as to how effective such a preferential credit policy has actually been in terms of encouraging export expansion. It would appear that even though credit diversion has occurred, Korean export growth has been spectacular. One might suggest two possible reasons for this, aside from the contribution of other policy measures such as exchange-rate policy. First, there are various costs involved in seeking to divert credit, so that it has been far from complete. Second, as suggested by Cole and Patrick in chapter 2, the relending of credit by export-oriented enterprises at significantly higher interest rates is an important source of profits to them. Since their eligibility for preferential credit treatment depends on their export performance, the latter is thereby indirectly encouraged. We have here an illustration of how regulatory measures can create patterns of economic behaviour that were not anticipated by the authorities. The entire subject is one that warrants considerable further investigation, as the authors themselves recognise. Such an investigation would also have to encompass an evaluation of the efficiency of the preferential credit policy. There is some evidence that more capital-intensive sectors are characterised by higher loan–value-added ratios, higher degrees of credit diversion, and lower gross rates of return to capital, than more labour-intensive ones, but have also increased their share of total manufacturing exports. While this would appear to constitute prima facie evidence of static inefficiency, one has to consider social rather than private rates of return (inclusive of external effects, for example), and dynamic as well as static efficiency aspects.

The chapter on 'ASEAN: Financial Development and Interdependence' by

Lin See Yan raises some thought-provoking issues. All the ASEAN countries have, since the 1960s, experienced increased 'financial deepening', as measured, for example, by M2–GNP and Total Financial Asset–GNP ratios. The more rapidly growing ASEAN economies, namely Malaysia and Singapore, also experienced the most rapid pace of financial deepening, tending to support the Shaw and McKinnon theses[6] as to the existence of a complementary relationship between real and financial development.

However, the extent and growth of financial interdependence among the ASEAN economies has been much less spectacular. 'Financial interdependence' was shown to be a multi-faceted concept. Among its many indicators are: 'the extent to which the settlement of external debt outstanding among ASEAN countries occurs; common listing in the stock exchange; and the simultaneity of movements in inflation, real money balances, exchange rates, and interest rates in the region'.[7] Financial interdependence as defined by these criteria has been shown to be very weak, with the exception of somewhat stronger financial ties between Malaysia and Singapore, on account of historical, geographic, and socio-economic links.

In this connection, two issues require further analytical consideration. First, is increased financial interdependence necessarily a desirable goal? McKinnon[8] has suggested that the more successful a country is in mobilising financial resources domestically, the less, ceteris paribus, its dependence on external finance. Similarly, suggestions that the Singapore dollar be promoted as a regional 'vehicle currency' for the settlement of third-party trading transactions have been resisted by the Singaporean authorities, on account of fears that the domestic economy would be destabilised by portfolio shifts on the part of foreign asset-holders between Singapore dollars and other assets. Secondly, are the 'beneficial' forms of financial interdependence, if any, independent of the extent of trade and investment flows among the ASEAN nations? Various schemes currently being mooted to enhance financial linkages, such as the development of an ASEAN Bankers' Acceptances Market, would appear to suggest that the answer is in the main negative.

A more detailed discussion of the Thai experience is provided in chapter 6 by Cole, Chunanuntathum, and Loohawenchit. Financial deepening, as measured by the M1–GDP and broader ratios, has occurred consistently steadily over the 1960–82 period, reflecting both the rapid growth of income and the maintenance of high positive real rates of interest on most financial assets during most of the period. At the same time, the M1–GDP ratio has declined, due essentially to the offering of higher rates of return on competing assets, and to improved efficiency in the use of transactions balances. As in other developing countries, commercial banks dominate the financial system, being responsible, for example, for 70.3 per cent of total deposit mobilisation in 1982. However, finance and security companies have succeeded in obtaining a rapidly rising share of total deposit mobilisation, rising 0.73 per cent in 1969 to 16.41 per cent of 1982.

The latter phenomenon is in part symptomatic of the fact that the Thai financial system continues to be somewhat repressed. There is strict control over the issue of new licences for banks, and the latter are also subject to more stringent ceilings on interest rates than finance and securities companies are. Commercial banks have also, since 1975, been required to channel a certain minimum percentage of their total deposits to the agricultural sector, while there also exist several other financial institutions, such as the Industrial Finance Corporation of Thailand, the Government Housing Bank, the Small Industrial Finance Office, and others, which 'perform specialised functions with a basic aim of providing subsidised credits to government-designated priority sectors'.[9] A large, unregulated money market continues to exist. It also appears that some participants in this market have access to bank credit, and relend some of the funds to earn higher returns on riskier loans.

The authors also undertake a regression analysis of the demands for the various types of financial assets, the explanatory variable being various interest rates and GDP. In general, the signs were as expected, except that the inflation rate enters positively in the demand for savings deposits, which the authors attribute to the tendency for higher inflation rates to induce a shift away from currency and demand deposits towards savings deposits, the latter being also highly liquid. The interest rate on finance-company promissory notes, which is less stringently regulated than interest rates on bank savings and time deposits, appears to reflect movements of interest rates in the unregulated markets fairly well. Among other things, this may assist in explaning why GDP is the only significant explanatory variable in the demand for finance-company promissory notes.

In Part III, international issues are dealt with more specifically. Hewson's chapter on 'The Internationalisation of Banking' covers three areas The first deals with the broad trends in the phenomenon of international banking. The distinguishing features of international banking transactions are the dominance of the interbank market, the wholesale nature of the market, the virtually complete freedom for interest rates to respond to supply and demand forces, the formal linking of most loan rates to deposit rates, the largeness of the loans and thus the need for syndication, and the typical lack of government regulation. Hewson identifies the two main functions of multinational banking as liquidity distribution and liquidity creation. Multinational banks can be conceived of as operating collectively as an efficient distribution mechanism, for shifting funds of similar liquidity from lenders to borrowers on a global scale. The system also creates liquidity through maturity transformation, such as turning 3–6 month OPEC deposits into 10–15 year loans to oil-importing countries. Loan/deposit interest spreads are narrower than in domestic banking partly because multinational, offshore banking is free from domestic banking regulations, and partly because the syndication of loans spreads both maturity transformation and default risks. In commenting upon this, David Schulze suggested a third reason: significant economies associated with increasing deposit and loan sizes. Richard Cooper, however, disagreed, arguing that the so-called economies of scale really stemmed from indivisibilities. Were it not so there would be only one international financial centre in the world. Schulze also posed the question whether the narrower loan/deposit spread of offshore banks does not reflect a systematic underestimation of risks. This would appear to be so in the case of sovereign risks. Moreover, as Chia Siow Yue pointed out, Eurocurrency-type loans are not appropriate for balance-of-payments financing or development financing of developing countries. Witness the debt-rescheduling problem!

Hewson defines multinational or offshore banking as those transactions with residents or non-residents in foreign or domestic currencies from an offshore base. This is to be distinguished from 'traditional international banking' encompassing home-based transactions with residents and non-residents in foreign currencies, and transactions with non-residents in domestic currency.

Chia Siow Yue suggested a distinction between international financial centres and regional financial centres. The former, such as London and New York, have a global character while the latter have extra-regional sources and/or uses of funds. Regional centres may be further classified into 'booking centres' like Singapore and 'collection centres' like Bahrain. Chia also mentioned the benefits of hosting offshore activities such as providing complementary financial services and extending the international connections of city-states like Hong Kong and Singapore, providing financial access for capital-scarce countries like the Philippines, and providing an intermediate step towards financial liberalisation, as in Tokyo. However, as Chia pointed out, there are also costs of establishing financial centres such as heavy investment in the financial, communication and transportation infrastructure, the loss of autonomy in monetary policy and the possibility of capital outflows.

The second area of Hewson's chapter covers offshore banking in the Asian-Pacific region, with special reference to Singapore. The internationalisation of banking in the region went through the same three stages of development as other centres: expansion of traditional international banking from the mid-1950s to the mid-1960s, development and spread of offshore banking, mid-1960s to the end of the 1970s, and a period of slower growth, rationalisation and consolidation, from the early 1980s to date. Other important developments include the significant increase in both credits from and deposits with international banks by most countries in the region, the generally greater prominence of international banking business in the balance sheets of most banks, the significant relaxation of exchange markets, and the very rapid development of a number of regional financial centres.

Singapore developed as a financial centre because of a favourable time zone, proximity to Asia and its capitals, strong domestic economic performance, substantial financial and telecommunications infrastructure, pleasant living conditions and most importantly the continuous support and encouragement provided by the government. Despite such encouragement Singapore remains essentially a funding centre, complementary to Hong Kong, and has failed to attract a significant portion of the deposits of countries in the region. Domestic monetary restrictions gave rise to round-tripping and swap transactions. Augustine Tan pointed out in discussion that the later may also be a reflection of interest arbitrage while the movement of Singapore dollars to Hong Kong may be a means of tax avoidance, as Singapore residents are taxed on ACU interest. He also questioned Hewson's assertion that the ACU is heavily underwritten by the government and its instrumentalities. Hewson claims that the Singapore dollar is more internationalised than desired by the government. The domestic banking system remains underdeveloped and insulated, dominated by four Chinese banks; constrained and distorted by the large savings garnered by the Central Provident Fund (CPF). Tan disagreed with Professor Hewson's point that the CPF artificially stabilises the Singapore dollar; rather the strength of the latter derives from prudent fiscal policy, low inflation and a climate of confidence that engenders capital inflow.

The third part of Hewson's chapter deals with Australia banking. Australian banks were generally slow to internationalise because of heavy protection and oligopoly, the relatively slow process of internationalisation of Australian corporate activity, the ability of Australian banks to service corporate needs through domestic banking, the protective nature of the domestic foreign-exchange market and the slow recognition of profit opportunities available in overseas banking activities. Foreign banks in Australia control about two-thirds of merchant banking and 38 per cent of finance-company activities. There are also over a hundred representative offices of foreign banks. However, direct access by foreign banks to trading or commercial banking is quite restricted. Australia has accelerated the process of financial deregulation, including tender sales of government securities, abolition of exchange controls, free floating of the Australian dollar and the licensing of non-banks as foreign-exchange dealers. Foreign banks are likely to be required to have Australian equity participation. Banks from countries like China, Japan, Singapore and New Zealand are likely to be treated differently from other foreign banks. In Hewson's view, the factors favouring an offshore banking centre in Australia include a time-zone advantage, a natural deposit and loan base and potential business with New Zealand, Indonesia, Papua New Guinea and the Pacific Islands. In support of the second factor, he pointed out that Australia has ranked as either first or second largest Asian borrower in the syndicated loan market; in June 1983 Australia absorbed US$10.3 billion loans from overseas banks. Moreover Australia's GDP is more than half the sum of national products of ten major Asian countries, excluding Japan. The Asian–Pacific region can readily support another offshore centre. The question is whether the Australian government would have the kind of vision, purpose and persistence to develop it.

In response, Chia Siow Yue emphasised the difficulties of distance and isolation. Australia would have to improve on her transport, communications and access to information. Moreover, Australia would have to provide concessions and liberalise banking regulations.

Dr Lee's chapter on 'Developing Asian Financial Centres' compares the development of offshore financial centres (OFC) in Singapore, Hong Kong and the Philippines. Singapore and Hong Kong provide 'financial entrepot services' in that funds are primarily borrowed from overseas and relent overseas. Manila, on the other hand, is domestically oriented with resident non-bank customers taking up the bulk of deposits and loans. Kiyoshi Kojima commented that it might be better to describe these centres as developing ones whose own currencies are used for local transactions only, in contrast to developed centres like London and New York whose currencies are internationalised.

Lee notes the considerable financial deepening of the Singapore economy, while the development of the OFC has made it more open. The OFC was established in 1968 and went through several stages of growth and consolidation. The net size of the centre is now about 6 per cent of the Eurodollar market, narrowly defined. The establishment and rapid growth of the centre was due to the vigorous encouragement of the Singapore government which progressively deregulated the market and offered several tax concessions. These included the abolition of exchange controls (1978), the abolition of the withholding tax of 40 per cent on interest earned, the concessionary 10 per cent tax on loan interest and offshore income and the drastic reduction of the ad valorem duty on ACU offshore loan agreements from 0.5 per cent to a limit of US$500. In fact, the tax system discriminates in favour of the OFC. Nevertheless, a separation fence exists between the OFC and domestic banking, although there has been some erosion.

The Singapore OFC is marked by the predominance of interbank funds. In 1968–70, deposits were collected largely from Asia and invested in London or New York; since then this pattern has been reversed. The loans are mainly denominated in US dollars. The market is principally short-term in nature and, in contrast to Manila, residents take up a small and declining proportion of deposits and loans. Longer term financing is available through the Asian Bond Market which was launched in 1971. As elsewhere, the interest-rate spread is lower for the OFC than for domestic banking. However, interest rates in Singapore have been consistently lower than OFC rates, reflecting the strength of the Singapore dollar and its tendency to appreciate. Unlike Hong Kong, the Monetary Authority of Singapore exercises prudential supervision.

Ralph Bryant pointed out three policy dilemmas for Singapore. The goal of developing the OFC can lead to a further erosion of the separation fence. Moreover, it can work at cross-purposes with the desire for prudential financial regulation and supervision. Finally, the greater financial interdependence increases the vulnerability of the economy to external shocks. It would take careful balancing of policies to minimise the conflicts.

The laissez-faire atmosphere of Hong Kong has produced a different kind of OFC from that of Singapore. There are more financial institutions; financial regulations and supervision are lax and the OFC is integrated with, rather than segregated from, domestic banking. As a result, the growth rate of assets of financial institutions has been higher in Hong Kong than in Singapore. The contribution of the financial sector in Hong Kong is also much higher than in Singapore. However, the system is inflation-prone and promotes a shift to the use of foreign money. The latter was accelerated during the recent political crisis.

According to Ralph Bryant, three policy issues face Hong Kong: the adequacy of scope and intensity of prudential financial supervision; managing the transition to 1997; and the wisdom of continuing with the present financial arrangements and policies. Lee proposes either a central bank or the strengthening of the Exchange Fund to provide better financial control.

The key to Hong Kong's and its OFC's future, however, lies with China. The recent agreement between China and Britain provides for a special administrative zone with considerable autonomy. Whether this will restore confidence remains to be seen. Traditionally, as Lee notes, Hong Kong has served China as an entrepot, as a window to international trade and finance, a source of tourism, remittances, investment opportunities and capital.

Lee points out that the Manila OFC was developed to prevent capital flight. That this is so may be seen in the preponderance among non-bank customers of resident deposits and loans. The centre experienced little growth between 1972–76 because of overly restrictive regulations. However, there was rapid growth after 1976 and by September 1983 the centre commanded funds totalling nearly 11 per cent of Singapore's OFC. A separation fence exists between Manila's OFC and domestic banking as in the 1968 Singapore model. The problems facing the Philippines in its attempt to develop its OFC include a highly regulated and inward-looking economy, an underdeveloped financial infrastructure; inadequate telecommunications; sluggish growth rates in 1980 –84; and political instability and the consequent debt problem. Lee recommends financial liberalisation, to the extent allowed by the crisis.

The foreign-exchange markets of the three financial centres are characterised by the predominance of third-currency and interbank transactions. Their forward markets are relatively underdeveloped.

Chapter 10, on the 'Internationalisation of the Tokyo Financial Markets', deals with the reforms of the Japanese financial system, particularly the liberalisation of the Tokyo capital market and the internationalisation of the yen. In Sakakibara's view, the Tokyo capital market is already considerably internationalised and deregulated; especially with the impetus of computers and electronic banking, internationalisation is inevitable. There has been a rapid expansion of financial operations of non-financial corporations, and the outstanding government bonds amount to 39 per cent of GNP. These factors should at least lead to deregulation of the short-term financial markets. However, there are five unsatisfactory features: administrative controls on call and bill transactions through six money dealers; the bulk of national bonds are traditionally underwritten by a captive syndicate; private bond markets are dominated by four major securities companies and eight commissioned banks; restrictive membership (excluding foreigners) of the Tokyo Stock Exchange; and the fixed commission structure for stock brokerage.

Sakakibara next deals with the Hosomi proposal for an International Banking Facility (IBF). This would be implemented gradually, step by step, taking care to maintain a separation fence between offshore and domestic banking. Financial institutions would set up special separate IBF accounts which would be prohibited from maintaining yen settlement accounts and from negotiable CD, BA issues. Non-bank residents would not be allowed to have IBF deposits, which would be exempt from interest rates, reserve and deposit insurance requirements and the withholding tax on interest. Permissible IBF assets would include advances and loans to non-residents, non-resident bonds, loans/deposits with other IBFs and overseas financial institutions, and loans/deposits with the domestic and overseas main and branch offices of financial institutions with IBFs.

The general reaction of the Japanese financial community was that the pace of internationalisation of the yen and deregulation would be too rapid. They also objected to the two-tier system, separating the IBF from domestic banking. The possibility of leakage of Euroyen into the domestic market would dilute the Central Bank's control of the money supply. Besides, they felt that the offshore yen market was already big enough.

A Japanese–American financial agreement was reached in May 1984. It allowed for deregulation of European impact loans, further liberalisation of CD-related issues and the possible creation of a TB market. Furthermore, there would be deregulation of Euroyen bond issues. Lastly, the Japanese would consider the membership issue in the Tokyo Stock Exchange. Sakakibara maintained that deregulation should proceed first with the interbank market, followed by the wholesale market, then deregulation of interest rates for large deposits, and finally the desegmentation of banking business. His chapter provoked considerable comment.

Robert Chia questioned whether the highly lucrative Japanese pension-fund market, estimated to be worth US$50 million, would be opened to foreigners, whether foreign acquisition of Japanese banks would be allowed, and queried the impact of the development of the Euroyen market on the Asian dollar market.

Zenta Nakajima commented that as far as the interbank market is concerned, there are now practically no binding official regulations. Moreover, the Bank of Japan had never disapproved of direct bank dealing. He was concerned about the possible adverse effects of too-sudden deregulation of interbank deposit rates. In his view financial internationalisation implies capital mobility which would restrict the scope of monetary and fiscal policies. It would also lead to a more pronounced synchronisation of domestic and US long-term interest rates.

Lawrence Krause pointed out that the yen–dollar imbalance had little to do with alleged Japanese manipulation of the yen or the financial-market restrictions; rather it had to do with the asymmetry of monetary and fiscal policies in the US and Japan. Richard Cooper thought that the real intent behind the US push for liberalisation of the Japanese financial system was to deflect attention from more central US–Japan frictions, particularly in trade relations. Shinichi Ichimura commented on the anomaly of Tokyo's relatively weak position as a financial centre, given Japan's economic prominence. He thought that the third world would benefit from internationalisation of the Japanese financial system through better access to the market and yen financing.

Grubel's chapter on 'Trade In Financial Services' defines the two tasks of the financial service industry (FSI) as the clearing of payments among economic agents, whether foreign or local, and intermediating between ultimate savers and borrowers of funds. The latter involves not only the sale and ultimate redemption of financial obligations but also the brokering of existing debt instruments.

Data on the actual contribution of the FSI to GDP are not readily available. The category 'Finance, Insurance and Real Estate' (FIR), as a proportion of GDP, ranges from 9.6 per cent for Canada to 20.7 per cent for the US; for Indonesia it is 4.9 per cent, for Malaysia 8.3 per cent, for Singapore 17 per cent and for Hong Kong 20.8 per cent. These figures are for 1980 and include the contributions of insurance and real estate. From the figures available for Canada it would appear that the contribution to GDP of FSI proper is relatively small at 2.3 per cent. This conclusion was challenged by Edward English and Heinz Arndt, whose figures showed 8 per cent for Canada and 11.3 per cent for the US. It is clear that more detailed study would be necessary to unravel the true picture.

Grubel defined trade in financial services as that part of the value-added of financial intermediaries which is exported or imported. This is not the same as the international capital flows which are enabled by these intermediation activities, and are different from the international factor-service flows, consisting of interest and dividends on foreign-asset holdings. Trade in financial services mainly takes the form of intermediate inputs into conventional traded goods and services and, one might add, international transfers of factors of production, particularly capital.

Unfortunately, balance-of-payments statistics do not include statistics on trade in financial services because, historically, these have been either intermediate inputs into exportables or they have been non-tradable. However, with the spread of multinational banks and enterprises and increased travel, financial services have ceased as non-tradables. To the extent that these are embodied in exports of goods and other services, a bias is involved. For small open economies like Hong Kong and Singapore this bias may be serious.

Grubel also distinguishes between four types of direct trade in financial services: traditional capital-flows intermediation; 'trade diversion' in financial services due to differential regulations and taxation, e.g. offshore banking; arbitrage between national money markets; and direct financial services and retail business, e.g. credit cards, travellers' cheques, futures trading.

Referring to the first type of direct trade in financial services, Grubel identifies Hong Kong and Singapore as regional, supranational financial centres whose comparative advantage grew from the imparted skills of British banking, central location, government support, human capital, good communications and favourable taxation and regulatory environment. He predicts that the Hong Kong and Singapore financial centres will continue to grow as income and wealth grow in the Pacific region.

Technological changes and differential regulation have made financial services increasingly tradable. Capital-market efficiency has increased in financial centres like Hong Kong and Singapore. On the other hand the costs are in terms of reduced national economic sovereignty and greater susceptibility to cyclical and random disturbances. In Richard Cooper's view, Hong Kong and Singapore have managed to reduce these costs by a strict separation between offshore and domestic banking and by effective management. He predicted, however, that the Asian currency business could shrink as deregulation becomes more general.

Heinz Arndt questioned whether differential regulations were the entire rationale behind the development of offshore banking. He also pointed out that, though no attempt has been made to measure trade in financial services, the qualitative evidence leaves very little doubt that trade in financial services has grown very rapidly in the last two decades, even faster than the output of such services. Cooper pointed to the fact that, over the last thirty years, trade in services, including financial services, had grown faster than trade in goods. This was particularly striking for Singapore. He also expected the share of international financial services in GDP to grow in the immediate future.

Yoshitomi's chapter on 'Recent US–Japan Financial Interactions Under Flexible Exchange Rates' addresses four issues: the characteristics of recent misaligned dollar–yen exchange rates and the new dilemma facing Japanese macropolicies; US–Japan financial interdependence under flexible exchange rates; the nature and persistency of the current-account surplus of Japan; and the role of the Japanese financial market for world economic development.

In 1984 Japan's current-account surplus was estimated to be US$3.1 billion or nearly 3 per cent of GNP. This is largely a reflection of US budget and trade deficits. The US budget deficit has helped to trigger strong US economy recovery since early 1983, accompanied by high real interest rates. Consequently the US dollar is highly overvalued, causing a huge current-account deficit of $81 billion in 1984 and nearly $100 billion in 1985. The net result is that the US absorbs world savings amounting to almost 3 per cent of her GNP.

Yoshitomi dismisses the proposal to increase Japanese domestic spending for three reasons: fiscal policy should be aimed at achieving domestic rather than external equilibrium; under floating rates, fiscal policy cannot achieve the switching required because of full employment at home and because the yen exchange rate is externally determined; and, moreover, this would boost the already high level of real interest rates in the world, without increasing world savings. An interest-equalisation tax plus investment-tax credit would have questionable effectiveness as they may reduce capital outflow to the US and thereby increase US interest rates.

Yoshitomi states that theoretically it cannot be predetermined whether an expansionary fiscal policy at home causes the exchange rate of the home currency to appreciate or depreciate. The simulations by the Economic Planning Unit's World Econometric Model produced the following results: (1) the effective exchange rate of the US dollar increases when US fiscal policy is expansionary because higher interest rates attract net capital inflow, outweighing the worsening of the current account, in contrast to other countries' experience; (2) the effect of US fiscal policy expansion is transmitted to real GNP of other countries with greater force under flexible than under fixed exchange rates; (3) high US interest rates are transmitted to other countries to a much lesser extent under flexible rates than under flexible exchange rates, because of the depreciating Deutschmark in response to US fiscal expansion; (5) for Japan, there is a trade-off between higher GNP and higher net real exports because the latter trigger US protectionism. The net implication of (4) and (5) is that the economic independence of Japan and West Germany is reduced. Monetary policy in those countries becomes more hesitant for fear of inducing a further depreciation of their currencies through lower interest rates. For this reason, real long-term interest rates of most industrial countries tend to converge to levels in the US. This is reinforced by the increasingly near-perfect substitutability between domestic-currency-denominated bonds and US-dollar bonds.

Commenting next on the nature and persistence of Japan's current account surplus, Yoshitomi points out that, under normal circumstances, the size of the surplus should be only about 1.5 per cent of GNP instead of the current 3 per cent. Japan's progression to the position of international creditor in the 1970s was accompanied by a shift towards large budget deficits and a steady shift towards production of knowledge-intensive as well as high value-added products.

As to the role of the Japanese financial market, Dr Yoshitomi believes that Japan will borrow short-term by providing yen-denominated liquid assets for non-residents, and lend long-term via direct investment, portfolio investment, syndicated loans and foreign aid. In 1982 Japan was a large exporter of long-term direct investments, loans and securities, but official transfer was small. Her direct investment is diversified among US, EEC and developing countries while her loans and trade credits went mostly to developing countries, small OECD countries and international organisations. Capital movements in the form of securities and bonds were two-way, centring on OECD countries.

Yoshitomi claims that the coexistence of high employment, Japanese budget deficits and current-account surpluses has necessitated the liberalisation and internationalisation of the Japanese financial market. Domestically, the substantial accumulation of national bonds (40 per cent of GNP in 1983) has led to pressure to deregulate interest rates in secondary markets plus the weakening of detailed segmentations among various financial institutions. Internationally, decontrol of foreign-exchange regulations has been de facto since 1977 and de jure since December 1980. There have also been freer forward market transactions and freer use of Euroyen markets for residents and non-residents since April 1984.

In conclusion, Yoshitomi notes: the contribution to world economic development through better and freer portfolio selection and improved allocation of resources as a result of the rapid integration of the Japanese financial market into the world system; the loss of some autonomy in economic management and development because of the US-exerted influence on interest rates and monetary policy; and the potentially greater contribution to the world economy via Japan's capital exports through better macroeconomic coordination between Japan and the US.

Daniel Kane questioned whether the last conclusion meant reducing Japan's chronic payments surplus or better allocation of resources and queried the implications for other Pacific countries. In his view the US deficit is a structural, not cyclical problem, not amenable to measures of coordination. Political factors are also at work. Hence what is required to resolve the problem is US policy change in combination with market forces.

Francis Chan complained about the lack of background material and information about the EPA World Economic model. He thoughts that Japan's problem of the current-account surplus is not new but reflects a persistent trend, and he believes there is a deflationary gap not properly measured by the rate of unemployment.

Ronald McKinnon questioned the stability of the EPA model finding about the asymmetric responses of the US and other countries to fiscal expansion. He gave two reasons: the expectations of US financial markets being shaped by the Reagan deficit and the unwillingness of Volker to finance it; also, capital controls existed before in Japan, weakening the capital-account effect.

In chapter 13, de Macedo provides some interesting perspectives on problems of macroeconomic coordination between open economies related by trade and financial ties. Under certain conditions, he demonstrates that coordination of monetary policy between such economies, accompanied by maintenance of fixed exchange rates between them, leads to the attainment of full employment and a common inflation rate, whereas a 'non-cooperative' solution, in which they engage in 'competitive' appreciations designed to lower domestic inflation rates, will lead to the perpetuation of unemployment. As Kong-Yam Tan pointed out, it would be interesting to extend the model to allow for the asymmetry resulting from one country playing a reserve-currency role, as the United States presently does.

The analysis suggests that complete flexibility of exchange rates may not be in the best interests of most countries: indeed, de Macedo argues that exchange rates, both real and nominal, have tended to be highly volatile in the 1970s, and that this volatility reflects largely the role played by unanticipated 'news', including the initiation of sudden, unannounced policy changes. Richard Cooper's reflections on this issue merit extended quotation. Most news is extremely noisy, in the sense that it contains little information or that the information will be quickly reversed in its implications for exchange rates. And yet exchange rates do seem to respond to such noisy news. This suggests that the dealers are playing the foreign-exchange market on its day-to-day dynamics, rather than on the economic fundamentals which will determine exchange rates over the longer run. This process can be disturbing to economies because movements in nominal rates typically imply movements in real exchange rates as well, and real exchange rates influence investment and trading decisions in the goods market. High variability in nominal exchange rates would not matter very much if future exchange rates showed greater stability, since traders could then hedge in the futures market. But futures rates show the same high degree of variability as do spot rates. So traders face considerable uncertainty with respect to their international transactions, and while any single short-term transactions can be hedged in the sense that the proceeds of a foreign-currency sale in domestic currency can be known with certainly by selling the foreign currency forward, most traders do not make their decisions on a 90- or 180-day basis alone. Engaging in international trade requires longer-term investments than these, investments that cannot be hedged in the forward market. Thus there is considerable investment uncertaintly arising from high variability of exchange rates. Early studies of floating exchange rates showed no apparent deterrent effect of exchange-rate variability on trade. That is hard to believe on a priori grounds, and more recent studies do show some considerable effect of exchange-rate variability on trade. For example, a 10 per cent increase in the variance of the dollar–Deutschmark rate has recently been reported to reduce German trade by about 2 per cent.

In view of this, countries around the Pacific have been wise to tie their currencies to something so long as the tie does not become unduly rigid. They should not hasten to embrace free floating.

Naya and James's chapter deals with 'External Shocks, Policy Responses And External Debt of Asian Developing Countries'. Since the oil crisis of 1973 to the present, there has been a quantum jump in external debt of oil-importing developing countries in Latin America, Asia and the Sub-Sahara. The developing countries of Asia have had to adjust to two oil shocks followed by serious world recessions, high interest rates and world inflation. Over the last two years, their problems were compounded by a market slowdown in new commercial bank lending, resulting in negative net capital inflow. Asia's first debt crisis occured in late 1983 when the Philippines asked for rescheduling of her debts. The austerity measures implemented by developing countries could stifle world economic recovery. There is also the danger of defaults triggering a financial breakdown and world depression, though the signs for the present are hopeful.

The emphasis of the Naya–James chapter is on the relationship between domestic efforts to mobilise and efficiently allocate investment resources and debt-servicing capacity. Twelve developing Asian countries (DACs) are grouped into three categories: the four newly industrialising countries (NICs), Singapore, Hong Kong, Taiwan and South Korea; the four middle-income and natural-resource-rich countries of Southeast Asia, Malaysia and Indonesia (both net oil exporters), Thailand and the Philippines; and four countries, Burma, India, Pakistan and Sri Lanka, which are lower income, agrarian and inward-looking.

The balance-of-payments (BOP) impact as a percentage of GNP averaged 17.5 per cent during 1974–82, with higher figures for the smaller countries like Hong Kong, Singapore, and Sri Lanka. There was, however, a favourable effect on the two oil exporters, Indonesia and Malaysia. Decomposition of the BOP impact revealed that between 75 per cent and 80 per cent was due to the unfavourable terms of trade, and the balance was due to declines in export volumes. The exceptions were two of the newly industrialising countries and Pakistan. This was thought to be prima facie evidence that oil prices had a more severe impact than the world recessions.

The DACs adjusted to the external shocks in four ways: by increasing export market shares; increasing import substitution; lowering growth rates; and resorting to external borrowing. The NICs relied mainly on increasing exports and less on import substitution. Only Singapore had much recourse to net external financing. The Southeast Asian oil importers increased their export market shares to some extent but resorted mainly to external borrowing. The latter was the predominant means of adjustment for the South Asian countries. The two net oil exporters were better off but had to deal with adverse exchange-rate consequences for non-oil sectors as well as income distribution problems.

The authors thought that debt in DACs had been due to high productivity, resulting mainly from investments in domestic energy development, agriculture and industrialisation. The emergence of the debt problem was due to two causes: the unexpected deterioration of external conditions, and reductions in foreign aid. However, the debt-servicing burden in Asia is still less than that of countries elsewhere. The concept of the critical interest rate (CIR) was employed to identify the factors which affect debt-servicing capacity, such as the GDP growth rate, incremental capital–output ratio (ICOR) and the marginal saving rate. The CIR was supposed to indicate the level of real interest rate on the external debt of a country under which its external debt will grow at the same rate as its GDP. In other words the CIR is the maximum interest rate which can be paid on external debt without increasing the ratio of debt outstanding to the GDP.

For the NICs the CIR decreased slightly from 1976–82, mainly due to the falling ICOR. The CIR for the Southeast Asian group was lower than for the NICs but declined rapidly from 8.2 per cent in 1966–75 to 5.9 per cent in 1976–82, mainly due to the increase in ICOR. The CIR for South Asia was low, about 5 per cent, and it increased slightly during 1976–82. Thus, on average, the CIR showed that the long-run debt-serving capacities of the DACs have deteriorated. However, they continued to be highly productive in the use of external finance. More favourable external conditions would be helpful, particularly in the areas of protectionism, inflation, interest rates and capital flows. Interestingly, the more open, outward-looking countries are generally much stronger in debt-servicing capacity than inward-looking ones. The Philippines had the lowest trade–GDP ratio and was the most protectionist of the group; it was also the only country to require debt rescheduling.

However, Mukul Asher queried the paradoxical high growth-rate response of the Philippines, Pakistan and Sri Lanka. He also objected to the use of ICOR for long-run analysis. Luo Yuan-Zheng thought that the world recessions were more important in causing the decline of economic growth in the DACs. He felt there was a need for stringent and internationally coordinated efforts to cope with the present world debt crisis.

Taken singularly and collectively, the following chapters provide a considerable body of information and new data on the patterns of financial development within and between the nations of the Asian–Pacific region. In Parts I–IV a major theme emerges, namely, the issue of government regulation of the financial sector with its predictable and unexpected, desirable and not-so-desirable consequences. On this broad issue, and on the related issues of the future trends in, and desirability of, deregulation, the internationalisation of banking, the Asian debt problem and US–Japan financial relations, there is considerable divergence of prognoses and data, as the above comments on each chapter indicate. This divergence of views may in part reflect different national experiences of these events. Whatever the reason, there is immense value in having delineated and examined these issues on the basis of the thoroughgoing research, analysis and the collected data presented in the chapters that follow.

Part I The Process of Financial Development

2 Financial development in the Pacific Basin market economies

DAVID C. COLE AND HUGH T. PATRICK

The past two decades have witnessed the rapid development of the market economies of the Pacific Basin, together with even more rapid growth in international trade flows and economic interdependence.[1] Commensurate with the real economic performance has been the increasing role of domestic and foreign finance, and the accelerated development of financial institutions, markets, and instruments.

This process of economic and financial development has on the whole been highly successful, but it has by no means been smooth for the region as a whole or for individual countries. The two oil crises, world inflations and the recessions of 1973–75 and 1980–83 were profound shocks to all the region's economies. They were compounded by major changes in the international financial system; the adoption of flexible exchange rates; an increasingly large and efficient bank-based international capital market; and the accumulation of large foreign debts. In addition, each Pacific Basin economy over the past decade has experienced its own problems of domestic adjustment to political change, internal disruption or external shock.

The reactions among the Pacific Basin economies have varied considerably, reflecting specific national attributes and circumstances such as the level of development, economic structure, financial system, and economic policies pursued. In general, the inflations of the 1970s put severe pressure on those financial institutions which were subject to interest-rate ceilings. Gaps widened between regulated nominal interest rates and market-clearing rates, and financial repression was a short-term consequences in almost all Pacific Basin economies. In some countries, however, the longer term response has been to generate new, more flexible financial policies of liberalisation and deregulation.

The purpose of this paper is to provide a broad comparative overview of domestic financial development in the market economies of the Pacific Basin. We identify major patterns and raise some major issues. Our analysis has been guided by the following questions:

— What have been the patterns of financial development in these countries?
— Has the balance changed over time between the modern and traditional, the formal and the informal financial sectors and have these changes affected the growth of the economy?

39

— Which parts of the financial system seem to be most effective at mobilising and allocating financial resources?
— How have governmental policies affected the growth structure of the financial system?
— Is the new emphasis on financial liberalisation and deregulation likely to result in greater integration and efficiency of the financial sector?

Our main concern is with the thirteen major Pacific Basin market economies: the economically more advanced countries of Australia, Canada, Japan, New Zealand and the United States; and eight Asian developing market economies of South Korea, Taiwan, Hong Kong, Singapore, Malaysia, Thailand, Indonesia, and the Philippines, on which we focus particularly.[2]

We do not include the People's Republic of China or other Asian communist nations in our discussion since finance has played only a subsidiary role in national savings and investment allocation behaviour in such planned, socialist economies. While still a small portion of total tangible assets, currency in circulation in China increased at an 8.8 per cent average annual rate between 1957–81, and individual deposits at 11.9 per cent. Over the past few years, China has been re-evaluating the role of finance, concomitant with other economic reforms.[3]

After some cautionary points, and a discussion of the relationship between financial development and economic growth, we take up the institutional aspects of the various national financial systems. The relative importance of financial instruments and how well they fulfil their major functions are analysed in the third section. While there is no single proxy that adequately summarises financial deepening and development, for the developing countries change over time in the ratio of M2 to GNP is the best available. Those changes are presented in the fourth section. To supplement that analysis, we then discuss the overall growth and evolution of the national financial systems. These first five sections deal primarily with the regulated segments of the system, but it must be borne in mind that the unregulated segments are of substantial importance, and we take up the relationship between the two in the sixth section. Financial liberalisation and deregulation is discussed in the seventh section, and we conclude with some thoughts about the prospects for reforms and development.

SOME CAUTIONARY POINTS

Understanding what is going on in finance and making cross-country comparisons involves a number of major problems. The first is that the real-world finance is often quite different from what is generally observed or statistically recorded. Finance is the most mobile and fungible of economic goods, involving high degrees of substitutability among different types of financial claims, albeit with differing degrees of liquidity, once commitments are made.

A second point is that national differences among Pacific Basin countries in institutional arrangements, markets, and government policies are even more extreme and important in finance than in agriculture, manufacturing, or infrastructure. The hand of history is heavier. Standard typologies based on criteria relating to the real economy, developed versus developing, industrial NIC versus near-NIC, are less relevant to financial development. Economies such as Hong Kong and Singapore have become highly developed international financial centres while in some other countries financial repression has affected the symmetry of financial and economic development.

Third, the financial system is considerably larger and more complex, especially in the developing Asian market economies, than is commonly recorded in the financial statistics. The total financial system is in fact composed of two broad sectors. The sector commonly thought of as comprising the commercial banks, savings banks, insurance companies, development banks and other 'modern' financial institutions, is licensed to operate by the government, which exercises a greater or lesser degree of supervision and regulation. The activities of this component, which we term the regulated financial sector, in general are recorded. The other broad financial sector is unlicensed, unregulated, and its transactions are usually unrecorded. This sector goes by many names; informal, curb (or kerb), traditional, free-market or black-market, none of which captures its essence fully; we follow the terminology of Cole and Park in calling it the unregulated financial sector.[4] We recognise that the dichotomy between licensed and unlicensed, or regulated and unregulated, simplifies what may alternatively be thought of as a spectrum involving different degrees of restriction or freedom in financial activity. The nature and interplay of these two components of the overall financial system is an important feature both of the historical process of financial development and of the way resources are raised and allocated, and monetary–financial policies implemented. These relationships are especially important in countries where the regulated financial sector is repressed by intentional or inadvertent government policy.

Fourth, the need for caution in the use of monetary and financial data cannot be overemphasised, especially in the developing Asian economies. As a general rule for the regulated financial sector, data on quantities, amounts of deposits, loans, and the like, are good, but data on actual prices, especially effective lending rates as distinct from nominal rates, are poor and in some countries virtually non-existent. In contrast, the domestic unregulated financial sector can often generate reasonable data on market-clearing interest rates. In some economies, most notably Korea and Taiwan, the central bank regularly collects kerb-market interest-rate data as a gauge of monetary and financial conditions. Given the difficulties of measuring real rates of return on physical capital, the unregulated market rate is a reasonable proxy for the marginal efficiency of capital.[5] However, because of its unregulated and often illicit nature, data on the quantities of financial claims in the unregulated financial sector are sparse, episodic, and weak.

It might be noted that the largest unregulated financial market is highly efficient, enjoys economies of scale, and both its prices and quantities, with some exceptions, are recorded. We refer to the Euro- and Asia-dollar markets. While nations may be able to regulate the participation of institutions domiciled in their territory, or regulate the inflow or outflow of funds, they cannot regulate the totality of institutions and transactions in the international currency markets.

The quantitive macro data on the regulated financial sector—currency in circulation, demand deposits, savings and time deposits, M1, M2, and other monetary measures, loans and other assets or liabilities of commercial banks and other modern financial intermediaries—are commonly regarded as the most reliable of national economic statistics. After all, they are collected by central banks and other regulatory authorities, and are based on individual-institution balance-sheet data. However, in some countries, banks make loans that are not recorded on their balance sheets. Compensating deposit balances are used against loans in most Asian countries, particularly Japan and Korea; this device raises the effective nominal interest rate but also overstates loans and deposits. 'Currency in circulation' may be used extensively outside national boundaries, as with the Singapore dollar in Southeast Asia and the US dollar everywhere. It has been estimated that in recent years approximately $5 billion a year of $100 bills flow out of the United States in unrecorded transactions. In Korea, where large-denomination currency does not exist, certified bank drafts are used as a means of payment. In many Asian countries, cheques on personal demand deposit accounts are considered unreliable, so that funds are transferred through bank drafts or sight bills on grain traders. National differences in definitions of M2 weaken international comparisons. These examples reinforce the simple point that one must know the data well and use it with caution.

At the micro level, data problems are even more severe. While large projects and their financing are highly visible, and information is available on a few large enterprises, the hard fact is that for most financial transactions we do not know at all well who really borrows, how much, on what terms, and for what purpose. Accordingly, free-market-determined interest rates are important price signals, and reference points. In highly regulated or repressed financial systems, unregulated markets play this important role.

Other data problems plague our understanding of financial development. Only in Korea and Thailand are there direct estimates of savings; in most Asian developing countries domestic private saving is a residual dependent upon investment estimates. Recent international comparisons indicate that real investment is seriously overestimated in some developing countries such as the Philippines where restrictions remain severe.[6]

Savers and investors make decisions based on current and expected real interest rates, not nominal interest rates. Expectations of future inflation are central to these decisions, yet economists have no satisfactory way of measuring expectations. Distributed lags are an artful construct but they have only a weak behavioural basis. There are theoretical as well as substantive empirical estimation problems in determining which price index to use—consumer prices, wholesale price, or GNP deflator.[7]

The coexistence of recorded and unrecorded components in the financial system, the various techniques which result in misestimations of quantities and prices within the regulated sector, and the paucity of data on effective (nominal) interest rates pose severe problems for monetary and financial analysis. The reality is that measures of financial development, financial deepening and the like, combine in some unknown way shifts in claims between the recorded and unrecorded sectors, with actual changes in demand for total financial assets, or changes in types of instruments, compensating deposit balances, and the like. Yet we can only use the data that exist; and it does provide considerable evidence though regarding it as finely honed is unreasonable. So we, like others before us, proceed to calculate financial ratios as evidence of financial development, while urging appropriate caution in their interpretation.

FINANCE AND REAL GROWTH

There was a tendency in the aftermath of the Keynesian revolution for economists to think that money and monetary policy were much less relevant to economic growth than fiscal policy and foreign-capital inflows. In the 1970s, the pendulum swung the other way. Monetarists claimed that controlling the money supply was the main instrument for controlling inflation, and some suggested that price stability and financial growth were the keys to economic growth. Now after a decade of experimentation we have seen, most notably from the US but also from Japanese experience, that restrictive monetary policy, if pushed hard enough, can halt inflation even in the face of expansionary fiscal policy, but at a high cost in terms of growth of output, employment and human welfare, not only in the restricting country but also throughout the world.

In some countries, during some periods, there has been a positive association between the rate of economic growth and the recorded growth of financial intermediaries. In other instances the relationship has been negative or simply obscure. Often it is not possible to determine whether there has been a real change in the level of financial intermediation or merely a shift of activity between the unrecorded and recorded parts of the financial system. Even such a shift is considered by some to affect the rate of economic growth, because they believe that the modern, recorded part of the financial system is likely to allocate resources more efficiently than the informal, unrecorded financial institutions. Others have suggested that the unregulated markets give better guidance for allocation decisions.

The theoretical case for the role of financial intermediation in economic development generally is well understood.[8] Practically every kind of productive activity—in agriculture, manufacturing, infrastructure, domestic and foreign trade, and by large units or small—requires some form of finance. The financial system provides the medium of exchange; it allocates resources to investment; it provides a return on and presumably affects the level of savings; it pools, transforms and distributes risk; it is an important locus of the implementation of stabilisation policy. However, the relationships between financial and real development are complex and difficult to specify because of significant feedback interactions. They are difficult to measure because of severe data problems, as already discussed.

For most of the Pacific Basin economies, financial development has been documented through national case studies, and also to some extent by cross-country comparisons utilising pooled cross-section and time-series data.[9] The specific conditions, experiences, institutional arrangements, and behaviour of individual countries loom importantly in cross-sectional studies; country dummy variables are typically significant and sizeable. Nevertheless these studies suggest that the most important factor influencing financial development in the Pacific Basin and other market economies has been real economic growth. The reverse causality (from the financial to the real side) is much more difficult to demonstrate empirically but is, in our view, of much greater importance than is usually believed. Real economic growth goes hand in hand with an increasing amount and diversity of activity of financial institutions, markets, and instruments. Financial deepening, as measured by increases in ratios of different types of recorded financial assets to total assets or GNP (see Figure 2.1), is a common, but not universal tendency, at least until high levels of income are achieved.[10]

The major inhibitor of financial development has been inflation. Rapid,

Figure 2.1   Fitted trends in monetary and real growth, 1960–1981

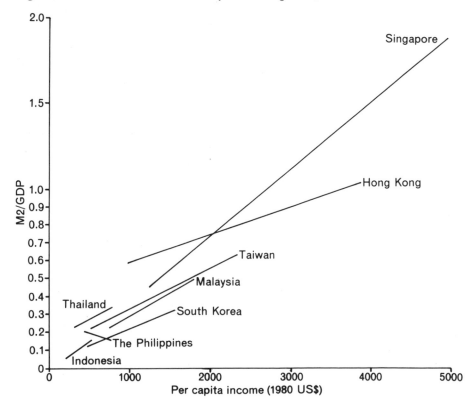

erratic inflation has generally retarded financial development, brought on financial repression and in extreme cases resulted in implosion of the financial system, as happened in China in 1948, Korea in 1945 and 1950, and Indonesia in the mid-1960s.

Other important variables affecting financial development are the real interest rate and the ease of access to financial institutions and their services. For example, recent empirical studies of a sample of Asian developing countries suggest that real deposit rates have a positive but quantitatively very modest effect on the national savings rate and a somewhat stronger effect on the financial mobilisation of savings, by increasing the demand for financial assets.[11] There is some questionable evidence that allocative efficiency of investment is increased as well.[12] Nonetheless, it must be said that on the whole the empirical testing of these relationships has been limited, and constrained by problems in data and model specification.

Government policies have had an extremely important, if at times inadvertent and indirect, role in financial development. Even in those countries where the objective has been to have competitive, effectively functioning financial markets, some government regulation has generally been considered essential for prudential purposes; to maintain depositor safety and to prevent the disruptive shocks of bank runs and financial panics. But in practice, most governments have gone far beyond prudential regulation and have adopted policies that tended to restrict the development and growth of competitive financial markets. Governments have used the financial system to achieve other policy goals: cheap financing of fiscal deficits; maintaining an overvalued exchange rate and/or otherwise insulating domestic from international financial markets; attempting to accelerate economic development by low-interest-rate policies; and/or allocation of credit through regulated financial institutions on preferential terms to selected categories of users. In pursuit of these other goals, governments have relied on direct controls rather than market forces: ceilings on deposit, loan and other interest rates; direct controls over high-powered money and bank credit and direct qualitative controls over their allocation; control of the exchange rate and foreign financial flows.[13] The result has been repression of the regulated financial sector: credit rationing, markets not clearing, distorted financial allocation. The unregulated sector on the other hand has been stimulated by, and has expanded to resolve, the pervasive disequilibria in the regulated sector. The nature of this interaction and its effects on economic growth will be discussed in a later part of this chapter.

Recently in some countries there has been a significant move away from the more pervasive forms of regulation of financial prices and market shares. This has blurred the boundaries of institutional specialisation, narrowed the spreads between interest rates of regulated and unregulated markets and led to greater competitiveness among financial institutions. It is still too early to assess the ultimate effects of such deregulation on the development, efficiency and stability of the several national economies. In a later section of this chapter we will review the regulatory patterns of individual countries and comment on their recent trends and prospects.

FINANCIAL STRUCTURE IN THE PACIFIC BASIN ECONOMIES

Gurley and Shaw suggested some years ago that the main determinants of the size and structure of a financial system were the level of economic development, and the extent to which the system was relied upon to intermediate between savers and investors.[14] The developed countries of the Pacific Basin provide three quite different models of financial intermediation. The United States, Canada and Australia have relied most heavily on direct financing through sale of debt and equity. Consequently intermediation by the banking system has been less important and the size of the banking sector relatively small. Japan on the other hand has relied heavily on indirect finance through the banking system so that the banking sector is relatively large. Singapore and Hong Kong, which we include among the financially developed economies, follow the British and Swiss model of serving as international financial centres, offering banking services to neighbouring countries. Consequently, their banking sectors as well as other financial services are highly developed.

In a more general sense, we can say that the size and structure of the financial system of a given country reflects both the demands placed upon that financial system and the extent to which the system meets those demands. The indications are imprecise because institutions and instruments generally satisfy more than one type of demand or serve more than the national market, and also because the unrecorded parts of the system tend to fill in when the recorded part is not performing adequately. Nevertheless, it is possible to match up certain

Table 2.1 Main types of financial instruments and their functions

Instrument	Main function	Secondary functions
Currency	Small transactions	Store of value, tax evasion
Demand deposits	Large transactions	Payment guarantees
Time deposits	Accumulation	Store of value, payment guarantees
Bonds	Accumulation	Speculation
Stocks	Control	Accumulation, speculation
Insurance	Risk protection	Accumulation
Foreign currency	Store of value	Transactions, tax evasion
Foreign deposits	Store of value	Accumulation, transactions, speculation
Foreign securities	Accumulation, store of value	Speculation
Credit association deposit	Accumulation	Social interaction
Claim on informal financial institution	Accumulation	
Loan, private	Accumulation	Social relation

types of financial instruments with certain basic financial functions and then assess whether the recorded supplies of those instruments within a country are consistent with expected demands for them. In those instances where the recorded supplies are unusually large, it seems reasonable to ask whether those instruments are meeting other types of demands, or the demands emanating from some other source. Similarly, if the recorded supplies of particular instruments in one country are low compared to those in other countries one may ask whether some other type of instrument is filling the normal function of the recorded instrument that is in limited supply.

The major functions of financial instruments are familiar. They include: transactions medium, store of value, payment guarantee or financial collateral, accumulation of wealth, accumulation of power or control, dispersion of risk, and speculation. Some of these functions overlap, and some others might be added; we cite them as illustrative, and use them in Table 2.1 to indicate the main and secondary functions of selected types of financial instruments.

We turn next to an analysis of the relative importance of some of these financial instruments in the major Pacific Basin countries and try to assess how well these instruments are fulfilling their major functions. Table 2.2 shows the ratios of various financial aggregates to GDP or GNP for thirteen economies in 1980. The spectacular success of Hong Kong and Singapore in specialisation in international and domestic financial services, moves them out of the increasingly

Table 2.2 Ratios of monetary and financial aggregates for selected Pacific Basin countries, 1980 (per cent)

	Monetary aggregates[a]			Recorded financial claims[b]		
	Currency	M1	M2	Broad money[c]	Securities[d]	Total
Developed countries						
New Zealand	2.1	10.7	25.8			
Australia	4.1	14.1	44.5			
Canada	4.3	12.0	53.9	64	125	189
United States	4.4	16.1	61.9	90	130	220
Japan	7.4	29.6	88.1	141	99	240
Singapore	13.5	25.1	61.6	70	130	200
(including Asian currency units)			(171.0)			
Hong Kong[e]	7.4	27.9	106.2	132	192	324
Less developed countries						
Indonesia	4.7	9.3	15.2	18	0	18
The Philippines	3.2	7.2	18.0	30	18	48
South Korea	4.3	9.1	30.4	37	14	51
Thailand	6.2	9.4	32.7	43	16	59
Malaysia	8.6	17.6	47.8			
Taiwan[f]	7.7	18.7	59.3			

Notes and sources:
a Monetary aggregates are derived from IMF *International Financial Statistics*. The denominator is GDP. The numerator is the average of end-of-month values.
b Recorded financial claims are from tables prepared by the Capital Markets Department of the International Finance Corporation in March 1983. The denominator is GNP.
c Broad money is financial aggregate composed of currency, all deposits, and any negotiable financial instruments with maturities of one year or less.
d Securities consist of the current market value of bonds—any negotiable debt instrument with a maturity of more than one year; shares—shares in a corporation which can be bought or sold in the secondary market. Preferred as well as common shares are included.
e From *Hong Kong 1983*.
f From *Taiwan Statistical Data Book, 1982*.

ambiguous developing-country category into the financially developed category.

As table 2.2 indicates, currency is a low fraction of GDP in the most developed countries, somewhat higher in the less developed countries, but unusually high in Singapore. New Zealand and the Philippines on the other hand have relatively low currency ratios. What explains these outlying cases?

Singapore's currency serves as an important transactions medium and store of value in many parts of Southeast Asia. It has been a strong currency, having appreciated relative to the US dollar by 41 per cent between 1970 and 1979. Singapore is an important trading centre for both the legal and illegal trade of Southeast Asia and some of this trade may be paid for with currency rather than transfers through bank accounts. Also, Singapore is a major world financial centre, as indicated by its generally high financial ratios.

The more interesting question is not why Singapore's currency ratio is so high but why Hong Kong's ratio is not higher, since Hong Kong serves many of the same trading and financial functions as Singapore. Is it that Hong Kong's currency was less strong than Singapore's during the 1970s, or that Hong Kong's currency is issued by two commercial banks rather than a central monetary authority and therefore is perceived as less reliable, or that potential users of its currency are geographically less proximate?

Japan has a relatively high currency ratio for a developed country. Individuals and small businesses typically use cash rather than cheques as means of payment. With credit cards, electronic transfers and on-line computer networks among banks and their branches, Japan may bypass altogether the personal cheque phase of finance.

New Zealand's currency ratio is low relative to other developed countries, as are its M1 and M2 ratios. The Philippines has the lowest currency and M1 ratios of the less developed countries listed in Table 2.2, although the demand deposit ratio is slightly above that in Thailand. This is not just a one-year phenomenon; the M1 ratio declined from 12.5 per cent in 1961 to 7.0 per cent in 1982. Apparently, Filipinos have responded in an increasingly sophisticated way to the inflations of 1970–74 and 1978 to the present, to negative real interest rates in the banking system, to the turmoil of occasional bank runs and failures which have plagued the banking system, and to the opportunities of financial access to Hong Kong and Singapore.

Japan's postwar pattern of indirect finance evolved in the 1950s and 1960s, a time of increasingly high savings rates and few alternatives to time and savings deposits in banks or in the postal savings system, despite the fact that real interest rates on such deposits were close to zero. The financial system has become substantially more open, competitive and flexible in the past decade, with huge new issues of government bonds and a large and dynamic stock market well beyond the 1980 ratio given in Table 2.2 Singapore's high M1 and M2 ratios are explained in large part by its role as an international financial centre and by the strength of its currency. Even so, these ratios understate the total level of bank deposits in Singapore, because they do not include the deposits in the Asian currency units (ACUs) which are treated as separate entities by the Monetary Authority of Singapore. For purposes of intercountry comparison, especially with Hong Kong, where no such distinction is made, it seems appropriate to include the ACU deposits in an expanded M2 ratio. At the end of 1980, these ACU deposits amounted to 109.4 per cent of Singapore's GDP, thus raising the composite M2 ratio to 171 per cent, by far the highest of all the countries included in Table 2.2.

Since the difference between currency and M1 is demand deposits, and that between M1 and M2 is time deposits, we can identify those countries with unusually small or large ratios of demand and/or time deposits to GDP. Japan and Hong Kong have demand deposit ratios of 22 and 20.5 per cent, well above those of the other countries. Thailand has a demand deposit ratio of 3.2 per cent. The average demand deposit ratio is 11 per cent for the other developed countries and 8 per cent for the LDCs. Thus, it appears that demand deposits are held for more than transactions purposes in Japan. On the other hand, the demand deposit ratio is very low in Thailand. As discussed in chapter 6 on Thailand, savings deposits and overdraft loans are easily converted into cash or demand deposits, so that demand deposit balances are kept at low levels.

The country with the lowest time deposit ratio is Indonesia (5.9 per cent). The highest time deposit ratios are in Japan (58.5 per cent), Hong Kong (78 per cent), and Singapore (146 per cent including the Asian currency unit deposits). The low level of time deposits in Indonesia reflects both incomplete recovery from the hyperinflation of the 1960s and the inclination of many Indonesia individuals and businesses to hold deposit balances abroad, especially in Singapore. The absence of any restrictions on transferring funds in and out of both Indonesia and Singapore, and the considerable amount of commerce between the two countries has resulted in very close linkages between the two financial systems. Because of the stability and strength of Singapore's currency, in contrast with continuing inflation, several devaluations and negative real interest rates in Indonesia, it is readily understandable why so many Indonesians use the easily available Singapore financial services. The high deposit ratios in Singapore and Hong Kong are the counterpart of the offshore banking activities of Indonesians and others in Southeast Asia.

Consistent information on other types of financial assets is available for only nine of the thirteen countries in Table 2.2. The Capital Markets Department of the International Finance Corporation has been compiling statistics since 1977 on short-term liquid assets and longer term securities. The former are incorporated in 'broad money', which includes M2 and all other deposits in non-bank financial institutions plus all other negotiable financial instruments with maturities of less than one year. The securities include stocks and bonds issued by both corporations and governments that are publicly traded.

As can be seen in Table 2.2, 'broad money' is substantially greater than M2 in all of the developed countries, but not very different in three of the four LDCs. Only the Philippines shows a substantial difference. This difference indicates the relative importance of non-deposit liabilities of commercial banks or of deposit institutions other than commercial banks. The surge in money-market funds accounts for part of the difference in the US between 'broad money' and M2.

Securities comprise the largest part of total financial claims in all the developed countries except Japan. But securities clearly are of secondary importance in four LDCs for which we have data. Indonesia, which has no domestic public debt and a very limited capital market, has practically no securities. The Philippines on the other hand, with its more sophisticated stock market, has a ratio of securities to GNP equal to its M2 ratio. Securities plus near money (the difference between M2 and 'broad money') account for more than half of total recorded financial claims. The availability of these alternative financial instruments helps to explain the low monetary ratios in the Philippines.

Turning from the instrumental to the institutional perspective, we present in Table 2.3 some comparative data on the role of commercial banks in the financial structure of the Pacific Basin economies. More detailed statistics on the institutional structure of each country are presented in appendix 2A.

Commercial banks play a major, indeed frequently dominant, role in the financial structures of all countries. In those countries where security issues (direct finance) are important, other financial intermediaries play a somewhat larger role. Insurance, pension funds and similar financial assets are income-elastic. Government-sponsored specialised financial institutions exist in all countries; they are relatively more important in the developing countries, where they serve mainly as conduits for foreign official credits or domestic government funds.

Table 2.3 Commercial banks: numbers of offices and share of total financial assets

| | Number of bank offices | | | | Percentage of total financial assets | | |
| | Head offices | | Total offices | | | | |
Country	Domestic banks	Foreign banks	Domestic banks	Foreign banks	Total	Domestic banks	Foreign banks
Hong Kong (1980)	34	79	na	na	67.4	32.7[a]	34.7[a]
Indonesia	76	11	1 010	20	84.2	78.2[b]	6.0
South Korea	18	44	1 047	44	44.9	39.4	5.5
Malaysia	22	16	462	146	55.3	38.5	16.8
The Philippines (1980)	28	4	1 501		49.7	43.3	6.4
Singapore	13	37	181	37	48.3	12.9[c]	35.4[c]
Taiwan	24	27	734	27	68.0	62.6	5.3
Thailand (1981)	16	14	1 556		67.7	63.3[d]	4.4[d]
Australia	12	—	5 108	—	25.7	25.7	—
Canada	11	44	7 414	75[e]	50.2	48.4	1.8
Japan	86	75	8 367	na	35.4	34.0	—
New Zealand	4	—	1 000	—	36.2	36.2	—
United States	14 435	279	39 242	67	43.8	39.3	4.5

Notes: All figures are at year-end 1982 unless otherwise noted.
    a   1979 data.
    b   Includes the State Development Bank (Bapindo).
    c   1978 data.
    d   Total commercial bank loans in 1979.
    e   Estimate.

Sources: Official statistical publications of each country; Lee and Jao (1982) *Financial Structures and Monetary Policies in Southeast Asia* for selected pre-1980 data; Patrick and Moreno (1984) 'Philippine Private Domestic Commercial Banking, 1946–1980' for the Philippines.

Most countries have extensive branch banking systems. The United States is unique in its degree of reliance on unit banks. Foreign banks are, not surprisingly, very important in Singapore and Hong Kong, and of considerable importance of Malaysia. Elsewhere they engage in limited domestic banking, though they are a significant conduit of trade credit and foreign non-governmental loans. The commercial banking systems are predominantly government-owned in Indonesia, Taiwan and, until recently, Korea. The banking system is mixed in Australia, Malaysia, New Zealand, the Philippines and Thailand, with one or two large state-owned banks competing with a substantial number of private banks. Canada, Hong Kong, Japan, Singapore, and the United States have privately-owned commerical banking systems.

FINANCIAL GROWTH IN THE ASIAN DEVELOPING MARKET ECONOMIES

Another perspecitve on financial development in the Asian region can be obtained by tracing the evolution over time of the key financial ratios. While the best measures would relate total financial assets to total real assets, such data are not available even for the regulated financial sectors. Lee and Jao provide a variety of measures of financial deepening in Hong Kong and the ASEAN nations between the mid-1960s and 1979–80.[15] In our judgment the best available measure for a large number of developing countries over a number of years is the M2 to GDP ratio. We have used pooled cross-section and time-series data for eight Asian countries over 21 years (1960–1981) to derive an estimate of the main determinants of the M2 ratio.[16] We then use the trend value of this ratio from the pooled data to compare with the actual ratios of individual countries over time. Country differences are captured most effectively by estimating separate intercepts for each country and then determining common coefficients for the two explanatory variables. The regression results are as follows:

$$M\,Two = .228\,YDPC - .003\,DP + .169\,(HK) + .009\,(IN) + .000\,(KO)$$
$$(12.63) \qquad (-0.78) \quad (8.00) \qquad (7.3) \qquad (8.1)$$
$$+ .044\,(MA) + .013\,(PH) + .074\,(SG)$$
$$(8.3) \qquad + (7.4) \qquad + (5.9)$$
$$+ .002\,(TA) + .050\,(TH)$$
$$(7.6) \qquad (5.6)$$

$R^2 = .90$ T-statistics in parentheses
where
M Two = Ratio of M2 to GDP
YDPC = GDP per capita in thousands of 1980 US dollars
DP = Percentage change in the GDP deflator during the previous year (a proxy for price expectations)

Note: Variables adjusted to correct for autocorrelation. See appendix 6A for a description of the methodology.

The positive influence of per capita income on the M2 ratio is strong and significant as expected. Past change in prices causes expectations of further price change and as expected has a mild negative (though statistically insignificant) impact on the demand for money.

We use this regression to estimate the trend in the relationship between values of the M2 ratio and per capita dollar income. We then compare the actual value for each country with the trend value.

The results are depicted in two figures. Figure 2.1 shows the fitted trends of M Two relative to YDPC for each country and the trend for the pooled data from all eight countries. In Figure 2.2, we provide a freehand rendition of the approximate path of M Two and YDPC for each country over 21 years from 1960 to 1981. The latter figure smooths out somewhat the year-to-year changes and gives an approximate moving average. The main line for Singapore includes the Asian currency unit deposits. In Figure 2.2, the dashed line, Sn[1] shows M Two without the ACU deposits, as reported in *International Financial Statistics*. Clearly, including the ACU deposits for Singapore makes a big difference and,

Figure 2.2   Patterns of monetary and real growth, 1960–1981

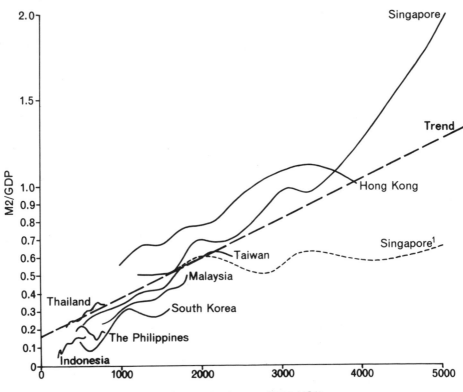

we believe, gives a more accurate indication of Singapore's financial development.

The two figures show both the real economic growth and the real financial growth of each country over the two decades. Some countries have achieved spectacular income growth. Some have also achieved higher-than-trend financial growth. Generally economic and financial growth have gone together and there is a strong positive slope for the whole group. The Philippines is the only economy in Figure 2.1 with a negative slope, indicating a decline in the M Two ratio. It is also the country with the poorest record of income growth.

Figure 2.2 gives a better sense of the changes in the M Two ratio over time. Some economies, Malaysia, Taiwan and Thailand, have had quite steady growth of the M Two ratio. Hong Kong's ratio, after a long period of steady growth, has turned down in recent years, whereas Singapore's ratio, which includes the ACU deposits, after some distinct oscillations has risen sharply in recent years. These opposite movements in Hong Kong and Singapore suggest a shift of intermediation from one to the other. The other three countries, Indonesia, Korea and the Philippines, also show some distinct oscillations, which reflect changes in inflation rates, real interest rates or other government policies. We have not attempted to refine the statistical analysis of such country variations in this chapter.

FINANCIAL SYSTEM EVOLUTION

Probably the most important fact in Pacific Basin financial development is that each economy's financial system has dynamically and often dramatically evolved and grown over the past three decades. In each case the current state of the financial system has been much shaped by history. Central banks, insurance companies and all the other institutions of the modern financial sector, which emerged and evolved in the West over the past several centuries, have provided the models for the modern, regulated financial institutions for all the Pacific Basin economies. Often the Western banks and other financial institutions have served as the carriers and implementors of specific institutional arrangements.

There were two patterns. The newly settled colonies, the United States, Canada, Australia, and New Zealand, received and adapted the British model. The United States, however, in achieving independence before the development of modern banking, came to have a unique, locally based banking structure because of its emphasis on local autonomy. The Asian nations all had informal, unregulated, 'traditional', market-determined financial systems before Western penetration. Governments issued coins and currency and engaged in some regulation, but financial activities, which in some countries came to be quite sophisticated, were predominantly outside regulatory control. Onto this 'traditional' sector were grafted 'modern' financial institutions, predominantly through colonisation.[17]

Only Japan and Thailand were never formally colonies. Japan autonomously crafted its own eclectic financial system combining British, Continental European and American features.[18] Thailand's banks initially were branches of foreign banks; British influence was strong, but in recent years the new Chinese–Thai-owned banks have grown most rapidly.[19]

In the other countries, banks followed the colonial flag; foreign banks established branches or subsidiaries mainly to facilitate foreign trade, gradually expanding to providing working capital for predominantly expatriate domestic production and commerce. It has made some significant institutional difference for each country whether the first banks were from the United Kingdom, the Netherlands, Japan, France, or the United States.

Newly independent governments in the early postwar period set as one of their first objectives the achievement of financial autonomy. Each newly independent Asian nation dealt with the problem of foreign ownership and control of domestic financial institutions differently, but some features were similar. Central banks were established in all economies but Singapore and Hong Kong; foreign-owned banks were nationalised in some countries, and in all cases brought under substantial national regulatory supervision; the entry of new foreign banks was prohibited or severely restricted; a domestically owned system of various types of financial institutions was developed with active government encouragement and often government ownership. Beyond that, national policy and experience varied widely. The Philippines in the 1950s and 1960s encouraged new commercial bank entrants, thereafter severely limiting entry. In contrast Korea did not allow the establishment of new commercial banks. In virtually all cases specialised government-owned institutions were established for specific purposes, notably in long-term development finance, export credit and rural credit.[20]

Following an initial spurt, new entry in the regulated sector became almost as difficult for domestic banks as it was for foreign banks. Finance came to be seen as the handmaiden of development policy. Because the Pacific Basin economies in general pursued relatively conservative fiscal policies, the financial system was used to fund government deficits less than in many Latin American countries. However, by applying high required reserve deposits at the central bank on commercial banks, private savings were mobilised by the authorities in some countries for reallocation to preferred uses through government or private financial institutions.

The government policies of strengthening national autonomy, tightening regulation of the organised financial sector, and directing finance toward particular development objectives had profound consequences for the structure and performance of the financial system in each country. Specialised institutions and preferential allocation of cheap credit created segmented financial markets and market niches. Arbitrage among these markets was restricted in the regulated sector, which created opportunities for the unregulated sector, a topic discussed in the next section. Market niches also created vested interests in the status quo; this has made liberalisation of the financial system politically difficult. Excess demand for funds, in a situation of low-ceiling interest rates in regulated markets, resulted in credit rationing and the creation of substantial rents, depending upon the degree of financial repression. The allocation of these rents among political leaders, financial institution bureaucrats, and powerful large borrowers has been decided at least as much through political bargaining as through economic calculations.

Government-owned financial intermediaries have often become bureaucratic, inflexible, unable or unwilling to respond quickly to changing market conditions and opportunities. The extensive degree of government regulation and distortion of financial markets has made access to cheap credit an important domain of elites, cliques, cronies—those able to exert influence on the government for their own benefit.

An important policy issue in most countries has been the degree to which the government should actively foster the institutional development of a modern financial system, termed supply-leading;[21] or passively allow institutions to be established and grow in response to increasing demand for financial services, demand-following. Success in supply-leading institutional development requires that the institutions relatively quickly become effective mobilisers and allocators of private savings, so that they become capable of operating without further government subsidy, direct or indirect. Such success evidently depends on whether the financial system is operating in a competitive, market-driven environment or a restricted, directly controlled, financially repressed environment; and in practice, whether the financial institutions are owned privately or by the government.

The Japanese government successfully created a privately owned commercial banking system very early in its modern development by providing government deposits and endorsing private banknote issue.[22] These institutions then were able to become real banks; mobilisers of private savings rather than mere conduits of government funds in a context of no controls over interest rates on loans or deposits. On the other hand, in a comparative study of securities markets in developing countries, Wai and Patrick found that the costs of supply-leading special incentives for securities markets were likely to outweigh the benefits, and concluded that a demand-following policy, with appropriate levels of regulation for prudential purposes, was preferable.[23] These findings are reinforced by Korean experience as described by Cole and Park.[24]

The actual experience of the Pacific Basin developing economies in supply-leading institutional development suggests that such a policy approach frequently has been misused. The real success stories, Singapore and Hong Kong, simply allowed easy entry in a competitive, market-oriented system. In contrast, Korea, the Philippines, and Indonesia in particular created subsidised and typically government-owned financial institutions, as vehicles to allocate cheap credit to preferred borrowers as a means of circumventing financial markets, thereby contributing further to the degree of financial repression. Supply-leading policies were perverted from their originally proposed market orientation.[25] Government savings institutions such as postal savings, agricultural cooperatives, insurance/provident funds, have had at best modest success in mobilising private resources on a voluntary basis. Such institutions have been little more than captive conduits for official foreign loans or government funds. All in all, the verdict is still out regarding the relative merits of supply-leading and demand-following approaches to financial-system-institution building.

Consistent with its European banking heritage, Asian banking generally has not followed the American twentieth-century model, of loans based on appraisal, of the overall creditworthiness of the borrower rather than the nature of the collateral. Virtually all domestic banks in the Asian–Pacific region require specific collateral for loans and for debenture issues. This difference in banking practice has come to pose difficulties, particularly for the Japanese monetary authorities and financial institutions as they move toward internationalisation of the Japanese financial system. Japanese banks, and presumably local and other foreign banks which also require specific collateral for loans to companies in Asian–Pacific developing economies such as Thailand, have found that American banks are prepared to lend to prime customers without such collateral requirements.

One of the most important, and least studied, features of the financial systems of the Asian–Pacific developing economies has been the emergence of large, family-owned financial and industrial conglomerates. Clan-based or extended-family-based banking, finance, commerce, and industry is perhaps the dominant form of large-scale industrial organisation throughout Southeast Asia.

In Japan, the prewar *zaibatsu* were broken up by the Allied Occupation authorities, and were replaced by much looser-knit but nonetheless important 'groups' of affiliated firms based on management alliances, with banks and trading companies typically at the core.

In Korea, family-based industrial conglomerates, *chaebol*, emerged as an important feature of industrial development after independence, and especially in the rapid growth of the past two decades.[26] Much of their success has been based on preferential access to credit. A crucial issue for the Korea government has been the appropriate ownership and control of the commercial banking system.[27] The five large commerical banks, all but one established and owned by the Japanese in the colonial era, were first taken over by the Korean government, then sold to wealthy entrepreneurs in 1957, repossessed from Syngman Rhee's cronies by the new military government in 1961 and in 1982–83 once again sold to private owners. As is discussed later, it remains to be seen whether this new effort at financial divestiture will be successful, and to what extent the banks will become tools of the *chaebol* conglomerates.

In the Philippines, private commercial banks are predominantly owned or controlled by one or several individuals and their families, and lend extensively to related enterprises.[28] Government and private credit has been allocated to financial institutions and businesses controlled by individuals close to the current government, especially during the severe economic difficulties of the past several years.

Family networks, notably ethnic Chinese, extend across Southeast Asian countries as well as within them. Through these sophisticated financial networks, funds can be readily transferred from one country to another and from one use to another. According to Wu and Wu, ethnic Chinese direct and indirect (concealed) ownership of banks and other financial institutions in Hong Kong and Southeast Asia is extensive. To quote them, 'It is probably safe to say that Chinese funds have been a primary factor in making Singapore and Hong Kong the principal financial markets serving Southeast Asia'.[29] While we know relatively little about the nature, extent, mechanisms, amount of funds involved, performance, or efficiency of these financial networks, we believe they are ubiquitous, readily accessible to those whose personal trust and creditworthiness are well established, involve large amounts of funds and are efficient.

THE INTERPLAY BETWEEN REGULATED AND UNREGULATED FINANCIAL SECTORS

We have stressed that conceptually the financial system is divided into two sectors, regulated and unregulated, and that the unregulated, or informal, sector is of substantial importance in the financially developing Pacific Basin economies. This importance has several dimensions: its size; its relative efficiency in the mobilisation and allocation of funds; and its use as an effective mechanism for adjustment to the distortions imposed by policy repression of the regulated financial sector. The unregulated sector combines two strands of financial intermediaries and activities, which can be termed the 'traditional' and the 'urban informal'.

Traditional institutions, markets, and financing arrangements flourished before the establishment of modern commercial banks and they continue to play an important role in many countries, notably for small-scale finance. They include moneylenders, pawnshops, rotating credit associations,[30] as well as friends and relatives. These are often efficient suppliers of small amounts of credit; they are flexible, non-bureaucratic, capable of making quick decisions, and have superior information on borrower creditworthiness and superior ability to collect loans. On the other hand, in comparison with commercial banks in a competitive, market-oriented financial system, traditional markets tend to be segmented, lack mechanisms for pooling funds and risks, and are unable to achieve economies of scale. Depending on the scarcity of viable alternative sources of funds, moneylenders can exploit market power in lending and in receiving funds on deposit.

In theory, over the course of economic and financial development as a regulated modern financial sector arises, the modern and traditional sectors become increasingly integrated, and the organised modern sector gradually takes on and absorbs many of the financial activities of the traditional sector. Vestiges remain but are quantitatively not very important. The main exception is the continuing major role of internal finance, including friends and relatives, for the establishment of new small businesses; venture-capital institutions are still the exception, not the rule.[31]

In the urban centres, which are the base of the regulated financial system of banks and other 'modern' financial institutions, a variety of informal, kerb markets have evolved and often thrived. To some degree they represent the continuation and metamorphosis of traditional institutions. They also reflect considerable financial innovation; they include bill brokers, finance companies and the like.

Where there are interest-rate controls that result in substantial distortion of interest rates on loans or deposits from free-market-equilibrium values, strong incentives are created not only for illicit payments to those controlling the allocation of such funds, but also for the emergence, or continuation, of informal, parallel markets in which funds are traded at more realistic, competitive prices. Furthermore, if the credit of regulated institutions is initially channelled to certain uses, frequently in conjunction with below-equilibrium interest rates, and those uses are less profitable than other opportunities currently available, parallel financial markets are likely to assist with the reallocation of credit from the less to the more profitable uses at market-clearing prices. Such reallocations of credit may be for relatively brief periods of time in individual cases, but if they are a continuing phenomenon they can have a significant effect on the allocation of capital.

In general, it can be said that the parallel, informal, unregulated urban financial markets serve those who do not have access to the regulated institutions or who cannot meet all their needs from the regulated institutions, and those who are in a position to arbitrage between the two markets. If such arbitrage is extensive then the actual prices for finance are likely to be similar in the two types of markets. But if the barriers to entry and to arbitrage are effective, the prices may diverge substantially.[32] The irony of any attempt to compare the two types of markets is that, as we have already stated, it is generally possible to obtain reasonably reliable information on the quantities of claims of the regulated institutions but not of the unregulated institutions. On the other hand, while the official prices in the regulated institutions and the prevailing market prices in the unregulated markets may be known, it is difficult to obtain reliable information on the surcharges extracted in connection with the allocative process of the regulated institutions. Consequently, it is impossible to make reliable comparisons of either the quantities transacted or the prices of the two types of institutions. Such comparisons must inevitably be based more on impressions and anecdotal information than on hard evidence.

The unregulated financial market is large and still plays an important financing role in all the financially developing Pacific Basin economies. The relative importance of the unregulated sector is greater the less developed the economy and the more repressed the regulated banking and financial system. Put another way, most bank loans go to large enterprises in industry, commerce and agriculture. Large enterprises produce only a small proportion of GDP. For example, at least three-quarters of private bank loans in the Philippines go to the 1000 largest corporations, which produce only one-tenth of GNP.[33]

In contrast, despite numerous efforts in recent years to provide credit services to farmers through government-supported institutions, sample surveys in many Asian developing countries continue to report that most credit needs of rural inhabitants are met through informal channels. In only a few countries, such as Korea and Taiwan, has organised institutional credit to farmers achieved significance. Even so, governments have typically provided more formal institutional support and subsidised credit for farmers than for small business.

It is always going to be exceptionally difficult to obtain even crude guesses of the size of the unregulated sector, at any point in time, much less for changes over time. Case studies and surveys of urban as well as rural households, small business, and large enterprise sources and uses of funds are the most likely sources of evidence, but very little actual research has been done.[34] There are occasional flashes of illumination. For example, a Korean government decree of August 1972 required all informal-sector loans to enterprises to be registered and renegotiated or be invalid. The suddenly available data indicated that informal-sector lending to enterprises amounted to about one-half of commercial bank lending.[35] A study of household savings in financial form in Thailand indicated that, in 1977–81, 33 per cent was channelled through the unregulated, informal financial sector, a decline from 57 per cent in 1961–66.[36] Wells cites rural credit surveys which indicate very high (88–100 per cent) reliance on informal sources of credit in the late 1960s in Malaysia.[37]

The data presented in Table 2.2 and attendant discussion provide indirect evidence on the relative importance of the unregulated sector. Where the regulated sector provides minimal levels of financial services we can be quite sure those services are being supplied, even more than would normally be the case, by the informal, unregulated sector. Wide spreads between nominal loan interest rates in the regulated and unregulated financial markets also suggest above-normal opportunities for action by the unregulated institutions. In Korea between 1963–78, the interest-rate gap ranged between 22–46 percentage points.[38] In Taiwan, the gap between commercial bank deposits and loan rates and those in the 'unorganised money market' were 10–20 percentage points between 1970 and 1983.[39] Fragmentary evidence suggests a gap in Philippines interest rates between bank deposits and unregulated deposit substitutes in the late 1970s–early 1980s of the order of 10–20 percentage points.[40]

We believe that the unregulated sector in most cases is a more effective, efficient and equitable mobiliser and allocator of funds than a highly repressed regulated sector. Market determination of interest rates provides appropriate signals and incentives. Entry is relatively easy and case studies suggest that competition is substantial (even among moneylenders). However, private and social benefits and costs may differ significantly. In the unregulated market it is possible to conceal income and wealth and thereby to evade taxes, which raises private benefits above social benefits. On the other hand, the addition of risk premiums to normal interest rates, to offset potential costs of government crackdowns on what are often regarded as illegal rather than free-market activities, tends to lower private relative to social benefits. The analogue in the regulated institutions is the payoffs for allocation of low-cost loans that cause private benefits to diverge from social benefits and also distort income distribution. Nonetheless, because it provides a mechanism for the rechannelling of official cheap credit to more efficient uses and for the redistribution of available funds in periods of sharp inflationary surges or monetary contractions, the unregulated sector typically plays a complementary rather than substituting role in repressed regulated financial systems.[41]

Furthermore, the unregulated sector may play a key role in making effective the subsidies implicit in the low-interest-rate loans of the regulated sector. At least this is the case if the allocators of the low-interest loans do not extract all the economic rents from the original borrowers. The export-credit subsidies in Korea provide an example of how the system works.

In the latter half of the 1960s, Korean exporters were able to obtain a 90–120-day loan at 6 per cent per annum interest, for an amount equal to 80 per cent of their export order upon presentation of a valid export letter of credit to a Korean commercial bank. The loan was automatic as long as the exporter had a good performance record, so there was little opportunity for the loan officer or the bank to impose any extra charges. Because the borrower often did not need that much credit in order to prepare the goods for shipment, he could either use the funds for his other business activities or lend them out in the unregulated market at 25–30 per cent per annum. If he relent the money at 30 per cent for 90 days, he could realise a gain of 4.8 per cent of the value of the export order, thus producing an interest subsidy of nearly 5 per cent on the exports. Without the unregulated market, the implicit subsidy would have depended on the return on his other activities or the short-term savings deposit rate in the commercial bank, which being only 5 per cent per annum was less than the interest on the loan. Accordingly, most exporters were heavy borrowers from the regulated commercial banks and heavy lenders in the unregulated markets. The interest-rate differential helped to keep profits up and export prices down. While the World Bank and the IMF lauded Korea's export performance, they often criticised the low-interest loans to exporters, the lack of control over increases in export credits, and the misallocation of resources by the unregulated credit markets, without acknowledging that all these features were contributing, albeit indirectly, to the export performance.

Unregulated financial sectors are still of some significance in the financially developed Pacific Basin economies. Moneylenders, finance companies, and other unregulated or semiregulated intermediaries continue to make high-risk, small-scale consumer or business loans at high interest rates in the United States ('loan sharking'), Japan (*sarakin*), Singapore ('six-five system') and elsewhere. But it is more than that. Virtually all the financially developed economies have had, and indeed still have, some regulations which control some interest rates and/or otherwise restrict competition.

The collision of the inflationary surges with regulated ceilings on interest rates in the 1970s brought about various innovations in virtually all the financially developed countries whereby funds moved into newly developed unregulated or less regulated instruments and markets. In the United States ceiling interest rates on bank deposits were effectively imposed until 1982; large depositors escaped to, and indeed were an important cause of the development of, the unregulated Eurodollar market and the market in negotiable certificates of deposit in the 1960s. Small depositors shifted funds into the money market in the late 1970s, when the gap widened between interest rates in the uncontrolled money market and those for controlled bank deposits. In Japan, credit rationing of small business had the result that large enterprises, trading companies in particular, became significant de facto financial intermediaries, borrowing huge sums from city banks and relending (at unregulated and unknown rates) to small companies through trade credit, which forms a much larger share of business assets and liabilities in Japan than elsewhere.[42] In New Zealand, lawyers created unregulated 'solicitors' nominee companies' in the mid-1970s which accepted deposits and made mortgage loans, accounting for more than 11 per cent of total mortgage finance in 1977.[43] In Australia, as in many developing Pacific Basin economies, the share of largely unregulated finance companies increased significantly from 2 per cent to 14 per cent in 1978.

FINANCIAL LIBERALISATION AND DEREGULATION

From time to time governments have attempted to offset and to curb inflation and to reduce or end financial repression by policies of financial liberalisation and, more recently, deregulation. Financial liberalisation was implemented in the 1950s and 1960s in several Asian economies (Taiwan, Korea and Indonesia), defined and given academic respectability by McKinnon and Shaw in the early 1970s, and taken up as the new orthodoxy by the IMF and World Bank in the late 1970s and early 1980s. Recently, it has been redesignated as deregulation, following the US example, and is being tried on in various forms by Japan, Korea, Indonesia, Thailand and the Philippines. We review these experiences briefly because they have been and are likely to be important features of future Asian financial development.

The early 'liberalisation' programs in Taiwan (1950s), Korea (1965), and Indonesia (1968) consisted mainly of raising nominal interest rates on the time deposits of banking institutions above the prevailing inflation rates. Loan rates were also increased but not always as much as deposit rates. The governments retained their controls over bank interest rates, credit allocations and entry of new financial institutions, so that the extent of liberalisation was quite limited. The increased deposit rates did raise the demand for time deposits and added significantly to the resources of the banking system. The matching expansion of bank lending went mainly into new private-sector investment which in turn contributed to higher growth with less inflation. Although these cases of limited liberalisation were quite successful at the time, the policies were largely rescinded after several years, at least in Korea and Indonesia, as the governments reduced nominal bank deposit rates below OPEC-induced inflation rates and M2 ratios levelled off. Also, it was never clear how much of the growth in bank deposits resulted from a shift out of unregulated financial assets.

Many Pacific Basin economies have responded to the inflationary pressures of the second oil crisis by initiating or contemplating extensive programs of financial liberalisation and reform. These efforts have focused on deregulation: withdrawal (or substantial reduction) of government controls over the pricing and allocation of finance, and greater reliance on market forces and indirect controls for the exercise of monetary policy. In some countries, such as the United States, Japan, Korea and the Philippines, financial institutions have been allowed to expand their range of services and create new instruments, thereby reducing market segmentation. However, in general the entry of new institutions has not been made substantially easier.

While the United States has long had a very large, sophisticated, and market-oriented financial system, there were, nonetheless, restrictions which inhibited competition: interest-rate ceilings on deposits; restrictions on the development of close deposit substitutes; and domestic geographic restriction to banking within state (and in some states, local) boundaries. Inflation in the late 1970s created a large gap between regulated and unregulated rates, and the pace of financial innovation in unregulated markets quickened. In a burst of reaction to public discontent Congress enacted the Depository Institution Deregulation Act of 1980, and, in the Reagan Administration's spirit of extensive deregulation, subsequently passed the Depository Institutions Act of 1982. This Act was necessary to enable banks and savings institutions to compete effectively against the burgeoning money-market funds. The pace of subsequent change has been bewilderingly rapid: new financial services, new roles for old institutions, vigorous competition in retail as well as wholesale financial markets. The pendulum between regulation to reduce the chances of banker moral hazard and to enhance depositor safety and confidence in the financial system, and deregulation to enhance competition, efficiency and consumer welfare, has swung far toward the latter. The United States now has the most free-market-oriented, competitive, vigorously functioning financial system in its history— with attendant potential dangers. It is premature to judge the longer run effects and implications.

Japan too, over the past decade, has been pursuing a path of rapid financial liberalisation, both domestically and in its international transactions, from an initial level of considerable financial repression.[44] In the 1950s and 1960s financial regulation rather successfully kept interest rates below equilibrium levels and allocated credit to large, rapidly growing enterprises. The degree of repression was mitigated by modest inflation rates, very high and rising savings, tax inducements to hold savings in time deposits, and the lack of viable deposit substitutes. While inflation was one source forcing change, more important since 1975 has been the huge sustained issuance of government bonds in what had become a Keynesian economy of continuing very high rates of saving and only moderately high rates of investment. Moreover, large corporations found themselves with surplus funds on which they wanted competitive interest-yields. To this has been added foreign pressures on Japan to liberalise its foreign transactions and foreign access to the Tokyo capital market. Liberalisation has proceeded rapidly due mainly to market pressures; the Ministry of Finance has persisted in resisting and slowing the pace even though change is widely regarded as inevitable.

The Canadians deregulated interest rates and reduced controls over entry of new banks in the Bank Act of 1967, which implemented many of the recommendations of the Porter Commission *Report on Banking and Finance* of 1964.[45] The results have generally been favourable in terms of increased competition and expanded services, but there is continuing pressure to reduce the barriers to functional diversification.

Australia and New Zealand present quite disparate cases of financial reform.[46] New Zealand in 1976 began a five-year process of liberalisation of interest rates, activities of financial institutions, and financial markets—only to reimpose interest-rate ceilings and other instruments of financial repression in late 1981 in order to 'fight inflation by reducing the cost of credit'. Australia began partial deregulation from 1979, removing interest-rate ceilings on deposits but not on loans, and establishing the Campbell Committee which made a comprehensive review, entitled *The Australian Financial System: Final Report of the Committee of Inquiry* (December, 1981, preceded by a 1980 interim report).

In Korea, the government was greatly embarrassed by the involvement of its own commercial banks in the 'kerb market scandal' of 1982 and sought to resolve the problem by selling its shares in five government-owned commercial banks to the general public. The ostensible purpose was to reduce the degree of government involvement in bank operations and rely more on market forces. Also it was hoped that a freer banking sector would draw business away from the unregulated financial institutions.

Ownership of the banks has passed mainly into the hands of the large industrial-trading groups, *chaebol*, whose affairs are so intimately intertwined with those of the government that it is difficult to differentiate national interest from entrepreneurial self-interest. While the government is undoubtedly sincere in its expressed intent to disengage from day-to-day direction of the banks, such a policy will probably be difficult to implement, especially in the current politico-economic context of Korea.

The 1982 Korean reforms ended the preferential interest rate on export credits by reducing the rate on essentially *all* loans to 10 per cent and on time and savings deposits to 8 per cent.[47] The hope was that the early 1982 decline in the inflation rate to unprecedentedly low levels would persist and, despite the misgivings of many, that hope was fulfilled; the consumer price index increased only 5 per cent in 1982, and 2 per cent in 1983 and early 1984. Sustained price stability will eventually alter Korean inflationary expectations. This, combined with the current 9–9.5 per cent nominal yield on deposits, could bring about a substantial shift of claims from the kerb market to the regulated financial institutions, and eventually a further lowering of nominal interest rates throughout the financial system.

We predict that, if inflation rates in Korea can be kept below 5 per cent and real bank deposit rates above 5 per cent for several years, the banking system will move up to levels more typical of a country with Korea's per capita income. We doubt, on the other hand, that the Korean banking system will become very free of government direction, unless the doors are opened considerably wider for the entry of new financial enterprises, both domestic and foreign. One fear is that this would lead to Japanese domination of the Korean financial system, something no self-respecting Korean government will permit.

Deregulation in Indonesia was initiated dramatically on June 1 1983 when, without prior notice, the government removed controls over the interest rates on deposits and loans (excluding priority credits) of government-owned banks and eliminated credit ceilings on all banks. A second step, in January 1984, was to introduce central bank rediscounting privileges for private as well as state banks and to initiate the periodic auction of central bank securities as instruments for controlling the reserve base. These instruments are not yet developed to the point where they can impose any real restraint on credit and monetary expansion. The government-owned banks have, however, been slow to commit their excess liquidity to loan expansion and are still inclined to listen carefully for guidelines from the central bank.

Indonesian authorities keep saying the government-owned commercial banks should behave more like competitive private banks, but old habits are difficult to change. There are still severe restrictions on foreign banks in Indonesia; no offices outside Jakarta and only two branches within Jakarta for already licensed banks, and no new permits for foreign banks. Domestic private banks are becoming more aggressive in their deposit mobilising and lending activities, but they too are restricted and still handle much of their business through Singapore and Hong Kong.

As in Korea, the main reason for the continuing restriction on the entry of new branches of foreign and domestic private banks is the fear that Indonesian banking will be dominated, in this case, by the Chinese of Southeast Asia. Consequently, future growth of the financial system and continuation of governmental guidance within Indonesia will probably be predicated upon the maintenance of a reasonable share of the market for Indonesian financial institutions, whether owned by government or private citizens. And, ironically, the excess demand for financial services in Indonesia will continue to spill over into the Chinese-run financial markets of Singapore and Hong Kong.

The Philippines in 1980 initiated an ambitious program of financial reform which focused primarily upon institutional change but also had the goal of interest-rate liberalisation.[48] A series of laws was enacted to increase competition among financial institutions by allowing all institutions a wider range of activities, thereby reducing market segmentation. Functional differences among various types of thrift institutions were eliminated and they were allowed to compete directly with commercial banks for demand deposits. Other institutions were allowed to convert to commercial bank status. Perhaps most importantly, very large commercial banks (by Philippine standards) were allowed to become 'universal banks' by engaging in investment banking, including direct equity participation in industrial enterprises as well as the underwriting of new securities issues. Interest-rate ceilings on deposits and term loans were removed in 1981 and on short-term loans in 1983. However, they were apparently replaced by a cartel agreement (the Manila Reference Rate) supported by considerable governmental suasion.

The Philippine financial reforms have been substantially undermined by ensuing events. The financial system, always subject to the turmoil of bank runs, was subjected to a major crisis in the spring of 1981, triggered by the flight of a highly respected business leader who left large debts behind. The world recession, combined with domestic policies and conditions, forced a number of major enterprises into insolvency or even virtual bankruptcy. Many, especially cronies of the First Family, were bailed out by loans and infusions of equity from the very large government-owned financial institutions. Another banking crisis occurred in spring 1984 as a consequence, in part, of government efforts to control rampant inflation by restrictive monetary policies. Add in the over-whelming problems of the recent, ongoing foreign-debt crisis and high levels of domestic political turmoil and one has the recipe for aborted, or at least delayed, financial reform.

Where do the Pacific Basin economies fit, as of mid-1984, along the spectrum between the poles of completely free financial markets with unrestricted entry and a high degree of integration, and at the other extreme, highly controlled and segmented formal financial systems with substantial spillover into unregulated markets? Appropriate criteria include: market versus authority determination of deposit, loan, and other interest rates; ease of entry and latitude of permitted activities for financial intermediaries; competitive market allocation of various forms of financial claims.

One important litmus test on financial repression is whether ceiling interest rates are set, formally or informally, by the monetary authorities, or by banks allowed to engage in collusive price-fixing behaviour, or whether interest rates are determined, like other prices, through the demand for and supply of financial claims in the marketplace. The key interest rates are on commercial bank loans, time and savings deposits, and long-term credit. Table 2.4 provides a subjective ranking, in clusters, of Pacific Basin economies from more to less market-determined financial systems as of mid-1984. It also provides our assessment as to whether major interest rates are determined by market forces, or (relatively low) nominal ceiling rates are set by the monetary authorities or by agreement among the banks. As Table 2.4 indicates, most rates are regulated in most Pacific Basin countries. The issue really is one of degree: the gap between equilibrium and regulated rates, the responsiveness of administrators in adjust-

Table 2.4 Degree of financial restriction and nature of interest-rate determination (at mid-1984)

| Clustered ranking by degree of financial restriction | Interest-rate determination | | |
	Time and savings deposits	Commercial bank loans	Long-term credit
Singapore	Market	Market	Market
Hong Kong	Market	Market	Market
United States	Market	Market	Market
Canada	Market	Market	Market
Japan	Regulated	Market	Regulated
Malaysia	Market	Market	Regulated
Australia	Market	Regulated	Market
Thailand	Market	Market	Regulated
Indonesia	Market	Regulated	Regulated
Taiwan	Regulated	Regulated	Regulated
New Zealand	Regulated	Regulated	Regulated
South Korea	Regulated	Regulated	Regulated
The Philippines	Regulated	Regulated	Regulated

Notes: Long-term credit refers to government-bond-issue conditions or, if negligible, other major forms of long-term credit.
Regulated rates include both those which are administratively adjusted quite rapidly to changing actual market conditions, and those where adjustment is slow or inflexible.

ing regulated rates as market conditions change, the importance of credit rationing, the degree of financial distortion and repression.

The comparative evaluation provided in Table 2.4 represents our best judgment of the current situation (mid-1984). As the preceding discussion indicates, different countries have pursued different policies at different points in time, so that similar tables for earlier time periods would provide somewhat different results. Moreover, Table 2.4 is based on our informed but subjective and qualitative evaluation. More detailed country case studies and further cross-country research would yield more rigorously based conclusions, and presumably some reassessment of our results. We do not have any rigorous method for measuring or weighting these various factors, but offer our subjective evaluation for others to contest or reassess over time.

FUTURE PROSPECTS FOR FINANCIAL DEVELOPMENT

It is premature to predict how enduring and successful financial reform and development will be. Policies promoting financial reform can be adversely overwhelmed by unrealistic and rigid macroeconomic policies. A highly expansionary fiscal policy can generate inflationary pressures which monetary policy and the financial system cannot deal with, or can do so only at the cost of high real as well as nominal interest rates, as in the US since 1980. Or, as happened in Sri Lanka in the late 1970s, financial reform can result in a large-scale channelling of resources to unproductive public sector projects.[49] Exchange-rate controls, and a pegged rate, which result in an overvalued exchange rate appreciating in real terms with higher-than-world rates of domestic inflation, further undermine domestic financial reform programs, as in the Philippines. Deregulation and privatisation can result in a concentrated financial sector in the hands of a few wealthy families or industrial groups who take on undue risk or allocate funds to their own purposes, in expectation of government bail-out in emergency, such as in the Philippines[50] or the Chile fiasco of financial liberalisation.

Future financial development of the Pacific Basin economies will depend on the same variables as in the past: real economic growth; the rate of inflation; government policies on interest rates, entry of new firms and controls which foster liberalisation and deregulation, or, instead, financial repression; and the nature and degree of domestic political stability. On the whole we view the prospects as good. The Pacific Basin economies, both developed and developing, will outperform their counterparts in the rest of the world. Inflation is likely to be less rapid during the remainder of the 1980s than in the 1973–83 period. Governments appear to be pursuing more flexible, more economically oriented, more market-oriented policies. The trend is for increasingly variegated and sophisticated regulated financial structures, with decreasing market segmentation. The trend is toward a far wider range of financial services offered by commercial banks, though achievement of universal banking has a long way to go in most countries.

Yet we are far from sanguine. The overhang of third world debt, and the possibility of an international financial crisis, persist. The struggle to control inflation is not over; it is an ongoing battle both worldwide and in a number of countries with relatively fragile financial systems and/or misguided macroeconomic policies. Vested interests enjoying market-niche rents strongly resist financial liberalisation of their markets (witness the ongoing series of struggles in Japan). Political succession clouds the future of Hong Kong and, more immediately, the Philippines.

On balance, however, we regard the prospects for financial development and growth in the Pacific Basin economies as we do their real economic prospects, like a weather forecast: on the whole, good, but with occasional clouds and some locally severe disturbances.

3 Capital flows among Pacific Basin economies

TSAO YUAN

The Pacific Basin region has, in the past one-and-a-half decades, been one of the most economically dynamic regions in the world. The rapid growth of Japan as well as the industrialising countries in the region has meant that there have been increasing opportunities for closer economic integration, based on trade and capital flows. There is, therefore, interest in examining the extent of inter-dependence among the Pacific Basin countries. While the nature of the trade links has been relatively well researched,[1] the complementary picture of the pattern of capital flows is still relatively unexplored. The objective of this chapter is, therefore, to investigate the nature of capital flows among the countries of the Pacific Basin region.

This region is defined as the countries which border the Pacific Ocean and for the purposes of this chapter will exclude Latin America. The countries in this region can be broadly divided into two groups: the developed countries of Australia, Canada, Japan, New Zealand and the United States (US), collectively called the Pacific Basin Developed Five (PB5 for short), and the less developed countries of Indonesia, Malaysia, the Philippines, Singapore, Thailand, Hong Kong, South Korea and Taiwan, or the Pacific Basin Less Developed Eight (PB8).[2] The main focus of the discussion will be on flows from the PB5 to the PB8 and to a lesser extent on intra-PB8 flows. Intra-PB5 flows will not be discussed. The US and Japan are net capital exporters while the smaller countries of the PB5, Australia, Canada and New Zealand, as well as the PB8 countries, are in general net capital importers. One would expect, therefore, that the flows from the US and Japan to the PB8 countries would eclipse the flows from the other PB5 countries. At the same time, external sources of funds have been important to the PB8 countries. This has been not only to finance the excess of investment over domestic savings in the context of fairly rapid growth, but also to help ease the adjustment to the turbulent world economic conditions of the 1970s and early 1980s: the changes in their terms of trade due to the oil shocks and the volatility of the prices of raw materials, as well as the world recessions. There are, therefore, several interesting questions which can be asked with respect to captial flows in the Pacific Basin region. One of these is the role of external capital in the growth and adjustment of the PB8 countries.[3]

Another is the extent of financial interdependence and integration among the Pacific Basin countries. A third, which is a more narrow version of the second, is the focus of this chapter; the nature of the capital flows among the Pacific Basin countries.

The paper is organised around the demonstration of several themes in an attempt to provide an overview of capital flows in the region since 1970. By capital flows is meant those transactions which are recorded in the capital account of the balance of payments, as well as flows of official reserves. As comprehensive a treatment of all kinds of financial transactions will be discussed as data availability will allow.[4] The first issue to be discussed is the importance of capital flows from the PB5 to the PB8 countries, relative to flows from other sources and to other developing regions. It turns out that flows from the PB5 to the PB8 have been relatively important during 1972–82. This relative importance has also increased from the early 1970s to the early 1980s. Why have these flows been relatively important and become increasingly so? In the investigation of the more detailed pattern of flows a second theme emerges; that of the central role played by Japan in the region. While flows from the US are important because of their large absolute magnitude, flows from Japan to the PB8 are important because of Japan's relative concentration of its capital flows to this region. This is true for both official and private-sector flows. Third, from the viewpoint of the PB8 countries, the variation of these flows with growth is evident over time as well as across countries. Private-sector flows have risen in importance as compared with official flows. In terms of intra-PB8 flows, direct foreign investment is found to be not insignificant, particularly from the Asian newly industrialising countries (NICs). Within private-sector flows, loans have also become important relative to foreign investment for some countries. Fifth, the banking data available show that the PB8 countries are net borrowers, from the offshore centres in the region as well as from the US. In the conclusion, the hypothesis is raised that there has indeed been increasing financial integration among the Pacific Basin countries, because of improved technology and a greater degree of financial liberalisation (among other reasons). The chapter ends by raising questions which might prove to be fruitful avenues for further research in this area.

THE RELATIVE IMPORTANCE OF FLOWS FROM THE PB5 TO THE PB8 COUNTRIES

The OECD publications are one of the best sources of data available from which the geographical distribution of financial flows originating from most developed countries can be derived. They give data compiled from developed countries and institutions, and as such are subject to two main drawbacks:[5] the flows recorded are essentially one-way, with the 'net' flows eliminating repayment of principal and interest where relevant; and flows from other developing countries are not considered. They do give a breakdown of flows by type:

1 offiical development assistance (ODA), or official flows with a grant element of at least 25 per cent and with a maturity of at least one year;
2 other official flows (OOF), which are all types of official flows other than ODA;
3 flows originating from the private sector, comprising private direct investment, portfolio investment and export credits;
4 total flows, which is the sum of ODA, OOF and private sector flows.

Most of the flows will be discussed in net terms, not only to provide an estimate of the net transfer in any one year, but also because total flows are given only in net terms.[6] This source of data will be used extensively in the following discussion.

The nominal net flows from the PB5 to the PB8 countries are shown in Table 3.1. Total flows increased about fourfold between 1970 and 1982. The composition of total flows has, however, changed over time. In the early 1970s, ODA was of major importance, comprising slightly more than half of total flows. By 1980–82, official flows, including OOF, comprised only one-third of total flows, with private-sector flows comprising the other two-thirds.[7] The rise in importance of private-sector flows is possibly due to the increasing flows of private direct investment and public debt from banks and other financial institutions.[8] At the same time ODA from the PB5 has declined as the PB8 countries have risen on the development ladder; official flows from multilateral institutions have also increased in importance relative to official bilateral flows.

Table 3.1 Nominal net flows from the PB5 to the PB8, 1970–82 (US$ million)

Year	ODA	OOF[a]	Private-sector[a]	Total flows
1970	714.9 (5.12%)		682.4 (48.8%)	1 397.3 (100%)
1971	805.2 (55.3%)		650.5 (44.7%)	1 455.7 (100%)
1972	871.9 (53.1%)		771.3 (46.9%)	1 643.2 (100%)
1973	854.1 (34.8%)		1 602.2 (65.2%)	2 456.3 (100%)
1974	778.7 (45.2%)		945.2 (54.8%)	1 723.9 (100%)
1975	810.1 (22.5%)		2 795.2 (77.5%)	3 605.3 (100%)
1976	771.4 (23.8%)		2 468.1 (76.2%)	3 239.5 (100%)
1977	1 172.8 (30.2%)	1 241.7 (32.0%)	1 464.0 (37.8%)	3 878.1 (100%)
1978	860.9 (25.5%)	607.8 (18.0%)	1 908.4 (56.5%)	3 377.1 (100%)
1979	969.2 (28.1%)	623.4 (18.1%)	1 854.4 (53.8%)	3 477.0 (100%)
1980	1 804.2 (31.4%)	731.6 (21.2%)	1 633.3 (47.4%)	3 499.1 (100%)
1981	1 392.5 (17.0%)	328.9 (4.0%)	6 451.1 (78.9%)	8 172.5 (100%)
1982	952.9 (16.9%)	490.0 (8.7%)	4 186.6 (74.4%)	5 630.4 (100%)

Note: a   A separate breakdown of OOF and private-sector flows is not available before 1977.
Source: Computed from OECD Geographical Distribution of Financial Flows (various years) Paris.

One expects that the capital flows from the PB5 to the PB8 countries would have increased in relative importance over time. In order to assess the relative importance of these flows, however, there has to be some means of comparison. This is so, especially since net flows from the developed to all developing countries have also risen during the same period and the PB5 includes the two largest capital exporters in the world, the US and Japan. The method of comparison adopted is shown in the table below:

To	From	DAC countries PB5 Europe	Multilateral institutions	OPEC	All sources
PB8 Other less developed countries		x			T2
All less developed countries		T1			T

First, from the viewpoint of the PB8 countries, the ratio of flows from the PB5 relative to that from all sources, x/T2, is considered.[9] The trend over time of x/T2 shows us whether the PB5 have become relatively more or less important as a source of flows to the PB8. However, x/T2 may only be a reflection of T1/T, the flows from the PB5 to all less developed countries as a ratio of flows from all sources to all developing countries. Therefore, x/T2 will be considered relative to T1/T. If x/T2 is greater than T1/T at any point in time, then flows from the PB5 are relatively more important to the PB8 countries than to all less developed countries. If the ratio (x/T2)/(T1/T) increases over time, then these flows have increased in relative importance.[10] Second, from the source countries' point of view, the relative importance of the PB8 to the PB5, x/T, can be considered over time or in relation to the relative importance of the PB8 to all sources, T2/T. Again, if x/T is greater than T2/T at any point in time, then PB8 is more important as a destination for outward flows to the PB5 than to other sources. If (x/T1)/(T2/T) = (x/T2)/(T1/T) increases over time, the relative importance of the PB8 to the PB5 has increased. This analysis can be carried out by types of flow.

The composition of flows to the PB8 as well as all less developed countries by source, including x/T2 and T1/T, are given in Table 3.2. The most important point to note is that the PB5 has been the major source of net ODA, private-sector and total flows for the PB8 countries, with x/T2 being in general over 50 per cent for these flows. There is, however, a declining trend in x/T2, particularly for ODA. As for all developing countries, more ODA has come from multilateral institutions such as the World Bank, then bilaterally from the PB5 countries.[11]

The importance of the PB8 as a destination for flows from the PB5 and other sources is shown in Table 3.3. Here we see clearly that the flows to the PB8 as a ratio of flows to all developing countries from the PB5, x/T1, is higher than that from other sources for the various categories of flows, with only a few exceptions.[12] While the ratio of official flows from the PB5 to the PB8 has declined with the relatively rapid development of the PB8 countries, the ratio of private-sector flows has risen at least from the late 1970s to the early 1980s.

The data can be most concisely summarised by examining the ratio (x/T2)/(T1/T) as shown in Table 3.4. With only two exceptions, this ratio is greater than 1, implying that the PB5 to PB8 flows are important relative to flows from other sources and to other less developed countries.[13] This is true for official as

Table 3.2 Composition of net flows to recipient developing country groups: PB8 and all developing countries (per cent)

	1970	1971	1972	1973	1974	1975	1976	1977	1978	1979	1980	1981	1982
ODA: PB8													
PB5	77.2	70.9	74.3	69.6	63.8	62.2	59.4	56.9	61.3	58.2	55.2	61.3	51.9
Europe	18.1	21.2	17.9	19.0	20.0	18.7	16.5	15.9	13.5	17.7	25.6	22.6	27.2
Multilateral	4.7	7.9	7.9	11.4	16.2	19.1	18.2	19.4	20.0	20.5	16.8	13.8	17.9
OPEC	—	—	—	—	0.0	—	5.9	7.8	5.0	2.2	2.4	2.2	3.0
ODA: all													
PB5	51.7	49.9	47.5	36.4	31.0	26.3	26.0	24.6	23.5	24.6	22.2	23.9	28.0
Europe	32.4	33.0	35.2	32.8	27.9	26.6	27.0	28.5	26.9	31.5	30.9	31.3	31.9
Multilateral	15.9	17.1	17.2	19.2	20.6	20.7	21.6	26.1	23.1	21.3	22.7	23.9	24.3
OPEC	—	—	—	11.7	20.5	26.3	25.3	20.8	26.5	22.6	24.2	20.9	15.8
OOF: PB8													
PB5								34.0	38.2	35.9	38.8	16.1	18.1
Europe								6.4	4.9	0.4	0.7	4.7	6.2
Multilateral								57.4	56.9	63.7	60.5	79.2	75.7
OPEC								2.2	—	—	—	—	—
OOF: all													
PB5								25.5	35.9	24.0	24.6	15.4	23.1
Europe								9.3	17.9	16.8	24.6	25.8	21.4
Multilateral								50.0	46.3	59.2	50.8	58.9	55.6
OPEC								15.1	—	—	—	—	—
Pte: PB8													
PB5								18.9[a]	79.0	54.3	45.0	70.4	72.1
Europe								81.1	21.0	45.7	55.0	29.6	27.9
Pte: all													
PB5								32.3	38.5	38.4	25.2	52.5	50.4
Europe								67.7	61.5	61.6	74.8	47.5	69.6
Pte export credits: PB8[b]													
PB5										33.5	32.9	39.3	53.6
Europe										66.5	67.1	60.7	46.4

Pte export credits: all													
PB5										18.0	21.5	32.7	27.7
Europe										82.0	78.5	67.3	72.3
Pte direct inv: PB8													
PB5										74.6	78.6	95.3	93.9
Europe										25.4	21.4	4.7	6.1
Pte direct inv: all													
PB5										71.6	49.9	65.4	65.6
Europe										28.4	50.1	34.6	34.5
Total flows: PB8													
PB5	69.0	67.6	70.8	71.0	56.3	68.1	50.1	35.2	62.4	50.7	46.1	60.6	54.4
Europe	22.9	20.8	16.2	16.8	24.4	15.2	31.8	37.5	14.3	27.4	33.6	24.7	22.1
Multilateral	8.1	11.6	13.0	12.2	17.9	16.6	16.1	24.2	21.9	21.3	19.7	14.3	23.0
OPEC	—	—	—	0.0	1.3	0.1	2.0	3.1	1.3	0.5	0.6	0.4	0.5
Total flows: all													
PB5	46.6	50.2	52.3	53.0	41.1	40.8	33.0	28.9	33.1	32.3	23.9	38.8	38.5
Europe	41.3	36.4	34.5	28.5	32.4	31.1	38.5	47.8	45.7	47.1	51.0	39.6	39.2
Multilateral	12.1	13.3	13.2	13.1	14.5	14.1	14.7	14.5	12.0	12.7	15.2	14.3	16.5
OPEC	—	—	—	5.4	11.9	14.1	13.7	8.8	9.1	8.0	9.9	7.3	5.7

All categories of flows are on a net basis except for private export credits, which is in gross terms.

Notes: All: all developing countries.
Pte: private-sector flows
Pte direct inv: private direct investment.
—: nil.
blank: not available.
a See note 11 in text.
b In gross terms.

Source: OECD *Geographical Distribution of Financial Flows* (various years) Paris.

Table 3.3 Flows to thue PB8 as a percentage of flows to all developing countries, by source and type of flow (per cent)

	1970	1971	1972	1973	1974	1975	1976	1977	1978	1979	1980	1981	1982
ODA													
PB5	20.5	21.2	23.0	22.9	17.9	16.6	16.5	14.3	14.1	13.5	14.3	17.6	11.0
Europe	7.7	9.6	7.5	7.0	6.2	4.9	4.4	3.4	2.7	3.2	4.8	5.0	5.1
Multilateral	4.0	6.9	6.7	7.2	6.8	6.5	6.1	4.6	4.7	5.5	4.3	4.0	4.4
OPEC	—	—	—	—	0.1	—	1.7	2.3	1.0	0.6	0.6	0.7	1.1
All sources	13.7	14.9	14.7	12.0	8.7	7.0	7.3	6.2	5.4	5.6	5.8	6.9	5.9
OOF													
PB5								28.1	25.4	37.0	31.2	22.1	17.9
Europe								14.5	6.5	0.6	0.6	3.8	6.6
Multilateral								24.2	29.3	26.6	23.5	28.4	31.0
OPEC								3.1	—	—	—	—	—
All sources								21.1	23.8	24.7	19.9	21.1	22.8
Private-sector flows													
PB5								2.9	11.5	10.6	16.5	23.5	19.5
Europe								5.9	1.9	5.5	6.8	11.0	7.7
All sources								4.9	5.6	7.5	9.2	17.6	13.6
Private export credits, gross													
PB5										24.6	22.3	19.8	33.0
Europe										10.7	12.4	14.9	11.0
All sources										13.2	14.6	16.5	17.1
Private direct investment													
PB5										6.6	26.2	45.7	23.3
Europe										5.7	7.1	4.3	2.9
All sources										6.3	16.6	31.4	16.3
Total flows													
PB5	20.4	17.3	17.4	18.6	13.0	19.6	21.2	8.7	13.5	13.0	17.4	22.2	17.1
Europe	7.6	7.3	6.0	8.2	7.1	5.7	11.9	5.6	2.2	4.8	5.9	8.8	6.8
Multilateral	9.2	11.2	12.6	12.9	11.7	13.8	15.8	11.9	13.1	14.0	11.7	14.2	16.8
OPEC	—	—	—	0.0	1.1	0.1	2.1	2.5	1.0	0.6	0.6	0.7	1.1
All sources	13.7	12.9	12.9	13.9	9.5	11.7	14.4	7.1	7.2	8.3	9.0	14.2	12.1

Notes: All flows are on a net basis unless otherwise specified.
    —: nil.
    blank: not available.

Source: OECD Geographical Distribution of Financial Flows (various years) Paris.

Table 3.4 $(x/T2)/(T1/T) = (x/T1)/(T2/T)^a$

	1970	1971	1972	1973	1974	1975	1976	1977	1978	1979	1980	1981	1982
ODA	1.49	1.42	1.56	1.91	2.06	2.37	2.28	2.31	2.61	2.37	2.24	2.56	1.85
OOF								1.33	1.06	1.50	1.58	1.05	0.78
Private sector								0.59	2.05	1.41	1.79	1.34	1.43
Private export credit										1.86	1.53	1.20	1.94
Private direct investment										1.04	1.58	1.46	1.43
Total flows	1.48	1.35	1.35	1.34	1.37	1.67	1.52	1.22	1.89	1.57	1.93	1.56	1.41

Notes: All flows are given in net terms except for private export credit, which is in gross terms.

a Refer to text for the meaning of this ratio.

Source: OECD *Geographical Distribution of Financial Flows* (various years) Paris.

well as private-sector flows. For ODA and total flows for which data are available for 1970–82, this ratio rises over the 1970s, peaks at the end of the 1970s/early 1980s and falls slightly in the early 1980s. Comparing the early 1970s with the early 1980s one can see that this ratio has increased for both these types of flows. It is more difficult to discern a time trend for private-sector flows as data are available only from 1977, and for private direct investment, from 1979. However, for total flows at least, the flows from the PB5 to the PB8 countries have increased in relative importance from the early 1970s to the early 1980s.

This observation, however, raises the question of why the PB5 to the PB8 flows have been relatively important and why this relative importance has increased. In an attempt to answer this question, it seems helpful to examine these flows in greater country detail. One conclusion from this discussion is the central role played by Japan and secondarily by the US.

THE IMPORTANCE OF JAPAN

Among the PB5 countries it is to be expected that flows from the US and Japan would be of major importance. This is indeed borne out by Tables 3.5, 3.6 and 3.7, which show net flows of ODA, total flows and OOF and private-sector

Table 3.5   Country matrixes: net ODA (US$ million)

From To	Australia	Canada	Japan	New Zealand	USA	Total
(a) 1970–72 average						
Indonesia	19.8	6.1	113.6	0.7	190.3	330.5
Malaysia	3.5	2.8	9.2	0.6	3.0	19.1
The Philippines	0.7	0.0	50.8	0.1	32.0	83.6
Singapore	0.7	0.5	6.3	0.1	0.0	7.6
Thailand	4.2	0.8	16.0	0.2	31.0	52.2
Hong Kong	0.0	0.0	0.1	0.0	0.0	0.1
South Korea	0.4	0.9	107.9	0.1	193.3	302.6
Taiwan	0.0	0.0	4.4	—	−2.7	1.7
Total	29.3	11.1	308.3	1.8	446.9	797.4
(per cent)	(3.7)	(1.4)	(38.7)	(0.2)	(56.0)	(100.0)
(b) 1980–82 average						
Indonesia	46.3	20.8	314.8	4.2	97.3	483.4
Malaysia	8.1	1.0	68.5	0.4	1.0	79.0
The Philippines	13.7	1.5	147.0	1.2	53.0	216.4
Singapore	1.6	0.4	7.3	0.1	—	9.4
Thailand	10.3	7.5	191.5	1.5	19.0	229.8
Hong Kong	0.1	—	1.5	—	—	1.6
South Korea	0.2	0.2	125.2	0.1	7.0	132.7
Taiwan	—	—	−1.1	—	−8.0	−9.1
Total	80.3	31.4	854.7	7.5	169.3	1 143.2
(per cent)	(7.0)	(2.7)	(74.8)	(0.1)	(14.8)	(100.0)

Source: OECD Geographical Distribution of Financial Flows (various years) Paris.

Table 3.6 Country matrixes: net total flows (US$ million)

To	From Australia	Canada	Japan	New Zealand	USA	Total
			(a) 1970–72 average			
Indonesia	21.8	6.1	228.3	0.7	178.3	435.2
Malaysia	4.9	1.1	35.8	0.6	5.7	48.1
The Philippines	0.6	4.8	112.2	0.1	53.0	170.7
Singapore	1.6	1.0	38.5	0.1	1.0	42.2
Thailand	5.0	0.7	27.0	0.2	27.7	60.6
Hong Kong	2.5	0.0	238.5	0.0	−6.7	243.3
South Korea	0.4	2.7	206.9	0.1	188.0	398.1
Taiwan	0.0	−0.7	91.7	—	18.7	109.7
Total	36.8	15.7	979.9	1.8	465.7	1 498.9
(per cent)	(2.5)	(1.0)	(65.3)	(0.1)	(31.1)	(100.0)
			(b) 1980–82 average			
Indonesia	60.7	18.9	1 223.1	4.2	433.4	1 740.2
Malaysia	22.0	2.1	257.0	0.4	308.0	589.2
The Philippines	17.6	3.6	299.1	1.2	107.7	429.2
Singapore	26.2	0.9	282.7	0.1	330.7	640.6
Thailand	15.3	14.7	362.8	1.5	166 7	561.0
Hong Kong	35.0	0.0	226.3	—	336.0	597.3
South Korea	0.2	59.5	307.9	0.1	364.0	731.7
Taiwan	0.0	0.0	170.1	—	291.0	461.1
Total	177.0	99.7	3 129.0	7.5	2 337.4	5 750.6
(per cent)	(3.1)	(1.7)	(54.4)	(0.1)	(40.6)	(100.0)

Source: OECD *Geographical Distribution of Financial Flows* (various years) Paris.

Table 3.7 Country matrixes: net OOF and private-sector flows

To	From Australia	Canada	Japan	New Zealand	USA	Total
			(a) Net OOF, 1980–82 average			
Indonesia	−2.3	−2.0	23.5	—	62.0	−42.8
Malaysia	—	1.0	—	—	4.3	—
The Philippines	3.5	2.2	5.4	—	−20.3	−9.2
Singapore	—	0.5	—	—	−1.3	−0.8
Thailand	0.2	5.9	28.6	—	−1.3	33.4
Hong Kong	−0.2	0.0	—	—	17.3	17.1
South Korea	—	59.7	−0.8	—	212.7	271.6
Taiwan	—	—	—	—	242.7	242.7
Total	1.2	67.3	56.7	—	392.1	517.3
(per cent)	(0.2)	(13.0)	(11.0)	—	(75.8)	(100.0)
			(b) Net privates sector, 1980–82 average			
Indonesia	16.7	0.2	884.8	—	398.0	1 299.7
Malaysia	13.9	0.1	188.5	—	302.7	505.2
The Philippines	0.34	0.0	146.5	—	75.0	222.2
Singapore	24.6	—	275.4	—	332.0	632.0
Thailand	4.8	1.3	142.7	—	149.0	297.8
Hong Kong	35.1	—	224.8	—	318.7	578.6
South Korea	−0.1	−0.5	183.4	—	144.3	327.1
Taiwan	—	0.0	171.2	—	56.3	227.5
Total	95.4	1.1	2 217.6	—	1 776.0	4 090.1
(per cent)	(2.3)	(0.0)	(54.2)	—	(43.4)	(100.0)

Source: OECD *Geographical Distribution of Financial Flows* (various years) Paris.

flows respectively. What is interesting is that 65 per cent of total flows in 1970–72 and 55 per cent in 1980–82 came from Japan, with the corresponding figures for the US being 31 per cent and 41 per cent respectively.[14] In other words, flows from Japan have been of central importance, not only in the early 1970s and early 1980s, but throughout this time period.

It is worthwhile looking at the flows by type. In terms of net ODA, flows from Japan have increased absolutely as well as relatively, while flows from the US have declined absolutely. It appears that official flows from the US have become more non-concessionary in nature (see the net OOF country matrix, Table 3.7) while official flows from Japan are still largely in the form of ODA. In terms of net private-sector flows in 1980–82, again flows from Japan comprising 54 per cent of the total are larger than flows from the US, 43 per cent.

A breakdown of private-sector flows particularly into direct investment and portfolio investment would be interesting. Some OECD data exist for private direct investment and net export credits by country. Taking portfolio investment as private-sector flows less direct investment less net export credits the following details are revealed for 1980–82:

1 private direct investment flows from the PB5 to the PB8 comprise nearly 70 per cent of total private-sector flows, with export credits and portfolio investment comprising about 15 per cent each;
2 while the flows of private direct investment are slightly larger for the US than for Japan, the reverse is true for portfolio investment and export credits.

It is possible to put together data on foreign investment in each PB8 country by host country from other sources, as shown in Table 3.8.[15] Here we see the importance of both Japanese and American investments, particularly in the Philippines, Hong Kong and Korea. Table 3.9 shows foreign investment in the People's Republic of China (PRC). The US is the largest foreign investor in joint-equity ventures. Japan is as yet cautious regarding investing in the PRC and is a relatively small investor at present (although the investments in the first half of 1984 are larger). The Japanese, however, are the leading investors in offshore petroleum exploration and development, as shown in Table 3.9.[16]

Why are flows from Japan, and secondarily from the US, of central importance to the PB8 countries? Two sets of data, discussed below, are consistent in showing that the concentration of flows from Japan to the PB8 countries is much greater than that from the US. In other words, the PB8 is a much more important region as a destination for outward flows from Japan than it is to the US.

Table 3.10 shows flows to the PB8 countries as a percentage of flows to all developing countries from individual PB5 countries. This ratio is highest for Japan for all categories of flows except OOF. In 1980–82, for example, 43 per cent of total flows from Japan were channelled to the PB8 countries, while the corresponding figure for the US was only 12 per cent.

The data on foreign investment from the US and Japan from host country tell a similar story (see Tables 3.11 and 3.12). While firstly Europe and Canada and secondly Latin America are the most important regions for the US overseas

Table 3.8 Foreign investment in individual PB8 countries by home country (per cent)

From \ To	Indonesia	Malaysia	The Philippines	Singapore	Thailand	Hong Kong	South Korea	Taiwan
Australia	1.7	2.1	2.0		2.8	3.8		
Canada	0.1	0.4	2.2					
Japan	34.0	26.7	14.8	16.4	25.8	21.7	50.6	23.6
New Zealand	0.0	0.1						
USA	6.7	11.3	53.8	34.0	10.3	44.5	24.7	29.6
PB5	42.6	40.6						
Europe	16.1		16.7[a]	39.2	17.1	19.6[b]	11.4[c]	8.7
Indonesia		0.0						
Malaysia	0.1				2.5	0.6		
The Philippines	2.5	0.1			0.4	2.7		
Singapore	1.3	20.7	0.6		5.3	2.7		
Thailand	0.1	0.1				1.6		
Hong Kong	6.9	12.7	5.3		5.2			7.7
South Korea	1.3		0.3			1.1		
Taiwan	0.9	0.4			9.6			
PB8	13.1							
Others	28.2	25.4	4.3	10.4	21.0	3.2	11.7	30.4
Total	100.0	100.0	100.0	100.0	100.0	100.0	100.0	100.0

Notes: A blank signifies that separate data for that country are not available.

a   The Netherlands, the UK, Switzerland, France, West Germany, Sweden, Denmark, Luxembourg and Austria.
b   The UK, Switzerland, the Netherlands, Germany and France.
c   West Germany, the Netherlands, Italy and the UK.

Definitions of foreign investment and data sources by country

Indonesia: foreign investment: projects approved by the government; from Bank Indonesia *Indonesian Financial Statistics*. The period covered is accumulated investment from June 1967 to June 1983.

Malaysia: foreign investment in approved projects (in production) at end 1977; from UN ESCAP Secretariat at (1983) Table 10, p. 199. (See also text note 15.)

The Philippines: CB-approved direct foreign equity investments (inwardly remitted), cumulative from 21 February 1970 to June 1983; from the Central Bank of the Philippines.

Singapore: gross fixed assets in manufacturing; from Economic Development Board *Annual Report 1982/83*

Thailand: registered capital of firms granted promotion certificates as at end June 1984; from Bank of Thailand.

Hong Kong: overseas investment in Hong Kong manufacturing at end March 1980; from Centre of Asian Studies, University of Hong Kong.

South Korea: foreign investment in Korea (present approvals), cumulative 1962–81; from Economic Planning Board *Major Statistics of Korean Economy 1982*.

Taiwan: foreign investment cumulative 1952–83. The figure for Japan comprises both overseas Chinese and 'foreign' investment, and similarly for 'Others'. From Ministry of Economic Affairs Investment Commission *Statistics on Overseas Chinese and Foreign Investment, Technical Co-operation, Outward Investment, Outward Technical Co-operation* Republic of China, December 1983.

Table 3.9(a) Percentage of foreign joint-equity ventures in the People's Republic of China, by country

Country	Investment
USA	34.0
Hong Kong	26.0
The Philippines	10.7
The United Kingdom	10.2
Norway	6.8
Japan	6.4
Belgium	2.6
Sweden	1.9
Switzerland	1.3
France	0.0
West Germany	0.0
Thailand	0.0
Austria	0.0
Others	0.0
Total	100.0

Table 3.9(b) Foreign funds absorbed for offshore petroleum exploration and development

Projects	Accumulated projects by end of 1982	Accumulated foreign investment agreed by end of 1982 (US$10 000)	Accumulated foreign investment realised by end of 1982 (US$10 000)
Total	**13**	**116 972**	**48 666**
1 Sino–Japanese co-development of Chengbei oil field in Bohai	1	10 908	2 249
2 Sino–Japanese co-development of western Bohai	1	60 000	14 785
3 Sino–French co-development of central Bohai	1	8 000	8 166
4 Sino–French co-development of northeast part of Beibu Gulf	1	10 100	12 502
5 Sino–US (Arco) co-development of Yingge Sen in South China Sea	1	17 000	—
6 Geophysical prospecting area	8	10 964	10 964

Table 3.10 Net flows to the PB8 countries as a percentage of flows to all developing countries from individual PB5 countries, by type of flow and period

	Australia	Canada	Japan	New Zealand	USA	PB8
ODA						
1970–72 average	13.9	3.6	72.1	10.3	16.3	21.6
1980–82 average	15.1	4.2	38.8	14.8	3.8	14.3
OOF						
1980–82 average	7.2	10.6	10.8	—	36.2	23.7
Private sector						
1980–82 average	68.1	1.1	49.1	—	12.2	19.8
Total flows						
1970–72 average	8.8	2.4	62.6	8.3	8.4	18.4
1980–82 average	24.7	4.5	42.8	9.5	12.0	18.9

Note: A separate breakdown of OOF and private-sector flows is not available before 1977.

Source: Computed from OECD *Geographical Distribution of Financial Flows* (various years) Paris.

investment, the PB8 countries are the most important region for Japanese investment after North America.[17]

Why are the PB8 countries more important to Japan than to the US? The reasons for this are not entirely clear. Some may attribute this to geographical proximity, so that the PB8 countries are to Japan what the Latin American countries are to the US. Some explanations regarding the motivations for US and Japanese direct investment in the PB8 countries have been advanced.[18] The

Table 3.11(a) Foreign investment from the USA (US$ billion)

	Total asset of allied foreign affiliates				Net claims of US parents on their foreign affiliates
	1966		1977		1982
All countries	109.4		443.4		221.3	
Developed countries	78.8	(100.0%)	320.0	(100.0%)	163.1	(100.0%)
Canada	29.2	(37.1%)	83.1	(26.0%)	44.5	(27.3%)
Europe	40.2	(51.0%)	188.4	(58.8%)	99.9	(61.2%)
Japan	3.4	(4.3%)	25.9	(8.1%)	6.9	(4.2%)
Australia	4.5	(5.7%)	17.2	(5.4%)	8.7	(5.4%)
New Zealand	0.3	(0.4%)	1.0	(0.3%)	0.6	(0.3%)
(South Africa)	1.2	(1.5%)	4.5	(1.4%)	2.5	(1.5%)
Developing countries	26.3	(100.0%)	108.7	(100.0%)	53.2	(100.0%)
Latin America	18.1	(68.8%)	71.3	(65.6%)	33.0	(62.2%)
Other Africa	2.9	(11.0%)	8.6	(7.9%)	5.1	(9.5%)
Middle East	2.3	(8.7%)	13.4	(12.3%)	2.7	(5.1%)
Other Asia and Pacific	3.1	(11.8%)	15.4	(14.2%)	12.4	(23.2%)
Indonesia	0.21		3.02		2.41	
Malaysia	0.13		0.87		1.03	
The Philippines	0.91		1.89		1.43	
Singapore	0.06		1.54		1.80	
Thailand	0.17		0.66		0.59	
Hong Kong	0.26		2.50		2.98	
South Korea	na		2.29		0.82	
Taiwan	0.11		0.88		0.62	
India	0.76		1.31		0.46	
Other	na		0.43		0.20	
International	4.3		14.5		5.1	

Note: The definitions for 1966–77 and 1982 are different, so that they cannot be directly compared (see text note 17).
na   Not available.

Table 3.11(b) Sectoral composition of US foreign investment in 1982 (per cent)

	Mining	Petro-leum	Manufac-turing	Trade	Banking	Finance	Other
Other Asia and Pacific	na	40.1	23.8	10.6	8.5	8.8	na
Indonesia	na	84.7	6.0	0.8	0.5	0.3	na
Malaysia	0.3	65.4	23.9	6.8	0.9	0.7	2.1
The Philippines	na	20.8	37.4	5.6	11.4	na	na
Singapore	0	39.1	31.3	10.0	7.0	9.5	2.5
Thailand	1.7	72.1	6.4	13.1	7.7	0.0	−1.0
Hong Kong	0	10.6	16.7	23.9	14.1	18.2	16.1
South Korea	0	na	19.6	8.0	16.0	na	na
Taiwan	0	10.3	58.4	12.7	16.3	0.6	1.8

Note: The definition of foreign investment is the same as in Table 3.11(a). These two tables are consistent for 1982.
na   Not available.

Source: US Department of Commerce Bureau of Economic Analysis Survey of Current Business April 1982 and August 1983.

Table 3.12   Overseas direct investment from Japan

	FY 1951-70		FY 1951-76		FY 1951-82	
	Value (US$ million)	Cumulative %	Value (US$ million)	Cumulative %	Value (US$ million)	Cumulative %
USA	701	19.6	4 081	21.0	13 970	26.3
Canada	211	5.9	586	3.0	1 255	2.4
North America	912	25.5	4 667	24.0	15 225	28.7
Latin America	567	15.9	3 302	17.0	8 852	16.7
Indonesia	242	6.8	2 709	14.0	7 268	13.7
Malaysia	50	1.4	353	1.8	764	1.4
The Philippines	74	2.1	355	1.8	721	1.4
Singapore	33	0.9	301	1.6	1 383	2.6
Thailand	91	2.5	228	1.2	521	1.0
Hong Kong	29	0.8	447	2.3	1 825	3.4
South Korea	32	0.9	689	3.6	1 312	2.5
Taiwan	85	2.4	226	1.2	479	0.9
PB8	636	17.8	5 308	27.4	14 272	26.9
Other Asia	115	3.2	155	0.8	280	0.5
Asia	751	21.0	5 463	28.2	14 552	27.4
Middle East	334	9.3	1 254	6.5	2 479	4.7
Europe	639	17.6	2 854	14.7	6 146	11.6
Africa	93	2.6	773	4.0	2 507	4.7
Australia	210	5.9	818	4.2	2 882	5.4
New Zealand	33	0.9	109	0.6	212	0.4
Papua New Guinea	33	0.9	122	0.6	177	0.3
Other	5	0.1	44	0.2	98	0.2
Oceania	281	7.9	1 093	0.6	3 370	6.3
Total	3 577	100.0	19 406	100.0	53 131	100.0

Note: Slight discrepancies are due to rounding off.

Source: Investment Division, Department of International Finance, Ministry of Finance (1983) *Private-Sector Overseas Investment* (in Japanese).

Japanese are concerned about continued supplies of raw materials and have therefore invested extensively in natural-resource-based industries in the region for export to its own market. Japanese investment in manufacturing is motivated by the wage–cost differentials at home and in these countries and at least initially was mainly in labour-intensive industries. American investment began earlier at the time when Europe was the most dynamic region in the world, in contrast with the later start of Japanese overseas investment and the emergence of the PB8 countries as a region of rapid growth. While mining, smelting and petroleum are important areas for US investment in the region its foreign investments have traditionally been in higher technology industries principally serving the domestic markets of the host countries.[19] Perhaps a clearer explanation would require the separation of factors into explanations for a one-time increase in the relative concentration of Japanese flows in the PB8 countries (static factors), and explanations for changes over time (dynamic factors). Several static factors can be offered as possible explanations for the importance of official flows from Japan in the region. The Japanese have an interest in preserving and enhancing the political stability of the region and in fostering friendly relations with its individual countries. This is especially so in view of geographical proximity of the PB8 countries to Japan and their comparative abundance of natural resources. The desire to compensate for the atrocities of World War II may be another contributory factor.

COMPOSITION OF FLOWS IN THE PB8 COUNTRIES: FLOWS FROM THE PB5

From the same OECD data set, the composition of flows to each PB8 country can also be obtained (see Tables 3.5, 3.6 and 3.7). Over time, the ratio of ODA to total flows has decreased for all countries except the Philippines. This is to be expected with growth. One of the most rapid reductions of the ratio of ODA was experienced by Korea, from 76 per cent in 1970–72 to 18 per cent in 1980–82, with OOF or official flows with less of a concessionary nature becoming more important and comprising 37 per cent of total flows in the latter period. In 1980–82 the largest absolute and relative amounts of ODA were received by the least developed countries among the PB8: Indonesia, the Philippines and Thailand. The two city-states and Malaysia had the highest ratios of private-sector flows, with Singapore experiencing the most rapid rate of growth of private-sector flows between the early 1970s and the early 1980s. This is consistent with balance-of-payments data that private investment is most important for Singapore and Malaysia, while other cateogories of long-term flows, particularly borrowing, are important for the other PB8 countries. OOF is important only for Korea and Taiwan.

Intra-PB8 flows of overseas investment

There is unfortunately no comprehensive data available on the capital flows among the PB8 countries. One is aware of the overseas Chinese network as mentioned for example by Arndt.[20] There are also periodic flows of substantial amounts of 'hot money', such as into Singapore in the early 1970s during the period of transition from fixed to floating exchange rates in the world and subsequent domestic property boom. There is, however, some documentation regarding foreign direct investment within the PB8 region, particularly by the four NICs (see Table 3.8). Hong Kong is one of the largest developing country investors.[21] Singapore is the largest investor in Malaysia, after Japan, because of the historical and geographical proximity between the two countries. Until 1979, slightly over 50 per cent of Korean and Taiwanese overseas investments were in Southeast Asia and ASEAN respectively (see Table 3.13 and 3.14). The motivations for a developing country to invest overseas are probably similar across each country, although with variations in the relative strengths of each factor.[22] The factors are:

1   investment in natural resources to acquire raw materials for home-country industries (important for Korea until the late 1970s);

Table 3.13 Korean overseas investment (US$ million)

	1968–79	1980	1981	1982	1983	(April) 1984	Total	Share (%)
(a) By region								
Southeast Asia	51.3	−0.4	8.9	6.2	25.1	5.2	96.3	23.6
Middle East	10.7	10.7	−3.0	7.4	1.9	—	27.8	6.8
North America	28.6	3.6	5.5	40.8	41.5	11.8	131.9	32.4
Latin-South America	5.3	2.1	10.0	21.7	11.6	1.8	52.4	12.8
Europe	3.9	0.3	1.1	2.1	1.9	0.2	9.5	2.4
Africa	24.7	−1.0	−1.6	−3.5	−0.7	0.3	18.2	4.5
Oceania	2.0	0.05	10.9	41.3	15.5	1.8	71.5	17.5
Total	126.5	15.4	31.7	116.0	96.8	21.2	407.6	100.0
(b) By industry								
Mining	1.4	1.8	10.0	89.8	46.0	4.0	153.0	37.5
Forestry	19.4	−0.1	11.0	6.9	15.1	2.5	54.8	13.4
Fisheries	10.2	−1.2	0.2	—	0.1	0.1	9.4	2.3
Manufacturing	21.2	3.8	3.0	5.5	25.5	5.7	64.7	15.9
Construction	16.9	7.6	−1.5	7.5	2.6	0.2	33.2	8.1
Transportation–storage	1.9	0.4	0.2	0.2	0.1	−0.2	2.6	0.6
Trading	24.6	3.7	4.3	5.0	11.4	1.0	49.0	12.0
Real estate	15.2	0.5	4.5	−0.1	—	—	20.1	4.9
Other	15.6	0.0	0.0	1.2	−3.9	7.9	20.8	5.3
Total	126.4	15.5	31.7	116.0	96.8	21.2	407.6	100.0

Source: Korea Herald 4 July 1984.

2 investment to serve host-country markets as a defensive measure because of protectionist measures (applicable to both developing and developed host countries);

3 investment overseas because of quota restrictions on home-country exports and to take advantage of quota availabilities in other developing countries (important for the move overseas of Hong Kong textile and garment manufacturers);

3 investment in on-site trading, warehousing and distribution channels to serve overseas markets for home-country exports;

4 investment in civil construction and engineering-related areas (for example, Korean construction companies and workers in Singapore and the Middle East);

5 investment in high-technology companies in industrialised countries for the purposes of technology transfer back to the home country. The latter, as well as protection of markets, are important as reasons for Korean and Taiwanese investment in the US in the 1980s.[23]

Loans

The trend in external borrowing by the PB8 from all sources is similar to that discernible for all developing countries.[24] In terms of medium- and long-term (MLT) loans as shown in Tables 3.15 and 3.16, the trends in PB8 debt are:

Table 3.14 Taiwanese overseas investment (US$ million)

	Thailand	Malaysia	Singapore	The Philippines	Indonesia	USA	Others	Total
(a) By year and region								
1959–69	2.12	0.92	0.96	0.25	0.00	0.10	3.24	7.59
1970–75	2.21	0.27	2.31	0.31	2.43	2.00	9.35	18.86
1976	—	0.30	—	0.02	1.93	1.20	1.02	4.46
1977	0.10	0.62	0.33	9.28	0.78	1.65	1.02	13.79
1978	0.24	—	0.41	—	—	3.27	1.28	5.20
1979	0.15	0.97	0.30	—	3.70	0.62	3.63	9.36
1980	0.02	—	2.79	—	0.12	35.13	4.04	42.11
1981	0.07	—	0.74	—	1.96	1.65	6.35	10.76
1982	—	—	0.10	—	8.96	2.50	0.08	11.63
1983	1.76	3.00	0.91	0.25	—	2.86	1.78	10.56
1959–83	6.67	6.08	8.84	10.11	19.88	50.97	31.78	134.43
1959–79	4.82	3.08	4.31	9.86	8.84	8.84	19.54	59.26
(b) By industry and region								
Agriculture and forestry	0.20	—	—	—	0.23	—	—	0.43
Fishery and animal husbandry	—	0.01	—	—	—	—	3.78	3.79
Mining	—	—	—	—	—	—	—	
Food and beverages	1.40	—	—	0.25	1.50	0.24	4.15	7.54
Textiles	0.92	0.13	0.71	—	7.22	—	1.91	10.88
Garments and footwear	—	—	0.57	0.06	—	—	0.12	0.75
Timber	0.20	1.98	—	—	0.79	—	1.00	3.97
Paper products	1.76	0.08	—	—	5.88	—	—	7.64
Plastic products	0.06	—	1.26	0.07	0.27	6.00	1.49	9.22
Chemicals	0.25	0.11	0.85	9.18	3.60	24.00	0.20	38.08
Non-metallic minerals	—	—	2.33	0.10	—	0.46	9.04	12.05
Metal products	0.81	3.23	0.84	—	0.40	0.74	0.63	6.65
Machinery	—	0.12	—	—	—	0.25	—	0.37
Electrical goods	0.86	0.33	2.05	—	—	8.61	4.58	16.78
Construction	—	0.07	—	0.10	—	—	1.91	1.98
Trade	0.21	0.02	0.24	0.35	—	9.35	1.64	11.55
Banking	—	—	—	—	—	—	1.05	1.05
Services	—	—	—	—	—	0.75	0.12	0.87
Other	—	—	—	—	—	0.57	0.16	0.73
Total	6.67	6.08	8.84	10.11	19.88	50.97	31.78	134.32

Source: Ministry of Economic Affairs, Republic of China Statistics on Overseas Chinese and Foreign Investment, Technical Cooperation, Outward Investment, Outward Technical Cooperation December 1983.

Table 3.15 Sources of medium- and long-term loans for PB8 countries (excluding Taiwan): disbursementts (per cent)

	1970	1971	1972	1973	1974	1975	1976	1977	1978	1979	1980	1981	1982
Total concessional bilateral	27.2	22.0	25.3	23.1	14.5	9.3	9.4	8.0	7.0	7.2	8.3	10.5	5.7
—PB5 DAC	26.7	21.8	25.3	23.1	14.5	9.3	9.4	7.4	6.6	6.8	7.9	10.3	2.3
Europe DAC													3.4
—OPEC	0.1							0.6	0.4	0.3	0.3	0.2	0.0
—CPE													
—other bilateral	0.4	0.2	0.0							0.1	0.1	0.0	
Total official export credits	3.8	3.6	5.6	5.1	3.5	3.4	6.8	8.6	6.2	6.2	5.7	5.0	6.8
—PB5 DAC	3.8	2.9	5.1	5.1	3.5	3.2	6.6	7.5	5.6	5.6	5.7	4.3	5.3
Europe DAC													
—OPEC							0.2	1.1	0.5	0.6		0.0	0.0
—CPE										0.0		0.1	
—other bilateral		0.7	0.5		0.0	0.2	0.0	0.0	0.1	0.0	0.0	0.6	1.5
Total multilateral loans	4.8	7.6	6.6	8.1	8.7	11.2	13.1	11.1	10.7	11.6	11.7	12.2	14.0
Total private-source loans	20.8	29.6	31.1	31.4	33.3	47.4	44.8	46.0	54.1	54.9	47.1	45.2	51.7
Total public debt[a]	56.5	62.8	68.6	67.7	60.0	71.3	74.0	73.8	78.0	80.0	72.8	72.9	78.3
Total private non-guaranteed debt	43.5	37.2	31.4	32.3	40.0	28.7	26.0	26.2	22.0	20.0	27.2	27.1	21.7
Total public and private debt (US$ million)	2054.7 (100%)	2258.7 (100%)	3284.3 (100%)	3742.3 (100%)	5104.6 (100%)	7142.0 (100%)	7898.2 (100%)	8593.6 (100%)	11691.1 (100%)	13117.5 (100%)	13534.6 (100%)	17351.9 (100%)	18776.3 (100%)

Notes: DAC—member countries of the Development Assistance Committee of the OECD.
OPEC—Organisation of Petroleum Exporting Countries.
CPE—centrally planned economies.
a Public debt includes publicly guaranteed debt.

Source: World Bank Debtor Reporting System.

Table 3.16 Sources of medium- and long-term loans for PB8 countries (excluding Taiwan): debts outstanding and disbursed (per cent)

	1970	1971	1972	1973	1974	1975	1976	1977	1978	1979	1980	1981	1982
Total concessional bilateral	32.4	38.7	38.5	35.3	29.7								
—PB5 DAC	21.1	27.2	29.0	30.8	28.5	24.6	22.5	22.0	21.9	19.0	18.5	17.1	14.8
—Europe DAC													
—OPEC	—	—	—	—	—	—	—	0.1	0.2	0.3	0.3	0.3	0.3
—CPE	9.5	10.0	8.3	7.4	5.9	4.4	3.5	2.9	2.3	2.0	1.6	1.3	1.1
—other bilateral	1.8	1.5	1.2	0.4	0.9	0.7	0.5	0.4	0.4	0.3	0.3	0.2	0.2
Total official export credits	5.2	3.2	3.3	3.1	3.0	3.0	3.9	5.0	5.5	5.9	5.8	5.6	5.9
—PB5 DAC	2.5	2.4	2.6	2.6	2.5	2.6	3.6	4.4	4.9	5.3	5.4	5.1	5.1
—Europe DAC													
—OPEC	—	—	—	—	—	—	0.0	0.3	0.4	0.4	0.3	0.2	0.2
—CPE	2.5	0.5	0.3	0.3	0.3	0.2	0.2	0.2	0.1	0.2	0.1	0.1	0.1
—other bilateral	0.2	0.3	0.4	0.2	0.2	0.2	0.1	0.1	0.1	0.0	0.0	0.2	0.5
Total multilateral loans	6.5	6.5	6.9	7.6	8.2	9.6	11.0	11.4	12.1	13.4	13.4	14.3	15.0
Total private-source loans	23.5	22.8	23.9	24.8	25.7	30.9	30.7	35.1	37.5	40.3	41.4	41.5	43.7
Total public debt[a]	67.7	71.2	72.7	73.5	72.3	73.2	75.1	76.8	80.0	81.5	81.2	80.3	80.9
Total private non-guaranteed debt	32.3	28.8	27.3	26.5	27.7	26.8	24.9	23.2	20.0	18.8	18.5	19.7	19.1
Totall public and private debt (US$ million)	8384.6 (100%)	10586.9 (100%)	12789.9 (100%)	15210.3 (100%)	18933.5 (100%)	23832.5 (100%)	29450.1 (100%)	35746.4 (100%)	42862.0 (100%)	48540.7 (100%)	52277.7 (100%)	66732.9 (100%)	77689.1 (100%)

Notes: DAC—member countries of the Development Assistance Committee of the OECD.
OPEC—Organisation of Petroleum Exporting Countries.
CPE—centrally planned economies.
a   Public debt includes publicly guaranteed debt.

Source: World Bank Debtor Reporting System.

Table 3.17 Medium- and long-term public debt of the PB8 countries (excluding Taiwan) by source: PB5 or European DAC countries

| | Debt outstanding and disbursed | | | | | | Disbursements | | | | | |
| | Private credits | | | Official bilateral | | | Private credits | | | Official bilateral | | |
Year	Total (US$m)	PB5 (%)	Europe DAC (%)	Total (US$m)	PB5 (%)	Europe DAC (%)	Total (US$m)	PB5 (%)	Europe DAC (%)	Total (US$m)	PB5 (%)	Europe DAC (%)
1970	1 687.1	57.8	42.2	1 759.7	70.1	29.9	372.8	59.0	41.0	623.8	83.2	16.8
1971	1 837.3	63.4	36.6	1 977.2	75.2	24.8	631.6	72.1	27.9	557.2	85.1	14.9
1972	2 264.8	62.6	37.4	3 129.4	72.2	27.8	971.6	58.3	41.7	1 000.5	86.5	13.5
1973	2 919.0	60.5	39.5	4 059.4	76.3	23.7	973.6	76.5	23.5	1 052.4	86.5	13.5
1974	3 422.2	63.7	36.3	5 087.8	77.2	22.8	1 508.7	81.3	18.7	917.9	83.4	16.4
1975	4 429.6	67.9	32.1	5 896.1	76.8	23.2	2 825.4	85.2	14.8	895.4	83.4	16.4
1976	6 442.1	76.2	23.8	6 480.4	78.8	21.2	2 730.4	61.3	38.7	1 263.8	86.9	13.1
1977	8 348.0	71.4	28.6	7 658.7	80.3	19.7	2 966.9	52.5	47.5	1 315.2	85.2	14.8
1978	10 257.7	64.5	35.5	9 448.6	80.9	19.1	4 462.0	63.0	37.0	1 439.9	18.3	16.7
1979	12 810.1	59.6	40.4	11 586.2	80.6	19.4	4 461.4	60.4	39.6	1 761.1	89.0	11.0
1980	14 332.6	56.3	43.7	11 955.0	80.4	19.6	3 335.5	61.9	38.1	2 007.5	87.4	12.6
1981	15 989.1	59.2	40.8	13 950.7	84.0	16.0	3 014.6	43.4	56.6	2 543.2	81.2	18.8
1982	15 682.7	57.7	42.3	15 145.1	85.2	14.8	4 614.3	62.0	38.0	2 257.6	66.5	33.5
1983	17 566.2	59.5	40.5	16 133.7	83.4	16.6	5 362.2	56.6	43.4	2 876.0	81.6	18.4

Note: DAC countries—countries of the Development Assistance Committee of the OECD apart from the PB5 countries, the members are Austria, Belgium, Denmark, Finland, France, West Germany, Italy, the Netherlands, Norway, Sweden, Switzerland, and the United Kingdom, collectively described as the European DAC countries.

Source: World Bank Debtor Reporting System.

1   both the flows of disbursements, as well as the stock of debt outstanding and the disbursed (DOD), have increased about ninefold between 1970 and 1982 for the PB8 countries, excluding Taiwan—a significant and rapid increase;

2   the debt of the public sector and debts which are officially guaranteed (or public debt for short) have increased in importance compared with private non-guaranteed debt in both flows and stock terms;

3   the composition of public debt has shifted away from official to private sources, particularly to loans from private financial institutions;

4   among the official sources of public debt, loans from multilateral institutions have increased in importance, compared with official bilateral ODA and export credits.[25]

About 80 per cent of official bilateral disbursements of loans have originated in the PB5 countries, as compared with the European DAC countries during 1970–82 (see Table 3.17). The ratio for private credit is smaller for the PB5 countries but it has been in general over 50 per cent. The PB8 countries (excluding Taiwan) have borrowed more from the PB5 countries than from the European DAC countries. This points again to the importance of flows from the PB5 to the PB8 countries.

It is more difficult to obtain an accurate description of how the composition of private-sector flows from the PB5 to the PB8 countries has changed over time, and whether this has followed the pattern for all developing countries of the rising importance and dominance of bank credits as compared with direct investment.[26] There are, however, some data on the relative magnitudes of private investment and debt borrowed from private sources origination from all countries (and not merely the PB5). OECD data on the disaggregation of net private-sector flows into direct investment, portfolio investment and export credit for the PB8 countries from all sources, indicate that the ratio of direct

Table 3.18   Private direct investment and the net transfer of MLT public debt from private sources for the PB8 countries (excluding Taiwan) (US$ million)

Year	Flows of private direct investment	Net transfer of public debt from private sources
1970		16.9
1971		282.4
1972		537.3
1973		354.8
1974		882.0
1975		2 244.9
1976	1 357.0	1 905.7
1977	285.7	1 471.9
1978	1 177.5	1 724.5
1979	760.2	2 362.7
1980	1 703.5	2 122.1
1981	5 231.2	2 341.5
1982	1 870.7	3 522.6

Notes: Net transfer of public debt refers to disbursements less amortisation less interest, of loans borrowed by governments or guaranteed by governments.

Sources: For private direct investment, OECD *Geographical Distribution of Financial Flows* (various years) Paris; for public debt, World Bank Debtor Reporting System.

investment to private-sector flows has fluctuated but not declined from 1977
–82.[27] The series on the net transfer of MLT public debt (defined as
disbursements less amortisation less interest) from private sources, obtained
from the World Bank Debtor Reporting System, for the PB8 countries
excluding Taiwan, is perhaps a more accurate series on the flow of debt incurred
by these countries for private sources. While the flows of private direct
investment from the PB8 countries (excluding Taiwan) have fluctuated from
1977–82 there has been a steady increase in the net transfer of public debt from
private sources (see Table 3.18). With the exception of 1981, when the flow of
private direct investment was particularly large, the relative rise in the
magnitude of public debt from private sources can be seen. For all source
countries, therefore, there is some evidence that the composition of private-
sector flows has changed, with public debt from private sources rising in
importance compared with private direct investment.

Banking Data

Yet another category of data available is data on the net claims of banks by
country. In this section, data on the two offshore centres' net claims as well as
US banks' net claims for the PB8 countries are discussed. The main finding is
that the PB8 countries are net borrowers from the offshore centres as well as
from the US banking system.

The presence in this region of two major offshore centres, Singapore and
Hong Kong, raises the question of whether these offshore centres perform the
function of distribution of funds across regions. The data on the net claims of
Asia currency units in the offshore system in Singapore (see Table 3.19) show
that Asia has been a net borrower of funds from the system, while Europe and
all others (including the US) have been net lenders. Moreover, in the 1970s and
early 1980s, borrowing by Asia has in general increased. The data on net claims
by Hong Kong banks and deposit-taking companies (DTCs) on the banks of
each country give a more detailed country breakdown (see Table 3.20). The
banks in the PB8 countries (except Singapore) are net borrowers from both
Hong Kong banks and DTCs. The annual net flow is also positive, implying an
increase in the borrowing over time by these banks. The largest borrowers are
the Korean and Philippine banks. Singapore's position is unique because it is an
offshore centre. It is a net depositor of funds with the Hong Kong banks and the
DTCs. This is consistent with the relationships between the two offshore
centres, where Singapore is the funding centre and Hong Kong the booking
centre for loans.[28] The US and European, particularly the British and West
German banks, are net depositors in the Hong Kong banking system. The
offshore centres, therefore, do facilitate the borrowing of funds by the Asian
countries.

The US banks switched from being net borrowers to net lenders in the early
1980s, primarily due to the rapid increase in lending to the Latin American
countries as well as smaller deposits from Europe (see Table 3.21). The PB8

Table 3.19 Net claims and flows of Asian currency units in Singapore by region (US$ million)

End of year	Asia[a]	Europe	All others
	(a) Net claims by region		
1971	400	−352	−48
1972	966	−1 006	40
1973	1 205	−1 011	−194
1974	2 949	−2 538	−411
1975	4 233	−3 269	−964
1976	7 041	−5 753	−1 288
1977	7 655	−5 845	−1 810
1978	8 059	−5 445	−2 614
1979	7 886	−5 677	−2 209
1980	8 450	−5 654	−2 796
1981	12 960	−5 450	−7 510
1982	13 455	−6 407	−7 048
1983	13 473	−7 049	−6 424
1984 (June)	12 359	−8 816	−3 543
	(b) Net flows by region[b]		
1972	566	−654	88
1973	239	−5	−234
1974	1 744	−1 527	−217
1975	1 284	−731	−553
1976	2 808	−2 484	−324
1977	614	−92	−522
1978	404	400	−804
1979	−173	−232	405
1980	564	23	−587
1981	4 510	204	−4 714
1982	495	957	462
1983	18	642	624
1984 (June)	1 114	−1 767	2 881

Notes: a Includes the Middle East.
   b Net flow in year t equals net claims at end of year t minus net claims at end of year (t−1). A positive figure implies an increase in borrowing or a decrease in deposits by that region, and vice versa for a negative figure.

Source: Monetary Authority of Singapore.

countries are net borrowers from the US banking system, although as expected the size of borrowing is relatively small compared with the Latin American countries. Again, the largest borrower is Korea, with lending to the Philippines showing a marked increase from the late 1970s. It is interesting that Singapore has become a net depositor in the US banking system since 1981. This could be because of the sizeable investments of Singapore's official reserves in the US, managed by the Government Securities Investment Corporation (GSIC) which was established around that time.[29] Indonesia is a net depositor with the US banking system in spite of her substantial borrowings. This is perhaps due to the deposits of official reserves and foreign-exchange earnings of the country.[30]

CONCLUSION

The description of the geographical distribution of capital flows is difficult because of the lack of comprehensive data and information on the subject. This chapter has attempted to utilise whatever data are available in order to provide

Table 3.20 Net claims[a] of Hong Kong banks and deposit-taking companies (DTCs) vis-à-vis banks outside Hong Kong (HK$ million)

	March 1979		December 1979		December 1980		December 1981		December 1982		December 1983	
	Banks	DTCs	Banks	DTCs	Banks	DTCs	Banks	DTCs	Banks	DTCs	Banks	DTCs
Indonesia	-64	121	-425	234	-1588	-515	-3185	-1117	-2989	-880	-3257	-1138
Malaysia	-117	-20	-249	-322	146	-480	688	-213	-1	-368	442	3958
The Philippines	1330	327	1522	51	2141	1051	3588	841	5797	1387	8311	1331
Singapore	-7917	-7771	-7710	-8792	-14385	-10558	-15117	-22276	-7475	-27190	-13878	-23250
Thailand	427	320	240	113	108	-7	202	202	-272	360	1649	-167
South Korea	2629	299	3101	1097	3619	2536	5673	5282	8714	8934	13350	11921
Taiwan	321	586	954	628	1151	728	924	466	-1086	1168	534	229
PB8 (excluding Singapore)	4496	1633	5143	1801	5607	3313	7890	5461	10163	10601	21029	16134
People's Republic of China	4273	96	5592	32	5858	302	1948	-718	-5213	-930	-7862	-2150
Brunei	0	0	-10	—	—	—	—	—	—	58	-50	163
Japan	1208	776	1386	-19	-667	-474	1756	-1185	11611	-3684	6020	-7239
Australia	245	32	391	8	274	-44	356	243	549	54	2168	423
New Zealand	-30	-8	-12	-2	57	-1	-127	7	146	133	90	37
Other Asia and Pacific	5482	-38	5640	146	1768	652	-14693	1282	-12482	1639	-14774	1678
Asia and Pacific total	8207	-5280	10420	-6826	-1488	-6810	-17897	-17186	-2701	-19319	-7257	-14204
USA	-3540	-751	-3703	-683	-293	-805	-35	-868	-10088	-3977	-18450	-1969
Canada	78	-556	-237	-622	-283	-589	-89	-206	-41	-93	1670	-500
North America total	-3462	-1307	-3940	-1305	-576	-1394	-124	-1074	-10129	-4070	-16780	-2469
Europe[b]	-8525	-7396	-8773	-7592	-18266	-10115	-19039	-17377	-19586	-18916	-10083	-15820
Caribbean	-812	-604	-3603	-125	-4552	-1461	6376	-3082	10999	-8837	7536	-9530
Latin America	52	88	228	202	177	596	330	1676	406	1901	375	2565
Middle East	-3090	-974	-2113	-1980	-2279	-2305						
Africa	89	-40	-81	64	92	116	325	225	308	216	279	212
Unallocated	158	10	103	12	124	386	132	19	174	14	160	8
Total	-8382	-15503	-7219	-17550	-26771	-20987	-34874	-39146	-23154	-52938	-31731	-41691

Notes: a Net claims comprise both those denominated in Hong Kong dollars and those denominated in foreign currencies.
b Both Eastern and Western Europe.

Source: Hong Kong Monthly Digest of Statistics

Table 3.21 US banks' total net claims by country (US$ million)

Country	End of year								
	1975	1976	1977	1978	1979	1980	1981	1982	1983
Indonesia	-123	-122	-178	-251	-333	-429	-239	-460	-151
Malaysia	na	na	-30	26	67	143	-607	281	595
The Philippines	-166	91	-101	81	-7	132	1042	1911	883
Singapore	128	145	181	1023	482	149	-316	-1581	-4012
Thailand	268	165	100	350	687	443	57	62	349
Hong Kong	-330	-569	-546	258	182	-268	233	2091	1831
South Korea	1401	1544	1739	1659	2951	4447	5509	8037	8565
Taiwan	29	355	708	1301	767	1297	746	-174	-1838
PB8	1207[a]	1609[a]	2143	4447	4796	5914	6425	10167	6222
People's Republic of China	-100	-43	-41	-61	-5	191	-39	37	67
Japan	853	-3008	-4559	-7972	9200	7839	7970	14103	13936
Other Asia[b]	-6459	-8786	-8553	-5031	-13842	-12588	-10454	-8689	-7989
Total Asia	**-4589**	**-10228**	**-11010**	**-8617**	**149**	**1356**	**3902**	**15618**	**12236**
Australia	-1306	-1302	-233	135	83	251	486	-4066	-5416
Canada	272	-1128	-568	558	533	-1132	2979	4616	3861
Europe	-32628	-31960	-41826	-55782	-50330	-43931	-16503	-1293	-22658
Latin America[c]	8918	19853	22238	27744	20316	42393	56810	79248	66737
Africa	-1399	70	45	-146	-876	-2052	1082	3005	4511
Other	22	69	26	-106	-30	111	8	192	477
International and regional	-5671	-5670	-3175	-2517	-2282	-2182	-2669	-4823	-5755
Total	**-36381**	**-30295**	**-34504**	**-38733**	**-32433**	**-5185**	**46096**	**92498**	**53992**

Notes: New Zealand is not listed separately in this table.
  a Excludes Malaysia.
  b Includes the Middle East.
  c Includes the Caribbean.
  na Not available.

Source: US Department of the Treasury *Treasury Bulletin* (various recent issues).

an overview of the capital flows in the Pacific Basin region. In the discussion on flows from the PB5 to the PB8 countries, it was found that these flows are not only relatively important but have increased in importance. One of the main reasons for this is the dominant role played by Japan because of the importance of the PB8 countries as a destination for outward flows from Japan. While flows from the developed to the developing countries are therefore fairly well captured very few data exist on the flows among developing countries and from developing to developed countries. In terms of foreign investment, we have seen that flows from Asian NICs to the other PB8 countries have not been insignificant. The debt of the PB8 countries has risen substantially since 1970 and debt from private sources appears to have risen in importance relative to private direct investment. The banking data available show that the PB8 region has been a net borrower from the two offshore centres as well as from the US banks.

There are a number of questions which this chapter raises. First, the key role played by Japan has not been satisfactorily examined. The recent liberalisation of the Japanese financial markets may lead to even greater capital flows into and out of Japan. Second, the People's Republic of China may become an increasingly important actor in the region in the years to come and should be included in discussions regarding the Pacific Basin. Hopefully, more data will become available with growth in the country. Third, have the Pacific Basin countries become more financially integrated and interdependent? The evidence of a greater intensity of capital flows from the PB5 to the PB8 countries certainly points towards this, but financial interdependence is a larger issue than capital flows. Fourth, there have been recent trends towards greater financial liberalisation in the Pacific Basin countries, not only in Japan, but also for example in Australia and Korea. How would this affect the pattern of capital flows and financial integration? An observation which has been made is that the Pacific Basin countries have become more financially integrated for the following reasons:

1   the similarity in time zones allows for easier access to other financial markets in the region;
2   the greater use of electronic equipment and computers allows for a wider availability of information, a larger number of participants both in the home countries and overseas, and greater competition;
3   the relaxation of exchange controls enables investors to invest overseas as a means of diversification;
4   investments overseas also imply that less information is available to tax officials at home.

Whether these factors have indeed caused the Pacific Basin countries to become more financially integrated requires more rigorous investigation.

Part II   The Financial Experience of Asian-Pacific Nations

4 The development of equity and bond markets in the Pacific region

P.J. DRAKE

Financial transactions nowadays know few limits, and increasingly occur across national boundaries. National finance markets that once were separate now have many connections and national exchange controls are no longer workable. Essentially, the rapid internationalisation of financial activities has three causes: cost-diminishing technological advances in electronic systems for storing and transmitting financial information;[1] expansion of education in economics and finance, to the point where a level of understanding and knowledge thought professional a generation ago is now commonplace; and the current normative ascendancy of libertarian or anti-regulatory philosophies in economics. These influences are sweeping away barriers of nationalism and distance and broadening the area over which financing activities may be conducted profitably.

In developing countries, the business of raising capital through bond and share issues, and subsequently trading the securities so created is in its infancy. Yet the natural protection afforded to LDC securities markets by the inadequacies of transport, communications and information is being fast eroded. The pure theory of international trade suggests that securities markets would not be viable in all countries but would cluster at a few points on the globe, determined by the location of factor skills and by time zones. Even so there is point in contemplating the development of facilities for the issue and trading of stocks and bonds in countries where securities markets are not already well-rooted and bearing high volumes of transactions. The electronic data-processing revolution will narrow, but never eliminate, areas of informational monopoly. There will always remain an irreducible core of knowledge about financial transactors based upon personal judgments of character and ability.[2]

This is especially true where enterprising and growing firms are seeking to go public for the first time, as they may frequently do in developing countries which harbour the corporate form of business organisation. It will be hard for corporations and governments in any country to resist the pressures and inducements to issue securities which may be traded widely. Local securities markets are a necessary means of reconciling local knowledge with participation in the international financial circuits; a well-functioning domestic securities market is essential for any nation which wants to share in world economic growth, development and diversification.

Irrespective of the internationalisation of finance, securities markets have a useful role to play as any nation's industry, commerce and infrastructure grow. Given that a securities market imparts liquidity to long-term assets, the potential benefits are:

— a rise in the ratio of domestic savings to income;
— encouragement of capital inflow from abroad and discouragement of capital outflow;
— improved resource allocation, promoted by widening the range of borrowing and lending choices and increasing competition in financial activities;
— improved mobility of investible funds through further 'financialisation' of savings;
— enchanced scope for monetary policy measures.
    Securities markets are also a breeding ground for enterpreneurship, and for the skills of risk evaluation, portfolio selection and financial management.

A securities market in a developing country provides the means for non-coercive transfers of corporate ownership from foreigners to locals, if at the cost of some forgone increase in net domestic capital formation in so far as domestic savings are absorbed in buying up the equity of foreigners in existing capital stock and so constitute a monetary outflow.[3] Increased indigenous ownership does not necessarily ensure local control of companies, though.[4] Economists are on slippery ground when they contemplate the objectives of domestic ownership and control. Whatever the social or political desirability of these objectives, they are economically dubious: there is no a priori reason to believe that any increase in domestic ownership or control would lead to a rise in investment or output, to a social improvement in resource allocation, or to a 'better' distribution of income. It is worth noting the practical opinion of Robert Dickie, who accepts the diversification of corporate ownership towards local citizens as a goal of political economy, but does not believe that the raising of local capital by foreign firms will remove significant capital from the local economy, because the proceeds of public offerings of shares are 'almost always' used for new local investment rather than capital outflow.[5]

In contrast to my own optimistic view about securities-market development, the limited literature on the subject is mostly lukewarm[6] or pessimistic. Samuels and Yacout come to pessimistic conclusions by taking an 'efficiency' approach to the subject. They point out that the 'efficient markets' concept of Western financial analysts focuses exclusively on pricing or informational efficiency, and that a market which is efficient in this sense is not necessarily efficient according to operational, allocational or social criteria. They argue that securities markets in developing countries are unlikely to be efficient in the pricing sense, and that pricing inefficiency may be detrimental to the other efficiency goals.[7] In short, the establishment of stock exchanges that has occurred in over thirty developing countries rests on hopeful but uncertain arguments. This is fair opinion but the facts do not, I believe, warrant wholly pessimistic presumptions about the future.

In what follows, more space has been devoted to corporate securities, equity shares and bonds/debentures issued by companies, than to government securities; this is because long-term bonds issued by governments in the region generally have not attracted much uncoerced demand, owing to the common attempts by government to borrow long-term funds at less than market rates of interest. The relative neglect of government bonds in this chapter should not be taken to imply that they are inevitably an unimportant means of finance; it might be advantageous to the world economy if governments reverted to the nineteenth-century practice of borrowing long by the issue of bonds, available to domestic and foreign lenders, at rates of interest determined in a free market where adequate premiums for relative risks can be provided.

A securities market requires three basic components: private and public enterprises to issue securities; parties to subscribe to the issues; and parties to trade confidently in the securities created, so conferring on long-term financial instruments, bonds and equities, the precious characteristics of liquidity.

In any country, some greater or lesser degree of incentive may be required in order to foster the issue, acquisition or trade in securities; but the provision of market incentives is always a benefits-versus-costs issue, and the case for official intervention in the securities markets is at best a qualified one.[8]

The largely adequate demand for securities in either new issues or stock-exchange markets in countries where economic and financial development has progressed beyond rudimentary stages, stems from speculative interest and the unsatisfied portfolio needs of certain financial institutions. Demand for securities by pension and superannuation funds, life insurance companies, unit trusts and similar financial institutions is substantial and growing rapidly. Mistrust and inadequate yields are known in some Asian countries, but the main obstacle to large-scale and rapid development of securities markets is the chronic deficiency in the supply of securities arising from the sizes and forms of business organisations prevalent there. Local enterprises, regardless of size and industry category, are generally run by individuals, families or cohesive social groups; the corporation is not a favoured business form. On the other hand, enterprises owned and/or controlled abroad are usually companies even when, as in Malaysia, their activities are agricultural. Foreign and joint-venture companies commonly dominate the limited corporate sectors of developing countries.

Foreign owners and managers often have little need or desire to raise share capital locally, especially when bank credit is easy to obtain and access to foreign-capital markets is possible; but they may be persuaded, or can be obliged, to issue shares locally, in harmony with most governments' desire both to increase domestic-capital formation and to raise the share of local ownership. A government may justifiably regard the issue of shares or debentures locally as the price of admission to the local economy, though care and sensitivity are needed in framing and administering such regulations; excessive forcing of share issues may be counterproductive and restrict net capital inflow. Foreign owners will naturally be concerned about control of the company once local shareholders are admitted. In general, however, not even a large offering of local equity would deprive a foreign party of control; local ownership is likely to be diffused and local shareholders are unlikely to have the expertise to run the company even when they constitute a shareholding majority, unless a government or its agents is involved, as in the case of Pernas's takeover of Sime Darby (Malaysia). A public offering to local shareholders may not only allow foreign interests to retain control of the company, 'but also may provide it with nonfinancial benefits, such as some favour with the local government, a diminished risk of expropriation and a reduction of local prejudice against it.'[9]

Enterprises owned and controlled locally by families, clans or similar social groups have been noticeably unwilling to adopt corporate form, issue equity and admit outsiders even as minority shareholders. Large clan groupings which span several activities are often able to organise efficient capital markets internal to the group.[10] In Southeast Asia and the Pacific Islands, clannishness is reinforced among the Chinese and Indians by the fact that they are political minorities in all countries except Singapore, Hong Kong and Taiwan. Where the ethnic Chinese enjoy economic strength but are also politically vulnerable, their companies tend to remain private; where Chinese economic influence is not politically contentious, their companies are frequently public and their shares are traded on the stock exchange.[11]

There are obvious business reasons behind the reluctance of any private firm to admit outside shareholders: the risk of dilution, if not loss, of control; the risk that secret and valuable information may be disclosed to competitors; the possibility the firm's financial position may be fully disclosed to authorities, leading to increased tax liability or even confiscation; pressure from shareholders for dividend payouts, which may inhibit the reinvestment of profits by the firm and exacerbate cash-management difficulties.[12] Finally, firms may be deterred from issuing shares to the general public if governments hold down the issue price in the primary market. If a government opts for countervailing incentives to encourage close-held firms to open up and expand, it will need to provide legal sanctions to protect minority shareholders.

The family or group business is often buttressed by good banking connections, sometimes including interlocking ownership and control among banking, trading and industrial concerns, and with the easy access to bank credit which foreign firms usually enjoy too. Nominally short-term bank finance can be rolled over indefinitely to constitute a line of long-term funding which obviates the need to issue share capital and results in very high gearing ratios of debt to equity. This pattern of financing, which is available to most well-established firms above a certain size whether they be foreign, local or mixed enterprises, is reinforced to the extent that the rate of interest on bank credit may be artificially low, owing to financial repression. A liberal reform of interest rates would knock away this prop.

Government securities on issue in the developing countries of Asia and the Pacific are often in larger amounts than private enterprise issues, but they are nowhere plentiful and trade in them is generally very inactive. Governments are eager to borrow funds by the issue of domestic securities but the market is not usually eager to oblige them, especially when governments expect to borrow at below market rates of interest. There is in some countries so much reluctance to acquire government paper that issues are either negligible or are more or less compulsorily subscribed by financial institutions under official pressure.

In earlier times much infrastructure development in Asia and America, regardless of whether undertaken by state or private enterprise, was financed by the public issue of long-term bonds. Nowadays, public utilities are usually conducted by state enterprises and are commonly funded indirectly through central government budgets and borrowing programs. There is still potential for financing public capital works by direct long-term borrowing. The floating of bonds by public utilities would not only provide a supply of long-dated, fixed-interest securities in the local market but also relieve some of the demands upon general government revenue. Public-enterprise bond issues need not be confined to the local market in domestic currency: bonds could also be sold to foreigners and denominated in either domestic or foreign currency.

Governments should be committed to a general policy of monetisation and financial development, unregulated interest rates, and allocation of investible funds via an open market. These conditions will provide the most freedom and encouragement for the growth of all financial activities, including securities markets; conversely, while some forms of official intervention may be compatible with, or even necessary for, securities-market development, it will not occur when intervention and regulation are common.

Income-tax policy is also important. Incomes derived from the ownership of securities should be taxed neutrally with respect both to the different forms which the factor rewards to capital may take, whether dividends or interest, and to different categories of securities owners, whether individuals or institutions. Non-neutral taxes may lead to biases, for example, against equity financing and against individual share ownership. Capital gains realised by trading in the securities markets should be exempt from tax; these gains are properly regarded as the reward for successful risk-bearing, while capital losses result from risks which turn out to be bad. The prospect of tax-free capital gain is an important and legitimate attraction, for many investors the main reason, to participate in the securities markets.

Specific measures to foster the issue of private-sector securities include: the provision of tax concessions to issuing corporations; the reform of irregular tax administrations; restrictions on the provision of bank credit to undercapitalised firms, obliging them to approach the public for equity; requiring firms above a certain size, or of a certain type, to offer shares to the public; requiring foreign corporations to issue a defined proportion of equity to local shareholders.

Governments may also have to take steps to raise the performance of the local accountancy profession. The lack of an adequate number of competent, independent accountants and auditors will make it difficult to obtain the external audit of company accounts, without which neither the public at large nor potential overseas joint-venture partners would be prepared to acquire an equity interest. This difficulty afflicts some countries more than others; the quality of independent accounting services could be categorised as high in Singapore and Malaysia, medium in Thailand, and low in Indonesia; and it may be alleviated if branches of the 'big eight' international accounting firms are located in a country.

Table 4.1   Securities markets: outline ratios

Country	Year	Ratio of outstanding bonds[a] to GNP (%)	Ratio of outstanding shares[b] to GNP (%)	Ratio of total securities to GNP (%)	Turnover ratio[c] (%)	New issues ratio[d] (%)
Japan	1977	47	27	74	48	2
	1980	65	34	99	51	2
	1981	67	38	105	59	2
Hong Kong[e]	1977	—	32	3ℓ	29	2
	1980	3	189	92	45	3
	1981	3	168	171	52	5
Singapore[e]	1977	42	34	76	6	1
	1980	48	82	130	15	1
	1981	41	101	142	18	2
The Philippines	1977	14	11	25	14	1
	1980	13	5	18	32	2
	1981	13	4	17	na	—
Thailand	1977	11	4	15	144	6
	1980	12	4	16	26	3
	1981	11	3	14	11	5
Taiwan	1981	1	12	13	104	9
	1982	2	11	13	66	8
	1983	2	15	19	119	5
South Korea	1977	3	12	15	59	8
	1980	7	7	14	45	7
	1981	9	7	16	86	10

Notes: a   Corporate and government bonds at par value.
        b   Outstanding shares at year-end market value.
        c   Value of shares traded during year as a ratio of market value of shares outstanding at end of year.
        d   Value of new share issues during year as a ratio of market value of shares outstanding at end of year.
        e   The ratios for Singapore and Hong Kong are based on figures which include foreign as well as domestic securities.
        —   Negligible (less than 1 per cent).
        na   Not available.

Source: International Finance Corporation, based on central bank, government, stock-exchange and miscellaneous sources.

Table 4.2   Securities markets: features

Country	Number of listed stocks	Market capitalisation 1980 (US$b)	Equity trading volume 1980 (US$b)	Turnover 1980 (%)	Level of restriction on foreign investment
Japan	1 402 (1980)	357	157	44	Medium
Australia	1 082 (1980)	60	5	8	Low
Hong Kong	242 (1980)	42	19	45	Low
Singapore	263 (1980)	27	4	15	Low
Malaysia	250 (1980)	22	na	na	Low
The Philippines	195 (1980)	2	0.6	30	Low
Thailand	77 (1980)	1.2	0.3	25	Low
Taiwan	101 (1980)	0.1	4.5	74	Medium
South Korea	344 (1980)	4	2	50	High
Indonesia	19 (1983)	0.1	0.01	—	Medium/high
Fiji	8 (1982)	$F38.8m	$F0.11m	—	Low

Notes: na   Not available.
         —   Negligible.

Source: Data presented by A.W. van Agtmael on behalf of the International Finance Corporation (1982), and own estimates based on miscellaneous reports.

It is now time to review securities markets in Asia and the Pacific. In following these brief accounts of individual countries it will be helpful to bear in mind the statistics in Tables 4.1 and 4.2, which give a very broad outline of the relative size, depth and activity of the various markets, revealing at any rate the relative degrees of securities-market development. Ratios in columns 1 and 2 of Table 4.1 may give an exaggerated impression of the available supply of marketable securities since, in the countries concerned, large blocks of both bonds and shares are held permanently and never traded; conversely, column 3 may tend to understate market activity.

INDONESIA

In Indonesia, long-term securities are at present scarce. There are only nineteen equity stocks and three bonds listed on the infant Jakarta stock exchange, wherein trading is inactive. This is remarkable in a non-socialist nation with a population of some 150 million and plentiful and varied natural resources. So far as government is concerned, a requirement that its budgets be balanced precludes overt deficits and therefore direct borrowing from the public. In the private sector, shareholder ownership is limited first by the fact that government ownership and control pervade industry and commerce, extending into activities such as hotels, airlines, and agricultural estates which would be suitable for private-sector companies. Second, there are disincentives to going public with equity shares: disclosure, regulation, tax liability, dividend payout, cash-flow difficulties, and dilution of ownership and control. These are so considerable that the countervailing incentives held out by the government rarely indicate a net advantage to go public. Third, firms of a size and standing to contemplate issuing shares to the public find that debt finance is easy to obtain and very inexpensive relative to the costs of raising and servicing equity. Until June 1983 domestically owned companies were able to borrow at subsidised rates of interest from the state banks; promissory-note accommodation is readily obtainable from the authorised merchant banks; and it is not hard to tap foreign financial centres such as Singapore. Only those few companies which are virtually forced to go public do so; usually they contain large foreign interests. The result is that the official annual goal of ten new public company listings on the stock exchange has not yet been achieved in any year.

Rapid expansion of local equity and the development of a share market still constitute essential concomitants of the Indonesian government's determination to secure majority Indonesian ownership in the corporate sector. The potential for share issues is very substantial; compared with the nineteen listed public companies, there are some 800 foreign–Indonesian joint-venture companies for which the minimum targets for Indonesian shareholding are 30 per cent in respect of companies licensed before 21 September 1974 and 51 per cent in companies licensed after that date.

In order to foster the issue and trading of securities, the authorities have established a highly controlled and regulated system for share dealings; it is an open question whether it is counterproductive.

The exchange was reformed in 1977 under the management of a government agency, the Capital Market Executive Agency (BAPEPAM), responsible to the Minister of Finance; he is advised on capital-market policy and guidelines by the Capital Market Policy Council, consisting of five ministers of state, the governor of the central bank, and two senior government officials. The Capital Market Executive Agency is required not merely to operate the stock exchange but also to determine criteria for the listing of shares on the exchange, to evaluate and approve all companies which seek share listing, and to monitor the performance of companies which become listed on the exchange. These very substantial powers are exercised in bureaucratic detail to the point where some critics feel the regulatory framework is a handicap.

Another state-owned body, P.T. Danareksa (National Investment Trust), was established to promote public participation in corporate ownership. It does this, first, by acquiring block shareholdings in listed public companies. Danareksa then issues its own bearer certificates in smaller parcels 'back-to-back' with its block of shares in each company, or issues unit trust certificates against a basket of shares held in its portfolio. In the former case the bearer certificates can be purchased at state bank branches throughout Indonesia without transaction fee. The fact that Indonesia's only stock exchange is in Jakarta imposes considerable extra transactions costs on those who wish to deal directly on the exchange but reside elsewhere. Danareksa undertakes to repurchase its certificates at the prevailing price of the underlying share. Danareksa also buys and sells on the stock exchange, seeking to stabilise share prices within a narrow band (4 per cent daily amplitude); finally, it is an important underwriter of new share issues.

Danareksa must be offered the opportunity to subscribe to at least 50 per cent of each new issue of shares, although it is not obliged to subscribe any part. In practice, Danareksa has exercised its subscription rights, putting a major floor under the market for new issues. In general, they have been oversubscribed, often by 50 per cent or more. This suggests that there is no deficiency of demand for shares among Indonesians; foreigners are not allowed to purchase shares in new issues or on the stock exchange. There is less cause for optimism when Danareksa's participation is allowed for, along with the relatively low prices at which the new issues have been offered to the public, and the small total of demands made upon the market: less than three issues per year on average. With the rise in new issue activity in 1983, when five companies sought public subscriptions for the first time, underwriters experienced difficulties in placing shares. Moreover, Danareksa still owns large shareholdings not yet offset by subscriber certificates.

Among listing criteria for the stock exchange are requirements that the company must have authorised capital in excess of Rp100 million of which at least Rp25 million has been fully paid up, and must have been operating profitably for the last two years with the most recent profit being in excess of 10 per cent of shareholders' equity. These requirements are not onerous and it may seem surprising that, despite the existence of some 3600 domestic and 800 joint-venture companies, only nineteen companies have been listed in the six years since the stock exchange was reopened, fourteen of them joint-venture enterprises with foreign interest. Until recently, the incentives to go public have not outweighed the disincentives. As is readily conceded by the Indonesian authorities, domestic companies are deeply committed to the family or group practices of tight management control, secrecy of information and reluctance to pay tax, while foreign-sponsored corporations have been inclined to delay the process of 'Indonesianisation'. The administration of taxation in Indonesia has been irregular, and businessmen's resistance to disclosure is extremely strong.[13] Stock-exchange listing is further impeded by requirements that a company seeking listing must have been audited by an independent public accountant for the preceding two years and have an unqualified audit report for the last year. Listed companies, of course, must also have independent annual audits. The number of accounting firms in Indonesia is quite small and very few are competent by international standards of accounting.

The government encourages share issues by substantial five-year tax concessions, up to a maximum relief of 80 per cent of tax due, for all companies which went public before 31 March 1984; coupled with this goes pressure on foreign joint-venture corporations, with the issuing of shares to Indonesians as the price of admission to the local economy. In addition to tax-rate concessions, companies which sell at least 15 per cent of their shares to the public may enjoy relief by tax-free revaluation of fixed assets and capitalisation of the resulting book profit; in subsequent years the revalued assets can be depreciated against current revenue and written off as a tax deduction. A further incentive to issue equity to the public is found in the fact that industrial-plant capacity, which is licensed and regulated by the Indonesian authorities, may be expanded when a manufacturing firm goes public. This practice favours such a firm against prospective new competitors.

In principle, there may seem to be an incentive for a company to increase its equity so as to obtain a sounder balance between equity and debt funding. In practice this incentive is missing because of the ease of obtaining credit and the low risk attached to it, on the one hand, and the relatively high cost of servicing shareholder funds, on the other. Listed companies are virtually required to pay annual cash dividends of 15 per cent on capital. For example, in 1981 the listed company P.T. Goodyear paid out Rp7.2 billion in dividends whereas its profits were only Rp5.0 billion. It is very costly for a company to service equity at the rate of 15 per cent on capital cash outgoings after tax in comparison with, say, a comparable rate of tax-deductible interest payable to a bank or NBFI lender. Moreover, the high rate of dividend makes it very hard for a company to amass reserves which could form the basis of internally financed expansion. The dividend requirement constitutes a very big disincentive to going public.

The fourteen joint-venture enterprises with foreign interests listed at the end of 1981 have overseas affiliates in six cases from the USA, three from Japan, two from the Netherlands and one each from the UK, Canada and Germany. Four of the six companies most recently listed are of Indonesian origin. Danareksa dominates the secondary share market on the stock exchange and, following the government's desire, ensures that the share-price fluctuations are narrow so as to engender confidence among inexperienced and prospective investors. The conjunction of virtually fixed share prices, resulting from Danareksa's intervention, with the apparent obligation of listed companies to pay out a 15 per cent annual cash dividend, means from the investor's point of view that a share investment looks very much like a fixed-price, fixed-income instrument, or in other words a bond.

As the number of listed companies grows, the Indonesian authorities will need to shift their concern from fostering the supply of shares to promoting demand and securing investor protection and efficiency in the secondary market. Danareksa's focus on the stability of both share prices and dividends must first be relaxed. A true equities market cannot develop until participants are exposed to the possibilities of capital gains and losses, and companies freed from the mandatory, high-rate, annual dividend. Share prices and yields will then be related to economic performance, achieved and expected. In 1983 there was a sign that Danareksa would no longer intervene to support the price of each and every share; with nineteen issues now capitalised at over Rp100 billion, universal support is anyway beyond Danareksa's resources.

Some tax exemption of the income from shares is already offered to shareholders, but does not generally serve to make shares so attractive as time deposits in state banks; it depends in each case on the tax status of the holder. There is a strong latent demand for rupiah assets, such as shares and bonds, from insurance companies and pension funds which enjoy steady and large inflows of premium money; but the demographic profile of the population to whom these premiums relate is such that the insurance institutions are at present not interested in trading shares so much as in holding them; bonds might suit better.

The bond market in Indonesia was revived in 1983 with three issues by state-owned enterprises: P.T. Jasa Marga, a toll-road and bridge developer, for a total of Rp64 billion; Bank Pembangunan Indonesia, or BAPINDO, for Rp25 billion; P.T. Papan Sejahtera, a housing-finance concern, for Rp6 billion. These issues were largely provoked by the inability of the central government, in the face of a diminishing budget surplus, to fund the capital works of highway, telecommunication and housing authorities or to incur debt in order to do so. Since this incentive on the supply side coexists with a large and unsatisfied demand from institutional investors such as pension funds and insurance companies for local-currency, long-term, fixed-interest securities, there are good prospects for substantial growth in bond issues and trading. An important corollary of the supply of long-dated, fixed-interest, state-enterprise paper will be diminution in the need for Danareksa to impress the characteristic of fixed yield on to shares: differentiation between the two types of financial asset should improve the marketability of both.

FIJI

A miniature of Indonesia's experience is found in the recent securities-market development in Fiji. A stock exchange was established in 1979 on the initiative of the Fiji Development Bank, as its wholly-owned subsidiary. It is expected that the exchange will ultimately assist financial development generally and promote local share ownership of foreign companies operating in Fiji. More immediately, the Development Bank finds itself acquiring a portfolio of shares which it wishes to sell to the public; and there is a Fiji unit trust which needs facilities to acquire and trade in securities. The stock exchange is tiny: only eight companies are listed, mostly owned and controlled abroad, and the volume of trading is minuscule; 8000 shares in three listed companies were the total of trade in the final quarter of 1982. The volume of business is too small to support brokers; buyers and sellers of shares deal through the stock-exchange office. The exchange does not offer underwriting service and there is not yet any public new-issue activity. Listing requirements are modelled on those used in Australia.

There are on issue in Fiji Government Development Bonds (and 91-day Treasury Bills), Fiji Development Bank Bonds and Fiji Electricity Authority Bonds. Little trade occurs in these long-term instruments, although the Central Monetary Authority, soon to become the Reserve Bank, publishes prices at which it will deal in them.

KOREA

As for the Korean Stock Exchange, it opened earlier, in 1956, but dealt only in government bonds until the early 1960s. A handful of public-enterprise and commercial-bank securities were traded on the exchange for the next decade. Development of securities markets was stunted by attractive alternative investment opportunities in real estate and informal money lending, as well as by the reluctance of firms to seek equity capital on the public market.[14] The corporate sector in South Korea has always been characterised by tight ownership and control. The controlling interests' strong desire to preserve their position goes a long way towards explaining the underdeveloped market.

Before the mid-1960s, the corporate sector consisted predominantly of small to medium-sized firms, founded on private capital and expanded through reinvestment of profits. Thereafter the economy grew very fast, and companies responded by drawing on outside loan funds rather than on shareholders. This strategy was consistent with traditional business philosophy and was also most expedient at the time. Debt finance was readily available from both domestic and foreign lenders at very favourable relative rates of interest. Foreign loan funds still constitute over one-fifth of all long-term financing of Korean corporations. Domestic loans came principally from the banks—54 per cent of total corporate borrowing in 1968–71—in accordance with government policies; but there have been significant borrowings from informal financiers also.

In 1968 the Korean authorities tackled the underdeveloped securities market by introducing measures designed to promote both the supply of and demand for corporate securities, as well as taking steps to reduce the attractiveness of speculation in real estate. The Law on Fostering the Capital Market of 1968 provided tax exemptions for dividends and debenture interest. In 1974 further incentives to share acquisition included concessional credit for those who wished to subscribe to new issues and low-interest government loans for financial institutions for the purpose of underwriting share issues.[15] New share issues offered at par value were below their anticipated market values so that 'stag' premiums would be available to those who obtained new shares and resold them on the stock exchange. The underpricing led to oversubscription and wild speculation. The underpricing discouraged the existing owners of companies from making public issues or else encouraged them into dubious practices.[16] Circumstances were ripe for firms to favour friends and benefactors when allotting new shares.

On the supply side, the 1968 law held out concessional rates of corporate income tax and accelerated depreciation provisions on fixed assets for corporations open to the public; but securities continued to fall short of demand, which had grown significantly. From 1968 to the end of 1972, only 32 new firms issued shares to the public, making a total of 66 companies listed on the stock exchange by the end of 1972.[17]

In 1972, therefore, the authorities took a large step in the Public Corporation Inducement Law which empowered the Minister of Finance to designate eligible corporations and force them to make public issues. Those who responded were rewarded with tax benefits, those who resisted were subject to sanctions.[18] In 1972, again, company borrowings from Korea's large unregulated money market were arrested by an emergency decree: existing unregulated or informal loans were protracted to long terms at reduced rates of interest. The decree 'not only greatly reduced the capitalized value of outstanding loans, but also raised the public's perception of the risk of lending money to the unregulated institutions ... Furthermore, the informal money market loans made by large stockholders or executives to their firms ... were converted into capital subscriptions by the decree'.[19] Largely in consequence, the Korean stock market expanded considerably and rapidly. Companies listed on the exchange went from 42 in 1969 to 355 in 1979, with particularly noticeable growth after the 1972 Inducement Law. Over the same decade, shareholders rose from 54 000 to 872 000.[20] Turnover on the exchange increased significantly too.

Despite various financial measures designed to encourage equity funding and deter private loans to corporations, reliance upon outside funds rose in the late 1970s to the point where, by 1980, 78 per cent of funds then raised came from outside the firm. The ratio of outside liabilities to equities for Korean corporations was estimated by a World Bank team at 82:18, in 1980 and 1981. This extremely high and burdensome ratio is the outcome of a conjunction between a business philosophy antipathetic to widening the equity base and practices and policies which have made debt funding attractive. Korean companies are still largely family concerns, often interlocked into groups whereby different corporations within the group work in different industries under overriding and co-ordinated direction from the centre. Controlling interests would resist any attempt to increase equity capital to an extent which would strain the contributing capacity of the major shareholders or risk diluting their interests by admitting outside equity in excessive proportions. Korean companies have further been wary of enlarging capital because of the difficulty of servicing it, given the traditional practice of meeting shareholder expectations of annual cash dividends at rates comparable with those obtainable on bank fixed deposits. Concessional rates of interest on loans from a highly directed banking system, a tax regime which encouraged tax-deductible interest payments on regular loans, and a sizeable unregulated money market were further elements of institutional bias against equity funding. Finally, a Securities and Exchange Commission regulation which requires that all equity be issued at par value inhibits new issues by those corporations whose shares may be standing above par in the secondary market.

At a time of economic stagnation and falling profitability the fixed-interest obligation of corporate debt becomes exceedingly burdensome. In 1982 the Korean authorities undertook two measures which are likely to alleviate the difficulties of companies, a reduction in the maximum interest rate on domestic currency loans to 10 per cent and a proposed reduction in the basic rate of corporate income tax to 20 per cent, from a range of 33–38 per cent. Further reforms are under consideration. They include: promotion of securities investment trust companies; reforms of the ownership structure and portfolio rules of life insurance companies; establishment of private-sector pension funds; and provision of easier access to the stock market by foreign investors. All these measures could be expected to enhance the demand for securities.

No specifically supply-side measures are proposed although two major further recommended reforms would, if achieved, work to stimulate both the supply of and demand for marketable securities. First, it is desirable to abolish the SEC rule requiring share issues to be offered at par. This is a substantial disincentive to companies with good prospects and valued above par. In such circumstances a par issue would give away too cheaply claims on the future profits of the enterprise. It would be preferable to allow the company to issue shares at a price above par and put the excess into a share-premium reserve. The abolition of the par-only issues rule would also open the way for the introduction and issue—at appropriately graded prices—of such hybrid instruments as debentures or preference shares with attached rights of conversion into common stock. Second, the reduction of the double tax on corporate profits, which are taxable when earned, and again when distributed as dividends, would make both the issuance and the ownership of shares more attractive. A combination of all these policies would generate both demand and supply pressures, which should interact dynamically and lead to an enlarged and more active market for equities.

Korean companies were long unwilling to issue bonds or debentures and the rather inactive market in such instruments was, until 1972, confined to government paper, largely held by government-controlled financial institutions. Following a fall in bank-deposit interest rates and the introduction of a corporate bond guarantee system, it became feasible for firms to issue bonds at competitive rates of interest and the issues proved appealing to investors.[21] The volume of corporate bond issues rose from W86.3 billion in 1976 to W1036.1

billion in 1981; in the same years, government issues were W263.0 billion and W765.2 billion respectively. Since 1978 the value of bond issues has exceeded that of increases in paid-up share capital. The rapid growth of corporate bond issues in Korea in the period 1979–81 may result from the very tight monetary policy of those years; even the largest firms found it extremely difficult to obtain bank credit and had to raise funds at high interest rates via debenture issues and from non-bank financiers.

Government intervention in the Korean securities markets has been frequent and extensive. The leading authorities conclude: 'The longer-term securities markets are, however, very much a product of governmental incentives and direction. While they have led to some broadening of the ownership of major corporations they have not generated significant amounts of new capital or reduced the heavy reliance on bank and foreign-loan financing, nor have they much effect in reducing the direct links between government and the principal owner–managers of the large corporations.'[22]

THAILAND

In Thailand, a Bangkok Stock Exchange opened in 1962 but, consequent upon a report by E.A.G. Robinson, it was closed in 1975 and in its stead was established the Securities Exchange of Thailand (SET). The war in Vietnam was then at its climax; there was little Thai confidence in the stock market. Only eleven companies were initially listed on the SET and the share price, set at 100 on opening day, 30 April 1975, fell to 76 by March 1976.

The SET acts under the general supervision and control of the Minister of Finance and its membership is limited to thirty firms which must be approved and licensed by the Minister. The board of directors of the Exchange consists of four persons appointed by Cabinet, four elected by and from the members, and the general manager. The Securities Exchange of Thailand Act makes the SET responsible to government and gives the Exchange the functions of securities commission as well as of securities market, so that both new issues and secondary trading come within its domain. The Exchange also allows the trading of unlisted but 'authorised' securities. The procedures for listing new stocks provide for oversight and final approval by the Minister of Finance and, as recommended by Robinson, there is some tax remission for listed companies. The Public Company Act of 1978 provides for the profits of companies listed on the SET to be taxed at the rate of 30 per cent, compared with 35 per cent for unlisted companies.[23] This is not a substantial incentive for a firm to go public, especially in view of the fact that closed and clannish businesses are strongly established in Thailand.

Interest and confidence in the Thai stock market grew very rapidly from 1977. Listed companies rose from 39 in 1977 to 61 in 1978, rather surprisingly since there seems to have been no significant direct subsidy to promote listing; subscriptions to new issues were very strong, B7.0 million in the two years 1978–79; the number of shareholders per company and the total number of shareholders both rose, with the latter exceeding 100 000 by 1979; the average value of daily trade recorded on the SET in 1978 was B217.5 million. There have been no restrictions on foreign investment in Thai companies through the stock exchange, although foreign ownership of companies is as a general rule limited to 49 per cent. Share prices rose rapidly during 1977 and 1978 but then declined sharply in 1979. The SET share-price index went from 80 at the end of 1976 to 180 at the end of 1977, 230 at the end of 1978 and 140 at the end of 1979; by the end of 1982 it was 120. Turnover, in billions of baht, plunged from 57.3 (1978) to 6.6 (1980) and 2.9 (1981).

The collapse of the market in 1979, while owing something to international influences such as oil-price rises and general payments and debt difficulties, has been attributed chiefly to domestic causes: excessive trading by uninformed and inexperienced speculators, easy availability of generous margin finance, lack of laws and rules to prevent market manipulation, sharp practice, and operational inefficiencies among brokers. The failure of a large listed finance company was also very damaging to confidence in the market. All these weaknesses were revealed also in Australia's stock-market boom and bust between 1967 and 1972. The stock-market fall was very damaging to investor confidence and now makes it difficult to revive demand for securities. Many investors and speculators are locked into large holdings of shares which they can only sell at substantial loss. The same applies to the two government rescue funds which bought falling stocks in 1979 in order to prevent a near-total collapse of prices

Overall, there is a very large volume of shares which are held unwillingly but cannot be quit at any realistic price. The demand for securities can hardly be strong; investors are naturally fearful of abuse of the market by insiders and will not commit their funds. It seems essential for the Thai authorities to implement stringent and prominent measures to prevent insider trading and other forms of manipulation; they should also require improved standards of disclosure and accountability from firms. Paradoxically, of course, companies will probably become less willing to issue shares to the public as the regulatory requirements are increased. Considerable tax compensation may be needed as an inducement. The need to raise equity capital in Thailand is very great, if development is to be financed in the private sector without either relying on foreign investment or consolidating the economic power of traditional or privileged groups in the community. Potential shareholders are not lacking in Thailand; there is a burgeoning professional and managerial class, and there are fast-growing institutions such as insurance companies and pension funds. Few of these are likely to be interested in the stock market without prior improvement in the regulatory framework and probably also significant tax incentives.

A little needs to be said about the bond market. Trading in corporate debentures has never been significant, but in government bonds was substantial in 1975 and 1976. Since then the market for government bonds has not been active because coupon rates of interest have been unrealistically low and the bonds have been held reluctantly by banks, acting under compulsion. The market value of listed bonds at the end of 1979 was B392 million compared with the then B21 784 million market value of listed shares.

THE PHILIPPINES

In the Philippines, institutionalised trading of securities goes back over fifty years to the establishment of the Manila Stock Exchange in 1927. The Manila market has been dependent historically upon resource-related stocks and its vicissitudes have generally reflected the fortunes of copper and gold mining and, more recently, oil exploration and extraction. The biggest postwar boom in mineral stocks occurred in 1954–56, when the mining-share index multiplied fivefold. There was a further surge in share prices in the late 1960s which petered out because of political instability. Following the imposition of martial law in 1972 and the implementation of measures to foster the securities market, share prices rose again in the mid-1970s, but the market has been in a slump since 1979 and in 1981 recorded its lowest trading figures for nine years. It has always had a noticeably speculative tone; perhaps because of this, and the adoption of US models of securities regulation, the Philippines has long had a Securities and Exchange Commission with wide powers and supportive laws.

In 1963 the Makati Stock Exchange near Manila was formed; it did not begin business until 1965, when the opposition from the Securities and Exchange Commission was overruled in the courts of law. Competition between the Makati and Manila exchanges has promoted trade and reduced the rate of brokerage. Stocks may be, and commonly are, listed on both exchanges but brokers cannot be members of both. Broker commission on Makati has been 1 per cent since the inception of that exchange; Manila formerly charged 1.5 per cent but since 1972 has adopted the Makati rate. Business is fairly evenly divided: 53 per cent Makati and 47 per cent Manila in 1978, compared with the 70:30 split in Manila's favour in 1971. There is a third exchange, also in Manila, the Metropolitan Stock Exchange; but its business is less than 1 per cent of the total trade value. Another stock exchange in outlying Cebu was opened in 1972 but closed two years later for want of business.

Little non-speculative buying and selling of stocks and bonds has occurred in the Philippines. There is the familiar supply problem of close-held firms, reluctant to go public for fear of disclosure and loss of control, with little difficulty in obtaining bank credit at low rates of interest, while the banks in turn have enjoyed low-cost deposits. On the demand side, long-term securities have been unattractive compared with real-estate and money-market invest-ments. There have also been institutional deterrents to holding stocks or bonds. First, the highly regulatory and interventionist style of the central bank has led to segmentation of the financial markets. Second, the commercial banks have been wary of acquiring long-term securities because of the lack of last-resort discount facilities which might have conferred liquidity. Similarly, insurance companies and pension funds, with a pattern of liabilities appropriate to a portfolio of long-term assets, find long-term securities risky because the secondary market for them is so thin. Third, merchant or investment banks, which were established in the expectation that they would underwrite corporate share issues, have concentrated their efforts on short-term financing, which generates mainly promissory notes.

These were the circumstances existing in 1980 when the authorities undertook bold actions to make the environment attractive to issue and hold securities. First, and most important, was liberalisation of interest rates; the consequent rise in bank borrowing rates made it relatively attractive for firms to seek funds direct from the public through stock and bond issues. Second, the central bank established lender of last resort facilities for licensed banks and provided very attractive rediscount arrangements for long-term paper; a big incentive for the banking system to acquire such securities was created. Merchant/investment banks were given access to the central bank's rediscount window and were allowed to undertake trust and foreign-exchange operations. A new class of banking institution was created, combining commercial banking with certain merchant-bank functions such as equity participation and the underwriting of new issues. These institutions are subject to constraints, in that not more than 35 per cent of their paid-up capital may be invested in any one enterprise and their aggregate holdings of equity shares may not exceed 50 per cent of their net worth. It is expected that these 'expanded banks' will foster new issues, in which they will retain significant equity.

The Securities and Exchange Commission is about to acquire powers to require companies to issue shares to the public where it judges this to be in the national interest. A local-share-issue requirement is now enjoined on foreign pioneer companies: all companies registered with the Board of Investment and having more than 30 per cent of their issued stock held abroad must offer at least 10 per cent of their equity to the Philippine public within a year after registration.[24]

These measures are directed at establishing an environment in which securities issues will be elicited or provoked, where an active secondary market may be developed to provide the essential liquidity on which successful new issues depend, and whereby institutions and individuals may be readily able to vary their security portfolios and convert securities into cash. It remains to be seen whether these measures will prove effective in eliminating the bias against long-term investment. There is a long way to go. The 196 equities currently listed on the stock exchanges represent only 0.5 per cent of all companies registered with the Securities and Exchange Commission. Perhaps the underlying economic and political difficulties in the Philippines discourage stock-market development to such an extent that financial measures may be of little avail.

TAIWAN

Taiwan has experienced significant financial deepening over the last twenty years or so. The ratio of M2 to GDP rose from an average of 28.5 per cent over 1961–65 to 77.3 per cent over 1981–83; in the same periods, the average ratios of net private national saving to national income were, respectively, 9.5 per cent and 16.9 per cent. The ratios of bonds and stocks to national income have not shown commensurate increases, however, Government bonds outstanding remain of relatively low value, while corporate finance in Taiwan is characterised by a low proportion of bond and equity financing and a heavy dependence on bank credit.

Short-term credits extended by banks have been regularly rolled over to provide a supply of long-term funds, as in other developing countries. Since firms prefer bank financing and as corporate-bond issues typically require bank guarantees, the corporate-bond market is small, even though the use of corporate bonds has increased in recent years. Public demand for government bonds has remained weak because of their relatively low interest rates. Corporate and government bonds have largely been purchased by financial institutions. The bond market in Taiwan needs to adopt more flexible pricing, promote the use of convertible bonds, and develop secondary trading.

The Taiwan Stock Exchange is Taiwan's sole stock exchange, established in 1961. Its two listed categories of stocks, A and B, differ according to the size of paid-up capital, the structure of assets in relation to liabilities, net profit rates and number of shareholders. Category-A requirements are more stringent and if a company fails to maintain them for two consecutive years it is relegated to category B. A category-B company rising to the category-A standards is elevated accordingly.

A Securities and Exchange Commission (SEC) was established in 1960 and is now supervised by the Ministry of Finance. The major functions of the SEC are creating conditions in which fair trading practices and the efficient allocation of investible funds will occur. The SEC monitors Taiwan's securities industry, which includes thirteen banks and fourteen private companies licensed as brokers; twelve companies licensed as traders; one securities finance company (Fuh-Hwa) and one international investment trust. Of the twelve traders, five are investment companies and seven are trust and investment companies licensed to underwrite new stock issues. Traders deal on their own account, while brokers deal on behalf of clients.

In October 1982 the SEC established an over-the-counter securities market in which only securities traders are allowed to participate. Currently trading is limited to government bonds, bank debentures and corporate bonds. Transactions in other securities such as the shares of unlisted venture-capital firms will be added in the future to help promote high technology ventures and technical upgrading. Fuh Hwa Securities Finance Company, established in 1980, has paid-up capital amounting to NT$400 million and bank credits of NT$5000 million. It provides loans to customers for transactions in securities, and executes safekeeping operations. International Investment Trust Company Ltd was incorporated in 1983 for the purpose of channelling foreign investment and fund management. Its paid-up capital is provided 51 per cent by six banks and one overseas Chinese group within Taiwan, and 49 per cent by nine foreign financial institutions.

Interposition of the investment fund between overseas investors and the local stock market is designed to minimise the risks associated with direct foreign access to the stock market. Indirect investment through the fund allows international investors to participate in Taiwan's stock market while providing local authorities with means of monitoring and regulating the total flow of foreign private capital, and minimising its speculative elements through selective allocation of fund untis. The first issue of certificates in Taiwan Fund amounted to US$41 million. The Fund's dividend and interest income from local sources will bear Taiwan income tax at the rate of 20 per cent; but the Fund will be subject to no other Taiwan tax on its income, its capital or its capital gains from securities dealing. Only those who are regarded as non-resident foreigners and who are foreign nationals or overseas Chinese may subscribe for the fund units.

The extraordinarily high turnover ratios in Taiwan—74 per cent in 1980, 104 per cent in 1981, 66 per cent in 1982 and 119 per cent in 1983—show that the stock market has been seen more as a vehicle for gambling than for serious investment. More confidence in the fairness of trading is needed. The securities market will not serve as an efficient means of allocating capital resources until it is clear that price movements in the market result from the well-informed judgments of many buyers and sellers, not from manipulation of short-run supply and demand by insiders and professional gamblers.

The Securities and Exchange Commission has a responsibility to build confidence in the trading market. Rules should be adopted to define fair trading practices. Inspection of brokers and traders and monitoring of market behaviour for irregularities need to be strengthened. Accounting and disclosure requirements for listed firms have to be improved. Adequate accounting practices are needed if reliable data, upon which to evaluate equities, are to be provided to the public. For all these tasks, a substantial improvement in the quality of professional staff is required within and beyond the SEC.

MALAYSIA AND SINGAPORE

Malaysia and Singapore can be treated together, because of their shared political and economic development until 1965, the fact that their joint stock exchange persisted until 1973, and their extremely close relationship even today. The development of their securities markets provides a remarkable contrast with neighbouring Indonesia. Whereas the latter's capital market is a delicately nurtured plant, characterised by few securities and feeble trade, the market in Malaysia–Singapore has been a vigorous tropical growth, with many instruments and high levels of activity in both primary issues and secondary trading, requiring more than occasional containment by the authorities.

Before achieving independence from Britain, Malaysia and Singapore shared a financial system similar to that in other British colonies. The paramount— indeed for long the only—financial institutions were the commercial banks, chiefly British. An inter-bank market in domestic currency and foreign exchange was well developed but there was no long-term capital market. London was ultimately both the repository of local long-term savings and the main source of long-term funds for investment. Neither government nor private enterprise had any particular need to attempt to tap whatever long-term savings could have been provided by local residents.

Stock and sharebrokers have operated in Malaysia and Singapore since the late nineteenth century, providing facilities for the purchase and sale of shares in companies, incorporated locally or abroad and operating in the area, and of British stocks and bonds. Although these brokers formed themselves into the Malayan Stockbrokers' Association in 1937, securities trading was not done publicly until 1960. In that year the brokers' association became the Malayan Stock Exchange, with nineteen member firms, and next year continuous trading was introduced, with the Singapore and Kuala Lumpur trading room linked by direct telephone in 1962.

Not only were neither government nor corporate demands made on long-term local savings in the colonial era, but even when local-currency securities were issued in the 1960s this was initially in response to a burgeoning demand for securities, rather than to corporate or government demand for long-term funds generating a supply of securities. The issue of securities began in Malaysia with government bonds being created in order to satisfy the portfolio needs of the Employees Provident Fund (EPF), private pension funds and other financial institutions in receipt of flows of long-term savings. The EPF source of funds consists of captive savings, compulsorily deducted at point of payment, from the incomes of government employees. Some idea of the significance of these funds can be gained from the fact that the EPF acquired 80 per cent of the M$336 million of Malayan government bonds issued between December 1961 and June 1964. In Singapore, the Central Provident Fund was similarly the dominant holder of long-term government debt.[25]

The volume of Malaysian government long-term debt issued has risen very rapidly, from M$889 million in the period 1961–65 to M$3879 million in 1971–75, and to M$9370 million in 1976–80. In 1981 alone the figure was M$3806 million.[26] The principal owners of long-term government debt are the social-security institutions and the banks, in conformity with requirements to hold stated proportions of local assets against deposit liabilities: the growth of Malaysian government securities is a demand-following as distinct from a supply-leading phenomenon. Although the Malaysian authorities have never needed to foster the supply of government paper in advance of demonstrated demand for it, they have been obliged to initiate measures to stimulate secondary trade in bonds, ensuring their liquidity. Bonds have been made tenderable at their par values in payment of estate duty; banks and other financial institutions are able to count bonds as part of their liquidity requirements; and the access of local discount houses to the lender of last-resort facilities of the central bank is conditional upon their assets consisting of government bonds, with remaining maturities of up to three years, and treasury bills. Even so, the secondary market in government bonds is not busy; without these measures it would have been extremely inactive.

The market for corporate securities in Malaysia is much more lively, although the funds raised there through primary issues have, until lately, been small in relation to the amounts raised through the issue of government bonds. Issues and placements of corporate shares and debentures raised M$264 million in 1961–65, M$559 million in 1966–70, M$632 million in 1971–75, and M$869 million in 1976–80.[27] In 1981, however, a spate of new issues in Kuala Lumpur raised M$900 million, as companies took advantage of strong demand for equity shares, and so avoided the more costly funding avenue of bank credit.

Similarly in Singapore the funds raised by the public sector have been, cumulatively, well in excess of the amounts raised by the corporate sector. In none of the seven years 1972–78 inclusive did the public sector's share of total new capital raised fall below 65 per cent and in 1977 it reached a peak proportion of 97 per cent. Bursts of new corporate capital raising occurred in 1961–64, 1973 (S$331 million), 1976–76 (S$314 million), and 1978 (S$190 million), with the latter year seeing the flotation of ten new share issues.[28]

Speculation was an important element in the buoyant Malaysian–Singapore share market of 1981, as so often during the market's 22–year lifetime.[29] Some speculation in new issues and in the trading of existing shares is necessary for an active stock market, but the investing public should be not left to the mercy of professional gamblers. Accordingly the Singapore government in 1973 established a Securities Industry Council (SIC) which administers the Securities Industry Act to curb insider trading and market manipulation, a Code on takeovers and mergers, and corporate disclosure policy. The SIC may also advise the stock exchange on the listing and delisting of Securities and the administration of trading. Likewise the authorities in Malaysia have provided a legal framework against excessive speculation and market manipulation.

In Malaysia, as well as a Security Industry Act 1973–1983, there has been since 1968 a Capital Issues Committee(CIC), consisting of the Governor of the Central Bank, the Registrar of Companies, and representatives of the Ministers of Finance, Trade and Industry, and of the private sector; this is charged with overall supervision of the issue of shares and other corporate securities. The CIC examine prospectuses and related documents of any intended new issue, and they regulate the timing and pricing of issues. In accordance with the New Economic Policy, companies issuing shares must reserve a designated proportion for subscriptions by the *bumiputra* or indigenous Malays. Most such allocations are taken up by the National Investment Trust (Pernas) acting on behalf of the *bumiputra*.

Far from implementing measures designed to promote the supply of corporate securities, the Malaysian authorities have been obliged to control the volume and timing of corporate fund-raising from the public. The reasons for this are to be found in the good health and prospects of the Malaysian economy; the desire of foreign enterprises to establish themselves in the economy on a joint-venture basis; the keenness of individual Malaysians to acquire shares, especially those of companies affiliated with giant international firms, and to speculate; and the determination of successive governments to ensure that a majority of corporate equity is acquired eventually by local citizens, particularly the *bumiputra*. The combination of these elements has produced a stream of share issues locally without overt official economic measures to promote the supply of securities.

By the end of October 1978, 254 companies were listed on the Kuala Lumpur Stock Exchange with a total nominal paid-up capital of M$5901 million, compared with 138 companies with a total nominal paid-up capital of M$708 million at the end of 1961.[30] These companies consist of local and foreign domicile enterprises, the latter including Singapore and Hong Kong corporations, and divide into plantations, tin production, financial institutions, properties and industrials. The last category accounts for about half of the listed companies; and almost all the industrial capital raised in Malaysia has been by firms of foreign origin. Local-company flotations have been notably in the fields of property development.

In Singapore, on 30 June 1981, 270 companies were listed on the Stock Exchange, 103 (38 per cent) of them incorporated in Singapore, 158 (58.5 per cent) in Malaysia and nine elsewhere. The intertwined nature of the Malaysian and Singapore share markets is further emphasised by the fact that, in 1975, 63 per cent of shares listed in Singapore were held by Singapore residents and 22 per cent by Malaysian residents.[31]

HONG KONG

In Hong Kong the style of economic organisation and administration that goes with being a British colonial territory has precluded government borrowing; no government securities are issued nor are any intended. Securities markets in Hong Kong deal in private-sector securities, of both domestic and foreign origin. Within these stock-exchange markets, government intervention is minimal and the absence of adequate investor protection has been lamented.[32]

Hong Kong's stock exchanges are highly developed and active as trading posts but, on the whole, they have not been very effective in raising new capital through the flotation of shares or debentures. The uncertain political future of Hong Kong, vis-à-vis China, has fostered very short-term investment philosophies in local businessmen; the objectives of quick capital returns, expansion or diversification (preferably the latter) through reinvestment of profits, and the spreading of capital risk by acquiring overseas assets, are strong within the family and clan concerns which dominate Hong Kong business. In the colonial-type monetary system, the currency stock is backed 100 per cent by foreign exchange, restrictions on foreign-exchange transactions are minimal, and little regulation is imposed on a highly competitive banking sector; this provides a haven for internationally footloose funds whose owners may wish to gamble on the Hong Kong stock exchanges.

Trading in shares in Hong Kong apparently began in the late nineteenth century. By the time of World War II, there were two rival stock exchanges, one European and one Chinese; these were merged in 1947 and continued as the sole exchange until 1969. Business up to that date was parochial and not very active, and the market was both highly sensitive to political disturbances and, because of its thinness, vulnerable to manipulation.[33] In 1969 changes set in: turnover on the exchange expanded rapidly, from a daily average of HK$10.2 million in 1969 to HK$193 million in 1973; three rival exchanges were founded, in 1969, 1971 and 1972; foreign stocks began to be quoted; and a substantial, boom in new issues occurred. The new issues—as in Malaysia and Singapore previously—were oversubscribed many times, with subscription money coming from all quarters of the community. Whereas only 59 shares were listed on the Hong Kong Stock Exchange in 1968, there were some 190 listed stocks on the four exchanges by the end of 1972 and 242, including 27 foreign stocks, by the end of 1978.

As in Singapore and Malaysia, again, the increased supply of securities was due primarily to the local listing of shares of international enterprises, especially British companies operating in the region. Foreign broker firms were admitted to the exchanges too. 'Increased participation by international investors and the listing of foreign stocks, dramatised sometimes by large-scale mergers and takeovers, has helped to further the trend of internationalisation of both cities [Hong Kong and Singapore]'.[34] Hong Kong attracts particularly 'overseas Chinese in the Asian and Pacific region and institutional investors in the United Kingdom'.[35]

No fiscal incentive is offered to companies to go public, but shareholders are not taxed on dividends or capital gains. For most of the decade since 1973 there were relatively few new listings and little company funding was raised by share issues. In 1980, however, a resurgence of new issues saw almost HK$4.5 billion raised through the issue of loan stock with warrants, a type of convertible debenture.[36] New issues have been highly variable in proportion to domestic gross capital formation: minimum 1.2 per cent, maximum 42.2 per cent, mean 10.9 per cent over the years 1961–77.[37] Hong Kong's important manufacturing industries have preferred bank credit to new equity funds; only 16 per cent of stock-exchange-listed companies in 1978 were engaged in manufacturing, compared with 43 per cent in real estate.

The stock-exchange market in existing shares has always been volatile. Boom and bust occurred in 1971–74, with the share-price index climbing to a peak of 1775 in March 1973 before collapsing to 150 in December 1974 (31 July 1964 = 100). Dishonest and dubious practices were widespread during this period and so a Securities Ordinance was enacted and a Securities Commission appointed in 1974, but insider trading is still prevalent.[38] The market continues to be variable: average daily turnover went from HK$24.5 million in 1977 to HK$105.2 million in 1979; the share-price index rose to around 800 in early 1980. The great uncertainty about Hong Kong's future makes the market wax and wane as China blows hot or cold about the financial future of the free-enterprise island on its doorstep.

A major internal problem is the rationalisation of the four competing stock exchanges, in which a total of over 2000 persons are engaged as brokers, advisers and support staff. Members of one exchange are formally prohibited from joining another but this barrier is easily circumvented. Companies can list on more than one exchange and all the major companies do so. The listing requirements are nominally similar but there seems to be a qualitative deterioration in their application on the weaker exchanges; at the margin, unsound firms may obtain listing and be a hazard for investors.

Plain corporate debt securities have had little appeal to either firms or investors in Hong Kong. For firms, low taxes on company profits have diminished the inducement of tax-deductibility of interest paid on bonds/debentures and reinforced the predilections for retained earnings as a source of funds. For investors, foreign fixed-interest instruments, freely obtainable from Hong Kong, have been so attractive as to inhibit a local variety. Hong Kong has become a leading centre for the international bond market. As Michael Skully has noted, the policy of 'intervention only when necessary' has been a major reason for Hong Kong's present position as an international financial centre beloved of free-wheeling investors and speculators.[39]

AUSTRALIA

Securities markets in Australia are older, wider and deeper than in Asia and cannot be described and analysed to a similar extent; but some recent Australian experience may provide lessons for securities markets elsewhere in Asia and the Pacific, particularly in relation to corporate shares and debentures. Although the Australian bond market is substantial and government and semi-government bonds are listed on the stock exchanges and traded there in growing volume, most trade in such instruments still occurs among banks, NBFI and a few other large principals.

Australia's stock-exchange markets have developed entirely without official promotion, support, intervention or, until lately, regulation. No tax incentives are offered to companies which issue shares, to those who subscribe to new issues or to those who acquire shares in the secondary market. On the contrary, the tax system tends to discourage both the issue and the acquisition of shares. Neither the federal nor the State governments have intervened in the pricing of new issues nor in the determination of share prices on the stock exchange. And the regulations aimed at eliminating abuse of the share markets are of quite recent vintage.

Australia's stock-exchange system is complex. It has six major stock exchanges, nominally separate and autonomous but in fact interdependent and in close and constant communication with one another, and 590 brokers formed into 115 broking firms employing 3008 persons, on 1980 figures. Although there is an active exchange in each of the State capital cities—but not in the national capital, Canberra—and all stocks are multi-listed, trade is dominated by the Melbourne and Sydney exchanges which together account for more than 90 per cent of national turnover by value. The number of companies listed in Australia is high by international standards but declined by a third between 1972 (1584) and 1982 (1033). On 30 June 1982 the total market value of shares was $A38 billion, $A28.5 billion of it industrials and $A9.5 billion mining stocks.

During the 1970s the new-issue market was relatively inactive; whereas Australian companies in 1955/56 and 1965/66 raised 20 per cent of funds from share issues, this source declined to about 3 per cent in 1972/73, before recovering to about 10–12 per cent in the late 1970s. Tax distortions made it more attractive for firms to incur debt than to issue shares. Moreover, in times of high and sustained inflation, as then experienced, the real burden of debt diminishes. On the demand side, and in common with the rest of the world during the inflation of the 1970s, the relative attractiveness of shares diminished in comparison with real assets; this was exacerbated in Australia by non-neutral tax conditions which made the acquisition of other assets, notably real estate, much more attractive than the holding of shares.

A significant consequential feature has been the marked shift of share ownership from individual Australians to institutions such as life-insurance companies, superannuation and pension funds and unit trusts, and to non-residents. In broad terms the proportion of shareholdings in individual hands fell from 80 per cent to 40 per cent between 1950 and 1980; only about 4 per cent of Australians currently own shares as individuals. There is also a high concentration of shareholdings in individual companies among a few life-insurance offices and superannuation funds. Tax arrangements have much to do with these developments: individual Australian taxpayers are liable for personal income tax on dividend receipts from companies; the dividends received by life offices, superannuation and pension funds, and unit trusts are either tax-free or taxed at lesser rates than those applicable to individuals. In any case the companies will have paid tax on profits before distributing dividends from such profits, so that dividends flowing to individuals are subject to double tax.

Demand for company securities in Australia was also damaged severely by the market crash of 1970/71 which ended a mining-based share boom begun in 1967. The collapse of this boom revealed many grave defects in the share markets. Insider trading, market manipulation, abuse of privileged positions, deception, misuse of trust funds and other improprieties were uncovered by a government committee set up to examine allegations of unsatisfactory practices in the securities markets. Among many other things, some stockbroking firms were found to be fragile and/or incompetent, and the stock-exchange system of self-regulation was judged inadequate to sustain public confidence in the share market. Accordingly, Australia in 1981 adopted new companies and securities industry legislation. The relevant Acts and Codes are administered by a National Companies and Securities Commission (NCSC) in conjunction with a Corporate Affairs Commission in each State. It becomes a nice point whether official regulation, previously inadequate, is now so excessive as to give rise to needless costs, delays and inflexibilities in financial management. The NCSC has to strike a workable balance between the efficiency of the securities market, on the one hand, and the maintenance of honesty within the market and public confidence about it, on the other.

The self-regulated stock exchanges in Australia were in an important sense anti-competitive, closed shops where established stock-brokers controlled limited entry into the broking industry and set brokerage uniform rates. These cosy arrangements have lately been disturbed by Australia's Trade Practices Commission, which has ruled that the stock exchanges must devise new and non-restrictive rules for admission and that the prices for broker services must be determined competitively. It may appear paradoxical that these liberalising judgments have been made at the very time that official regulation of the stock exchanges is increasing. In reality, the regulations administered by the NCSC are not anti-competitive but anti-monopolistic in the sense that they aim to prevent abuse of privilege and exploitation of inside information. All the authorities share the same objective of a stock market which is open, well informed and honest, so that fund raising and share trading can be conducted efficiently and with public confidence.

REGULATION: SOME GENERALISATIONS

Legislation and regulatory practices have not been adequate to ensure clean markets in most countries of the region then. Doubtful activities, such as preferential share allocations and insider trading, have gone so far unchecked as to threaten confidence even in the Australian and Hong Kong markets, let alone those that are less developed. As Kane has pointed out, regulations can make competition fairer either by shackling the less regulated or by unshackling all participants. 'If considerations of efficient production were all that mattered the unshackling strategy would clearly dominate. However, political concerns and responsibilities for improving the performance of the national economy and bolstering the stability of the financial system complicate the problem.'[40] Indeed; and the latter considerations are paramount for developing countries.

In order to promote and maintain confidence in the securities market and financial stability generally, governments must act resolutely to protect investors from dishonesty. This is easier said than done. In most countries of the region it will be difficult to draft and adopt suitable laws and rules, and to find competent persons to administer them. Then there is the overriding issue of determining the appropriate degree and form of regulation in the economic and social context of each country. There is a tension between competition, profitability and cost-minimisation, on the one hand, and fair play and market confidence, on the other.

Laws should not be of such an oppressive and distrustful character that they undermine the potential attractions of the securities market, especially the prospect of capital gains; room must be left for profitable speculation under fair trading conditions. Excessive regulations may stifle the workings and natural development of the securities markets with cumbersome and costly requirements. Moreover regulations may, perhaps unintentionally, give rise to, or protect, monopolistic positions for certain participants in the markets; hence the recent moves in several developed countries, including Australia, towards *deregulation* in order to maximise the potential benefits of competition, flexibility and speed of action within the securities markets. On the other hand, those who participate in the securities markets may reasonably expect that commercial law will protect them against fraud and dishonesty.

Laws which protect investors without weakening the market need to accommodate a multiplicity of interests. Conventional securities-market laws attempt to protect investors and reinforce market confidence primarily through disclosure requirements imposed on issuers of securities, avenues of legal redress for aggrieved minority shareholders, and anti-fraud provisions. If developing securities markets are to gain the confidence of investors, especially of international investors able to choose between markets, all these types of requirements may be necessary. The first two have obvious drawbacks, though. Compliance with disclosure laws imposes extra costs on issuers, not only in the production of the required information but also with respect to the effect of its public release upon the competitive position of the firm. In a developing country in which corporate disclosure has not previously been generally accepted, the competitive costs of disclosure may seem forbidding and the requirements may also engender non-economic anxieties. For cultural as well as economic reasons, privacy is especially important to the typical controlling kin-group; disclosure laws, however necessary to attract international investors, may have a counter-productive effect on the development of an active securities market by deterring local firms from going public.

Similar consequences may flow from the traditional legal methods of protecting minority shareholders, which consist not only of disclosure requirements and independent auditing but also of legal actions which may be initiated by individual shareholders. The potential for such actions is likely to be viewed as undesirable by members of a closely-held enterprise. In a society where privacy and personal control are highly valued, such remedies will increase the perceived costs of inviting public shareholder participation and may alone be sufficient to preclude it. All told, the costs of compliance with disclosure requirements, the competitive risks of revealing information and the potential for action by minority shareholders may well outweigh any attractions or incentives that are attached to going public.

Yet an unregulated market may permit conduct which investors view as unfair or dishonest, and which may result in losses of confidence such as have occurred, for example, in Thailand, Hong Kong and Australia. Even the 'stagging' which appears to have a powerful effect on the success of new issues may in the long run undermine the confidence of investors; for the 'stag' profits are usually obtained on a preferred basis by persons close to the issuers or underwriters, while investors from the general public end up, via the secondary market, paying a higher price for the investment risk. It may be necessary to enact laws to prevent privileged share placement (which tends to frighten many investors away), insider trading, market manipulation and even short selling, and to provide civil remedies for persons adversely affected by such practices. There was no legislation against insider trading in any of the markets mentioned above when public confidence in them declined.

There seems to be no reason to expect that laws aimed at preventing fraud, manipulation and other dishonest or unfair practices would deter owners of private firms from going public. The case for requiring detailed and expensive disclosure by issuing firms is weaker, because of its probable disincentive effect on these firms. Any discouragement that investors may take from undemanding disclosure laws may be ameliorated by incentives to acquire shares. The final object of securities markets legislation is to cleanse the market, not kill it.

CONCLUSION

This survey of securities market developments in several countries of Asia and the Pacific has covered a variety of markets exhibiting different performances and different degrees of official involvement. The viable, active and larger markets in Australia, Hong Kong, Singapore and Malaysia all evolved without official stimulus and suffer no, or negligible, official intervention in the markets. On the other hand, the still-delicate infant market in Indonesia has been directly established by government, and the prices and quantities of stocks issued and traded are ultimately determined officially. In Korea, Thailand and the Philippines, governments promote and/or influence the markets, in various ways, without conspicuous success. The lesson seems to be that official promotion and intervention is not a sufficient condition for the development of an effective securities market, and may not even be a necessary one. A liberal financial policy, it seems, is most likely to foster the flotation and trading of both corporate and government securities. Governments should eschew any ambitions to control interest rates, dividends, security prices and the allocation of credit. Two things seem especially to be avoided: non-neutral income taxes which are very inhibiting to securities market development; and non-market determination of security prices, especially of corporate new issues, which are likely to be inimical to economic and social development.

The elimination of financial repression generally may be expected also to erode the strikingly common preference among firms for loans over equity finance. Their equally widespread resistance to disclosure and 'outsider' shareholder participation is a more intractable problem: it springs from deep sociological roots and is fortified by political uncertainties. Financial liberalism will, at least, do nothing to entrench it. Financial liberalism does not mean that governments should abstain from any involvement with the securities market. The liberal approach may be compatible with issuing government securities; with encouraging companies, including foreign-owned companies, to issue equity; and with legislation for investor protection.

Concerns for political security, economic growth and financial stability have a keener edge under present conditions, where financial interdependence among nations is considerable and is growing but where a high total of LDC international debt overhang is weakening the international credit of all developing countries. Sound local securities markets are necessary both to facilitate the raising and allocation of local savings and to encourage the support of overseas portfolio investors.

5 ASEAN: financial development and interdependence

LIN SEE YAN

The Association of South-East Asian Nations (ASEAN) was formed in 1967 with the signing of the ASEAN Declaration. Among the principal objectives of the Association, as laid down in the Declaration, are: the acceleration of economic growth, social progress and cultural development in the region through joint endeavours in the spirit of equality and partnership; the promotion of regional peace and stability; and active collaboration and mutual assistance on matters of common interest in the economic, social, cultural, technical, scientific and administrative fields. ASEAN comprises Indonesia, Malaysia, the Philippines, Singapore and Thailand, and in January 1984, Brunei was admitted as the sixth member of the Association. For the purposes of this paper, ASEAN will refer only to the original five, since Brunei is a recent member.

In its formative years, the activities of ASEAN were centred on getting to know both each other and ASEAN itself and its potential. As ASEAN entered its second decade in the 1970s, it became more active in the economic sphere. The Agreement on ASEAN Preferential Trading Arrangements was signed in 1977 as a step towards cooperation in expanding trade among members through the use of regional trade preferences. The value of intra-ASEAN total trade (exports plus imports) increased at an average annual rate of 18.7 per cent during the period 1968–75, and rose to 22.8 per cent per annum between 1975 and 1982. Intra-ASEAN total trade accounted for nearly 20 per cent of the region's total world trade at the end of 1982, up from 15 per cent at the end of 1975. The growth in intra-ASEAN trade reflected rapid economic growth in the region. Also, there has been considerable financial development in each of the member countries of ASEAN since the 1960s. This chapter examines relationships in finance development in the ASEAN countries, and the process of financial deepening in each country and the region as a whole. In the next section, there is a brief discussion of development and financial deepening which highlights the importance of money and finance in an exchange economy and discusses some of the important measures of financial deepening. Next is presented an overview of financial deepening in the ASEAN countries, then an attempt is made to determine whether financial development in the ASEAN region has given rise to financial interdependence among the five nations.

DEVELOPMENT AND FINANCIAL DEEPENING

As an economy grows, it generates a growing demand for financial services. It is no longer interesting to determine if this is a demand-following phenomenon:[1] that is, modern financial institutions and their related financial services are created in response to the demand for these services in the real economy. Empirical studies have shown that it is not clearcut whether the growth of financial institutions leads or follows economic development. What is certain is that monetisation and the growth of financial intermediaries and intermediation are closely related to economic growth and development in a market-oriented economy. This is certainly true in the case of the ASEAN countries.

The theory of finance and economic development dwells heavily on the relationship between financial and real variables in the economy. Historically it has been shown that most countries, especially the more developed countries, accumulated financial assets more rapidly than real wealth or output. Gurley and Shaw[2] demonstrated that in the process of economic development, as per capita incomes rose, financial assets increased more rapidly than national output. Based on the experience of the mid-1960s, the ratio of financial assets to real wealth (GNP) was 10–15 per cent in countries such as Afghanistan and Ethiopia, 30–60 per cent in more prosperous countries like Brazil, Korea, Mexico and Venezuela, and more than 100 per cent in Japan, Switzerland, the United States of America and the United Kingdom. Applying the flow concept to this ratio, Goldsmith[3] found that the growth of financial assets rose more than proportionately to the growth in GNP. The use of money and financial instruments, relative to real output, in the development or modernisation process, has been referred to as financial deepening by Edward Shaw[4]. That is, so long as the accumulation of financial assets takes place at a pace faster than the accumulation of non-financial wealth, there is evidence of financial deepening in the economy.

There are numerous indicators of financial deepening. Included amongst the more interesting measures are the following:

1   the financial interrelations ratio, defined as the ratio of total financial assets to national wealth or national ouput. This is the broadest measure of the relative size of the financial superstructure. The flow concept of this ratio, in terms of both the absolute change and the percentage change, is a good measure of the extent of financial deepening. The net issues ratio, which is the ratio of the absolute change in total assets in the financial system to the change in national output shows the growth in the absolute size of the financial system relative to growth in national output. The income elasticity of net issues, that is, the ratio of the percentage growth in financial assets to the percentage growth in GNP, is another indicator of financial deepening. A value greater than unity for these ratios, especially the last, indicates growing financial deepening;

2   the maturity structure of equity securities, loans and deposits;

3   the ratio of financial instruments issued by financial institutions to those issued by non-financial institutions. This provides an indicator of the degree of institutionalisation of the financial process;

4   the relative size of the main groups of financial intermediaries in the financial system;
5   the layering ratio, which is the ratio of the combined to the consolidated total assets of the financial system. This measures the degree of interrelations existing among financial institutions;
6   the relative size of internal and external financing of the main non-financial sectors. Within external financing, the share of the different domestic lenders, particularly financial institutions, and foreign lenders is significant.

Many of these indicatores cannot be readily used, given the poor data base in many countries. ASEAN is no exception. Constrained by what is available, a number of simple yet meaningful indicators of monetisation and financial deepening can be easily computed, including the ratio of money (M1 and M2) to GNP, per capita deposits and the number of persons per banking office. A number of ratios have been computed for the ASEAN countries to determine the process of financial development in the region. These are discussed in the next section.

FINANCIAL DEVELOPMENT IN THE ASEAN COUNTRIES

The economic growth of the ASEAN countries has been remarkably good, especially in the 1970s. The ASEAN economies experienced real growth of between 6.4 per cent per annum and 9.1 per cent per annum during this decade. These exceeded the averages experienced in all the major industrial countries, including the United States and Japan, where real output rose at an average rate of 3.1 per cent per annum, 1.9 per cent per annum and 4.9 per cent per annum, respectively, in the same period.

Table 5.1   GDP growth in ASEAN

	1982 GDP per capita (US$)	Real GDP (average annual percentage growth)			
		1966–70	1971–80	1981–82	1966–82
Singapore	6 044	12.8	9.1	8.1	10.1
Malaysia	1 774	5.4	8.0	5.7	7.0
The Philippines[a]	785	4.8	6.4	3.2	5.5
Thailand	759	8.6	6.9	5.2	7.2
Indonesia	589	6.2	7.8	5.0	7.0

Note: a   Growth rates refer to real GNP.

Sources: IMF International Financial Statistics, and various national sources.

Among the other macroeconomic variables, of particular significance has been the high level of savings and investment in the ASEAN countries. The ASEAN economies are basically trade-oriented, especially Malaysia and Singapore, with a strong export sector. These indicators show that Singapore leads the ASEAN economies in terms of economic performance, followed by Malaysia and Thailand, while Indonesia and the Philippines lag somewhat behind.

Table 5.2   Macroeconomic ratios for selected Asian countries

Country	Savings		Investment		Exports	
	1970	1980	1970	1980	1970	1980
ASEAN						
Indonesia	10.4	26.0	13.8	21.9	33.7	50.5
Malaysia	17.9	29.5	17.7	30.1	44.4	56.2
The Philippines	20.6	25.1	16.0	25.6	14.8	16.3
Singapore	21.3	29.8	32.2	39.9	81.1	181.4
Thailand	22.6	19.2	24.0	26.3	16.6	19.8
South Asia						
Burma	9.1	17.9	10.1	19.6	5.6	8.6
India	15.9	21.0	15.8	18.8	3.8	5.0
Pakistan	5.9	13.6	13.7	15.5	2.5	10.2
Sri Lanka	na	12.9	18.5	31.0	16.0	26.2

Notes: All values expressed as percentage of GNP.
             na   Not available.

Source: Asian Development Bank *Key Indicators of Developing Member Countries of ADB;* IMF *International Financial Statistics.*

Let us now examine the process of monetisation and financial deepening in the ASEAN region. The selection of indicators in Table 5.3 summarises the evolution of monetisation and financial deepening in the five ASEAN countries over the years 1965–82. Before examining the ratios presented, a few remarks on their limitations are in order. First, the data shown for the total assets of the financial system in the five countries are in fact the 'combined' assets of all the financial institutions that make up the system, not a consolidated aggregate. That is, intra-sector or intra-institution transactions have not been eliminated. Second, the data may not be strictly comparable because of differences in the scope of coverage of the institutions that make up the financial system in each country. For example, the financial system of Malaysia covered in this study is comprehensive and includes all the financial institutions in the economy, whereas that of Singapore includes only the monetary authority, commercial banks, finance companies, merchant banks, discount houses and post office savings bank, including the Asian dollar market. Other development finance institutions and provident and pension funds have not been included. Nevertheless, despite their limitations, the indicators portray a generally consistent picture for our purposes. Indeed, these ratios reflect the overall development of the financial structure in each ASEAN country over a period of time, although some caution should be exercised when making cross-country comparisons.

On the whole, the indicators shown in Table 5.3 indicate that the degree of monetisation in the ASEAN region has been significant over the 1965–82 period. The use of narrow money (M1), relative to GNP, has stabilised in Indonesia and Malaysia and declined in the Philippines, Singapore and Thailand. But increasing use of broad money (M2) is evident in all five ASEAN countries, as shown by the consistent rise in their M2/M1 and M2/GNP ratios during that period, reflecting the rapid growth of financial intermediation throughout the region. In 1982, the M2/M1 ratio in Singapore, at 2.80, is comparable with 2.26 in the United States and 2.64 in the United Kingdom.

Table 5.3 ASEAN: selected measures of monetisation and financial deepening, 1965–82

	Indonesia 1965	1975	1982	1966–82	Malaysia 1965	1975	1982	1966–82	The Philippines 1965	1975	1982	1966–82	Singapore 1965	1975	1982	1966–82	Thailand 1965	1975	1982	1966–82
M1/GNP	0.11	0.11	0.12		0.18	0.20	0.21		0.11	0.09	0.07		0.30	0.26	0.26		0.15	0.12	0.10	
M2/GNP	0.11	0.17	0.21		0.28	0.46	0.64		0.21	0.17	0.23		0.56	0.62	0.73		0.25	0.35	0.34	
M2/M1	1.00	1.60	1.72		1.61	2.29	3.02		1.85	1.87	3.35		1.87	2.35	2.80		1.6	2.97	4.64	
Currency/M1	(0.73)	(0.49)	(0.41)		(0.56)	(0.51)	(0.46)		(0.57)	(0.46)	(0.54)		(0.51)[a]	(0.47)	(0.49)		(0.63)	(0.78)	(0.79)	
M2 per capita (nominal US$ terms)	..	36	121		86	349	1091		39	62	182		285	1530	4314		32	121	325	
Per capita deposits (US$)	..	26	89		61	283	958		34	61	169		211	1426	4510		21	101	288	
Persons per banking office ('000)	134[b]	151	149		35	30	23		91[c]	44	28		12[b]	9	7		64	46	30	
Total financial assets/GNP	0.20	0.43	0.55		0.76	1.23	1.80		0.64	1.07	1.30		0.86	0.46[d]	2.74[e]		0.49	0.65	0.95	
Assets/GNP[f]																				
Central Bank	0.13	0.19	0.24		0.04	0.22	0.23		0.13	0.23	0.27		0.14[g]	0.21	0.27		0.22	0.19	0.21	
Commercial banks	0.07	0.22	0.24		0.26	0.50	0.83		0.29	0.43	0.48		0.81	1.08	1.56		0.22	0.39	0.53	
Total banking system	0.20	0.41	0.48		0.30	0.72	1.06		0.42	0.66	0.75		1.08[g]	1.29	1.83		0.44	0.58	0.74	
Net issues ratio[h]																				
Financial system,				0.55				1.86				1.41				2.87[i]				1.00
of which																				
—Central Bank				(0.24)				(0.26)				(0.30)				(0.28)[j]				(0.21)
—Commercial banks				(0.24)				(0.90)				(0.51)				(1.62)				(0.56)
Income elasticity of net issues																				
Financial system,				1.19				1.43				1.40				1.48[k]				1.32
of which																				
—Central Bank				(1.11)				(1.85)				(1.42)				(1.39)[j]				(0.99)
—Commercial banks				(1.23)				(1.58)				(1.29)				(1.27)[j]				(1.42)
—Total banking system				(1.16)				(1.52)				(1.33)				(1.34)[j]				(1.26)

Notes:
a At end 1966.
b Position at end 1970.
c Position at end 1964.
d Including assets of the offshore Asian dollar market, the ratio would be 3.84.
e Including assets of the offshore Asian dollar market, the ratio would be 9.76.
f Ratio of average rates of growth of assets to average rates of growth of GNP.
g Position at end 1967.
h Ratio of change in assets to change in GNP.
i Including assets of the offshore Asian dollar market, the ratio would be 10.4.
j 1968–82.
k Including assets of the offshore Asian dollar market, the ratio would be 2.04.

Source: IMF *International Financial Statistics*, and various national sources.

The 1982 ratios in Malaysia (3.02) and the Philippines (3.35) were as high as in Japan (3.05) and Australia (3.68). The relatively high ratios of M2 to GNP in Singapore (0.73) and Malaysia (0.64) are again comparable with the ratio in Japan (0.93). The M2/GNP ratios in the other three ASEAN countries are close to those in the United States (0.35), the United Kingdom (0.39) and Australia (0.43). To a large degree, the lower M2/GNP ratios in these industrial countries reflect the maturity of their financial structures and the growing importance of non-bank financial instruments. It is also undeniable that the growth of near-money in ASEAN has been quite profound, reflecting not just growing monetisation, especially in the non-urban areas, but also growing sophistication in financial intermediation. The monetisation process in the ASEAN region is also reflected in the growth of the per capita M2 and per capita total bank deposits, although a wide gap remains among the individual member countries. Singapore, the most financially developed among the ASEAN countries, has a broad network of banking offices, each serving an average of only 7 300 persons in 1982. This development is reflected in a high per capita M2 of US$4 314 and per capita deposits of US$4 519. By contrast, in Indonesia, with a vast and relatively underdeveloped economy, each banking office served an average of 148 700 persons in 1982. Furthermore, a large part of the rural population is not served by banking offices, which tend still to be concentrated in the major towns. Indonesia has the lowest per capita M2 and per capita deposits in the region.

With the growth of new and more specialised financial institutions and the growing sophistication of the traditional banking institutions, the size of the financial superstructure of the ASEAN region has expanded impressively over the past two decades. The financial interrelations ratio, or the ratio of total financial assets to GNP, has increased significantly in all five countries between 1965 and 1982. During this period, financial deepening in the region has been significant, with the income elasticities of net issues of the financial system ranging from 1.19 in Indonesia to 1.48 in Singapore (or 2.04 if we include the Asian dollar market), with an average of 1.36 for the region as a whole. This implies that financial assets have increased at a much more rapid rate than non-financial wealth in the ASEAN countries. It is interesting to note that the income elasticities of net issues for the periods 1966–70, 1971–75 and 1976–80 separately show that in Indonesia the fastest rate of financial deepening was recorded during 1971–75, in Malaysia and the Philippines, during 1966–70, and in Thailand, during 1976–80. In Singapore, the rate of financial deepening progressed during each of the periods. Nevertheless, in all five ASEAN countries, the income elasticities of net issues peaked in the 1981–82 period, suggesting a culmination of the process of financial deepening in the 1980s.

It is not disputed that the process of monetisation and financial deepening has been significant in the ASEAN region. Much of this phenomenon reflects the close relationship between economic progress and financial development in all five nations. For example, Singapore and Malaysia, the relatively more developed and rapidly developing economies in terms of growth of output, experienced greater financial deepening than the other ASEAN members. By

Figure 5.1   ASEAN countries relationship between per capita GNP and M2/GNP
and financial assets/GNP (1982)

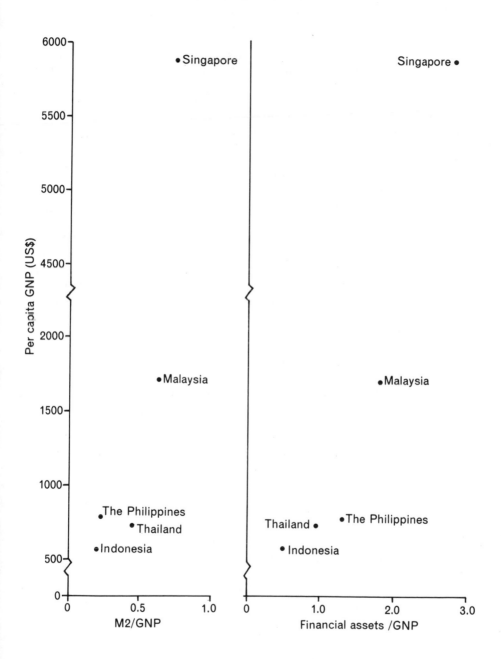

contrast, Indonesia seems to have lagged behind in both economic growth and financial development, resulting from the slower process of financial liberalisation in Indonesia. In 1983, the state banks, which dominate Indonesia's financial structure, were allowed to determine their own interest rates. Until then, the central bank stipulated and subsidised the deposit rates paid by the state banks, inhibiting the mobilisation of savings and attracting funds to the informal money market where interest rates were high. Indeed, this market expanded significantly at the expense of the formal financial system. This problem of a thriving informal money market also hindered financial development in Thailand. A graphical presentation of the relationship between economic progress and financial development in shown in Figure 5.1

ASEAN FINANCIAL INTERDEPENDENCE?

Recent literature on financial interdependence among nations has concentrated mainly on the degree to which nations are able to insulate their national economies against external economic and financial developments, through variability in their exchange rates. When any two nations fail to insulate themselves, they are considered financially interdependent. Wang[5] studied monetary interdependence from a slightly different perspective. Besides analysing the transmission of inflation among several countries in the Pacific region, he also studied the simultaneity among the countries of movements of interest rates, exchange rates and money supply. Here we will examine the existence of any financial interdependence among the ASEAN countries, given that there is some degree of economic interdependence among the five nations, based on their trade relations. This 'interdependence' is not broadly based, even though intra-ASEAN trade represented nearly 20 per cent of the region's total world trade in 1982; the bulk of this trade was transacted among Singapore and Malaysia and Indonesia (see Table 5.4), and mainly between the first two.

Financial interdependence is being examined from the perspective of a number of important financial relationships, including: the extent to which the

Table 5.4 ASEAN: economic interdependence, 1982

	Indonesia	Malaysia	The Philippines	Singapore	Thailand
Indonesia	—	0.001	0.003	0.053	0.002
Malaysia	0.001	—	0.005	0.141	0.014
The Philippines	0.003	0.005	—	0.007	0.001
Singapore	0.053	0.141	0.007	—	0.027
Thailand	0.002	0.014	0.001	0.027	—

Notes: Economic interdependence (Aij) is defined as for all Aijs (i = j):

$$A_{ij} = \frac{(B_i) + (B_{ij})/2}{Y_iY_j}$$

where B_{ij} = imports of country j from country i;
Y_{ij} = nominal GDP of country i.

Source: Based on Kano (1980).[6]

settlement of external payments and receipts is within the ASEAN countries or by ASEAN currencies; the degree to which ASEAN banking is conducted within ASEAN; the amount of external debt outstanding among ASEAN countries; common listing in the stock exchange; and the simultaneity of movements in inflation, real money balances, exchange rates and interest rates in the region. Because of serious data constraints, the assessment of financial interdependence is only adequate for Malaysia. If the statistics are reliable and complete, setting aside valuation, timing and coverage distortions, Malaysia's financial relations with each member of ASEAN should mirror each ASEAN member's financial relations with Malaysia. Nevertheless, the analysis should be interpreted with caution.

As indicated, the bulk of intra-ASEAN trade is transacted between Singapore and Malaysia, and Singapore and Indonesia. The predominance of Malaysia–Singapore trade is also reflected in the settlement of international financial transactions by Malaysia (Table 5.5). About 51 per cent of the total external payments and receipts of Malaysia were settled in the ASEAN region in 1982, but nearly the entire volume of these settlements was made via Singapore. By contrast, the use of ASEAN currencies for settlements within ASEAN has not been significant. About 70–80 per cent of external payments and receipts were settled in US dollars. It is quite clear that there is insignificant financial interdependence among ASEAN countries as far as the conduct of international settlements is concerned.

Banking interdependence within ASEAN is difficult to assess because of limitations of data. However, the broad thrust of relationships among banks within ASEAN can be traced. Singapore lies at the heart of ASEAN's banking relations, both among its members and with the rest of the world. Despite this, the banking bonds between Singapore and Indonesia, Thailand and the Philippines are not strong since, for historical reasons, the last three countries continue to look outside ASEAN for their external settlements and correspondence relations, as well as international banking ties generally. It must be noted, however, that the strength of financial links between Singapore and Indonesia cannot be discussed from official statistics, partly because of strict exchange controls in Indonesia and partly as a result of many trading accounts between the two countries being settled through inter-company accounts, where they are not reflected in the banking statistics.

Within ASEAN, the banking relations between Malaysia and Singapore are unique. Indeed, up until 1965, these two countries shared a common currency and banking system which did not change till the mid-1970s. Their currencies ceased to be 'customary' tender only in 1973, by which time the common stock exchange was separated and the sterling area exchange-control system abandoned. Nevertheless, the strong banking links between Malaysia and Singapore, as can be seen in external assets and liabilities of Malaysian banks (Table 5.6), continue to reflect the widespread traditional cultural, economic and social ties. Nearly 50 per cent of the banks outstanding gross external assets and liabilities in 1982 were in Singapore. Of the total amount of $3564 million of foreign borrowings outstanding at the end of 1982, $1828 million or 51.3 per cent was

Table 5.5 Malaysia: international financial statistics, 1982

International financial payments, by country

	Indonesia	The Phil(-)ippines	Singapore	Thailand	Subtotal	USA	Japan	Other	Total
M$ million (percentage of total)	321 (0.4)	291 (0.4)	39 815 (49.4)	814 (1.0)	**41 241** **(51.1)**	7 077 (8.8)	5 725 (7.1)	26 595 (33.0)	**80 638** **(100.0)**

International financial payments, by currency

	Rupiah	M$	Peso	S$	Baht	Subtotal	US$	Yen	Other	Total
M$ million (percentage of total)	1.1 (..)	8 319 (10.3)	6 (..)	5 770 (7.2)	34 (..)	**14 140** **(17.5)**	56 268 (69.8)	2 911 (3.6)	7 319 (9.1)	**80 638** **(100.0)**

International financial receipts, by country

	Indonesia	The Phil(-)ippines	Singapore	Thailand	Subtotal	Brunei	USA	Japan	Other	Total
M$ million (percentage of total)	252 (0.3)	557 (0.7)	38 503 (49.3)	477 (0.6)	**39 789** **(50.9)**	180 (1.2)	8 088 (10.4)	3 361 (4.3)	26 684 (34.2)	**78 102** **(100.0)**

International financial receipts, by currency

	M$	S$	Subtotal	US$	Yen	Other	Total
M$ million (percentage of total)	9 243 (11.8)	1 332 (2.3)	**11 065** **(14.1)**	64 991 (83.2)	456 (0.6)	1 580 (2.1)	**78 102** **(100.0)**

Source: Bank Negara Malaysia.

Table 5.6 Malaysian banks: external assets and liabilities

	M$ million	Percentage of total
1 Total external assets	2889.3	100.0
(of which: in Singapore)	(1410.3)	(48.8)
Amounts due from banks and financial institutions outside Malaysia,	2252.2	77.9
of which from		
—Indonesia	0.7	
—Singapore	1316.2	
—The Philippines	16.7	
—Thailand	41.1	
—ASEAN	1374.1	47.6
Trade bills outside Malaysia	480.7	16.6
(of which: Singapore)	(26.3)	(0.9)
2 Total external liabilities	3924.1	100.0
(of which: to Singapore)	(1820.0)	(46.4)
Amount due to banks and financial institutions outside Malaysia,	3563.9	90.8
of which to		
—Indonesia	124.7	
—Singapore	1659.7	
—The Philippines	3.8	
—Thailand	39.5	
—ASEAN	1827.7	46.6
Trade bills payable outside Malaysia	22.8	0.6
(of which: Singapore)	(2.3)	(0.1)
3 Net external liabilities	1034.8	100.0
(of which: Singapore)	(409.7)	(39.6)
Net amounts due to banks and financial institutions in ASEAN.	453.0	(43.8)

Note: At end of 1982.

Source: Bank Negara Malaysia.

due to banks and financial institutions in the ASEAN region. Of this, $1660 million (90.8 per cent) was due to institutions in Singapore. Similarly, of the total outstanding amount due from banks and financial institutions outside Malaysia at the end of 1982, the ASEAN countries as a group accounted for 61 per cent (of which, Singapore, 95.7 per cent). This is not surprising, since sixteen foreign banks operate branches in Malaysia, of which five are Singapore banks. Singapore banks accounted for 7.9 per cent of the total assets, 8.5 per cent of total banking deposits and 9.2 per cent of bank loans of all banks in Malaysia. The Singapore banks source their 'net working funds' (effectively their capital) from Singapore, as do most other foreign banks, since Singapore acts as the regional headquarters for many of them. Under this arrangement, surplus funds are invested in the Asian dollar market in Singapore. Five Malaysian banks have a presence in Singapore and most international banks have relations with banks in Malaysia through their offices in Singapore. However, the bulk of this business is denominated in US dollars.

It has been established in the preceding pages that interdependence within ASEAN is only significant between Malaysia and Singapore. Another indication of this is the heavy two-way dealings on both the Kuala Lumpur Stock Exchange (KLSE) and the Stock Exchange of Singapore (SES). The latest information shows that 53 of the total of 273 companies listed on the KLSE are incorporated in Singapore. These companies have a total paid-up capital of M$4.2 billion, representing 29.8 per cent of the total capitalisation of all companies listed on the KLSE. On the other hand, of the total of 315 companies listed in the SES, 179 are Malaysia-incorporated companies with a total paid-up capital of M$9.1 billion or 45.2 per cent of the total capitalisation of all companies listed on the SEA. Participation in either the KLSE or the SES by other ASEAN countries is negligible and there is no meaningful participation by Singapore and Malaysia in the capital markets of the other members.

Finally, the country and currency make-up of the nations' total external debt provide yet another indication of financial interdependence within ASEAN. In Malaysia, this debt totalled about $31 billion at the end of 1983 and almost none of the official debt has anything to do with ASEAN (Table 5.7). Of the private debt, only about 8.6 per cent ($715 million) is denominated in ASEAN currencies, mainly the Singapore dollar. Since Singapore is a financial centre, about 10 per cent of Malaysia's total debt is booked out of Singapore and the involvement of the other ASEAN countries is negligible. Unfortunately, data for the other ASEAN countries are not available but indications are that the involvement of Singapore or the Singapore dollar in this debt make-up is negligible.

To summarise, there is as yet no significant interdependence among ASEAN members in banking and finance. However, there is financial interdependence between Malaysia and Singapore, reflecting traditional economic, social and cultural ties rather than the impact of evolving cooperation within the framework of ASEAN.

Yet another approach to the study of financial interdependence is to observe the simultaneity of movements in relevant monetary indicators, in particular

Table 5.7　Malaysia: external debt outstanding (M$ million)

	Guaranteed loans	Private loans	Federal government	Total debt	Percentage of total debt
Total outstanding, of which:	4 944	8 340	17 662	30 946	
by currency					
—Singapore dollar	—	674	—	674	2.2
—Brunei dollar	—	41	—	41	
by country					
—Singapore	82	3 070	—	3 152	10.2
—Brunei	—	34	—	34	
—The Philippines	—	6	—	6	
—Indonesia	—	4	—	4	
—Thailand	—	3	—	3	
—ASEAN	82	3 117	—	3 199	10.3

Note:　At end of 1983.

Source:　Bank Negara Malaysia.

inflation, money supply, exchange rates and interest rates, in the ASEAN countries (Figure 5.2 to 5.4, Tables 5.8 and 5.9). The price trends in Figure 5.2(i) and 5.2(ii) show; simultaneity of price movements in the ASEAN countries; significant variations in the degrees of inflation, with Malaysia and Singapore being the low-inflation nations; strong correlation between ASEAN inflation and world inflation, as well as inflation in the industrial nations; ASEAN inflation is generally below world inflation rates, especially in the latter years of the 1970s and in the 1980s. Much of ASEAN's inflation is imported, as reflected by the strong correlation with world inflation. The different inflation rates in individual countries are a function of monetary growth, the fiscal deficit and changes in interest and exchange rates. The main points to note are: that the simultaneity of price movements in ASEAN does not reflect financial inter-dependence in the absence of dynamic growth in intra-ASEAN trade; and the general lack of banking and related interdependence within ASEAN implies that inflation is not readily transmitted within the region. The lack of transmission of inflation in itself reflects the absence of financial interdepend-ence.

Figure 5.3 shows the movements of real money balances (real M1) and indicates that: there is broad simultaneity in these movements for ASEAN, although the high correlation falls in the 1980s during a period of important

Figure 5.2 (i)   Consumer price movements

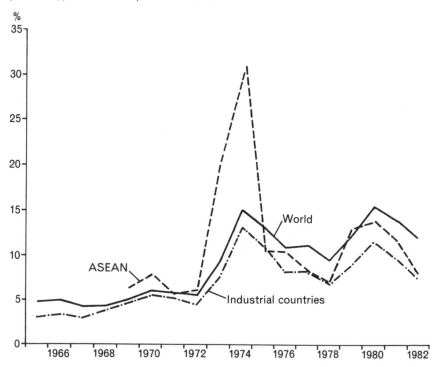

Figure 5.2 (ii)   Consumer price movements in ASEAN countries

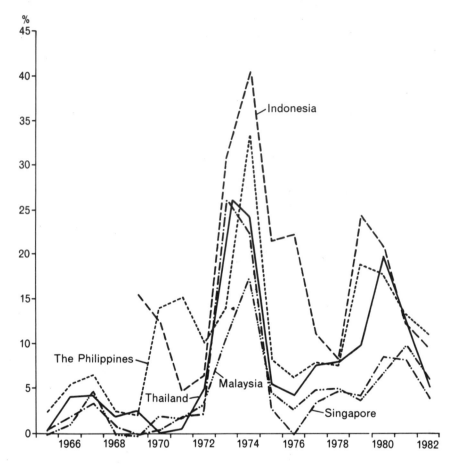

structural adjustments in most ASEAN countries; the movements in prices track changes in money growth with a lag. This close correlation between movements in prices and money balances should not be surprising. Experience in ASEAN suggests that the simultaneity in movements of these aggregates does not necessarily indicate strong financial interdependence, for very much the reasons stated in the last paragraph. Furthermore, it is extremely difficult to demonstrate convincingly that a price movement in any particular ASEAN economy is significantly affected by changes in money balances in any of the other ASEAN members. Even for Malaysia and Singapore such a hypothesis is unlikely to be true, given the openness and market-oriented nature of the two economies.

Changes in interest rates (Figure 5.4 and Table 5.8) and exchange rates (Table 5.9) within ASEAN display much less simultaneity in their movements, either for each aggregate or between them, for ASEAN as a whole. That this is

Table 5.8 Lending rates[a] in selected countries

	At end of year				
	1970	1975	1980	1982	1983
USA	6.75	7.25	21.50	11.50	11.00
UK	8.00	12.00	14.00	10.00	9.00
Japan	7.46	8.38	8.16	6.28	5.89
Australia	7.75	11.75	13.50	15.00	12.75
Indonesia	—	—	21.00	22.00	19.75
Malaysia	8.00	8.50	8.50	12.50	11.00
The Philippines	—	14.00	16.00	18.00	18.00
Singapore	8.00	7.08	13.60	9.33	8.98
Thailand	—	10.50[b]	16.50	16.00	16.00

Note: a   Refers to prime lending rates or the national equivalents.
          b   1976 Bangkok rate.

Sources: Morgan Guaranty Trust *World Financial Markets*, and various national sources.

Figure 5.3 Annual growth in real money balances

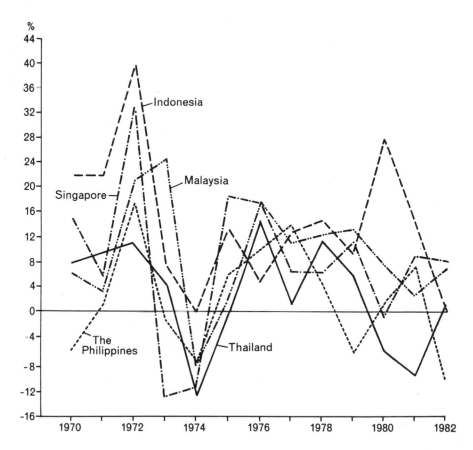

Figure 5.4   Interest rate movements in ASEAN countries

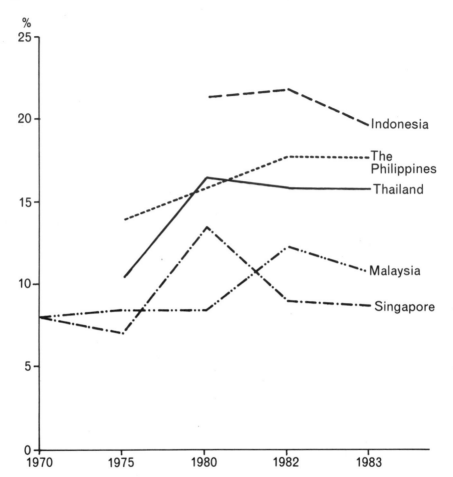

so reflects the 'controlled' or 'managed' nature of these aggregates in most of
ASEAN, and the implementation of structural changes in at least three of the
ASEAN economies, namely Indonesia, the Philippines and Thailand. For
example, the persistent devaluation of the Indonesian rupiah and the Philippines peso, and to a lesser extent, the Thai baht, vis-à-vis the US dollar, is
contrasted with the relative stability and appreciation in the 1970s of the
Singapore and Malaysian dollars. The close relationship between the values of
these two latter currencies throughout the period 1965–82 is striking. The
movement of ASEAN currencies is thus very difficult to interpret in terms of
their relevance to financial interdependence. The same is true in the case of
interest rates, where 'official management' is probably far more prevalent, in
view of the political sensitivity of high interest rates, for a wide cross-section of
national economies.

Table 5.9 Changes in exchange rates against the US dollar

Year	Singapore (S$) Rate	Change[a] (%)	Malaysia (M$) Rate	Change[a] (%)	The Philippines (peso) Rate	Change[a] (%)	Thailand (baht) Rate	Change[a] (%)	Indonesia (rupiah) Rate	Change[a] (%)
1965	3.0658	0.08	3.0659	0.24	3.9100	—	20.8300	0.02	na	na
1966	3.0675	−0.06	3.0688	−0.09	3.9042	0.15	20.7960	0.16	na	na
1967	3.0800	−0.41	3.0674	0.05	3.9250	−0.53	20.7540	0.20	153.6700	na
1968	3.0800	—	3.0649	0.08	3.9300	−0.13	20.8220	−0.33	300.0800	−95.28
1969	3.0792	0.03	3.0611	0.12	3.9325	0.06	20.8970	−0.36	326.0000	−8.64
1970	3.0942	−0.49	3.0797	−0.61	5.9060	−50.18	20.9280	−0.15	365.0000	−11.96
1971	3.0267	2.18	3.0202	1.93	6.4317	−8.90	20.9280	—	393.4200	−7.79
1972	2.8092	7.19	2.8048	7.13	6.6711	−3.72	20.9280	—	415.0000	−5.49
1973	2.4436	13.01	2.4426	12.91	6.7563	−1.28	20.6520	1.32	415.0000	—
1974	2.4369	0.27	2.4071	1.45	6.7881	−0.47	20.3750	1.34	415.0000	—
1975	2.3713	2.69	2.4016	0.23	7.2473	−6.77	20.3790	−0.02	415.0000	—
1976	2.4708	−4.20	2.5416	−5.83	7.4403	−2.65	20.4000	−0.10	415.0000	—
1977	2.4394	1.27	2.4613	3.16	7.4023	0.50	20.4000	0.00	415.0000	—
1978	2.2740	6.78	2.3160	5.90	7.3653	0.50	20.3360	0.31	442.0500	−6.52
1979	2.1746	4.37	2.1884	5.51	7.3776	−0.16	20.4190	−0.41	623.0600	−40.95
1980	2.1412	1.54	2.1769	0.53	7.5114	−1.81	20.4760	−0.28	626.9900	−0.63
1981	2.1127	1.33	2.3041	−5.84	7.8997	−5.17	21.8200	−6.56	631.7600	−0.76
1982	2.1400	−1.29	2.3354	−1.36	8.5400	−8.11	23.0000	−5.41	661.4200	−4.69
1983	2.1280	0.56	2.3390	−0.15	13.9900	−63.82	23.5000	−2.17	996.0000	−50.59

Notes: a   A positive figure denotes appreciation against the US dollar; a negative figure denotes depreciation against the US dollar.
na   Not available.

Source: IMF *International Financial Statistics*.

CONCLUDING REMARKS

Overall, financial interdependence among the ASEAN five is still in its infancy, despite the remarkable progress made over the past 25 years in financial development and growing evidence of financial deepening throughout ASEAN. With ASEAN's rapid development, the relationship between economic progress and financial growth has become increasingly close and mutually reinforcing, even though the degree of financial deepening relative to development has varied significantly among individual countries. Nevertheless, a degree of financial interdependence does exist between Malaysia and Singapore, a relationship born not from the existence of ASEAN but out of history, geographic proximity and close cultural, social and economic ties. Because of the export- and import-oriented nature of their economies, the fortunes of ASEAN are dependent on the vagaries of the international business cycle and the economic developments and performance of the major industrial countries, notably the United States and Japan. The persistence of inflation or high interest rates, or low growth and high unemployment in the United States have effects on the well-being of ASEAN more profound than the onset of similar phenomena in any of the ASEAN states.

Nevertheless, the seeds of economic and financial interdependence have been sown and they will take time to germinate. Together with the increasingly bold steps that are being taken to promote intra-ASEAN trade and greater complementarity in industrial development, new measures are being designed and implemented to strengthen ASEAN financial integration. One of the first steps was taken in 1977, when the ASEAN central banks and monetary authorities established the ASEAN Swap Arrangement. This Arrangement comprises a 'pool' of US$200 million, to which each member country contributes US$40 million, and provides each member country with short-term financial support up to a maximum of US$80 million. All members have benefited from the Swap Arrangement. Some progress has also been made in the development of an ASEAN Bankers' Acceptance market, and the ASEAN Finance Corporation (AFC), which was established in 1981, has already started a pilot project. So far, an amount of $4.9 million has been issued in Singapore to finance Malaysia–Singapore trade. The AFC has also been actively involved in mobilising resources to finance ASEAN joint-venture projects. At the end of 1983, the AFC had secured some $35.5 million of commitments for investment in ASEAN projects, of which about $15 million had already been drawn down. Finally, the ASEAN Reinsurance Pool was launched in 1982 to facilitate an exchange of reinsurance business among ASEAN insurers.

Much more remains to be done. ASEAN is still a long way from achieving the level of financial integration and interdependence of the European Economic Community (EEC). New ideas are being promoted to foster the growth of ASEAN financial interdependence, especially the settlement of intra-ASEAN payments, the promotion of flow of development finances and venture capital and the generation of new lines of balance of payment support, including export finance and export credit insurance. ASEAN is politically committed to the pursuit of economic development as the only way to a better life for its people. Part of its development strategy envisages the promotion of greater self-reliance through the growth of intra-ASEAN trade and finance. The attainment of greater financial interdependence remains a necessary condition for the 'great leap forward' of ASEAN.

6 Modelling of financial markets in Thailand in an asset–demand and institutional framework

DAVID C. COLE, SUPOTE CHUNANUNTATHUM AND CHESADA LOOHAWENCHIT

Although there is fairly widespread agreement on the major functions of a financial system, there are signficant differences in the relative importance ascribed to the different functions, and different analytical models are used to illuminate particular functions. The generally agreed major functions of a financial system are to provide: a medium of exchange and store of value; a mechanism for intermediating between savers and borrowers/investors; a means of spreading and reducing risk; and finally, one of several instruments for stabilising prices, incomes and the balance of payments.

In recent decades, most attention has been focused on the fourth function and the quantity theory, and its extension into the Polak–IMF models, has vied with neo-Keynesian IS–LM models to elucidate the link between monetary policy and stability. Financial intermediation has been the second most important function, and has been the focus of the Gurley, Shaw, Goldsmith and McKinnon models of determinants of the real size of the financial system.

The transactions and store-of-value functions of money, which were central to the earlier Cagan model of hyper-inflation, have taken on new importance as a consequence of new transactions media such as credit cards and electronic transfers, and new savings media such as money-market funds and sweep accounts. These new institutions have highlighted the close substitutes for money, the consequences of overregulation of monetary institutions and the potential for innovation as a result of technological breakthroughs in communication. They have also created statistical and analytical confusion over what is money.

Diffusion of risk has been the focus of portfolio models following Markowitz and Tobin. With the growth of multi-national corporations, the shift to flexible exchange rates and emergence of instantaneous linkages between all major financial markets, both the need and the opportunities for asset diversification to reduce risk have grown rapidly. Increased volatility of interest rates and prices of fixed-income securities has added further to the speculative and risk-avoidance demands for cash as a hedge against price declines of other assets.

Recently, the Walrasian general equilibrium models, which have been used to study processes of structural adjustment, have been expanded to include financial variables and prices. Such models, which include both quantities and prices of several categories of inputs and outputs, inevitably contain many variables. Consequently, the range of financial variables (quantities and prices of financial instruments) must be constrained. Also, the initial structure of the economy is depicted at a given point in time, which leaves out any trends of structural change or prevalence of structural distortion at that particular time.

The model of the Thai financial system that we will present in this paper is designed to explore how and how well that system has been fulfilling its main functions over time. Though we will not analyse the function of financial institutions in risk-spreading and risk-reducing, our modest model and the accompanying analysis can, at the minimum, serve to enrich the general equilibrium analysis. It may indicate, moreover, that the structure and functioning of the financial system are too complicated to be captured realistically in the few aggregate variables of a general equilibrium model.

THEORETICAL MODEL

The underlying theory of our model is: a) that there is a demand for financial instruments and institutions to serve the several functions already mentioned; b) that the demands for financial services are functionally related mainly to the level of economic activity but also to other structural characteristics of the economy; c) that there are many alternative types of financial instruments and institutions which are readily substitutable; d) that if some instruments and institutions are not serving particular needs efficiently, alternatives will be substituted.

Information on financial institutions and instruments is incomplete for all economies but the degree of completeness is positively related to the level of economic development and inversely related to the extent of repression or regulation of the financial sector. Thus, part of the rise in the ratio of financial claims to national product, that has been noted to occur in connection with increases in per capita income or reductions in McKinnon- and Shaw-type financial repression, undoubtedly reflects a shift from unrecorded to recorded financial claims and institutions.

Our analysis will show what has happened to the recorded parts of the Thai financial system over time and try to identify and quantify the major determinants of the demand for financial services.

In the process, we shall note some cases where there appears to be a diminished demand for the services provided by the recorded financial institutions. This may reflect an actual decline in the demand for that service or a shift in demand from the recorded to the unrecorded part of the system. We will explore these cases and attempt to evaluate their real significance, often, of necessity, in qualitative rather than, quantitative terms.

THE AGGREGATE FINANCIAL RATIOS

As shown in chapter 2, the Thai financial system as measured by the ratio of M2 to GDP has exhibited consistent steady growth closely following the trend derived from the cross-section of eight Pacific Basin economies (Table 6.1).

Table 6.1 Actual M2/GDP ratio for Thailand compared with estimate from eight Pacific Basin country regressions

Year	Actual	Estimated	Actual as a percentage of estimated
1960	0.213	0.205	104.0
1965	0.244	0.220	110.9
1970	0.281	0.245	114.7
1975	0.320	0.256	125.0
1980	0.327	0.302	108.3
1982	0.355	0.312	113.8

Note: These ratios are based on the average of end-of-month M2 levels for the year and the GDP for the year. All subsequent ratios use end-of-year financial data.

The broader financial ratios, including the claims on financial institutions other than banks, show similar increases, roughly doubling between 1963 and 1982. Table 6.2 shows the ratio of financial assets to gross domestic product for 1963–82.

These rising ratios of financial claims to GDP are clear evidence of growth of the formal, recorded financial system. They reflect a rising demand for the financial assets of these institutions and a growing capacity of these institutions to meet the demand. As the recent World Bank report on the Thai financial system noted: 'Thailand's record of financial deepening and sophistication over the past quarter century is among the more impressive in the developing world'.

COMPOSITION OF FINANCIAL ASSETS

While the overall financial ratios have been rising steadily, there have been some remarkable substitutions resulting in a sharp decline of some asset ratios and a rise of others. Most notably, the ratio of M1 to GDP has declined by nearly 50 per cent over two decades. This reflects a drop in the currency ratio from 11.5 per cent of GDP in 1960 to 6.26 per cent n 1982 and in the demand-deposit ratio from 5.2 per cent in 1963 to only 2.65 per cent in 1982. Table 6.3 provides the statistics on the ratio of transaction balances to gross domestic product for 1960–82.

The decline in these ratios since 1960 has taken them from levels that were average for other Asian developing countries to levels which are now well below the average.

On the other hand, the quasi-money and M2 ratios for Thailand, which were

Table 6.2 Ratios of financial assets to gross domestic product, 1963–82 (expressed as percentages)

Institution	1963	1964	1965	1966	1968	1970	1972	1974	1976	1978	1980	1982
Commercial banks												
—demand deposits	4.45	4.31	5.13	4.88	5.12	4.86	5.15	4.14	3.96	3.61	3.02	2.13
—savings deposits	2.18	2.42	1.52	1.79	1.91	1.93	2.26	2.27	2.57	2.99	3.91	6.90
—time deposits	6.21	7.12	7.52	8.60	11.24	14.34	19.02	18.22	22.13	23.35	22.02	25.73
Total deposits[a]	12.84	13.85	14.17	15.27	18.27	21.13	26.43	24.63	28.66	29.95	28.95	34.76
Finance companies	na	na	na	na	na	0.37	3.02	5.04	5.43	7.79	6.78	8.80
Life insurance companies	na	na	na	na	na	0.64	0.68	0.59	0.70	0.75	0.79	1.04
Credit finance companies	na	na	na	na	na	na	na	0.19	0.14	0.22	0.29	0.38
Government savings bank	3.17	3.32	3.51	3.60	4.26	4.30	4.85	4.17	3.92	3.65	3.55	3.73
Bank for agriculture and agricultural cooperatives	0.07	0.06	0.05	0.03	0.09	0.12	0.18	0.24	0.40	0.42	0.30	0.36
Government housing bank	na	na	na	na	na	na	na	0.05	0.49	0.72	0.95	0.51
Industrial finance corporation of Thailand	—	—	—	—	—	—	—	—	—	—	—	—
Small industrial finance office	—	—	—	—	—	—	—	—	—	—	—	—
Pawnshops	—	—	—	—	—	—	—	—	—	—	—	—
Agricultural cooperatives	na	na	na	na	na	na	na	0.01	0.02	0.01	0.03	0.03
Savings cooperatives	na	na	na	na	na	0.01	0.02	0.02	0.03	0.05	0.06	0.08
Currency	9.78	9.73	9.64	9.24	9.11	8.72	9.28	7.54	7.63	7.03	6.68	6.26
Total	25.86	26.96	27.37	28.14	31.73	35.29	44.46	42.48	47.42	50.59	48.38	55.95

Notes: a   Total deposits in commercial banks exclude intercommercial banks, other financial institutions, foreign, government and municipality deposits.
na   Not available (refers to financial institutions without any public deposits).

Source: Bank of Thailand and National Economic and Social Development Board.

Table 6.3   Ratios of currency and demand deposits to gross domestic product held by the public, 1960–82

Year	Currency held by the public	Demand deposits held by the public	Currency and demand deposits held by the public
1960	(11.20)	(7.48)	(18.68)
1961	(11.04)	(7.74)	(18.78)
1962	(10.30)	(7.09)	(17.39)
1963	9.78 (9.85)	5.20 (7.61)	14.98 (17.46)
1964	9.73 (9.76)	4.92 (7.54)	14.65 (17.30)
1965	9.64 (9.70)	5.68 (7.30)	15.32 (17.00)
1966	9.24 (9.31)	5.21 (7.21)	14.45 (16.43)
1967	9.07 (9.15)	5.43 (7.35)	14.50 (16.50)
1968	9.11 (9.16)	5.69 (7.46)	14.80 (16.62)
1969	8.52 (8.56)	5.48 (7.23)	13.99 (15.79)
1970	8.72	5.57	14.29
1971	9.03	5.80	14.83
1972	9.28	5.80	15.08
1973	8.61	5.21	13.82
1974	7.54	4.70	12.24
1975	7.45	4.25	11.71
1976	7.63	4.40	12.03
1977	7.27	4.00	11.27
1978	7.03	4.23	11.26
1979	7.32	3.69	11.01
1980	6.68	3.50	10.18
1981	6.05	2.96	9.02
1982	6.26	2.65	8.91

Note: Figures in parentheses refer to the old series.

Sources: Bank of Thailand and National Economic and Social Development Board.

Table 6.4   Comparisons of Thai financial ratios with averages for fifteen Asian countries.

	CU/GDP	DD/GDP	M1/GDP	QM/GDP	M2/GDP
Regional average	0.09	0.07	0.16	0.13	0.30
Actual Thai ratio in 1960	0.11	0.05[e]	0.17[e]	0.04	0.21
Actual Thai ratio in 1982	0.06	0.03	0.09	0.33	0.42

Note: e   Estimate.

quite low relative to the regional average in 1960, had risen to relatively high levels by 1982 (Table 6.4).

The obvious question is, why did the components of M1 shrink to such a low level relative to GDP, and why did quasi-money (the time and savings deposits of the banking institutions) rise to such a high ratio? If M1 is viewed as mainly fulfillng the transactions demand for money, how does the Thai economy make do with a transactions medium that is only about two-thirds of the expected level, and with a demand-deposit component that is less than half of the estimated or average level? Are there alternative financial assets which are meeting the transactions demand? Are they part of the recorded assets or are they in the unrecorded part of the financial system?

Similarly, if quasi-money is viewed as mainly fulfilling the savings-intermediation and risk-dispersion functions, why have Thai households and businesses turned so strongly to the banks to meet these demands? What attraction have the banks offered? Have other forms of saving become less attractive? Are the other forms part of the recorded or unrecorded system? Does quasi-money fill some of the apparently underserved transactions demand?

The remaining section of this chapter will attempt to shed light on these questions, first through discussion of the roles of various formal and informal institutions in meeting these demands, and then by presentation of some quantitative estimates of the demand for the main components of M2.

THE RELATIVE SIZE OF VARIOUS FINANCIAL INSTITUTIONS

The formal financial assets are supplied by a number of financial institutions. There has been a change in the structure and deposit mobilisation since the end of the 1960s. Table 6.5 and Figure 6.1 provide the relative size of the domestic deposit mobilisation during 1969–82.

The dominance of the commercial banking system is vividly seen with the annual share of the total deposit mobilisation being 70.28 per cent in 1982. The commercial banking system is composed of sixteen Thai or domestically incorporated banks and fourteen foreign-incorporated banks.

Thai banks dominate nearly all domestic commercial banking with 97.51 and 94.14 percentage shares of total deposits and credit respectively. This outcome is attributed to the Thai government policy of restricting foreign banks' operations, allowing each of them generally only one branch. Nearly all branches of foreign banks operate only in Bangkok, while the Thai banks, in a branch banking system, have spread out to all 72 provincial areas since 1967. There was also free branch opening for the period up to 1962. Though

Table 6.5 Shares of total deposits and deposit equivalents by financial institutions (expressed as percentages)

Institution	1969	1971	1975	1980	1981	1982
Commercial banks[a]	80.52	79.91	70.93	69.68	69.58	70.28
Finance and securities companies	0.73	3.63	14.36	14.90	15.94	16.41
Life insurance companies	2.13	2.10	1.55	1.73	1.81	1.93
Credit finance companies	na	na	0.41	0.64	0.75	0.70
Government savings bank	15.86	13.87	9.85	7.84	7.27	6.99
Bank for agriculture and agricultural cooperatives	1.02	0.44	2.33	2.91	2.85	2.51
Government housing bank	na	na	0.45	2.10	1.58	0.95
Industrial finance corporation of Thailand	—	—	—	—	—	—
Small industrial finance office	—	—	—	—	—	—
Pawnshops	—	—	—	—	—	—
Agricultural cooperatives	na	na	0.05	0.06	0.06	0.07
Savings cooperatives	0.05	0.06	0.06	0.14	0.16	0.16
Total (B million)	34 487	47 252	122 028	311 582	373 681	460 030

Notes: a   Including commercial banks incorporated abroad.
           na   Not available.

Source: Bank of Thailand.

Figure 6.1   Shares of total deposits and deposit equivalents by financial institutions

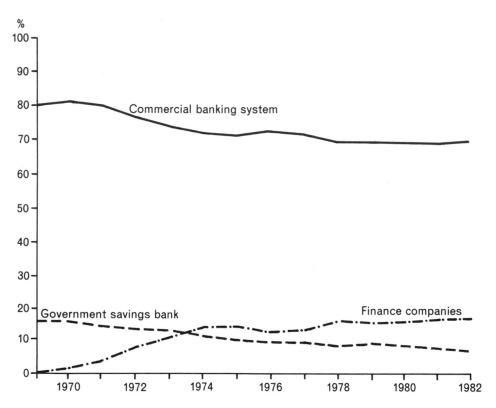

permission for a new branch needed to be granted by the monetary authorities, a permit could be quite easily obtained. It was not until the middle of the 1970s that certain conditions and restrictions were imposed including, for example, a minimum purchase of government securities as well as compulsory channelling of as much as 60 per cent of deposits as loans in the locality of a new bank branch office.

Certain areas in Bangkok are now regarded as crowded banking places where entries are quite restricted though they are not completely closed. The number of bank branches increased during 1960–82. In 1982, there were 1613 Thai commercial bank branches with 30 per cent and 70 per cent in Bangkok and the provinces respectively. The numbers of commercial bank offices per one million persons in 1982 were 26.31 and 92.06 for provincial areas and for Bangkok respectively, compared with 12.52 and 62.98 in 1969.

There has also been a limited entry for new Thai banks. The latest Thai bank is the Asia Trust Bank, which was established in 1965. It has operated as a finance and remittance house since 1949. The Krung Thai Bank was established in 1966 as a result of a merger of two ailing government-owned banks, the Bank of Agriculture and the Provincial Bank. So there have been no new bank licences for a period of almost twenty years.

Finance and securities companies had a rapidly rising share in total deposit mobilisation. Their market share was initially negligible at 0.73 per cent in 1969 but rose to 16.41 per cent in 1982. Though the absolute deposits at commercial banks and public demand for financial assets at other financial institutions did not fall, the relative shares, particularly of the commercial banks and the Government Savings Bank diminished from 80.22 per cent and 15.86 per cent respectively in 1969 to 70.28 per cent and 6.99 per cent in 1982. The growth of the finance and securities companies took place due to two major factors. Firstly, with a more flexible structure of deposits and higher rates of interest paid to their depositors as compared to bank depositors, finance and securities companies could (and still can) compete with commercial banks despite temporary setbacks in many finance companies after the collapse of the short-lived stock market boom from 1977–79.[1]

Secondly, there has been, as mentioned above, strict control over the issuing of new licences for banks. There is also control of activities which banks are allowed to do as well as regulation with respect to banks' compulsory asset-holding. Before 1972, the establishment of a finance and securities company did not require an authorisation by the financial authorities. However, the Executive Council Decree No. 58, issued in 1972, stipulated that finance companies must first be authorised by the Ministry of Finance. The finance and securities companies then proliferated from very few towards the end of the 1960s to as many as 127 by 1982. Table 6.6 and 6.7 provide some statistics on the numbers of headquarters and branch offices of various formal financial institutions in Thailand in recent years.

There are several other financial institutions which have been set up by specific statutes enacted by the government. These include the Industrial

Table 6.6 Numbers of headquarters of financial institutions in Thailand

Institution	1969	1975	1980	1982
Commercial banks[a]	29	29	30	30
Finance and securities companies	34	114	128	127
Life insurance companies	11	11	12	12
Credit finance companies	na	28	33	33
Government savings bank	1	1	1	1
Bank for agriculture and agricultural cooperatives	1	1	1	1
Government housing bank	1	1	1	1
Industrial finance corporation of Thailand	1	1	1	1
Small industrial finance office	1	1	1	1
Pawnshops	156	250	321	325
Agricultural cooperatives	72	578	875	971
Savings cooperatives	104	147	304	449
Total	411	1162	1708	1952

Notes: a   Including commercial banks incorporated abroad.
         na   Not available.

Source: Bank of Thailand.

Table 6.7   Numbers of branches of financial institutions in Thailand

Institution	1969	1975	1980	1982
Commercial banks[a]	574	866	1448	1613
Finance and securities companies	na	31	32	31
Life insurance companies	na	na	524	556
Credit finance companies	—	—	—	—
Government savings bank	264	308	379	402
Bank for agriculture and agricultural cooperatives	35	58	58	64
Government housing bank	—	—	—	—
Industrial finance corporation of Thailand	—	—	3	3
Small industrial finance office	—	—	—	—
Pawnshops	—	—	—	—
Agricultural cooperatives	—	—	—	—
Savings cooperatives	—	—	—	—
Total	873	1263	2444	2669

Notes: a   Including commercial banks incorporated abroad.
              na   Not available.
Source: Bank of Thailand.

Finance Corporation of Thailand (IFCT), the Bank for Agriculture and Agricultural Cooperatives (BAAC), the Government Housing Bank (GHB), the Government Saving Bank (GSB), and the Small Industrial Finance Office (SIFO). These financial institutions perform specialised functions with the basic aim of providing subsidised credit to government-designated priority sectors. Thus the IFCT, set up in 1959, basically provides long-term loans for relatively large industrial undertakings while the SIFO began to finance small industries after its inception in 1964. The BAAC, established in 1966, has been assigned to provide subsidised loans to farming activities. Since 1975, the government has forced the commercial banks to channel a certain minimum percentage of their total deposits to the agricultural sector. In 1982, for example, the target of this compulsory lending was 13 per cent of the total commercial banks' deposits outstanding in the preceding year. The GSB has been operating since 1946 to mobilise funds from the public for financing the government budget deficit. The GHB, on the other hand, was established in 1953 to provide housing finance for both middle-income and low-income families.

Despite the rapid expansion of financial assets held by the public at various formal institutions, there is still, as in any developing economy, a large unregulated or informal money market existing side by side with the formal money market. Aside from real assets such as real estate, gold, and direct or self-investment in productive businesses, direct lending to unincorporated businesses, farmers, and individuals for consumption is also prevalent. Moneylenders in rural areas also include relatively rich farmers. There is also widespread lending of cattle (real capital) for farming. Borrowers pay back using either money or harvested paddy output.

Another form of widespread informal lending is the well-known rotating credit society (or *Pia Huey* in Thai). This was formerly practised mainly among businessmen who formed a private borrowing–lending club in which each participant provided an agreed amount of money, which was then awarded by sealed bidding. The person who offers to pay the highest interest rate gets the money. But once he has received the money, he is not allowed to enter the following monthly biddings again. Moreover, he has to pay back some part of the loan in each month of later bidding. The monthly payment is, of course, equal to the fixed amount each person pays in originally, plus the monthly interest equal to what he has previously promised to pay. The last person in the rotating credit club gets all his money back plus all interest when the circle is completed. This may easily be more than a year if the club is large. In fact, this kind of informal lending is quite organised. The head of the rotating credit club is usually a respected and well-known person among club members. He is entrusted with responsibility for collecting money and overseeing the bidding process. In return, he is given the first-month borrowing with a zero (nominal) interest rate. It should be noted that this form of borrowing and lending has spread so widely that a number of companies have recently been set up to operate such businesses.

Direct lending among firms and individuals is usually not completely divorced from the formal money-market institutions. It is widely believed that there has been an increasing interest-rate arbitrage between the informal and formal money markets. Many money-lenders have access to bank credit and relend some of these funds to earn a higher return on a riskier loan in the informal money market. Many savers also lend directly, either to a middle person or an illegal finance company in the informal market for a much higher return than that prevailing in the formal money market. The middle person and the illegal finance companies, acting as intermediaries, then lend the money out to ultimate borrowers.

SUBSTITUTION AMONG FINANCIAL ASSETS

As analysed above, there was a rapid decline in the ratio of transactions balance (or M1) to gross domestic product from 1960 to 1982. This was, to a certain extent, a result of problems of definition regarding demand-deposit data published by the Bank of Thailand. Before the enactment of the Commercial Banking Act of 1962, there were no savings deposits at commercial banks. Only demand deposits and time deposits of different maturities, including those of less than three months, were available. Demand deposits could, however, be classified into two major categories: interest-earning deposits (4.5 per cent) and zero- or negligible-interest-earning deposits (0–0.05 per cent). Interest-yielding demand-deposit accounts were restricted to a maximum drawing of four cheques per month making them similar to savings deposits. This type of demand deposit was phased out a few years after the introduction of the Commercial Banking Act in 1962. Moreover, certain demand deposits were reclassified as time deposits in 1962 while time deposits with a maturity of less than three months were abolished in 1963.

Because of these problems of definition and policy changes, the demand-deposit figures derived under the old unadjusted series were higher than the new series (see Table 6.3) while time-deposit figures were lower under the old series as compared to the new series.

In spite of the data problem, the conclusion remains that there has been a rapid decline of the transactions balance relative to the national income although to a lesser degree than originally envisaged. Several factors were responsible for such a rapid decline.

One of these was the effect of a high rate of return from holding relatively safe financial assets, especially at commercial banks, beginning when the government raised the government bond rates to 6.00 per cent and 8.00 per cent in 1953 and 1956 respectively. The purpose of the cut was to reduce the financing of government deficits through credit creation by the Bank of Thailand, the central bank, which has always acted as a residual buyer of all government securities in public-debt management. With the maximum interest rates on one-year time deposits set by the Bank of Thailand at 8.00 per cent, and the return to monetary stability after the abolition of the multiple foreign-exchange rate system in 1955, the real rate of return for financial assets was quite high

Table 6.8 Nominal and real rates of interest paid by commercial banks and finance companies, 1961–82.

| Year | Rates at commercial banks | | | | Deposit interest rate at finance companies | |
| | Savings deposits | | Fixed deposits | | | |
	Nominal	Real	Nominal	Real	Nominal	Real
1961	4.50	3.09	8.00	5.61	—	—
1962	4.50	2.11	8.00	5.61	—	—
1963	4.50	3.53	7.42	7.03	—	—
1964	4.50	2.57	7.00	5.49	—	—
1965	4.50	3.56	7.00	6.06	—	—
1966	3.75	−0.18	7.00	3.07	—	—
1967	3.50	−0.82	7.00	2.68	—	—
1968	3.50	1.60	7.00	5.10	—	—
1969	3.50	1.13	7.00	4.63	9.08	6.71
1970	3.50	3.50	7.00	7.00	9.08	9.09
1971	3.50	3.00	7.00	6.50	9.19	8.69
1972	3.50	−1.29	7.00	2.21	8.60	3.81
1973	3.50	−12.09	7.00	−8.59	8.12	−7.48
1974	4.42	−19.83	7.92	−16.33	10.22	−14.03
1975	4.50	−0.76	8.00	2.74	9.36	4.10
1976	4.50	0.33	8.00	3.83	8.51	4.34
1977	4.50	−3.10	7.88	0.27	8.49	0.88
1978	4.50	−3.40	7.20	−0.70	9.45	1.55
1979	4.75	−5.12	7.43	−2.48	9.52	−0.39
1980	8.00	−11.68	10.80	−8.88	11.68	−8.00
1981	8.50	−4.18	11.00	−1.43	12.71	0.03
1982	9.00	3.77	11.43	7.20	12.45	7.22

Note: The saving rates of interest, which are tax-free, are the simple averages of monthly rates. The nominal rates for fixed deposits with at least one-year maturities are the simple averages of the rates of time deposits after taxes. The interest rates at finance companies are also simple averages of all deposit rates, less tax on interest income. The net nominal rates for saving and fixed deposits, as well as those for deposits at finance companies, are deflated by the consumer price index.

Source: Bank of Thailand and National Economic and Social Development Board.

during the period up to the early 1970s. Both the nominal and real rates of interest paid by commercial banks and the finance and securities companies during 1960–82 are shown in Table 6.8. During the years of high inflation between 1973 and 1981, the holding of transaction balances was subject to a heavy inflation tax. There was bound to be an accelerated move away from currency and demand deposits toward real and other interest-earning assets, particularly in finance and securities companies whose interest rates were more flexible. Finally, there were several upward adjustments of regulated interest ceilings both at the commercial banks and finance and securities companies during 1980–82.

Second, the government tax exemption of interest-income during 1961–77 increased the attractiveness of holding interest-bearing deposits during this period. This was especially so for savings deposits, which not only yielded a return but were highly liquid. Depositors were given passbooks and could make any number of withdrawals at any time. Even time deposits could be withdrawn before maturity if certain discounts were accepted. Furthermore, it was also convenient to deposit and withdraw money at commercial banks as there were large and rapidly increasing numbers of new bank branch offices, particularly in the Bangkok Metropolitan area where savings deposits were mainly concentrated. The introduction of computerised online services, especially since 1971 by the Bangkok Bank, the largest domestically incorporated bank in Thailand, also increased the potential for savings deposits as a substitute for transactions money. Customers of the Bangkok Bank were able to make both deposits and withdrawals from their savings and time-deposit accounts at any of its bank branch offices in the Bangkok Metropolitan area.

Furthermore, the existence of a system similar to the Automatic Transfer System (ATS) between demand and savings deposits makes it less necessary to hold large demand-deposit balances. The system makes it possible for customers to transfer money in their savings deposit accounts to their demand-deposit accounts whenever balances in the demand-deposit accounts were insufficient to pay for the amount written on their cheques. The system has been in use for some time, although it was not advertised as a service provided by banks. Customers had first to request such services and authorise banks to carry out such functions as there were no laws regarding such transactions. However, the system was finally given official approval in the late 1970s by the Bank of Thailand.

A third factor in the decline was that savings and time-deposit accounts have been accepted by commercial banks as collateral for borrowings since the 1970s, which makes it less necessary to hold transactions balances. In such cases bank customers are usually charged interest for their borrowings only a couple of percentage points above the interest rates paid on savings or time deposits, depending on the type of deposit collateral.

Fourth, the widespread use of an overdraft system also makes it less necessary to hold transactions balances. In 1982, the value of overdrafts was 48.32 per cent of the total commercial banking credit.

Finally, the financial system must have also increased its efficiency, allowing individuals and businesses to economise on their transactions-balance holdings. This greater efficiency is implied partially from the rapid increase in the velocity or turnover of demand-deposit balances from 3.47 times in 1965 to 20.14 times in 1982. Individuals and corporations, especially those in the Bangkok Metropolitan area, have become more sophisticated in their financial management. Many have been able to channel their excess money balances towards interest-earning assets both at finance companies and in the informal market. Finance companies have been able to offer to their customers higher interest rates together with short maturities including even one-day deposits or deposits at call. When the payments are due, many finance and securities companies even take care, if desired by their customers, to redeposit the money in the banks. As previously mentioned, finance and securities companies have been very aggressive in salesmanship.

ESTIMATES OF THE DEMAND FOR FINANCIAL ASSETS

In this section, linear regression models used for estimating five major types of recorded financial assets held by the non-bank public will be presented and discussed. The five types are currency, demand deposits, savings deposits, time deposits and promissory notes. In addition, an aggregate demand model of all financial assets recorded by the central bank was estimated.

The annual models were based on conventional theories which include income, various interest rates, and the rate of inflation as independent or explanatory variables. The specific variables included in the study are as follows:

CU = currency held by the non-bank public at year end (million 1972 baht)

DD = commercial banks' domestic demand deposits at year end (million 1972 baht)

SD = commercial banks' domestic savings deposits at year end (million 1972 baht)

TD = commercial banks' domestic time deposits at year end (million 1972 baht)

PN = promissory notes issued by finance companies at year end (million 1972 baht)

FA = all deposits and deposit equivalents held by the non-bank public at financial institutions as defined by the central bank at year end (million 1972 baht)

Y = gross domestic product (million 1972 baht)

r_s = interest rate on commercial banks' savings deposits at year end (per cent per year)

r_t = interest rate (net of tax) on commercial banks' time deposits with maturities of 3–6 months at year end (per cent per year)

r_f = interest rate on finance companies' promissory notes at year end (per cent per year)

P = inflation rate (per cent per year)

Table 6.9 Linear regression estimates of the non-bank public's financial asset holdings for 1982–83, without dummy variable

Independent variables	Dependent variables						
	CU (1)	DD (2)	SD (3)	TD (4)	PN (5)	PN (6)	FA (7)
Constant	5971.243	5449.505	7632.597	3324.768	-17476.930	-18652.15	1850.540
	(15.763)	(9.112)	(1.048)	(0.649)	(0.544)	(11.819)	(0.140)
Y	0.060	0.041	0.051	0.116	0.141	0.140	0.192
	(19.002)	(8.228)	(3.019)	(1.664)	(18.816)	(21.182)	(1.134)
$r_s - P$	-586.094	-963.961	1625.348	—	—	—	—
	(4.472)	(4.940)	(2.403)				
$r_f - f_s$	—	—	-3303.402	—	—	—	—
			(2.720)				
$r_f - r_f$	—	—	—	-2841.706	-416.765	—	-4091.843
				(3.176)	(0.645)		(2.221)
P	-572.250	-901.100	1379.152	-351.132	23.056	—	-534.445
	(4.341)	(4.330)	(1.919)	(4.131)	(0.313)		(3.011)
TD_{-1}	—	—	—	0.791	—	—	—
				(3.683)			
FA_{-1}	—	—	—	—	—	—	0.849
							(3.252)
R^2 adjusted	0.9780	0.8499	0.8542	0.9943	0.9658	0.9697	0.9926
DW	1.5753	1.1828	0.8811	1.4332	1.9700	1.6361	1.8181
SE	604.160	953.839	3194.927	2150.126	1773.434	1669.664	4578.376
F	297.739	38.739	30.290	827.826	132.746	448.689	574.604
N	1963–83	1963–83	1963–83	1964–83	1969–83	1969–83	1966–83

Note: Figures in parentheses are t-values.

D   =   dummy variable (= 0 for 1963–64; = 1 for 1982–83) to take account of changes in 1982–83.

The period covered in the study is 1963–83, except in the case of promissory notes and the total recorded financial assets, for which data were available only for 1969–83 and 1965–83, respectively. The equations were estimated with the ordinary least squares method and the best estimation results are shown in Table 6.9.

Since 1982, the central bank has liberalised the Thai financial system. Interest rates in the commercial banking system, which were in the past fixed by the central bank, were allowed to be determined by market forces for the first time under established ceilings for credit and deposit rates. Since the ceilings were fixed at rather high rates under conditions when international interest rates were moving down, market forces came into play for the first time. Furthermore, the year 1983 also saw a financial debacle in the finance company sector with a number of firms becoming insolvent. Because of such factors, a dummy variable taking into account the changes in 1982–83 was also experimented with and is shown in Table 6.10. Each of the recorded financial assets will not be discussed.

Table 6.10   Linear regression estimates of the non-bank public's financial asset holdings for 1982–83, with dummy variable

Independent variables	Dependent variables			
	DD	SD	TD	FA
Constant	4 129.831	4 840.290	121.677	−16 586.380
	(8.705)	(1.217)	(0.037)	(1.937)
Y	0.044	0.039	0.168	0.458
	(13.321)	(4.188)	(3.691)	(4.082)
$r_s - P$	698.780	822.746	—	—
	(5.049)	(2.116)		
$r_f - r_s$	—	−1 959.015*	—	—
		(2.826)		
$r_f - r_t$	—	—	2 994.686	−4 709.497
			(5.268)	(4.334)
P	−685.016	760.904	−201.222	−215.597
	(4.797)	(1.891)	(3.333)	(1.7748)
TD_{-1}	—	—	0.569	—
			(3.957)	
FA_{-1}	—	—	—	0.354
				(1.954)
D	−3 341.140	12 547.250	7 087.582	17 001.180
	(4.892)	(6.269)	(4.824)	(5.084)
R^2 adjusted	0.9361	0.9570	0.9977	0.9975
DW	2.5698	2.1635	1.9839	2.3838
SE	622.393	1 734.277	1 364.078	2 683.117
F	74.221	90.099	1 650.080	1 343.620
N	1963–83	1963–83	1964–83	1966–83

Note: Figures in parentheses are t-statistics.

Currency

The estimated results of currency demand agree closely with what was generally expected. All the major statistics were statistically significant with correct signs.

Currency was found to be positively related to GDP and negatively related to both the real interest rate on savings deposits and the inflation rate. The real interest rate on savings deposits was utilised here as the return on a substitute financial asset, since savings deposits are highly liquid in Thailand with few actual restrictions on withdrawals.

Demand Deposits

Similar to currency, demand deposits were found to be significantly and positively related to GDP and significantly and negatively related both to the real interest rate on savings deposits and the inflation rate. The other major statistics were also satisfactory except for the Durbin–Watson statistic which is in the inconclusive range. The introduction of a dummy variable for 1982–83 reduced autocorrelation somewhat. It also increased the R^2 value greatly but it did not change the level of statistical significance of the predictive variables.

Savings Deposits (SD)

The estimating equation for savings deposits confirmed expectations that they are related positively to GDP and the real rate of savings deposits.[2] An attempt to include the relative interest rate on savings and time deposits, to take account of possible substitution between the two types of financial assets, did not yield satisfactory results and was therefore abandoned. The attempt may have failed because of correlation among the explanatory variables.

Nevertheless, the relative interest rate between finance company promissory notes and savings deposits was found to be significantly and negatively related to savings deposits. This should not be taken to mean that finance company promissory notes are a major substitute for savings deposits. Instead, it could very well show the substitution of financial assets between the regulated and the unregulated markets. Since interest rates of finance companies[3] have always been allowed to fluctuate according to market forces under much higher interest-rate ceilings, they may very well reflect movements of interest rates in the unregulated markets. A lower (higher) interest rate on finance company promissory notes relative to the savings deposit interest rate could thus result in a shift of funds from (into) the unregulated money market into (from) savings deposits rather than a shift of funds from (into) finance companies. This view is supported by the estimation results on promissory notes of finance companies where there is no relation with the relative interest rate between promissory notes and savings deposits.

As for the inflation rate, a significant positive relationship was found, contrary to initial expectations, but there seems to be a logical explanation. One of the reasons why the transaction portion of money, as measured by currency and demand deposits, was low relative to GDP was the relatively high liquidity of savings deposits. The large network of bank branches makes it less costly to make frequent deposits and withdrawals while very few or no restrictions are actually placed on customers' withdrawals. Therefore, when the rate of inflation increases, people may shift their transactions balances from currency and demand deposits to savings deposits. Although there could very well be some shift out of savings deposits, it may not be enough to offset the inflow from currency and demand-deposit holdings resulting in a positive relationship with the inflation rate.

In general, the statistical significance of the savings deposits equation was also satisfactory except for the Durbin–Watson value, which is rather low. The inclusion of a dummy variable for 1982–83 improved the overall result significantly and also removed the autocorrelation problem.

Time Deposits

Since the time deposits in the past consisted of a high proportion with maturity periods greater than one year, a lag term of time deposits was included in the estimation. The statistical result was satisfactory. Both GDP and the lag term were positively related to time-deposit holdings. The coefficient of the lag term was found to be highly significant while that for GDP was somewhat less significant.

The relative interest rate between promissory notes and time deposits was found to affect time deposits negatively and significantly as expected. It should be pointed out here once again that the interest rate on promissory notes might have also taken account of movements of financial assets between the regulated and the unregulated financial market and not only of movements between time deposits and promissory notes.

In this case, the rate of inflation was found to affect time deposits negatively and significantly as expected. With the inclusion of a dummy variable for 1982–83, the estimation result improved somewhat, especially in the case of the Durbin–Watson statistic and the t-value for GDP.

Finance Company Promissory Notes

Since finance companies in Thailand are not allowed to issue deposits of any type, they rely instead mainly on promissory notes as a formal source of funds. The regression analysis did not indicate a significant relationship between promissory notes, various interest-rate measures and the inflation rate. The best estimates equation was the simple case where GDP was the only independent variable.

A likely explanation of this result could be government regulation of commercial banks, especially regarding the fixing of interest rates and the control on the number of banks. This, together with the fact that commercial banks in Thailand are under the control of families mainly interested in financing their own businesses, did not create sufficient competitive pressure in the banking system. The relatively high profitability of banks through a guaranteed interest margin coupled with the banks' inability or unwillingness to provide credit to businesses outside their family groups, resulted in the growth and proliferation of finance companies. Promissory notes of finance companies increased from only a mere 0.73 per cent of recorded financial assets in 1969 to 16.41 per cent in 1982. The growth factor seems to be more of an overriding determinant than other factors such as interest rates and the rate of inflation.

Another explanation could be that finance companies rely significantly on unofficial or informal sources of funds besides the use of promissory notes, for example, the issuing of predated cheques instead of promissory notes. This is an attempt to avoid both taxes and the maximum interest-rate ceiling allowed by the central bank. Since such informal fund sources were not and could not be recorded, the estimation of the demand for financial assets of finance companies was thus not complete and must be interpreted with care.

Aggregate Recorded Financial Assets

The statistical result in this case was more or less similar to the result for time deposits. This was because time deposits are the most important type of financial asset in the recorded financial system. Movements in aggregate financial asset holdings of the non-bank public closely followed movements in time deposits. Time deposits constituted as much as 50.30 per cent of the total recorded deposits in 1982.

CONCLUSION

Total financial growth and development in Thailand has been rapid over the last years. The more than doubling of the ratio of aggregate formal financial assets to the gross domestic product from 25.86 per cent in 1963 to 55.95 per cent in 1982 is impressive for a developing economy. The demand for financial assets has been strong due not only to the rapid growth of income but also other important factors including relative monetary stability and the nominally high regulated rate of interest, giving rise to a high positive real rate of interest during 1955–72. Interest-bearing financial assets are attractive outlets for wealth holdings.

Another important factor which has caused the public to absorb much of the interest-bearing deposits is the rapid expansion of commercial bank branches throughout the period after 1955. Although new licences for commercial banks have been restricted since 1965, opening new bank branches was relatively free for Thai banks, especially before 1962. It was only after 1975 that certain restrictions on branch expansion have been imposed, including, for example, compulsory government bond holding and minimum credit provision back to the area where deposits are originally mobilised. In this process of financial deepening, coupled with the increasing liquidity of interest-bearing savings deposits, the ratio of transaction balances to gross domestic product also fell rapidly during the last two decades ending in 1982.

A rapid emergence of finance and securities companies coincided with the beginning of the period of high inflation of 1973–81. The relatively higher and more flexible interest rate paid by finance and securities companies helped to circumvent much of the effect of inflation on financial asset holdings. There is also a relatively more flexible maturity structure in finance and securities companies. Despite a collapse of several finance and securities companies as well as credit finance companies after 1979, they have continued to provide competititon against commercial banks.

There was an upward adjustment in 1980 of the regulated ceiling rates of interest for financial deposits, both at banks and finance companies. With lower inflation rates, the real rate of interest for financial assets became a large positive figure again after 1981. The government has also attempted to pursue a more flexible interest-rate policy. The recent introduction of transferable certificates of deposits and secondary markets for government bonds by various commercial banks represents the beginning of a slightly more flexible financial market in Thailand.

There is presently some discussion of issuing more licences for new commercial banks as well as allowing specialised institutions and commercial banks themselves to perform more financial activities. This is particularly the case for the Government Savings Bank, whose mobilised funds have been almost totally channelled to finance the government's deficit. Whether these more liberalised financial measures will be successfully carried out by the government remains to be seen.

7 The financing of export-oriented growth in Korea

WONTACK HONG AND YUNG CHUL PARK

The economic performance of Korea together with the achievement of Hong Kong, Singapore, and Taiwan over the past two decades is often cited as one of the most striking features of modern economic history. These countries, known as the Asian NICs, have sustained rapid growth of output and employment through their successful promotion of manufactures exports.

From the mid-1960s onward, the Korean government has pursued an outward-looking development strategy which places emphasis on the expansion of manufactures exports. In order to promote exports, the government has provided the exporters, and those engaged in export-related production activities, with a wide range of incentives. Among them, interest-rate subsidies and credit availability have been the major export inducements. The financial incentives require extensive government intervention in the capital market. It is arguable that intervention is both more effective and more efficient than restrictions in the goods market as a means of inducing sectoral allocation of investment at certain stages of development. In Korea, however, the capital-market intervention has resulted in a high degree of financial repression, and the cumulative effect of the capital-market distortions has increased with the transition of the economy to a mature stage of development where allocational criteria are relatively more complex and difficult to devise.

The purpose of this paper is to analyse the effects on the sectoral factor and investment expansion of financing of the export-oriented growth in Korea during the past two decades. In sequence the discussion will treat: the system of export financing; credit rationing and government intervention in resource allocation in general; the association between subsidised credit rationing and the expansion of sectoral output and export; and finally the effect of the export financing system and government credit allocation in general on sectoral investment. Within a neoclassical framework of investment behaviour, the final section analyses empirically the issue of credit fungibility in Korea's manufacturing sector.

163

GOVERNMENT INTERVENTION IN RESOURCE ALLOCATION AND EXPORT FINANCING

The Korean government has intervened extensively in the allocation of resources by controlling interest rates and financial institutions. Most of the banking institutions have been arms of the government's industrial policy. The government has behaved as if, in the absence of intervention, some sectors that are important for development would not receive an adequate amount of credit while others would receive more than socially and economically desirable.

With the adoption of an outward-looking development strategy in the mid-1960s that placed emphasis on promoting exports, the government has sought to allocate a larger share of investment resources to the export-producing manufacturing sector. Due largely to this industrial policy, exporters and those engaged in export-related activities have been by far the most favoured borrowers at the banks in Korea. Exporters have access to short-term loans tied to the gross volume of export sales (the term of which does not in general exceed 30 days) and long-term loans for fixed investment in export-oriented industries. Export loans are all subsidised and preferential in that they carry interest rates lower than the general bank lending rates and are made available only to those who generate exports.

Short-term export loans are automatically extended without limit to those with valid letters of credit irrespective of the domestic value-added content of exports. They include loans for production and collection of export goods, domestic purchases as well as imports of raw materials for exports, agricultural and fisheries export preparations, and suppliers in foreign currency. Long-term export loans consist of foreign-currency loans supplied by domestic banking institutions within the limit of their foreign-exchange holdings, equipment loans for export industries and export–import bank loans for export on credit.[1]

As shown in Table 7.1, long-term loans as a percentage of the total export-related credit were negligible until the mid-1960s. Beginning in 1967, the long-term share has risen markedly, largely because of a sharp increase in foreign-currency loans. Excluding the foreign-exchange loans, the long-term share amounted to about 12 per cent between 1973 and 1980. It should be noted, however, that the institution of foreign-currency loans did not represent any new element in the export subsidy scheme. These loans partially replaced foreign loans, mostly in the form of suppliers' credit for which domestic banks provided payment guarantees and to which exporters had relatively easy access so long as the loans were for the financing of imported intermediate and capital goods to be used in export production. The partial substitution of foreign loans for foreign-currency loans by domestic banks was motivated by the government's effort to allocate more efficiently, and to mitigate the domestic liquidity effect of, growing foreign-exchange holdings.

The export financing system has provided a powerful stimulus to firms to export once they begin production. This system has spread the lendng activities of the deposit money banks more broadly throughout the manufacturing sector than would have been the case if the loans had been discretionary. It has also

Table 7.1 Export promotion loans extended by deposit money banks and ex-im bank (W100 million)

	1960	1970	1971	1972	1973	1974	1975
Total loans	243	8231	10897	13214	17471	26649	33463
—domestic currency	243	7224	9195	11980	15875	24278	29055
—foreign currency	—	1014	1573	1028	1281	1948	3436
—others[a]	—	43	111	206	315	423	912
Export promotion loans (1+2)	14	1616	2485	2318	4152	6526	8409
	(5.8)[b]	(19.5)	(22.8)	(17.5)	(23.8)	(24.5)	(25.1)
1 Short-term	14	602	908	1276	2502	3975	4062
—export promotion loans[c]	14	559	801	1084	2216	3595	3389
—negotiations of usance export bills	na	43	107	192	286	380	673
2 Long-term	—	1014	1577	1042	1660	2551	4347
—foreign currency loans	—	1014	1573	1028	1281	1948	3436
—equipment loans for export industries	—	—	—	—	350	560	612
—ex-im bank loans for export on credit	—	—	4	14	29	43	299

	1976	1977	1978	1979	1980	1981	1982	1983
Total loans	42289	55824	82848	111696	161002	210860	294596	312208
—domestic currency	37249	47090	66090	89778	122044	160091	202258	241503
—foreign currency	3461	5073	10989	17229	25961	27750	31588	31338
—others[a]	1579	3661	5769	7689	12997	23019	30750	39367
Export promotion loans (1+2)	10427	15115	26160	37648	56428	69574	81920	92326
	(24.7)[b]	(27.1)	(31.6)	(32.8)	(35.0)	(33.0)	(31.0)	(29.6)
1 Short-term	5635	8127	13033	18712	27309	31996	33935	39375
—export promotion loans[c]	4618	5672	8915	13278	19427	23419	23946	26996
—negotiations of usance export bills	1017	2455	4123	5434	7882	8577	9989	12379
2 Long-term	4792	6988	13122	18936	29119	37578	47985	52951
—foreign currency loans	3461	5073	10906	16254	23742	26303	30426	30542
—equipment loans for export industries	769	709	570	427	262	1799	1921	1855
—ex-im bank loans for export on credit	562	1206	1646	2255	5115	9476	15638	20552

Notes: a Includes negotiations of usance export bills and ex-im banks loans.
      b Percentage of total loans.
      c See text for the types of loans included.
      na Not available.

Source: Bank of Korea, Economic Statistics Yearbook.

eliminated much of the cost involved in obtaining the rationed loans of the banking system.[2]

Financial incentives in the form of availability of credit at subsidised interest rates induce domestic producers to sell abroad, rather than in the home market, as the incentives increase the effective exchange rate for exports. The automatic availability of credit also generates the powerful effect of encouraging investment in export-oriented industries. In a regime where strict credit rationing is administered, credit availability can be a far more important incentive than interest-rate subsidies.[3] When the official interest rates are often held below the expected rate of return to capital, and banks are the major source of credit, business enterprises are highly leveraged, and their liabilities are mostly short-term. Under these circumstances, bank credit can be critical for both the success and survival of firms.

In addition to the automatic availability of export-related credits, access to other types of bank credit has been better for exporters than for domestic-market-oriented firms for several reasons. In line with government industrial policies designed to direct more resources to export-generating sectors, financial institutions have been explicitly or implicitly encouraged to support exporters. Therefore, exporters have been treated as preferred customers in the rationing of credit by banks. From the viewpoint of the banks, exporters are also preferred borrowers because, unlike domestic-market-oriented enterprises, exporters are assured of credit so long as they maintain a certain rate of growth of export revenues. With a rediscounting facility at the central bank, discounting of export-related bills has been one of the major sources of bank profits. Indeed the banks have had every reason to attract exporters and then support them financially in preference to other customers.

The export financing system in Korea is geared to promote exports by making export sales more profitable and also by encouraging investment in export-oriented industries. The financial incentive scheme may not have always succeeded in keeping the real exchange rate favourable to exporters. However, the coupling of short-term export financing with the preferences given to exporters in the allocation of credit in general has meant that the Korean government has succeeded in allocating a large share of financial resources to exporters. One important question arising from these circumstances is whether the credit-allocation policy that favours exporters has contributed to the investment expansion in export-oriented manufacturing sectors? This question is important because if it can be shown that the allocation policy has had little effect on the investment in export-oriented industries, then one might doubt the efficiency of Korea's export financing scheme. We will return to this question in some detail.

CREDIT RATIONING IN KOREA

The most important form of government subsidy in Korea maintains extremely low real interest rates on bank loans by applying fixed nominal rates of interest and at the same time maintaining high rates of inflation through expansionary monetary policy. These low-interest loans are then rationed to the preferred sectors for export promotion.

Total loans provided through the deposit money banks (DMB), the Korea Development Bank (KDB) and the Korea Export–Import Bank (EXIMB) have steadily increased from about 15 per cent of GNP in 1962–66, about 32 per cent in 1967–71, about 39 per cent in 1972–76 and about 46 per cent of GNP in 1977–81. During 1962–66, the EXIMB did not exist but the KDB alone provided more than one-third of total bank loans in the form of discretionary policy loans. During 1967–76, the KDB and the EXIMB provided only about 15 per cent of total loans but, due to the rapidly expanding EXIMB activities since the late 1970s, their share in total bank loans expanded to about 18 per cent during 1977–81. Discretionary policy loans provided through the DMB were in the form of a machine-industry promotion fund, a term-loan fund, a medium-industry fund, an export-industry equipment fund, an industrial rationalisation fund, a foreign-loan fund, a national investment fund, and foreign-currency-loan fund, among others. These loans increased from about 10 per cent of total loans in 1962–66 to about 20 per cent in 1967–81. Therefore, the magnitude of loans formally designated as discretionary policy loans amounted to around 36 per cent of total bank loans during 1967–81.

Short-term export credits and loans for agriculture, fisheries and housing may be classified as non-discretionary policy loans. The magnitude of such loans was about 17 per cent of total loans during 1967–81. This implies that the proportion of formal policy loans slightly exceeded half of total loans (provided through the DMB, the KDB and the EXIMB) during 1967–81. However, commercial bills discounted and loans based on general banking funds were also rationed with the discretion of the government in Korea, and hence they should be regarded as non-policy but discretionary loans. The magnitude of such loans declined from about 30 per cent of total loans in 1967–71 to about 20 per cent in 1977–81.

Overdrafts, loans based on instalment savings deposits, loans for the popu-lace, remunerations (Citizens National Bank loans based on instalment savings deposits) and loans by the branches of foreign banks might be regarded as non-policy loans free of government discretion, though they still seem to have been subject to favouritism and political influence. The magnitude of such non-discretionary, non-policy DMB loans amounted to around 22 per cent of total loans during 1972–81.[4]

The real interest rate, the difference between the nominal interest rate and the rate of change in GNP deflator, on one-year time deposits amounted to about −10.7 per cent per annum on average in 1954–65, 10.0 per cent per annum during the high-interest-rate era of 1965–71, and −3.4 per cent per annum in 1972–81. The real interest rate applied to discounts of commercial bills amounted to −7.3 per cent per annum on average in 1954–64, 9.5 per cent annum per in 1965–71, and −1.7 per cent per annum in 1972–81.[5]

The weighted average real interest rate on foreign loans amounted to 2.1 per cent per annum during 1967–71 and −7.4 per cent per annum during

1972–76.[6] During 1977–79, Korea maintained a fixed exchange rate (at W484 per US dollar) in spite of the fact that domestic prices were rising at about 19 per cent per annum while the weighted average price level of its major trade partners, the US and Japan, was rising at about 6 per cent per annum, applying equal weights to both countries. Since the Eurodollar average interest rates amounted to about 11 per cent per annum during 1977–79, the real interest rates on Korea's foreign borrowing could not have exceeded −2 per cent during 1977–79.[7] Naturally, the foreign borrowings have also been strictly controlled by the government.

The total volume of domestic loans provided through the DMB, the KDB and the EXIMB amounted to about 39 per cent of GNP in 1972–76 and about 46 per cent of GNP in 1977–81. We may approximate the real interest rates on entire loans provided by all banking institutions in Korea with the real interest rates applied to the discounts of commercial bills.[8] On the other hand, the estimated average real rates of return on investment in the Korean manufacturing sector amounted to about 22 per cent during 1972–79. If we take the difference between the real rate of return on investment and the real interest rate as the subsidy rate associated with domestic bank loan allocations, the annual provision of credit subsidies in Korea amounted to at least 10 per cent of GNP each year on average in the 1970s. At 10 per cent of GNP, the domestic credit subsidy must be judged large enough to significantly affect the pattern of Korea's output and trade. Furthermore, there were also low-interest foreign loans allocated directly to entrepreneurs amounting to about 6 per cent of GNP each year on average in the 1970s.

SUBSIDISED CREDIT RATIONING AND EXPANSION OF SECTORAL OUTPUT AND EXPORT

In this section we will examine the association between sectoral credit rationing and sectoral factor substitution, and the expansion of output and exports in Korea during the period 1971–82. Most of the labour-intensive manufacturing sectors listed in Table 7.2, such as clothing, footwear, electronics, telecommunication equipment, miscellaneous manufactures, miscellaneous chemicals, metal products, electrical machinery and equipment, maintained very low loan–value-added ratios (L–VA ratios) amounting to around 60 per cent of the manufacturing average during 1971–82. The low L–VA of a sector does not by itself imply that the sector has received relatively unfavourable treatment in loan allocation. The very nature of the sector may not require a high L–VA ratio. However, given the subsidised rates of interest applied to bank loans, the below-average L–VA ratio implies the relatively small amount of subsidy allocation 'per value added' in the sector.

In spite of the relatively low L–VA ratios, all these labour-intensive sectors maintained very high 'gross' rates of return throughout the 1970s and the early 1980s.[9] Furthermore, most of these sectors achieved either significant factor substitutions or significant expansion of output or both. Although the share of

	Per worker fixed assets[a]		Gross rate of return on capital			Loan/VA (value added) ratio			Rate of increase during 1971–82		
	1971	1982	1971–73	1974–79	1980–82	1971–73	1974–79	1980–82	VA	pwFA	Exports
All manufacturing	1.14	9.27	32.3%	37.5%	37.4%	1.9	1.5	1.4	37.2	8.1	24.6
			Ratios to all-manufacturing average								
Very labour-intensive sectors											
Clothing and footwear	0.3	0.2	1.5	1.3	3.6	0.6	0.7	0.7	1.3	0.7	0.7
Electronic and telecommunications[b]	0.4	0.4	1.4	1.3	1.2	0.5	0.4	0.7	2.3	1.0	1.9
Miscellaneous manufactures[c]	0.4	0.4	1.3	1.3	1.1	0.4	0.6	0.6	1.0	1.2	0.5
Non-metallic minerals[d]	0.9	0.4	0.6	1.1	1.2	0.7	0.6	0.5	3.0	0.5	6.9
Moderately labour-intensive sectors											
Machinery (medium)	0.4	0.4	0.8	1.1	1.0	0.3	0.4	0.6	7.3	1.1	—
Miscellaneous chemicals	0.5	0.6	1.7	1.7	1.3	0.3	0.4	0.5	0.6	1.0	1.4
Metal products	0.4	0.6	1.1	1.3	0.9	0.4	0.5	0.8	2.2	1.5	3.5
Electrical machinery	0.8	0.7	1.3	1.2	1.1	0.6	0.6	0.7	1.2	0.9	1.8
Textiles[e]	1.0	0.7	0.9	0.8	0.9	1.0	1.2	1.1	0.9	0.7	1.0
Wood products	0.7	0.9	1.1	1.0	1.0	1.4	1.9	2.0	0.5	1.3	0.2
Capital-intensive sectors											
—Low return–high L/VA group											
Shipbuilding	1.5	1.3	0.3	0.4	0.6	2.7	1.6	1.1	9.6	0.9	8.4
Automobiles and parts	1.4	1.3	0.9	0.7	0.7	1.3	1.2	1.6	0.9	1.0	4.9
Machinery (large)	0.7	1.7	1.0	0.9	0.4	0.8	1.0	2.9	2.9	2.7	2.0
Non-ferrous metals	0.8	1.8	0.6	1.0	0.8	1.2	1.2	1.6	7.0	2.3	0.6
Industrial chemicals	4.7	1.9	0.8	1.0	0.9	1.4	1.1	1.2	0.7	0.4	2.7
Iron and steel products	1.5	4.1	0.7	0.8	0.7	1.7	2.0	2.0	3.8	2.8	5.0
Cement	5.1	5.8	1.0	0.9	0.7	1.8	1.3	1.2	0.4	1.2	2.2
—Other capital-intensive group											
Synthetic fibres	1.8	1.9	1.1	1.0	1.4	1.1	1.4	1.3	0.5	1.0	3.5
Rubber tyres	1.1	1.1	1.2	1.2	1.2	0.9	1.1	0.9	1.8	1.0	6.5
Glass and products	2.5	1.2	0.7	1.3	0.8	1.0	0.6	0.9	0.6	0.5	1.3
Pulp and paper	1.6	1.5	1.2	1.1	0.9	0.7	1.0	1.1	0.8	1.0	5.7
Sugar refining	3.7	3.3	1.5	1.8	1.9	0.9	0.8	1.1	1.1	0.9	8.7
Petroleum products	11.6	6.1	1.0	1.1	1.5	1.6	0.7	0.9	0.7	0.5	0.4

Notes: a   Per worker fixed assets (pwFA) in million won.
b   Radios and TVs, phonographs and tape recorders, other telecommunications equipment, household electrical appliances, and electronic parts and components for 1982 data. Data for 1971 exclude electronic parts and components.
c   Includes precision instruments (watches and optical instruments), leather products, plastic products and furniture.
d   Excludes glass and cement.
e   Excludes synthetic fibre yarns.

Sources: The Bank of Korea Financial Statements Analysis; KTA, Foreign Trade Statistics.

labour-intensive manufactures in total manufactures exports declined from about 90 per cent in 1970 to about 65 per cent by 1980, clothing, footwear, textiles and miscellaneous manufactures equipment were the major export sectors of Korea throughout the period 1970–80. Furthermore, the export of electronic and telecommunication equipment, metal products, electrical machinery, non-metallic mineral products and miscellaneous chemicals expanded very rapidly during the period.

Textiles and wood products were the most capital-intensive sectors among this labour-intensive manufacturing group. The textiles sector has consistently revealed relatively low rates of return, maintained the above-average L–VA ratios and yet achieved the below-average rates of output expansion and factor substitution. The wood products sector, which was the leading export sector of Korea in the late 1960s and early 1970s, revealed average or below-average rates of return during 1971–82 but maintained very high L–VA ratios and achieved significant factor substitutions. The share of textiles in total manufactures exports (12 per cent) did not change while the share of wood products dropped from about 14 per cent to 2.5 per cent during 1970–80. In spite of the very high L–VA ratios, the wood products sector revealed the poorest performance in output and export expansion among the labour-intensive group of sectors.

The capital-intensive manufacturing sectors, consisting, of shipbuilding, automobiles and their parts, large-scale machinery manufacturing, non-ferrous metal products, industrial chemicals including fertilisers, iron and steel products, and cement, revealed very low gross rates of return during 1971–73. And yet all these sectors maintained relatively high L–VA ratios during 1971–82, implying a relatively large amount of subsidy allocation per value added in the form of low-interest bank loans. The rates of return revealed by these sectors in the early 1980s (1980–82) were still very low.[10] In Table 7.2, these sectors are listed under the heading 'low return/high L–VA group'. Despite their low return, the shipbuilding sector achieved a significant output expansion, and the automobiles and parts and cement sectors achieved significant factor substitutions while the large-scale machine manufacturing, non-ferrous metal products, and iron and steel products sectors achieved both significant output expansion and significant factor substitutions during 1971–82. Furthermore, with the exception of non-ferrous metal products, the share of each of these capital-intensive manufactures in total manufactures exports significantly expanded during 1970–80. Indeed, shipbuilding and iron and steel have become major, if not the most important, export sectors of Korea since the late 1970s. In terms of rates of return and export expansion, the non-ferrous metal products sector revealed the poorest performance among the above capital-intensive group of sectors.[11]

In spite of the relatively low L–VA ratios, most of the labour-intensive manufacturing sectors constituted the major export sectors of Korea. On the other hand, despite very high L–VA ratios, many capital-intensive sectors failed to become the export leaders. However, some of them did become the leading export sectors while most of the other capital-intensive manufacturing sectors were able to achieve rapid export expansion in the 1970s. As a result, the share of capital-intensive manufactures in total manufactures exports expanded from about 9 per cent in 1970 to about 31 per cent in 1980. If we exclude textiles and wood products from the labour-intensive group of manufacturing sectors listed in Table 7.2, their share in total manufacturing fixed assets expanded from about 12 per cent to about 18 per cent during 1971–82. On the other hand, the share of the 'low return/high L–VA' sub-group of capital-intensive sectors in total manufacturing fixed assets expanded from about 30 per cent in 1971 to about 46.7 per cent in 1982. That is, the rates of expansion of the shares in total manufacturing fixed assets were very similar, about 50 per cent and 56 per cent, for both the very profitable labour-intensive subgroup and the much less profitable capital-intensive subgroup respectively.

The relatively low L–VA ratios maintained by the labour-intensive manufacturing sectors imply that these sectors received a relatively small subsidy per value added in the form of low-interest bank loans. However, the very nature of labour-intensive manufacturing may not require the maintenance of L–VA ratios as high as those in capital-intensive manufacturing. The fact that extremely high rates of return have been revealed in the very labour-intensive sectors, such as clothing and footwear, may imply that those sectors did not really need any subsidy at all. In other words, the labour-intensive manufacturing sectors might have required the maintenance of L–VA ratios equal to or even higher than those actually observed in Korea in the 1970s. The fact that these labour-intensive sectors revealed very high gross rates of return on capital throughout the period 1971–82 may imply that they required the 'subsidised' rates of interest for the loans allocated to them in order to achieve the rapid expansion of output and exports and the factor substitutions to accommodate rising wage rates. Abundant labour and low wage rates themselves might have been sufficient bases for a rapid expansion of outputs and exports of those sectors. Hence, whatever subsidy was given to them through the low-interest loans was a windfall income transfer, especially after the initial phase of infant export marketing. For instance, low-interest short-term trade credits have been allocated to all export activities at a uniform rate per dollar exported. As a result, there seems to have been enormous income transfers to the exporters of very labour-intensive goods. This may partly explain the phenomenal expansion of some business groups which have started mainly as exporters of clothing and footwear to become large conglomerates.

If the subsidised loans were allocated to selected entrepreneurs without any specified obligations, they would maximise the windfall income transfers from the government simply by investing in more profitable labour-intensive projects. However, even when subsidised loans were allocated on condition that capital-intensive projects were undertaken, presumably to generate external economies, the negative real interest rates applied to such loans meant that the entrepreneurs could still gain sizeable profits by obediently undertaking such projects instead of rejecting the loan rationing altogether. Furthermore, it is possible to make large profits by cheating the government and smuggling significant portions of such funds to other more profitable projects. This may partly explain aggressive diversification into the labour-intensive consumer goods, service and real estate sectors by some business groups which started mainly as the manufacturers of capital-intensive goods.

Most capital-intensive manufacturing sectors have maintained relatively very high L–VA ratios in the 1970s. Perhaps the nature of capital-intensive manufacturing might require the maintenance of L–VA ratios even higher than those observed in Korea. However, the very low gross rates of return revealed by most of the capital-intensive manufacturing sectors in Korea may imply that the substantial expansion in outputs and exports and the substantial increases in the capital-intensity of their production techniques may owe much to the subsidy element associated with credit rationing. It can be argued that such sector-specific subsidised credit rationing was an optimal growth policy for Korea, justified by the observed high growth rates of the Korean economy in the 1970s. Similarly, the accumulating foreign debt and the low growth performance of the Korean economy in the 1979–82 period raises suspicions about both the efficiency and the continued wisdom of the credit rationing system.

EMPIRICAL EXAMINATION OF CREDIT DIVERSION IN MANUFACTURING

Overview

In intervening in the financial markets, the government is not interested in the sectoral allocation of credit per se but in effecting the allocation of physical resources. As noted above, the Korean government has followed, for the past twenty years, an industrial policy designed to allocate more resources to export-producing manufacturing sectors. To what extent has the Korean government succeeded in attaining this objective? It is undoubtedly an extremely difficult question to answer even at a theoretical level and one that requires reliable microeconomic data for an empirical examination. The key to the answer lies in the fungibility of credit. If credit fungibility is easily achieved, the government cannot expect to be successful in effecting what it considers to be an optimal allocation of physical resources. But it is difficult to measure the degree of credit fungibility.

The fungibility issue could be examined at the two stages of the credit allocation process. At the first stages, which is related to the lending behaviour of financial institutions, it is possible that the financial intermediaries may simply evade or ignore the credit guidelines and directives. That is, the financial intermediaries themselves may be guilty of the credit diversion. This problem does not appear to have been serious in Korea because of the government's close supervision of the day-to-day operations of the DMB and other financial intermediaries.

At the second stage of credit allocation, which is related to the behaviour of borrowers, it is conceivable that a large part of bank credit has been diverted to the uses of real resources other than those designated by the government. One possible reason for this diversion is that the DMB and the KDB do not have an effective system of credit-use supervision. Even if they do have one, the management of these financial institutions would not be very much concerned about and hence would not actively supervise the actual use of bank credits, because the management is not responsible for the provision of directed and policy loans. The lack of autonomy in bank management may have aggravated credit diversion.

One piece of evidence supporting a high degree of credit fungibility is that firms invest heavily in real assets. A special measure issued in September 1980 shows that business groups and corporations hold a large share of their total assets in the form of real assets such as land and buildings.[12] Their holdings of these assets, the government points out, were far greater than the level that is normally required for their business operations. The presumptions here are that businesses invest in real assets as a hedge against inflation and a provision of collateral for bank loans, and that the bulk of their holdings were financed by bank loans in the first place. One large business group, which was once a ranking exporter, was so heavily involved in real-estate speculation financed by export loans that it went bankrupt in 1978 when its export earnings fell sharply and the real-estate boom cooled off. Undoubtedly, there have been numerous similar cases among smaller business groups.

Framework of Analysis

As the discussion in the preceding section suggests, the degree of diversion in credit use rests on a number of economic and institutional factors and its analysis is ultimately an empirical issue. In this section, we attempt to measure empirically the degree of credit fungibility in several sectors of Korea's manufacturing industry, using an investment demand model.[13]

Let us assume that there are two sources of funds for investment. One source consists of firms' internal reserves, the capital market, and the unregulated money market where funds are available by competition between firms. The second source lies in the organised financial institutions that allocate credit according to the priorities and criteria set by the government. Under this assumption, a sectoral share of total funds may be described by a weighted average of the sectoral shares of government-controlled and private funds,

$$F_i = \omega_1 GF_i + (1 - \omega_1) PF_i \qquad (1)$$

where F_i is the ith sector's total fund share, ω_1 is the weight for the government-controlled fund, and GF_i and PF_i are government-controlled and private fund shares in the ith sector, respectively. If credit fungibility is negligible, F_i is the sectoral share of nominal investment. In the absence of government intervention ($\omega_1 = 0$), F_i reflects a competitive sectoral allocation of investment resources. Recipients of government-controlled funds may not necessarily use the credit for the financing of the stipulated projects and may divert it to the financing of other investment activities. To estimate this credit-diversion effect, we introduce a fungibility parameter, γ, into equation (1).

$$FH_i = \gamma\omega_i GF_i + (1 - \gamma\omega_i) PF_i \tag{2}$$

where $0 \leq \gamma \leq 1$. FH_i is now the share of total funds in the ith sector that takes into consideration the possibilities of credit diversion. If one dollar of government-controlled credit allocated to the ith sector is completely diverted to another sector, then $\gamma = 0$ and $FH_i = PF_i$, which is the case of perfect fungibility. If there is no credit diversion, then $\gamma = 1$ and $FH_i = F_i$. In this case the government authorities can exercise almost complete control over the sectoral allocation of investment by manipulating GF_i.

In order to estimate the value of γ, we introduce a rationally distributed lag investment function developed by Jorgenson.[14] Investment in real terms, I_t, is defined by

$$I_t = NI_t + \delta K_{t-1} \tag{3}$$

where NI_t is net investment, δ is the rate of depreciation, and K_{t-1} is the stock of capital at $t-1$. Following Jorgenson and Kwack,[15] we assume that NI_t is described as

$$NI_t = \frac{\alpha}{(1 - \beta L)} \Delta K_t^* + \frac{\gamma}{(1 - \beta L)} FCR_t \tag{4}$$

where L is the lag operator, K^* the desired stock of capital at t, FCR is the real volume of government-controlled credit, and the fungibility parameter.

Equation (4) can be rewritten as

$$NI_t = \alpha \sum_{j=0}^{\infty} \beta^j \Delta K_{t-j}^* + \gamma \sum_{j=0}^{\infty} \beta^j FCR_{t-j} \tag{5}$$

By substituting equation (5) into equation (3) and from a repeated substitution, we obtain

$$I_t = \alpha \Delta K_t^* + \beta NI_{t-1} + \delta K_{t-1} + \gamma FCR_t. \tag{6}$$

Equation (6) is a general investment function, which is assumed to be applicable to the investment behaviour of all sectors of the economy.

The desired capital stock K_t^* is derived from the profit maximisation of firms over time,

$$K_t^* = \alpha V_t^n / q_t (\gamma_t + \delta - \dot{q}_t^E), \tag{7}$$

where α is capital share, V_t^n is nominal value added, q_t is the price of capital goods, and $\dot{q}_t^E$ is expected change in q.

In our study, we will estimate serveral versions of equation (6) mainly to examine the size of γ. It is easy to verify that γ in equation (6) is indeed the parameter measuring the degree of credit fungibility introduced in equation (2). To do so we write a sectoral investment function based on equation (6) as follows:

$$I_i = \alpha \sum_{j=0}^{\infty} \beta^j \Delta K_{t-j}^* + \delta K_{t-1} + \gamma \sum_{j=0}^{\infty} \beta^j FCR_{t-j}. \tag{8}$$

The first two terms of equation (8) represent the amount of real investment in the ith sector that will be realised in a competitive financial environment (I_i^*). The third term reflects the effect of government intervention on sectoral investment (γG_i) or the amount of investment induced by government credit allocation. Thus, sectoral investment I_i can be written as

$$I_i = I_i^* + \gamma G_i. \tag{9}$$

Multiplying both sides of equation (9) by the capital-good price q_i, we have

$$I_i q_i = I_i^* q_i + \gamma G_i q_i. \tag{10}$$

Dividing equation (10) by total investment, $I = \Sigma I_i q_i$, we have

$$\frac{I_i q_i}{\Sigma I_i q_i} = \frac{I_i^* q_i}{\Sigma I_i^* q_i} \cdot \frac{\Sigma I_i^* q_i}{\Sigma I_i q_i} + \frac{\gamma G_i q_i}{\Sigma G_i q_i} \cdot \frac{\Sigma G_i q_i}{\Sigma I_i q_i}. \tag{11}$$

Comparing equations (2) and (11), we know that

$$FH_i = \frac{I_i q_i}{\Sigma I_i q_i}, \frac{I_i^* q_i}{\Sigma I_i q_i} = PF_i, \frac{G_i q_i}{\Sigma G_i q_i} = GF_i,$$

$$\frac{\Sigma G_i q_i}{\Sigma I_i q_i} = \omega_1, \text{ and } \frac{\Sigma I_i^* q_i}{\Sigma I_i q_i} = 1 - \gamma \omega_1.$$

Estimation Results

In order to approximate the range of γ in manufacturing, it would be desirable to estimate equation (6) and its variants for the subsectors in Table 7.2. However, because of the unavailability of data, in particular capital stock, we have not been able to do so. For some variables, data are available for the period since the late 1960s, but this is not enough to conduct a meaningful time-series analysis. To obtain a sufficient number of observations, we have had to pool data by pairing subsectors of manufacturing.[16]

In our empirical examination, we have estimated equation (6) for the following seven sectors for the 1969–81 period.

Very labour-intensive	I	:	Clothing and footwear Miscellaneous manufactures
Moderately labour-intensive	II	:	Textiles Wood products
	III	:	Metal products Electrical machinery
Very capital-intensive	IV	:	Iron and steel Cement
Moderately capital-intensive	V	:	Pulp and paper Non-ferrous metal
	VI	:	Industrial chemicals Rubber tyres,
	VII	:	Machinery Transport equipment

As for the government-controlled credit variable (FCR), we have experimented with year-to-year changes in loans extended by the KDB and the DMB and in foreign loans. We have also used the sum of KDB and foreign loans, and of all three as a proxy for FCR.

KDB loans may be classified as genuine 'policy' or 'directed' loans in that they are extended in accordance with the criteria and priorities used for allocation by the government. Foreign loans must be approved by the government and are invariably tied to specific investment projects. These characteristics suggest that KDB and foreign loans combined may qualify as a good proxy for FCR. However, the sum of the two types of loans constitutes a relatively small part of the total volume of investment funds controlled by the government, as deposit money banks supply a sizeable amount of fixed investment financing in Korea. Therefore, when the sum of KDB and foreign loans is used as FCR, it may lead to an underestimation of the actual degree of credit fungibility because the variable represents only a part of the government-controlled investment fund. The variable may be statistically insignificant in estimated equations in those sectors which have limited access to KDB or foreign loans.

As an alternative to KDB and foreign loans, we have also tested change in DMB and foreign loans as a measure of FCR. While this variable covers a broader range of government intervention in loan allocation than KDB and foreign loans, it has also several defects. Although the government actively interferes with the asset management of DMB, it does not and in reality cannot control all lending activities of the banks. Some of the DMB loans are extended at the discretion of the banks themselves. More important, commercial banks theoretically specialise in supplying short-term loans for working-capital financing. It is therefore unrealistic to treat DMB loans as if they are all channelled to fixed-investment financing. To eliminate this bias, we have tried to divide DMB loans into short-term credit for working capital and long-term credit for fixed-investment financing. At the sectoral level, a lack of reliable data precludes such a division. There is, however, strong evidence that much of DMB credit has been used for long-term fixed-investment financing in Korea.[17] Although the DMBs may have some leeway in their asset management, they are supposed to follow the government's guidelines and directives for loan allocation. These considerations do suggest that DMB loans may not be as unrealistic as they appear as a proxy for FCR. Nevertheless, it is likely that the use of DMB loans in equation (6) exaggerates the degree of credit fungibility as they include short-term loans for working-capital financing. This problem is more serious when the sum of KDB, DMB, and foreign loans is used in the estimation.

Our estimation results are presented in Table 7.3 and from them we have reached the following tentative conclusions.

1　It can be seen that the investment demand model cannot be applied universally to all sectors of manufacturing. As evidenced by the poor explanatory ability of equation (6), the data do not seem to support the investment hypothesis in sectors I and V. This is true even when we take into consideration the use of pooled time-series data. The estimated equations also display considerable instability, making difficult the interpretation of some results.

2　From the perspective of our study, the results suggest a high degree of credit fungibility in Korea's manufacturing. This conclusion follows regardless of which credit variable among the three is used. When the sum of KDB and foreign loans is used as a measure of FCR, the credit term is significant in sectors II, III, IV, VII. The coefficient of FCR is highest in iron and steel, cement with 0.9, followed by 0.62 in textile and wood products, and 0.46 in metal products and electric machinery. The coefficient for machinery and transport equipment is about 0.33. While these figures indicate that KDB and foreign loans have been largely channelled to the sectors designated by the government, our confidence in these results is dampened by the fact that only in iron, steel and cement has ΔK_t^* an acceptable 't' value.

3　When KFL is replaced by either DFL (DMB and foreign loans) or KML (the sum of KDB, DMB, and foreign loans), the credit term becomes significant and has larger coefficients than before in sectors V and VI, while the opposite is the case in sectors III and VII. These results suggest that the credit variable that is appropriate for measurement of credit diversion is likely to differ from sector to sector.

4　On the basis of our results, one cannot establish any relationship between the degree of credit fungibility on the one hand and export performance or capital intensities on the other, in subsectors of manufacturing.

5　The degree of credit diversion is lowest in iron, steel and cement. This is true whichever credit variable is used in our estimation. One possible explanation for this is that this sector has been the major recipient of KDB

Table 7.3 Estimation results

Dependent Variables[a]	Very labour-intensive sector	Moderately labour-intensive sectors		Very capital-intensive sector	Moderately labour-intensive sectors		
	I	II	III	IV	V	VI	VII
Constant	2.100	−2.502	7.304	10.485	9.317	9.222	16.182
	(0.404)[b]	(−0.153)	(0.902)	(0.313)	(1.150)	(0.588)	(0.985)
K*	0.034	0.131	0.046	0.562	0.028	0.305	0.062
	(0.772)	(0.910)	(0.438)	(2.412)	(0.174)	(1.948)	(0.659)
K*	0.044	0.090	0.266	−0.080	−0.440	0.034	0.157
	(1.070)	(0.484)	(2.328)	(−0.301)	(−1.615)	(0.144)	(1.507)
KFL	0.462	0.616	0.456	0.895	0.117	0.176	0.333
	(0.694)	(1.453)	(1.109)	(2.053)	(0.466)	(0.577)	(1.383)
K	0.120	0.163	0.097	0.056	0.111	0.047	0.176
	(2.039)	(3.422)	(1.507)	(0.394)	(0.953)	(0.380)	(2.982)
NI	0.418	0.078	0.375	0.002	0.086	−0.072	−0.109
	(1.357)	(0.221)	(1.477)	(0.005)	(0.211)	(−0.189)	(−0.372)
R	0.371	0.681	0.646	0.512	0.305	0.548	0.694
Constant	3.633	−4.910	6.052	11.102	10.768	3.830	15.865
	(0.692)[b]	(−0.302)	(0.683)	(0.310)	(1.505)	(0.241)	(0.983)
K*	0.027	0.097	0.058	0.417	0.129	0.237	0.053
	(0.601)	(0.688)	(0.535)	(1.944)	(0.839)	(1.462)	(0.509)
K*	0.026	0.009	0.298	−0.031	−0.603	−0.905	0.148
	(0.586)	(0.042)	(2.624)	(−0.113)	(−2.589)	(−0.373)	(1.316)
DFL	0.074	0.420	0.137	0.794	0.516	0.307	0.038
	(1.138)	(1.606)	(0.448)	(1.620)	(1.888)	(1.239)	(0.258)
K	0.080	0.127	0.081	0.031	−0.010	0.091	0.184
	(1.186)	(2.542)	(1.171)	(0.214)	(−0.077)	(0.726)	(2.943)
NI	0.925	0.225	0.364	0.294	0.199	−0.115	−0.004
	(0.908)	(0.624)	(1.314)	(0.980)	(0.615)	(−0.317)	(−0.014)
R	0.041	0.689	0.624	0.471	0.425	0.579	0.658

	(1)	(2)	(3)	(4)	(5)	(6)	(7)
Constant	3.815	−5.025	5.130	2.719	8.585	1.750	15.311
	(0.729)[b]	(−0.321)	(0.604)	(0.035)	(1.165)	(0.124)	(0.947)
K*	0.025	0.124	0.061	0.414	0.115	0.217	0.060
	(0.554)	(0.912)	(0.568)	(2.204)	(0.737)	(1.521)	(0.573)
K*	0.023	−0.043	0.278	−0.036	−0.426	−0.181	0.150
	(0.516)	(−0.209)	(2.446)	(−0.146)	(−1.825)	(−0.805)	(1.338)
KML	0.082	0.499	0.246	0.898	0.294	0.486	0.060
	(1.223)	(1.973)	(0.961)	(2.572)	(1.659)	(2.296)	(0.449)
K	0.076	0.116	0.077	0.035	0.041	0.086	0.182
	(1.134)	(2.339)	(1.161)	(0.265)	(0.354)	(0.792)	(2.911)
NI	0.273	0.273	0.309	0.141	−0.052	−0.056	−0.018
	(0.834)	(0.776)	(1.125)	(0.505)	(−0.146)	(−0.170)	(−0.058)
R	0.408	0.709	0.640	0.564	0.400	0.653	0.661

Notes: a See appendixes 7A and 7B for a description of the variables
        b Figures in parentheses are t-statistics.

and foreign loans throughout the period under discussion. More important, to our view, is the fact that much of the investment in this sector has been undertaken by a public enterprise specialising in the production of iron and steel. Given this specialisation and the public nature of the firm, any efforts to divert funds to other ventures would have been easily detected and therefore unlikely to succeed. To these explanations we can add that the iron and steel industries are relatively efficient producers and exporters in Korea.

6 In contrast to the iron, steel and cement sector, the clothing and footwear, miscellaneous manufactures and very labour-intensive sectors are characterised by a relatively high degree of credit diversion. This appears to be the case regardless of the credit variable chosen for our estimation. The coefficient of ΔKFL, though high, is statistically insignificant and those of ΔDFL and ΔKML are less than 0.1. One possible explanation is that, given their low capital intensities, these sectors may not require as much long-term credit for fixed investment by comparison with the sectors with a higher capital intensity. Because of the relatively short-term nature of investment with high yields, the borrowers may not have had difficulty securing funds from sources other than the banks.

7 Industrial chemicals and rubber tyres (VI), and machinery and transport equipment (VII) account for a large share of KDB and foreign loans (Table 7.4). Unlike in iron, steel and cement the coefficient of the credit term for these sectors is either very low or statistically insignificant, suggesting a relatively high degree of credit fungibility. One possible reason for this may be that the borrowers in these sectors are usually large industrial groups, which have diversified their investments over a wide range of manufacturing activities and have better information about alternative investment opportunities. These conglomerates have a centralised unit that both oversees credit use and often acts like a financial intermediary. It mobilises funds from outside sources and then allocates between firms and investment projects of the groups. For these reasons, the borrowers in these sectors may find it easier to divert funds to uses other than those prescribed by the KDB and the government.

CONCLUDING REMARKS

The allocation of loans in Korea has been characterised by concentrated rationing to a small number of selected entrepreneurs. Almost all of Korea's manufactures exports have been carried out by or through these selected entrepreneurs. Therefore the financing of export expansion in Korea should imply the financing of this selected group of entrepreneurs and the export-oriented growth of Korean manufacturing should imply essentially the growth and export expansion of the same group.[18] The manufacturing firms not included in this group have had to depend almost exclusively on self-financing and kerb-market loans. Credit rationing has been concentrated particularly on

Table 7.4 Sectoral output, exports and loan allocation (expressed in percentage terms)

	Share in manufacturing output		Ratio of exports to output		Share in KDB and foreign loans to manufacturing		Share in DMB loans to manufacturing	
	1971–75[a]	1976–80[b]	1971–75[a]	1976–80[b]	1971–75[c]	1976–80[c]	1971–75[c]	1976–80[c]
I Clothing and footwear Miscellaneous manufactures	10.71	8.89	55.37	42.68	1.15	1.07	15.15	18.00
II Textiles Wood products	19.07	15.22	38.50	32.11	17.95	8.67	30.26	22.93
III Metal products Electrical machinery	8.47	10.48	41.47	36.37	4.85	5.31	5.31	10.40
IV Iron and steel Cement	9.35	11.35	17.98	17.12	25.22	33.43	8.58	9.01
V Pulp and paper Non-ferrous metals	3.17	3.14	7.19	8.51	3.56	7.12	4.68	5.77
VI Industrial chemicals Rubber tyres	12.81	13.64	14.32	17.19	15.25	18.69	12.52	13.06
VII Machinery Transport equipment	5.51	7.41	14.84	24.09	17.27	19.59	8.31	9.39

Notes: a Average of 1973 and 1975.
 b Average of 1978 and 1980.
 c Annual average.

Source: Bank of Korea, *Economic Statistics Yearbook* (various issues) and *Input–Output Tables* (various issues)

large company groups and as a result there occurred a concentration of export activities in Korea.

Considering the equity and efficiency aspects of credit rationing, one can conclude that the Korean government should start to reduce the excessiveness of credit rationing by enchancing as much as possible the role of the market mechanism in resource allocation. This conclusion is reinforced by the high credit fungibility in many subsectors of manufacturing. Our empirical examination shows that the Korean government has not been as successful as it may appear in influencing sectoral investment through directed allocation of bank credit.

Part III   The Internationalisation of the Financial Sector

8 The internationalisation of banking

JOHN HEWSON

Perhaps the most important development in international finance in the postwar period has been what is loosely referred to as the internationalisation of banking activities. It is important to see this in the context of what has been a fairly continuous postwar phenomenon; namely the internationalisation of most economic activities, most notably trade and investment as well as banking activities, as the world has become both economically and financially more interdependent. In this context the essential contribution of the international banking system is to ensure that global imbalances in the supply and demand for funds, risks, and other financial services are redistributed and matched in the most efficient way.

The purpose of this chapter is to review some aspects of the internationalisation of banking both generally and with particular reference to the Asian–Pacific region. I will concentrate my discussion of current developments in the region on developments in Australia concerning the internationalisation of Australian banking, the introduction of foreign banks and the viability of an 'offshore' banking centre in Australia.

SOME DEFINITIONS

The process of internationalisation of banking activities can be seen to have had several dimensions relating, most importantly, to whether it was conducted from 'home' or from an 'offshore base', whether it involved residents or non-residents and whether it was denominated in domestic or foreign currencies.

In these terms, 'traditional international banking' defines home-based transactions with residents and non-residents in foreign currencies and transactions with non-residents in foreign currencies and transactions with non-residents in the domestic currency. 'Domestic banking' is therefore home-based banking transactions with residents, denominated in the domestic currency.

Multinational banking, often (mis)called Eurocurrency banking or 'offshore' banking, applies to transactions with residents or non-residents in foreign or domestic currencies from an 'offshore' base.

Clearly several internal tiers of 'offshore banking' are possible: a pure offshore banking centre, confined to foreign-currency transactions with non-residents; an offshore banking centre with access for domestic residents, facilitating foreign-currency transactions with residents (hosts) as well as non-residents; and offshore banking with access for domestic banking business, perhaps on a limited basis.

The last tier—offshore banking in the domestic currency—makes it possible for the offshore market to transact in the domestic currency of the host. The desire could be to bring previously 'offshore' transactions in the domestic currency back 'onshore', as in the case of the IBFs in New York, or the proposed offshore banking centre in Tokyo.

BROAD TRENDS IN THE INTERNATIONALISATION OF BANKING

While hard data are not readily available on all these dimensions of international banking transactions on a global scale, let alone for the Asian–Pacific region, it is usually possible to muster sufficient evidence to suggest a significant 'internationalisation' of banking activities in all dimensions over the postwar period. Moreover, irrespective of the series chosen to measure international banking activities, it will almost certainly show a very rapid growth over this period, both in absolute terms and relative to most major macro aggregates, such as reserves, exports, domestic money or financial assets series, even allowing for the significant acceleration of postwar inflation. As a result, 'international' assets/liabilities have increased significantly relative to domestic assets in the balance sheets of most global banks.[1]

A crude classification of the postwar period would suggest three broad stages in the internationalisation of banking activities.

Stage 1.   The mid-1950s to mid-1960s saw the expansion of traditional international banking activity; foreign-exchange transactions, primarily trade-related and generally associated with the completion of the period of postwar reconstruction; the restoration of convertibility of most major currencies; the progressive liberalisation of capital movements and the internationalisation of corporate activity.

Stage 2.   The mid-1960s to late 1970s encompassed the development and spread of multinational banking activity, manifest in the rapid growth of the so-called 'Eurocurrency markets', initially in Europe but ultimately in all major geographical areas around the globe. In large measure, this development reflected a significant quest for cheaper and more efficient and diversified banking operations. A number of factors may be highlighted as important to the development of particular offshore centres. These include locational advantages such as position in the international time zone, proximity to a regional deposit or loan base, and considerations of political stability and risk diversification. Differences between banking controls in domestic and international markets are an essential requirement, especially the existence of reserve requirements on domestic deposits, interest-rate ceilings on domestic deposits and loans, and so on. Capital and exchange controls which serve to limit access to domestic markets, encouraging business to be done offshore, such as restrictions on lending by domestic banks to non-residents, various interest-equalisation taxes, deposit restrictions and the like are another factor. Differences in taxation of offshore and onshore income and differences in operating costs also facilitate the development of offshore centres.

Their growth was further accelerated in the 1970s by the move to more flexible exchange-rate regimes and the broadening and deepening of foreign-exchange markets which that implied; the global financing implications of the two oil price shocks and the role of international banks in recycling OPEC balance of payments surpluses. Increases in the development financing requirements of developing countries (quite independently of the oil shocks) in the context of their pursuit of more rapid growth, and the declining significance of aid and official finance and the quest by developed countries for expanded export markets were factors which also favoured the development of offshore centres.

This period saw a very rapid increase in the number of banks and other institutions involved in multinational banking, now no longer confined to major international banks as it was initially. This was accompanied by the rapid development of 24-hour dealing, where banks deal foreign exchange, deposits, loans and in fact most financial instruments, virtually continuously around the globe.

Stage two also saw significant shifts in domestic and international policy attitudes to the development of these offshore international banking activities, which fluctuated between the desire to control and to reduce (if not stifle) their rate of growth, to the desire to nurture, shore up and ensure their long-term viability. Correspondingly, a significant shift in the fortunes of particular financial centres occurred, primarily as a result of domestic policy initiatives. For centres like New York, for example, the reversal of earlier policy initiatives, and in fact the positive encouragement of the IBFs, has seen activities that were initially drawn offshore being encouraged back onshore, but not yet fully integrated back with domestic financial markets.

Other stage two developments have been a number of significant policy challenges posed for individual bank asset/liability management and strategy, domestic macro policy management and prudential supervision of international banking activities from both a 'home' and 'host' perspective; and finally, a challenge to theorists who rapidly recognised that 'domestic' explanations of banking behaviour (both macro and micro) were not readily transferable to the international arena.

Stage 3. Early 1980s to date has been a period of slower growth, rationalisation, and consolidation involving reassessment of risks and exposures, reassessments of banking presence in various offshore centres, and imposition (by self or regulatory authorities) of prudential restrictions relating to capital adequacy, liquidity and forex exposures in respect of international banking activities. This process was heightened recently by a spate of technical defaults by some major non-oil-producing LDC borrowers and by the domestically induced difficulties of a number of major international banks.

MULTINATIONAL BANKING

Finally, by way of background, it is instructive to briefly outline the broad features of an appropriate theoretical framework against which to analyse developments of multinational banking.[2] The broad dimensions of the framework stem directly from the distinguishing characteristics of international banking transactions, including: the importance of the interbank market—in excess of 70 per cent of multinational banking tansactions are with other banks; the wholesale nature of the markets where transactions are typically quite large and the freedom with which interest rates move in response to demand and supply factors.

A final distinguishing characteristic is the formal linking of most loan rates (some are still fixed) explicitly to deposit rates in the interbank market, such as LIBOR and SIBOR by way of a constant margin, and the frequent adjustment of those rates at certain pre-specified rollover dates, to mirror fluctuations in those deposit rates.

The margin is usually set and maintained on the basis of an initial assessment of the creditworthiness (or risk of default) of the borrower. The practical effect of this is that risks of interest-rate fluctuations can be (but are not necessarily) substantially shifted to the borrower, although the bank still relies heavily on the liquidity of the interbank market to enable deposit rollovers at the agreed date.

Other characteristics of international banking transactions are the large size of most loan demands such that they are generally syndicated by a number of banks as a means of spreading default risk. Also, there is a typical lack of government intervention or regulation of the offshore markets themselves. Hence there are usually no reserve requirements, interest-rate ceilings, maturity controls on either bank assets or liabilities and minimal exchange controls on offshore market transactions per se. The last decade has, however, seen an important shift toward increased 'surveillance', and in some cases regulation, in the name of prudential supervision by both, or either, home or host authorities.

From the point of view of constructing an appropriate theoretical framework these factors suggest that international bank balance sheets may look quite different to their domestic counterparts as the 'production process' is quite different from that of a domestic retail bank. To develop this, it is instructive to identify two main functions of multinational banking which might be called liquidity-distribution and creation functions.

At one level, multinational banks can be thought of as operating collectively as an efficient distribution mechanism for shifting funds of similar liquidity from lenders to borrowers on a global scale. Conceptually, this function can be performed without any change in the 'liquidity' of the banks' assets and liabilities. The economic rationale for this function is that multinational banks can do it more efficiently, at lower aggregate transactions costs and therefore with smaller spreads between deposit and loan rates than would be possible either in the absence of any financial intermediation, or by domestic banks dealing directly from their home bases, as in traditional international banking. The key to this function is clearly the interbank market.

At a second level, however, the international banking system also clearly performs an important liquidity-creation-function. As one example, it turns short-term OPEC deposits (3–6 months) into long-term (10–15 years, or even longer) balance-of-payments loans to oil-importing countries, increasing the liquidity of the global bank sector, which borrows long and lends short. Again the role of the interbank market is crucial. However, this time instead of merely distributing funds of like liquidity, it provides the wherewithal by which these long-term preferences of non-bank borrowers are made consistent with the short-term preferences of non-bank depositors. Essentially, as funds flow from ultimate depositors to ultimate lenders they will usually pass through several banks, each mismatching a little, so that in the aggregate the desired degree of liquidity transformation is achieved. The interbank market therefore also serves as the important mechanism by which the risk of liquidity transformation is spread across the whole multinational banking system. Clearly this is in sharp contrast to domestic retail banking where the risks of liquidity transformation are often borne entirely by the one bank, which accepts the deposit and makes the loan. Moreover, the domestic retail bank often carries the whole default risk, which is generally spread in multinational banking by syndicating the loan among a number of banks. As a result average loan/deposit spreads are usually somewhat higher in domestic markets than in offshore markets, even allowing for reserve requirements and other restrictions that can have a significant 'cost' impact on the production process of domestic retail banking.

Recognition of the basic wholesale, free-market structure of multinational banking that is so crucially dependent on the depth, breadth and efficiency of the interbank market should have an important bearing on the appropriate regulatory and prudential framework contemplated for the existing markets, or the development of any offshore banking centres.

INTERNATIONALISATION OF BANKING IN THE ASIAN-PACIFIC REGION

The experience of the region represents a microcosm of the global experience with the internationalisation of banking over the last couple of decades. Most importantly, the same three stages of development are evident for the major Asian financial centres as occurred with European centres (Table 8.1). However, the Asian experience has had a number of specific dimensions.

First, Asian countries have generally borrowed more from and lent more to the international banking community (Table 8.2).

Second, the relative importance of international banking business has in-

Table 8.1 Selected international banking aggregates (US$ billion)

	1965	1970	1975	1980	1983	1984
Global markets						
Gross external claims[a]	43	135	520	1585	2257	
Net international bank lending[b]	—	—	260	810	1085	1255 (Sep)
Gross size of Eurocurrency markets[b]	20	115	484	1538	2148	2222
Net marketing size of Eurocurrency market	—	65	250	730	—	—
Asian markets						
Singapore						
—ACU assets[c]	—	0.4	13	54	111	128
—ACU loans and non-banks[c]	—	—	3	12	30	34
—DMB—foreign assets[d]	—	0.5	11	44	88	98 (Aug)
Hong Kong						
—Total bank assets[e]	—	4	15	35	97	111 (Oct)
—DMB—foreign assets[d]	—	1	8	38	68	76 (Jan)

Sources: a Bank for International Settlements.
b Morgan Guaranty.
c Monetary Authority of Singapore.
d International Monetary Fund.
e *Hong Kong Digest of Statistics.*

creased quite markedly for major banks from most of the major countries in the region (Table 8.3).

Third, an important element in this internationalisation of regional bank balance sheets has been the desire to move operations offshore by opening branches in a number of centres both in the region and globally. Table 8.4 (a) attempts a comparison of the growth of overseas branches of the major banks from selected countries in the region. In each case the top ten banks were selected and ranked and their overseas branches were counted in the mid–1970s, and more recently (in 1983) at least some of the top ten banks from most countries showed some internationalisation of this type. While the pace differed markedly between countries—with the most expansive being banks from Hong Kong, Japan, Singapore and South Korea—Indonesia was stagnant and Taiwanese banks actually reduced the number of their overseas branches. The greatest increase in overseas operations was by the Hong Kong banks, especially the Hong Kong and Shanghai Bank with 65 new branches, followed by Japan (fairly evenly spread across the top ten banks), Singapore (concentrated in the United Overseas Bank) and South Korea (dominated by the Korean Exchange Bank).

Interestingly while some of this move offshore involved opening branches in Europe and North America, the predominant expansion was within Asia. Table 8.4 (b) selects one from each country and examines the geographical distribution of its new branches. For example, of the 65 new branches opened by the Hong Kong and Shanghai Bank since the mid-1970s, 36 were within Asia and 11 were in Africa; only 9 were in Europe and 5 were in North America. Similarly, 27 of

Table 8.2 Assets and liabilities of European international banks vis-à-vis selected Asian countries (US$ billion)

	December 1975		December 1980		December 1983		December 1983 (extended base)		September 1984 (extended base)	
	Assets	Liabilities	Assets	Liabilities	Assets	Liabilities	Assets	Liabilities	Assets	Liabilities
Japan	31.9	9.1	69.1	27.0	87.9	40.9	106.3	55.2	116.1	63.3
Australia	2.6	1.0	6.0	1.3	14.4	1.2	20.8	1.6	23.1	2.1
Singapore	5.8	4.7	21.8	18.5	40.2	31.1	53.3	46.2	60.0	55.1
New Zealand	0.8	0.2	1.5	0.3	2.9	0.5	4.3	0.6	5.0	0.9
Hong Kong	5.9	4.8	22.7	17.7	41.1	34.0	56.2	56.1	61.0	63.3
Indonesia	2.5	0.5	4.3	6.7	7.4	5.5	13.7	4.5	14.4	5.6
South Korea	3.3	1.2	14.0	3.3	19.2	3.2	29.3	4.9	30.2	5.0
Malaysia	0.7	0.7	2.3	3.6	6.0	3.6	11.4	4.2	11.7	3.8
The Philippines	2.0	1.7	7.0	3.5	8.0	2.7	13.7	2.4	13.7	2.2
Taiwan	2.1	1.5	5.1	4.8	4.7	9.2	6.8	12.0	5.9	15.4
Thailand	1.2	1.4	3.2	1.1	4.0	1.6	6.8	1.6	7.2	1.6
China	0.9	1.0	2.2	2.5	1.6	9.2	3.0	16.1	3.3	20.0
Pakistan	0.1	0.3	1.2	1.2	0.9	2.1	1.0	2.2	0.9	1.4

Source: Bank for International Settlements.

Table 8.3   Relative importance of foreign business of deposit money banks (per cent)

	1970		1980		1983		1984 (latest month)	
	Assets	Liabilities	Assets	Liabilities	Assets	Liabilities	Assets	Liabilities
Japan	2.3	2.9	4.3	4.0	5.2	7.7	4.8	8.1 (Aug)
Singapore	17.6	22.8	26.8	32.6	24.6	37.0	27.3	42.1 (Aug)
Australia	—	—	0.6	1.0	0.3	0.9	0.2	0.8 (Jul)
New Zealand	—	—	7.3	2.6	7.4	5.2	6.1	4.1 (Jul)
Indonesia	16.5	17.9	28.9	4.0	23.3	5.0	21.0	4.4 (Jun)
South Korea	3.0	9.9	12.0	21.6	10.4	24.8	9.2	24.2 (Aug)
Malaysia	7.1	6.9	6.6	9.9	10.0	12.9	7.7	12.0 (Aug)
The Philippines	7.4	10.2	13.9	31.0	12.0	32.2	13.8	37.2 (Aug)
Thailand	6.5	10.3	6.5	9.9	4.9	8.6	5.1	7.4 (Jul)
Pakistan	2.2	1.7	3.4	1.4	4.1	3.0	4.5	3.1 (Aug)

Source: As calculated by IMF *International Financial Statistics*.

Table 8.4(a)   Numbers of overseas branches of top ten banks in selected Asian countries

Rank Bank name	Mid-70's	1983	Change
Hong Kong			
1 Hong Kong & Shanghai Banking	68	133	+65
3 Shanghai Commercial Bank	0	1	+1
4 Bank of East Asia	2	2	0
5 Nanyang Commercial Bank	0	3	+3
6 Overseas Trust Bank (30 June 1982)	na	8	+8
8 Bank of Canton	3	3	0
Total	73	150	+77
Indonesia			
1 Bank Negara Indonesia 1946	3	3	0
Total	3	3	0
Japan			
1 Dai-Ichi Kangyo Bank	4	8[a]	+4
2 Fuji Bank	5	7[b]	+2
3 Mitsubishi Bank	4	7	+3
4 Sanwa Bank	8	13[c]	+5
5 Sumitomo Bank	6[d]	12[d]	+6
6 Industrial Bank of Japan	2	3	+1
7 Mitsui Bank	7	10	+3
8 Tokai Bank	2	7	+5
9 Bank of Tokyo	40[e]	45[f]	+5
10 Long-term Credit Bank of Japan	2	3	+1
Total	80	115	+35
Malaysia			
1 Bank Bumiputra (M) Bhd	na	6	+6
2 Malayan Banking Bhd	26	26	0
3 United Malayan Banking Corporation	9	9	0
Total	35	41	+6

Table 8.4(a) (Continued)

Rank Bank name	Mid 70's	1983	Change
Philippines			
1 Philippine National Bank	3[g]	4	+1
7 Allied Banking Corporation	na	3	+3
Total	3	7	+4
Singapore			
1 Development Bank of Singapore	na	4	+4
2 United Overseas Bank	4	32[a]	+28
3 Oversea-Chinese Banking Corporation	31	31	0
4 Overseas Union Bank Limited	19	18	−1
5 Chung Khiaw Bank	18	18	0
10 Lee Wah Bank	9	9	0
Total	81	112	+31
South Korea			
2 Korea Exchange Bank	9	19	+10
3 Hanil Bank Limited	na	5[g]	+5
4 Commercial Bank of Korea Limited	na	3	+3
5 Cho-Heung Bank Limited	na	4	+4
6 Korea First Bank	1	3	+2
7 Bank of Seoul & Trust Co.	na	4	+4
Total	10	38	+28
Taiwan			
3 First Commercial Bank	0	2	+2
5 International Commercial Bank of China	8	6	−2
7 Bank of Communications	2	0	−2
Total	10	8	−2
Thailand			
1 Bangkok Bank	15	12	−3
2 Krung Thai Bank	0	1	+1
3 Thai Farmers Bank	1	3	+2
4 Siam Commercial Bank	0	2	+2
Total	16	18	+2

Notes: Banks are ranked by total assets in the year to 31 December 1982, except for Japan, for which the period is the year to 31 March 1983. Japan's seven trust banks are ranked on the basis of their banking assets only; trust assets are not included.

       Of those banks with overseas branches among the top ten, each country's branches have been listed.
      a   Two subsidiaries.
      b   Two subsidiaries, two affiliates.
      c   One affiliate.
      d   One subsidiary.
      e   Five affiliates and associated banks.
      f   Eight affiliates and associated Banks.
      g   Including agencies.

Sources: Rankings—*Bankers Handbook for Asia 1983–84* (Guide to Banks and Finance Companies); numbers of branches—*The Bankers Almanac and Yearbook* (1975–76, 1984).

Table 8.4(b) Changes in numbers of branches of the most internationalised banks between 1975 and 1983[a]

Country	Geographical area									
	North America	South America	Central America	Europe	Asia	China	Middle East	Africa	Oceania	Total
Hong Kong Hong Kong & Shanghai Banking Corporation	+5	+1	+1	+9	+36	0	+1	+11	+1	+65
Indonesia Bank Negara Indonesia					0					0
Japan Bank of Tokyo	+1	+1	+1	+1	0		+1			+5
Malaysia Malayan Banking Bhd				0	0					0
The Philippines Philippine National Bank	-2			+1	+2					+1
Singapore United Overseas Bank				+1	+27					+28
South Korea Korea Exchange Bank	+5		+1	+2	+1		+1			+10
Taiwan International Commercial Bank of China	+1		+1		-4					-2
Thailand Bangkok Bank				0	-3					-3

Note: a   Counted at the end of 1982.

Source: *The Bankers Almanac and Yearbook* (1975–76, 1984).

the 28 new branches opened by Singapore's United Overseas Bank were in Asia. The Taiwanese banks shifted their focus from North America to Asia, although overall they trimmed their international operations. Only South Korea's Korean Exchange Bank and The Bank of Tokyo focused on North America and Europe more than Asia.

Fourth, there has been a significant relaxation of exchange controls in a number of major countries in the region including Japan, Singapore, Indonesia and more recently Australia and New Zealand, accompanied by the development of domestic foreign-exchange markets in these countries.

Finally, there was the rapid growth of a number of regional financial centres in the course of the last decade or so, especially Hong Kong, Singapore, Bahrain and to a much lesser extent Manila. These centres are providing an important link between the centres of North America and Europe and opening the way for global dealing in foreign-exchange deposits, financial-futures and in fact most financial instruments.

As Singapore stands out as perhaps the most successful global example of a conscious attempt to develop a regional financial centre and has served as something of a 'model' to be followed in other areas, I would like to offer several observations on the 'Singapore experiment'.[3]

The details of the development of Singapore as a financial centre are thoroughly described and examined in chapters 9 and 11 of this volume. And on face value, at least, the experiment appears to have been a notable success, primarily because of the careful way in which the Singapore government and authorities nurtured the development of offshore banking units through specific tax concessions, the gradual licensing of new offshore banks and the gradual dismantling of exchange, capital and monetary controls that ultimately produced a much closer integration of domestic and offshore financial markets.

Yet, despite the obvious success of Singapore's experiment it has not been without its difficulties. Singapore remains essentially a funding centre. Loan syndication remains focused in Hong Kong for a number of reasons, including Hong Kong's legal infrastructure, 'old boy' club-type network which makes syndication easy and taxation arrangements. Singapore and Hong Kong are therefore really complementary as financial centres in the region.

Although Singapore has something of a natural regional base in neighbouring Asian countries, it has apparently failed to attract a significant proportion of the potential deposit bases of neighbours; notably, the foreign reserves of countries like Indonesia and others are substantially held elsewhere and not necessarily in the region. The market is heavily underwritten by the government and its instrumentalities.

Singapore's monetary authorities still adhere to some quantitative domestic monetary controls even though they are quite inconsistent with the internationalised monetary system they have sought to create. The most significant of these are reserve requirements on Singapore dollar deposits and paying less than market rates of return on those reserve balances, but not imposing any reserve requirements on interbranch balances. This has given rise to two major forms of flow to circumvent the domestic requirements: borrowing in Singapore dollars by overseas branches or parent banks for on-lending to their Singapore branches; and swap transactions whereby Singapore dollars are swapped for US dollars (buy US spot and simultaneously sell them forward). For some reason the authorities have so far refrained from addressing this problem directly, preferring to rely on persuasion and cancellation of work permits.

Another difficulty is that the Singapore dollar has become somewhat more 'internationalised' than the authorities and/or the government apparently would like to see. There has been a fairly significant increase in both non-resident holdings of Singapore dollar deposits and non-resident borrowings in Singapore dollars since the abolition of exchange controls in June 1978. Also, despite some spin-off from the offshore banking system in terms of the development of Singapore's domestic financial system, that system remains particularly under-developed and insulated from direct foreign competition.

This state is the consequence of several factors, notably: the Singapore dollar deposit base is predominantly controlled by the four large Chinese banks, and these institutions in turn seem to enjoy a fairly 'unique' relationship with the monetary authorities. Perhaps more importantly, the development of the domestic financial system has been significantly constrained by the role played by the Central Provident Fund (CPF). Although undoubtedly an effective mechanism for mobilising household savings, the CPF imparts a consistent expansionary bias to monetary policy (the monetary policy task is to reverse to some extent the CPF's drain on the financial system) and constrains private financial behaviours and choice. It severely restricts the development of new private financial institutions and instruments because it channels the bulk of household savings through one government institution, which in turn becomes the primary holder of government debt as these funds are channelled to the government. It distorts the whole structure of domestic interest rates and reduces the role such rates can play in the process of monetary adjustment, as the government borrows the funds from the CPF at artificially low rates of interest. Finally, the CPF provides the wherewithal to artificially 'stabilise' the Singapore dollar, as substantial proportions of those funds are converted into foreign assets.

Looking to the future, the key to Singapore's success has been government political stability and will and the pace of real growth. The real question is how long both of these will be sustained.

INTERNATIONALISATION OF JAPANESE BANKING

By way of an aside, it is of interest to focus briefly on the internationalisation of Japanese banks. As evidenced in Table 8.5 all of the top ten Japanese banks have internationalised their operations noticeably in recent years, although by the standards of banks from most major industrial countries, the Japanese were late entrants to this process. As a result they have only started to dominate 'league tables' of international banks in recent years but already the Japanese banks rank first (Dai Ichi Kangyo), third (Fuji) and fifth (Sumitomo) in the world.

Table 8.5 attempts to summarise some of the available data bearing on the internationalisation of Japanese banks. It will be seen that between 1969 and 1983 Japanese banks opened a total of 110 foreign branches, 96 subsidiaries and some 240 representative offices around the globe (Table 8.5 (a)). Moreover, international banking business now accounts for an average of some 30 per cent of their total investments, produces around 37 per cent of total operating income and 12 per cent of operating profit of Japanese banks (Table 8.5 (b) and (c)).

As a counterpart there has been a very rapid expansion of lending overseas by

Table 8.5 (a)   Overseas network of Japanese banks

	1969	1979	1983	1983 minus 1969
Branches	58	127	168	110
Subsidiaries	8	73	104	96
Rep offices	35	158	275	240
Participation	na	na	na	

Source: Federation of Bankers' Associations of Japan.

Table 8.5 (b)   Ratio between foreign currency portfolio and total operating income (all banks; expressed in percentage terms)

	Fiscal year					
Ratio	1975 1st half	1980 1st half	1980 2nd half	1981 1st half	1981 2nd half	1982 1st half
Average outstanding portfolio in foreign currency/average total investments	13.5	17.4	19.5	22.0	24.0	29.5
Operating income in foreign currency/ total operating income	14.2	25.2	29.9	38.5	40.6	45.6

Source: Ministry of Finance, Japan.

Table 8.5 (c)   Weight of international banking (first six months of fiscal 1983)

	Outstanding portfolio of international banking	Operating income of international banking	Gross operating income[a] of international banking
	Total investment	Total operating income	Gross operating income
All banks	29.9%	36.6%	11.6%

Note: a   Gross operating income = Total operating income − operating expenses − transfer from provision for reserves for possible loan losses − other expenses

Source: Ministry of Finance, Japan.

Table 8.5 (d)   Loans outstanding to overseas borrowers

	1971	1975	1980	1981	1982	1983
All Japanese banks' overseas short-term loans outstanding						
Foreign-currency (US$100 million)	15	91	225	339	405	448
Yen-currency (¥10 billion)	—	0	4	14	18	21
All Japanese banks' overseas medium- and long-term loans outstanding						
Foreign-currency (US$100 million)	2	87	324	404	523	586
Yen-currency (¥10 billion)	—	5	210	233	299	398

Source: Ministry of Finance, Japan.

Japanese banks both short-term and long-term, totalling over US$103 billion at the end of 1983 compared to about $1.7 billion in the early 1970s. Much of the acceleration took place in the period since 1978 as Japanese banks stepped up their participation in internationally syndicated bank credits, initially medium- and long-term loans, but now also with short-term loans. There has also recently been a significant increase in overseas loans denominated in yen. At the end of 1983 about 10 per cent of overseas loans outstanding were yen-denominated.

Finally, two other dimensions of the internationalisation of Japanese banks are worthy of note. First, as at March 31, 1984 there were some 149 authorised foreign-exchange banks in Japan, of which 82 can now deal directly with overseas banks through correspondent agreements.

Second, there were about 75 foreign banks authorised to operate as branches in Japan, but their penetration of the Japanese banking market has generally been less than 3 per cent overall. To provide some further perspective, these foreign banks apparently account for about 15–18 per cent of the turnover of non-interbank foreign-exchange business, around 10 per cent of the gross earnings of foreign transactions but less than 1 per cent of the profit. This, combined with the more general concern about the fairly closed nature of the Japanese capital market has been the focus of considerable debate between the Japanese Ministry of Finance and the US Treasury, resulting in pressure from the US, and some, albeit limited, response from Japan, to internationalise the Japanese capital banking and money markets and in particular to expand access to banking and the issuance of Japanese securities. This pressure has also spawned the concept of an offshore banking centre in Tokyo, the prospect of which seems to have fluctuated directly with the intensity of US political pressure.

INTERNATIONALISATION OF AUSTRALIAN BANKING

As other chapters concentrate on the internationalisation of banking activities in a number of other countries of the Asian–Pacific region, I felt it appropriate and timely, given the ferocity of our recent domestic political debate and a number of significant recent developments, to examine the process of internationalisation of the Australian banking system. I will do so at two levels. First, I will comment briefly on the recent rapid increase in the overseas operations of Australian banks. Then I will discuss the entry of foreign banks into the Australian financial system and the possibility of establishing an 'offshore banking' centre in Australia. There are of course important links between these two dimensions of the issue.

Offshore Activities of Australian Banks

Like the Japanese banks, the Australian banks[4] were generally slow to internationalise, but they are now doing so with a vengeance. Even as I write one of our major banks, the ANZ, announced its takeover of the British bank, Grindlays (Table 8.6). Prior to the late 1970s they concentrated on the United Kingdom and neighbouring Pacific islands. But more recently they have moved significantly into the United States and major Asian financial centres. The relative significance of the UK has fallen from about 52 per cent to 36 per cent. However, Asian–Pacific centres in total have also decreased from 48 per cent to less than 40 per cent, although the relative significance of Hong Kong and Singapore has increased from 5 per cent to over 20 per cent. Table 8.7 indicates the form in which Australian banks operate overseas.

While it is not entirely clear why Australian banks were slow to move offshore, a number of factors are worthy of note, such as the heavily protected, quite isolated domestic banking system, in which the major banks enjoyed an oligopoly position and earned profits accordingly. This was reinforced by the relatively slow process of internationalisation of Australian corporate activity and the corresponding ability of Australian banks to service corporate needs from home base and a couple of offshore offices.

Other factors include the protective nature of the domestic foreign-exchange market, confined to banks and trade transactions with a relatively fixed spot rate, a controlled forward rate and a central bank willing to pick up the slack in

Table 8.6   Aggregate assets of Australian banks' overseas offices ($A million)

	June 1975	June 1980	June 1982	June 1983	December 1983
United Kingdom	1 452	4 164	5 967	7 256	8 054
United States	—	1 025	3 272	4 307	5 398
New Zealand	979	1 987	2 513	2 782	2 958
Hong Kong	—	374	901	1 366	1 691
Singapore	—	374	1 403	2 899	3 288
Papua New Guinea	209	320	338	336	333
Other Pacific countries	139	269	312	434	509
Total	2 779	8 138	14 706	19 380	22 232

Source: Reserve Bank of Australia.

Table 8.7 Overseas operations of Australian banks

Country	Form of representation[a]	Number of banks represented
Bahrain	representative office	1
Cayman Islands	restricted branch[b]	5
Channel Islands	branch	1[c]
China	representative office	2
Fiji	branch network[d]	2
Hong Kong	representative office	1
	deposit-taking company[e]	5[f]
Indonesia	representative office	2
Japan	representative office	6
Kiribati	agency	1
	branch	1
New Zealand	branch network[d]	2[g]
Papua New Guinea	branch network[d]	3[h]
Singapore	branch	4
Solomon Islands	branch	2[g]
United Kingdom		
—London	branch network[d]	3
	branch	4[i]
	representative office	1
—Manchester	representative office	1
United States		
—Chicago	limited federal branch	3
—Houston	representative office	2
—Los Angeles	agency	3
	representative office	1
	international banking facility[b]	2
—New York	branch	5
—San Francisco	agency	1
Vanuatu	branch	2
	restricted branch[b]	1
West Germany	representative office	1

Notes: a At Janaury 1983.
 b Offshore transactions only.
 c Wholly owned subsidiary.
 d Two or more branches.
 e Registered or licensed under Hong Kong Deposit-taking Companies Ordinance.
 f Three are wholly owned subsidiaries. one is partly owned. and one is a branch of a wholly owned subsidiary.
 g One is a partly owned subsidary.
 h Partly owned subsidiary.
 i Includes three banks owned by State governments.

the system, to sustain the set spot rate at the end of each day. The slow recognition of the profit opportunities available in overseas banking activities also retarded the Australian banks' move offshore.

Foreign Bank Participation in the Australian Financial System

One of the most controversial issues on the agenda of the last two Australian governments has been the possible entry of foreign banks into the Australian banking system. It has been the subject of constant debate and the focus of substantial parts of four recent public reports, the Campbell Report, the Martin Report, the Hamley Report and the Whitlam Report. The last two were confined specifically to the possibility of an 'offshore banking' centre being established in Australia, the former favouring Melbourne, the latter Sydney, as the focus of that market.

However, before briefly canvassing the recent decisions of the Hawke government on foreign bank entry and the possibility and viability of an offshore banking centre being established in Australia, it is important to note a few points by way of background.

The issue of foreign bank entry was blown out of proportion, given that banks had already significantly penetrated banking business as carried out through non-bank financial institutions in Australia. Foreign banks controlled about 66 per cent of merchant bank activity and 38 per cent of finance company activities. There are also over 100 representative offices of foreign banks 'illegitimately' doing banking business (specifically project finance) but booking it offshore. However, direct access to trading or commercial bank activity had been quite restricted although two foreign banks, the Bank of New Zealand and the Banque Nationale de Paris, were operating as branches under a special category of 'prescribed' banks.

The process of financial deregulation also had accelerated considerably in recent years, with the adoption of market-based or tender techniques for selling government securities, abolition of most major restrictions on banking and the abolition of most exchange controls, the virtually free floating of the Australian dollar, and the 'licensing' of non-banks. These non-banks previously ran a forward or non-delivery hedge market, fostered by a restriction on the official market that confined it to banks and trade transactions that forced them to operate under important timing constraints as foreign-exchange dealers.

Hence foreign bank entry became the last remaining 'significant issue'. However, given the most recent decision to allow non-bank access to foreign exchange, there were few areas of banking that were not accessible to foreign banks through a non-bank subsidiary. Hence the foreign banks entry issue really only related to access to the domestic payments system and to traditional domestic retail banking and to the 'special' relationship with the authorities, especially the Reserve Bank. Public opinion, previously declared government policy, and other internal party political pressure seemed likely to require any new foreign banks to begin operations in partnership with Australian interests. Moreover, the government had some declared international trade policy positions in relation to particular countries like China, Japan, Singapore and New Zealand, which produced an expectation that representative banks from those areas might be treated differently from the major international banks from the US and Europe, which were also seeking entry.

Finally, the previous Liberal government had commissioned the Campbell Committee to report on deregulation of the financial system and, in November 1981, that Committee had recommended that bank entry be relatively free provided applicants met certain minimum prudential and management standards. Specifically, it recommended that there should be no restrictions on the number of new licences (although it allowed for the possibility of phasing by a series of branches), nor on the type of activities, retail or wholesale, to be offered by the new banks (foreign or domestic), nor on branching, unionisation and so on, although minimum capital requirements might be necessary. It also bowed to the possibility of the government requiring for political reasons some Australian equity participation. After considerable public and internal party debate, the then Liberal Treasurer finally called for applications from foreign banks in January 1983, but the Fraser government was defeated in March 1983 before these applications were submitted.

Against this background, the incoming Hawke government deferred a decision until its Review Group, the Martin Committee, could report on the remaining recommendations of the Campbell Committee, including the issue of foreign bank entry, in the light of its political and social priorities. The Martin Committee therefore became a shrewd political device which served to keep the issue of financial deregulation in general, and foreign bank entry in particular, alive while the new Prime Minister and Treasurer could work to revise what had been long-term party opposition to these issues. The Martin Committee took a much more restrictive view than the Campbell Report and in January 1984 recommended the issue of four to six new foreign and domestic licences under noticeably tighter conditions as to range of services, Australian equity participation (to range from 50 per cent to preferably 66⅔ per cent), potential unionisation and so on. The Hawke government then used this Report to force a revision of its Party's opposition to foregin bank entry at the ALP convention in July 1984—which supported the entry of a 'small number of foreign banks' under similar conditions. It then called for applications from foreign banks prepared to meet the requirement of 50 per cent local equity in September 1984, due for submission before the end of November. At the same time the Bank of China was licensed as a special case and foreign banks were also allowed for a 12-month period to apply for a 100 per cent owned merchant bank. Some 42 applications were received for full bank licences and surprisingly, the government announced in February 1985 its intentions to license sixteen new foreign banks, as many as six of which will be 100 per cent foreign-owned, and representing a wide geographical distribution with three from Japan, one from New Zealand, one from Hong Kong and one from Singapore within the region, and five from North America and four from Europe. The criterion of selection indicated a requirement to meet prudential and management standards, as recommended by the Campbell Report.

While it is clearly too early yet to comment authoritatively on the likely impact of these banks—specifically until their final form and scale and direction of operations are identified—several general observations may be made. First, with the possible exception of one Swiss and one United Kingdom applicant, all serious contenders seem to have been successful. Second, while some four to five of the new applicants will offer a full range of retail and wholesale banking services the rest will be predominantly wholesale. At the retail level at least two of the new entrants should be significant competitors for the existing Australian trading banks, especially given their likely focus on high technology, systems-based retail outlets, which can be efficiently developed off a smaller capital than the labour-intensive, multitudinous network of existing banks. Competition will be fierce at the wholesale and retail level, although it can be expected that at least three of the Australian big four will remain dominant in the Australian dollar banking business because of their dominance of the retail base.

Finally, in its present form with a free forex market, significant foreign bank penetration and virtually no exchange controls, the Australian financial and banking system now represents one of the most open, internationalised and potentially competitive financial systems not only in the region but, more broadly, in the world. In time, its experience will provide a great opportunity for assessment of the merits and implications of an open financial development strategy.

AN OFFSHORE BANKING CENTRE IN AUSTRALIA

To conclude, let me offer a few comments on the potential viability of an offshore banking centre in Australia.[5] Australia enjoys some locational advantages over other centres in the Asian–Pacific time zone. Sydney and Melbourne would be the first centres to open each trading day, being two to three hours, according to the season, ahead of other Asian centres like Singapore. They would also offer the possibility of direct dealing with the West Coast (and possibly East Coast) US centres, as well as other Asian centres during the trading day. At our other extremity, Perth offers a trading overlap with Bahrain and London. Australia also has a natural deposit and loan base. Until recently, of course, the potential Australian business base of such a market was limited by a wall of exchange controls. In particular, Australian residents were prevented from holding significant amounts of foreign currencies, Australian financial institutions were prevented from third-currency dealing and, although generally allowed, overseas borrowings were often subject to cumbersome approval procedures and at times specific quantitative limits.

The potential of our domestic base is often discarded too quickly. To provide some perspective; in the last three years Australia has ranked as either the first or the second largest Asian borrower in the syndicated loan market. On the deposit side, Australians held only US$1.3 billion with major overseas banks at the end of 1983, a reflection of the exchange controls then obtaining. It is yet to be seen how much Australian residents will seek to hold in foreign currencies now these exchange controls have been abolished, but on the experience of other countries which have abolished exchange controls, holdings could increase quite dramatically. Finally, an important factor often overlooked is that Australia's gross domestic product is more than half the sum of national products of ten major Asian countries, excluding Japan.

However, the potential base for an Australian offshore market is not confined to Australian business. There is also the business of neighbouring countries, especially New Zealand, probably Indonesia, Papua New Guinea, and the Pacific Islands. Furthermore, it does not seem unreasonable to expect that on portfolio diversification grounds alone, an offshore market in Australia would also attract corporate and government business from elsewhere in the Asian–Pacific time zone.

The Asian–Pacific region can readily support another centre. The region is expected to be the major growth area of the 1980s. There is presently no financial centre in the southern half of this time zone. For the time being at least a centre in Australia could readily complement other Asian centres, particularly by adding additional depth and liquidity to the region's interbank market. Without wanting to overemphasise the point, a future shift of political balances in Asia, especially in Singapore and Hong Kong could greatly enhance the attractiveness of an Australian centre.

Against this background, and recognising that there are on balance no significant differences in operating costs between Australia and other Asian centres, the extent to which offshore business will be attracted to Australia will depend importantly on whether a centre in Australia offers much the same taxation and regulatory environment as exists in other Asian centres.

In fact, with the recent relaxation of exchange controls, the licensing of seventeen new foreign banks, and the opportunity for foreign banks to also operate a 100 per cent owned non-bank subsidiary and to apply for a foreign-exchange licence, all transactions which are traditionally defined as part of an offshore banking centre can already be done by these institutions. There is, therefore, no real need for a Singapore-style regulatory framework with separate OBUs and licence unless, of course, separate tax concessions are offered for offshore banking business.

In these terms, the question of offshore banking in Australia is therefore primarily a question of taxation and there are three levels to this issue: the need for exemption from State taxes such as stamp duties; the need for exemption from interest-withholding tax (IWT), at least on 'pure' offshore transactions between non-residents in third currencies; and the need for further tax concessions, for example to match Singapore in terms of a 10 per cent offshore profits tax on 'pure' offshore transactions.

As the State governments of New South Wales and Victoria are already broadly committed to removing all State tax impediments to the development of offshore banking transactions, the focus is presently on the second and third dimensions listed above. These matters are presently under review by a committee of officials established by the present Federal Treasurer. It seems likely that an exemption for IWT may be given for 'pure' offshore transactions, which was sufficient in Singapore's case to give the initial impetus to the development of the Asian dollar market based there and would, I believe, be enough to stimulate significant offshore business in Australia. The issue of concessional profits taxes is likely to remain the subject of debate for some time to come in Australia.

Nevertheless, I am reasonably optimistic that we will see the development of a regional financial or offshore banking centre in Australia, which will initially complement existing centres in Singapore and Hong Kong, and even Tokyo if it opens, as it would serve to deepen the regional interbank market. In time an Australian market will be more competitive, especially if the balance of growth and political stability is shifted somewhat away from other Asian centres.

9 Developing Asian financial centres

LEE SHENG YI

The Nature of Different Financial Centres

In well-developed economies with big industrial hinterlands, financial centres such as London and New York serve the purpose of lending out an excess of domestic saving as export capital.[1] London has the backing of not only the British industries but also the EEC industries; New York has the enormous American industries as its background.

In contrast, developing financial centres rarely have adequate industrial backing or sophisticated financial institutions. Some of them have been developed as 'tax havens', such as the Bahamas and the Cayman Islands, where the financial institutions and multinational corporations can escape the high taxation of the industrial countries where they have their headquarters. The time zone is another factor in international banking. For example, the Bahamas and the Cayman Islands are in the same zone as the United States; the Channel Islands of Jersey, Guernsey and the Isle of Man are in the same time zone as London. Bahrain is about halfway between London and Singapore. The spectacular rise of Bahrain as a financial centre in recent years is due partly to its time-zone advantage and partly to the geographical location of Bahrain in the midst of Middle East oil fields.

The developing Asian financial centres have different characteristics. Singapore and Hong Kong provide typical financial entrepot services. Funds are primarily borrowed from overseas and relent overseas; funds generated within Singapore and Hong Kong are limited because of the absence of big industrial hinterlands. Singapore's development as a financial centre with the Asian dollar market and Asian bond market is the result of government action plus international market forces. Hong Kong relies much more upon free-market forces for its financial development, although government regulations are beginning to increase. There is not a formal Asian dollar market in Hong Kong, although residents are free to deposit and to borrow in foreign currencies or domestic currencies. There is no exchange control.

The objective of the Philippines government in setting up the offshore banking system at Manila is primarily to conserve foreign currencies within the country, or to reduce capital flight as far as possible.

The possible rise of Tokyo as a financial centre would have much effect on the developing Asian financial centres. There are both complementary and competitive elements;[2] complementary, because the growth and prosperity of the centres would go together by way of external economy; competitive, because some of the deposit funds may be attracted to Tokyo, instead of Singapore and Hong Kong, and some of the lending activities may be 'booked' at Tokyo. Tokyo, with a huge industrial hinterland, would have a considerable advantage over Singapore and Hong Kong with respect to the provision of funds from Japan itself, instead of performing merely financial entrepot services. The nature of Tokyo as a financial centre would be parallel to that of London and New York. However, there is one more complementary aspect to be noted. It is hoped that Singapore will develop as a medium-grade technology centre, serving that need in Southeast Asia, whereas Japan is a high-level technology centre.

The outward-looking and inward-looking offshore banking systems have much effect on their respective foreign-exchange markets. The objective of this chapter is to focus on the financial centre development and foreign-exchange markets in Singapore, Hong Kong and Manila, and to analyse the major issues and future prospects.

SINGAPORE AS A FINANCIAL CENTRE

In Singapore, two banking systems progress side by side, the domestic banking system and the offshore banking system (Asian dollar market and Asian bond market).

Table 9.1 shows the total assets of the two systems, and their ratios to GDP. Statistically, the total assets of domestic banking units (DBUs) and Asian currency units (ACUs) cannot be added together because of the duplication arising from the transactions between the DBUs and ACUs of the same banks. The gross assets of the domestic financial system are only 38.5 per cent of those of the ACU; the percentage has been rapidly declining throughout the whole period of the 1970s and 1980s because of the higher growth rates of ACUs. Similarly, total assets of commercial banks as percentages of those of ACUs declined from 53 per cent in 1974 to 24 per cent in 1983.

Total assets in the domestic financial system as percentages of GDP increased rapidly throughout the 1970s and 1980s, implying financial deepening.[3] The corresponding percentage for ACUs rose even more—7.38 times GDP for ACUs, compared with 2.84 times for the domestic system in 1983.

The growth rate of total assets in the domestic financial system was about 21 per cent, which was lower than that of about 30 per cent in the ACU, in 1980–83 (Table 9.1, last column).

With financial centre development, the economy of Singapore has become more open (Table 9.2). The ratio of trade (goods and services) to GDP increased from 2.57 in 1968 to 4.08 in 1983. This very high ratio is due to the large entrepot trade, causing the value of trade to exceed GDP by two to four times.

Table 9.1 Total assets of financial institutions in Singapore, 1968–83

	S$ million					Growth rate (%)	
	1968	1974	1978	1980	1983	1968–83	1980–83
1 Total assets of commercial banks and merchant banks (domestic unit operation only)	3 674	12 659	21 726	34 499	59 915	20.5	20.2
2 Total assets of finance companies, POSB, CPF, discount houses and insurance companies	1 212	5 007	11 304	17 575	31 666	24.3	21.7
3 Total assets in domestic financial system (1 + 2)	4 886	17 666	33 330	52 074	91 581	21.6	20.7
4 Total assets of Asian currency units	93	23 495	58 501	113 871	237 928	72.8	30.3
5 GDP at current factor cost	3 971	11 738	16 475	22 382	32 252		
6 Item 3 as percentage of GDP	123.0	150.5	202.3	232.7	284.0		
7 Item 4 as percentage of GDP	2.3	204.0	355.1	508.8	737.7		
8 Item 3 as percentage of item 4	5 253.8	73.8	57.0	45.7	38.5		
9 Total assets of commercial banks as percentage of item 4	3 950.6	51.8	36.3	29.3	23.8		

Source: Various annual reports, and information from MAS and financial institutions; Ministry of Trade and Industry, Singapore Economic Survey of Singapore, 1983.

Table 9.2 Ratio of trade to GDP of Singapore, 1968–83 (US$ million)

	1968	1974	1978	1980	1983ᴾ
1 Exports of goods and services	4 914	19 646	31 331	53 617	64 876
2 Merchandise exports	3 891	14 155	22 986	41 452	46 155
3 Imports of goods and services	5 281	22 040	32 272	56 857	66 677
4 Merchandise imports	5 084	20 405	29 601	51 345	59 504
5 Total trade in goods and services	10 195	41 686	63 603	110 474	131 553
6 Total merchandise trade	8 975	34 560	52 587	92 797	105 659
7 Ratio of trade (goods and services) to GDP	2.57	3.55	3.86	4.94	4.08
8 Ratio of merchandise trade to GDP	2.26	2.94	3.19	4.15	3.28

Note: p   Provisional.

Source: Department of Statistics, Singapore *Economic and Social Statistics, 1960–1982* pp. 59–60, 68–9, 126–9; Ministry of Trade and Industry, Singapore *Economic Survey of Singapore 1983* pp.33, 98, 140.

Table 9.3 Loans and deposits of residents and non-residents in Singapore dollars and foreign currency in domestic banking units in Singapore, 1972–83 (S$ million)

End year	Residents in Singapore			Non-residents			Total		
	S$	FC	Total	S$	FC	Total	S$	FC	Total
Deposits of non-bank customers									
1972	4 387.1	20.8	4 407.9	291.7	37.1	328.8	4 678.8	57.9	4 736.7
1973	5 268.2	61.4	5 329.6	437.2	33.0	470.2	5 705.4	94.4	5 799.8
1974	5 984.3	67.8	6 052.1	469.4	64.2	533.6	6 453.7	132.0	6 585.7
1975	6 865.4	100.7	6 966.1	544.3	95.7	640.6	7 409.7	196.4	7 606.1
1976	7 517.5	153.7	7 670.8	681.5	136.3	817.8	8 199.0	289.6	8 488.6
1977	7 862.4	142.5	8 004.9	833.0	131.6	964.6	8 695.4	274.1	8 969.5
1978	8 749.2	78.4	8 827.6	1 082.7	135.4	1 218.1	9 831.9	213.8	10 045.7
1979	10 415.4	142.1	10 557.5	1 402.9	218.0	1 620.9	11 818.3	360.1	12 178.4
1980	13 796.9	185.3	13 982.2	1 766.7	286.1	2 052.8	15 563.6	471.4	16 035.0
1981	17 213.6	264.3	17 477.9	2 167.1	362.9	2 530.0	19 380.7	627.2	20 007.9
1982	19 941.1	241.5	20 082.6	2 693.3	532.9	3 226.2	22 634.4	774.4	23 308.8
1983	22 605.1	234.4	22 839.5	2 723.2	702.7	3 425.9	25 328.3	937.1	26 265.4
Loans and advances (including bills) to non-bank customers									
1973	5 489.4	253.8	5 743.2	129.8	398.2	528.0	5 619.2	652.0	6 271.2
1974	6 186.6	196.4	6 383.0	143.7	403.7	547.4	6 330.3	600.1	6 930.4
1975	6 838.7	314.0	7 152.7	142.2	534.3	676.5	6 980.9	848.3	7 829.2
1976	7 441.0	532.1	7 973.1	186.8	734.3	921.1	7 627.8	1 266.4	8 894.2
1977	8 203.5	640.7	8 844.2	200.9	1 137.9	1 338.8	8 404.4	1 778.6	10 183.0
1978	9 693.9	655.1	10 349.0	349.3	1 528.1	1 877.4	10 043.2	2 183.2	12 226.4
1979	12 221.7	691.2	12 912.8	885.90	2 208.2	3 094.1	13 107.6	2 899.4	16 007.0
1980	16 068.8	757.0	16 825.8	1 126.4	2 254.7	3 381.1	17 195.2	3 011.4	20 206.9
1981	20 968.6	694.6	21 663.3	1 507.0	2 058.8	3 565.9	22 475.6	2 753.4	25 229.0
1982	24 173.9	1 069.2	25 243.1	1 627.2	2 572.7	4 199.9	25 801.1	3 641.9	29 443.0
1983	29 279.6	1 075.2	30 354.8	1 426.5	2 264.5	3 691.0	30 706.1	3 339.7	34 045.9

Source: Unpublished data kindly supplied by the Monetary Authority of Singapore.

Taking a narrower definition, the ratio of merchandise trade to GDP was still high, increasing from 2.26 in 1968 to 3.28. Apparently, the increasing contribution of the service sector to GDP explains this phenomenon; in spite of the growing importance of manufacturing industries, trade remains the backbone of the economy.

It would be interesting to analyse the customer deposits and loans of residents and non-residents in Singapore, and furthermore the components of Singapore dollars and foreign currencies with respect to the DBU and to the ACUs. The notion of a financial centre in the broad and correct sense should include the foreign-exchange component of both DBUs and ACUs,[4] because when funds flow in and out of Singapore by way of depositing and borrowing, they affect both banking systems and the balance of payments. Obviously there is some interaction between DBUs and ACUs. Non-residents participate most actively in the ACUs with respect to deposits and loans but they also do participate in the DBUs (Table 9.3). For example, in 1983, non-residents shared 13 per cent of customers deposits and 11 per cent of customers loans in DBUs. In 1983, non-residents had 75 per cent of FC deposits, and 68 per cent of FC loans in the DBUs. Residents take only a small part of deposits and loans in ACU (see Table 9.3), and in FC deposits and FC loans in DBU. Furthermore, it should be noted from Table 9.3 that non-residents have deposited an increasing amount in Singapore dollars in the domestic banking system since 1977, owing to the strong Singapore dollar, and there is no evidence of a shift from Singapore dollar deposits to FC deposits by either residents or non-residents. Unfortunately, there is a tendency to regard the Asian dollar market and Asian bond market as the only part of the financial centre.

ASIAN DOLLAR MARKET

Strict banking regulations in the United States, coupled with strong demand for US dollars outside the United States, were the major factors in the establishment of the Eurodollar Market. The abolition of the withholding tax of 40 per cent on deposit interest, against the background of monetary stringency in the United States and Europe, started the Asian dollar market in 1968. Differential banking regulations and heavier taxation on the domestic banking system than on the offshore banking system explain the higher growth rates of the offshore banking system. Hence in recent years, international banking is progressing fast and international lending is greater than lending in the domestic banking systems. This serves as an impetus to the development of financial centres.

There are three basic conditions for the establishment of a financial centre and concomitantly the Asian dollar market (ADM): the free flow of funds, minimum taxation and a good financial infrastructure with numerous international financial institutions.

The free banking policy of Singapore provides the favourable background for the Asian dollar market.[5] The full liberalisation of exchange control as effective from June 1978 enables the free flow of funds in and out of Singapore for investment and payment purposes.

When the Asian dollar market was established in 1968, the Singapore government had the policy separating the domestic banking system from the Asian dollar market. Singapore residents were not permitted to deposit funds into the ADM, nor to borrow from the ADM to finance trade and investment in Singapore. Gradually, the demarcation line between the domestic banking system and the ADM has been reduced. Today, Singapore residents are liberally permitted to deposit funds in the ADM and to borrow from it with the approval of the Monetary Authority of Singapore.

Various tax concessions and fiscal measures have been used to develop the ADM and the Asian bond market, such as the abolition of the withholding tax of 40 per cent on deposit interest, the reduction of tax on loan interest and offshore income to 10 per cent and the drastic reduction of the ad valorem duty of the ACU offshore agreement from 0.5 per cent to the limit of S$500. In fact, taxation in the offshore banking system is lower than in the domestic banking system.

GROWTH IN AGGREGATE ASSETS

In the early years, total assets/liabilities of the ADM were multiplied by two to three times every year from 1968 to 1973. In the subsequent years 1974–81, the

Table 9.4 Consolidated assets and liabilities of Asian currency units, 1968–83 (US$ million)

End period		Assets					Liabilities	
	Number of ACUs	Loans to non-banks	Interbank funds	Other assets	Total assets/ liablities	Deposits of non-banks	Interbank funds	Other liabilities
1968	1	1.4	29.0	0.1	30.5	17.8	12.6	0.1
1969	9	0.9	120.5	1.6	123.0 (+303.3)	97.9	23.7	1.4
1970	14	13.9	370.2	5.7	389.9 (+216.9)	243.7	141.0	5.1
1971	19	188.8	850.8	23.2	1 062.8 (+172.7)	237.9	811.2	13.7
1972	25	600.9	2 331.1	44.1	2 976.1 (+180.0)	398.7	2 550.1	27.3
1973	46	1 214.3	4 691.9	101.0	6 277.2 (+110.9)	912.8	5 249.3	115.1
1974	56	2 629.4 (+16.5)	7 528.0	199.9	10 357.3 (+65.0)	1 614.2 (+76.8)	8 531.4	211.7
1975	66	3 303.4 (+25.6)	9 098.5	195.5	12 597.4 (+21.6)	2 067.7 (+28.1)	10 294.3	235.4
1976	69	4 048.3 (+22.5)	12 951.4	354.4	17 354.1 (+37.8)	1 960.3 (−5.2)	15 067.2	326.6
1977	78	5 281.2 (+30.5)	15 252.5	484.6	21 018.3 (+21.1)	2 254.6 (+15.0)	18 350.3	413.4
1978	85	6 376.8 (+20.7)	19 829.7	833.6	27 040.1 (+28.7)	3 600.0 (+59.7)	21 987.2	1 452.9
1979	101	8 484.0 (+33.0)	28 093.7	1 585.0	38 162.7 (+41.1)	5 760.5 (+60.0)	29 424.9	2 977.2
1980	115	12 402.3 (+46.2)	39 552.3	2 438.0	54 392.6 (+42.5)	9 250.5 (+60.6)	40 879.6	4 262.4
1981	132	19 452.2 (+56.8)	62 173.1	4 149.9	85 775.2 (+57.7)	13 555.6 (+46.5)	66 366.3	5 853.4
1982	150	27 606.3 (+41.9)	69 564.4	6 125.1	103 295.7 (+20.4)	17 629.7 (+30.0)	79 223.9	6 442.2
1983	160	30 384.6 (+10.1)	74 446.8	7 029.5	111 860.9 (+8.3)	20 619.9 (+17.0)	84 743.4	6 497.8

Notes: Asian currency units (ACUs) are separate accounting units of banks and financial institutions authorised by the Monetary Authority of Singapore to operate in the Asian dollar market.
Figures in paretheses are annual growth rates expressed in percentage terms.

Source: Monetary Authority of Singapore *Monthly Statistical Bulletin* (January 1984 and various other issues); *The Financial Structure of Singapore* (rev. edn, June 1980) p.64.

average annual growth rate was about 35.3 per cent (Table 9.4), which surpassed the growth rate of the Eurodollar market. The growth rate slowed down in 1982 and 1983, to about 20 per cent and 8 per cent respectively, owing to the international debt problem and the decline of international bank lending.

The number of ACUs operating in the ADM was increased from a few foreign banks in 1968–69 to 160 in February 1984 (Table 9.4). In recent years, the increase in the number of ACUs is mainly due to the offshore banks and merchant banks. At the end of 1983, the net size of the ADM was estimated to be about US$92.9 billion, if we exclude the inter-ACU loans. The net size of the ADM is about 6 per cent of the narrowly-defined Eurodollar Market as measured by the Bank of International Settlements.

The factors contributing to the rapid growth of the ADM and Asian Bond Market include the increasing number of ACUs, the favourable change in taxation and exchange-control regulations in 1976–78, rapid development of money and capital markets in Singapore, the recycling of the petrodollar, and above all the political and economic stability of Singapore. Freedom from banking regulations and reserve requirements and the lower income taxation in the offshore banking system contributed to its greater growth in comparison with the domestic banking system.

SOURCES AND USES OF FUNDS

One characteristic feature of the ADM is the predominance of the interbank funds, which constitute a much greater proportion of deposits and loans than in the domestic banking system. Interbank deposits and lending in the ADM constitute about three-quarters of total assets and liabilities, whilst non-bank deposits and lending to non-bank customers constitute only 20–25 per cent of the total.

In the early phase of 1968–70, deposits were collected in the Asian region by the ACUs, and remitted to London or New York for investment. In the latter phase, 1971 to the present, the reverse has happened as funds have been channelled from London, the Middle East and other places for investment in this region.[6] Thus in both lending and depositing, the ADM has assumed a regional character, with the predominant percentage for the Asian and ASEAN countries.

ACU loans are mainly denominated in US dollars. The principal industry groups financed include: non-bank financial intitutions; manufacturing; transport, storage and communication; general commerce; building developers, real estate agents and construction, and mining and quarrying, in that order of importance.

INTEREST-RATE MOVEMENT AND ITS REPERCUSSION ON THE DOMESTIC MONEY MARKET

Interest rates in the ADM are very volatile because of the nature of free banking, with keen international competition and without statutory reserve requirements. They follow closely the money and capital markets in New York, London and other financial centres. In fact, the ADM and the Eurodollar market can be said to be two facets of the same offshore banking system; funds flow freely between the two markets, and the deposit rates are almost identical.

Competition in the offshore banking system is greater than in the domestic banking system, there is no minimum reserve requirement, and the risk of default is smaller, most of the borrowers being internationally well-known big corporations. Consequently, the spread between deposit rate and loan rate is smaller in the former than in the latter.[7]

Interest rates in Singapore are usually slightly below the international level, because of the consistent inflow of foreign funds. The high and volatile interest rate in the ADM can make it difficult for industries, particularly small local entrepreneurs, to obtain finance. In order to alleviate this problem, the government has provided some special funds at lower interest rates to encourage exports and manufacturing industries.

TERM STRUCTURE OF ASSETS AND LIABILITIES

Table 9.5 shows clearly that the ADM is principally a short-term market. At the end of 1983, assets comprising mainly loans up to one month constituted 36 per cent of the total assets. Loans on demand and up to seven days constituted about 17 per cent of total assets; these are principally interbank funds and are similar to money at call and short notice in the domestic banking system.

At the end of 1983, the liabilities, predominantly deposits up to one month, constituted 47 per cent. Deposits within three months took up 77 per cent of the liabilities. Demand deposits and 'quasi-demand' deposits constituted 7 per cent and 15 per cent of total liabilities respectively. Trade financing and maintaining working balances are the main reasons for such short-term deposits.

Over time, the maturity structures of both loans and deposits have been changed (see Table 9.5). The anticipated rates of interest and inflationary expectation, and the alternative finance through bond issue, affect the maturity structures of both loans and deposits.

Table 9.6 shows the loans and deposits of non-bank customers, thus excluding the interbank funds. Residents take up a declining percentage of total deposits (from 24 per cent in 1973 to 14 per cent in 1983), although the absolute amount grew very rapidly in the fast-growing Asian dollar market. Similarly, residents have a declining percentage of total loans, from 15 per cent in 1973 to 9 per cent in 1983. Obviously, apart from interbank funds, non-residents have a much bigger share in the market, a characteristic feature of a financial centre. This point stands in contrast to the offshore banking system in Manila.

The loan/deposit ratio (Table 9.6, last column) shows an excess of deposits over loans in the early years of 1968–71, implying that deposit funds were collected in this region for investment outside the region. The reverse happened in the later years when funds were channelled from London, the Middle East

Table 9.5 Maturity structures of assets and liabilities of Asian currency units, 1970–83

	Assets (US$ million)								Total assets/ liabilities (US$ million)	Liabilities (US$ million)							
End of year	On demand	Up to 7 days	7 days to 1 month	Total up to 1 month	1–3 months	3–12 months	1–3 years	Over 3 years		Call deposits	Up to 7 days	7 days to 1 month	Total up to 1 month	1–3 months	3–12 months	1–3 years	Over 3 years
1970	na	na	na	274.3 (71.4)		105.7 (27.5)	4.1 (1.1)		384.1	na	na	na		268.5 (69.8)	114.0 (29.6)		2.2 (0.6)
1971	na	na	na	281.90	244.4	415.5	97.8	—	1 039.6	na	na	na	159.3	268.1	596.0	25.6	—
1972	na	na	na	679.8 (23.2)	766.7 (26.1)	1 234.4 (42.1)	251.1 (8.6)	—	2 932.0	na	na	na	711.8 (24.1)	841.0 (28.5)	1 277.3 (43.3)	118.7 (4.0)	—
1973	na	na	na	1 270.3	1 512.6	3 095.6	297.7	—	6 176.2	na	na	na	1 453.7	1 531.1	2 984.2	223.1	—
1974	na	na	na	1 968.0	2 859.3	4 545.9	784.3	—	10 157.5	na	na	na	2 776.0	2 692.4	4 485.1	218.3	—
1975	na	na	na	1 985.7	3 692.6	4 873.3	1 850.3	—	12 401.9	na	na	na	3 075.6 (24.8)	3 941.8 (31.8)	5 087.2 (41.0)	282.0 (2.3)	—
1976	na	2 706.4 (15.6)	3 380.1 (19.5)	6 086.5 (35.1)	4 743.0 (27.3)	3 623.5 (20.9)	554.3 (3.2)	2 346.8 (13.5)	17 354.1	963.4 (5.6)	3 269.2 (18.8)	4 307.0 (24.8)	8 539.6 (49.2)	4 851.4 (28.0)	3 364.4 (19.4)	271.6 (1.6)	327.1 (1.9)
1977	na	3 347.6	4 162.5	7 510.1	5 802.6	4 365.3	1 014.3	2 326.0	21 018.3	1 620.0	4 086.5	5 020.8	10 727.3	6 148.6	3 664.2	181.3	296.9
1978	na	3 862.3	5 445.8	9 308.1	7 633.2	5 550.7	1 313.4	3 234.7	27 040.1	1 810.1	4 146.8	6 446.8	12 403.2	8 173.5	5 622.3	568.9	272.2
1979	na	5 819.9	7 553.2	13 378.1	9 985.0	7 667.3	2 137.3	4 995.0	38 162.7	3 137.8	5 434.5	9 823.5	18 395.9	10 851.2	7 427.2	969.7	518.7
1980	na	7 918.4	9 814.2	17 732.6	14 552.0	11 746.8	2 991.3	7 369.9	54 332.6	4 527.0	7 303.4	12 293.7	24 124.1	16 372.9	11 126.7	1 656.8	1 112.1
1981	5 229.5	7 922.5	16 594.8	29 746.8	22 848.3	18 099.8	3 862.4	11 217.9	85 775.2	8 894.6	10 917.7	20 060.6	39 872.3	25 812.8	17 170.2	1 772.9	1 147.1
1982	4 999.9	9 679.8	19 937.8	34 617.5	25 758.3	21 745.6	4 408.1	16 766.2	105 295.7	9 639.7	13 630.7	24 575.5	47 845.9	30 615.1	21 560.2	1 813.6	1 461.0
1983	6 370.0 (5.7)	12 555.8 (11.2)	21 740.1 (19.4)	40 665.9 (36.4)	26 099.9 (23.3)	21 081.7 (18.8)	5 259.1 (4.7)	18 764.4 (16.8)	111 860.90 (100.0)	7 653.2 (6.8)	17 106.7 (15.3)	28 255.7 (25.3)	53 015.6 (47.4)	33 430.9 (29.9)	21 826.9 (19.5)	1 857.0 (1.7)	1 730.5 (1.5)

Note: Figures in parentheses are percentages of total assets/liabilities.

Source: Monetary Authority of Singapore *Monthly Statistical Bulletin* (January 1984 and various other issues); other information from MAS.

Table 9.6   Asian dollar market: customers, loans and deposits of residents and non-residents, 1968–83 (US$ million)

End of year	Loans and advances			Deposits			Loan/ deposit ratio
	Residents	Non-residents	Total	Residents	Non-residents	Total	
1968	na	na	1.4	14.6	3.2	17.8	0.08
1969	na	na	0.9	45.3	52.6	97.9	0.01
1970	—	13.9	13.9	87.0	156.7	243.7	0.06
1971	58.7	130.1	188.8	62.3	175.5	237.8	0.79
1972	157.6	443.3	600.9	118.0	280.7	398.7	1.51
1973	184.9 (15.0)	1 041.2	1 226.1	296.4 (24.2)	616.4	912.8	1.34
1974	349.9	2 347.8	2 697.7	488.7	1 125.5	1 614.2	1.67
1975	375.8	3 096.7	3 472.5	583.9	1 483.8	2 067.7	1.68
1976	508.1	3 878.5	4 386.6	364.8	1 595.5	1 960.3	2.24
1977	517.5 (9.8)	4 763.7	5 281.2	334.1 (14.8)	1 920.5	2 254.6	2.34
1978	793.7	5 583.1	6 376.8	777.8	2 822.2	3 600.0	1.77
1979	792.5 (9.3)	7 691.5	8 484.0	1 080.4 (18.7)	4 691.0	5 771.4	1.47
1980	1 117.4	11 284.9	12 402.3	1 647.3	7 674.9	9 322.2	1.33
1981	1 672.8 (8.6)	17 779.4	19 452.3	2 597.2 (19.0)	11 061.8	13 659.0	1.42
1982	2 284.5	25 321.8	27 606.3	2 439.0	15 190.7	17 629.7	1.57
1983	2 866.5 (9.4)	27 518.1	30 384.6	2 910.7 (14.1)	17 709.2	20 619.9	1.47

Notes: Residents include individuals and corporations which are registered or have permanent addresses in Singapore. Figures in parentheses are percentages in total loans/deposits.

Source: Monetary Authority of Singapore. See also R.I. McKinnon 'Offshore Markets in Foreign Currencies and Monetary Control: Britain, Singapore and the United States' in *MAS Papers on Monetary Economics* Singapore University Press, 1981, p.145.

and other places for investment in this region. Hence the ratio rose to the height of 2.24–2.34 in 1976–77, and became steady at the level of 1.4–1.5 from 1979 to 1983.

ASIAN BOND MARKET (ABM)

The Development Bank of Singapore and the government of Singapore released the first three bond issues in 1971 and 1972, initiating the government action to encourage the development of the ABM. The growth was rather sluggish in the early stages of 1971–75, particularly during the worldwide recession of 1974–75 (Table 9.7). There was no issue at all in 1974, when the international capital market was dull. In 1975, there were only three issues, amounting to US$47 million. The ABM has become increasingly active since 1976, in consonance with the Eurobond Market (EBM) and the world capital market. To date (up to February 1984) there have been 127 issues amounting to about US$5894 million. The Asian bond issues represented only 0.5 per cent of Euro issues in 1965 and 1.7 per cent in 1980.

In 1982, as a consequence of the mounting international debt problem, banks

Table 9.7 Asian bond issues, 1971–84

Year	Number of issues	Amount (million)	Coupon rate of interest (%)	Maturity (years)
1971	1	US$10	8.5	10
1972	2	US$20 DM100	7.75	10–15
1973	3	US$100	5.75, 6.5, 8.75	9–15
1974	0			
1975	3	US$47	9, 9.5	5–7
1976	9	US$247 DM50	6.5–9.5 or floating rate	5–15
1977	14	US$315 DM100 $A10	6–8.625 or floating rate	5–15
1978	12	US$220 SDR25 ¥15 000 DM40 $A15	9.5 or floating rate	5–15
1979	8	US$315 DM70	7 or floating rate	7–15
1980	18	US$659	7.25–12 or floating rate	3–8
1981	22	US$1001 +¥35 000	8.25 or floating rate	3–15
1982	16	US$900 +¥30 000	7.875–15.5 or floating rate	5–15
1983	15	US$1059.8	8–14.25 or floating rate	5–15
1984 (Jan Feb)	4	US$339.3	7–11.25	5–10

Notes: Coupon rates of interest refer to US$ bonds only.
Floating rates are usually 0.25 per cent above the six month LIBOR or SIBOR.

Sources: Monetary Authority of Singapore *Annual Report 1982/1983*; information from DIS (Daiwa International Securities Ltd).

became reluctant to expand their loans and loan syndication (see also Table 9.4). Asian bond issues did not increase much in 1982 and 1983.

The issuers and underwriters of Asian dollar bonds are drawn on a worldwide basis. They include companies, banks, financial institutions, governments and regional institutions. Since 1976, it has been a common practice to offer floating interest rates on the basis of LIBOR (London Interbank Offer Rate) or SIBOR (Singapore Interbank Offer Rate), as there is less risk to both issuers and subscribers from worldwide fluctuating interest rates, which rose sharply between 1979 and 1982.

New financial instruments have been introduced in recent years, such as the S$NCD (Singapore dollar negotiable certificate of deposit) in 1975, the US$NCD in November 1977, and SDR deposits in ACU in October 1979. The depository receipts of Singapore (DRS) were incepted in 1982, whereby investors in Singapore can indirectly hold shares in Tokyo and other countries.

The Asian dollar market is principally a short-term market, whilst the Asian bond market is a medium- and long-term capital market. They form complementary aspects of Singapore's offshore banking facilities.

HONG KONG AS A FINANCIAL CENTRE: THE MONETARY SYSTEM

Hong Kong has had favourable conditions to develop as a financial centre, notably a free money and exchange market and free gold market. Traditionally the Government has adopted a laissez-faire attitude, relying upon free enterprise and market forces for its development. However, in recent months the Government has introduced some regulations in the financial system, with the support of businessmen and bankers who feel that there is a need for some control.[8]

As a financial centre, Hong Kong still has an edge over Singapore. There are more international financial institutions operating in Hong Kong than in Singapore (see Table 9.8). There are also more international lawyers and accountants in Hong Kong who can process the contracts and documents of syndicated loans promptly. Hence Hong Kong is regarded as a 'booking' centre for lending, whilst Singapore is considered primarily as a funding centre for taking deposits. As there is no withholding tax on non-residents depositing in the Asian dollar market in Singapore, and there was such as tax of 15 per cent on foreign-currency deposit interest in Hong Kong prior to February 1982, deposit funds were attracted to Singapore. In Hong Kong there is no income tax on bank lending abroad since, according to Hong Kong tax law, income that is not generated within the territory of Hong Kong is not subject to tax. In Singapore, there is the concessionary income tax rate of 10 per cent, although banks can avoid it by not remitting the interest earning immediately as income. Furthermore, company income tax in Hong Kong is lower than that in Singapore. Because of the tax differential, financial institutions find it more profitable to lend out the funds or arrange loan syndication in Hong Kong than in Singapore.

Hong Kong tends to have a high growth rate accompanied by instability and a high rate of inflation. A fundamental weakness of the monetary system is that the system per se tends to be inflationary. Prior to June 1972 (the floating of the pound sterling), the two note-issuing banks, the Hong Kong and Shanghai

Table 9.8   Number of financial institutions in Hong Kong

		December 1969	December 1978	June 1980	June 1983
1	Licensed banks	73	88	113	132
	(offices)	(362)		(1078)	
2	Deposit-taking companies[a]	nil	241	283	352
	—licensed				26
	—registered				326
3	Representative offices of foreign banks	21	100	104	113
4	International money brokers				6
5	Local money brokers				5

Note: a   Deposit-taking companies (DTCs) include merchant banks and finance companies. The two categories of DTC—licensed and registered—were introduced in 1981. DTCs cannot accept small deposits by law, and there is restriction in the maturity of deposits.

Source: Hong Kong Banking Commissioner's Office; *Hong Kong Monthly Digest of Statistics* (various issues).

Banking Corporation and the Chartered Bank, offered sterling and other foreign exchange to the Exchange Fund in exchange for a non-interest-bearing Certificate of Indebtedness,[9] against which new notes are issued.[10] However, the two banks can have an authorised fiduciary issue to the maximum amount of HK$95 million, against the deposit of government securities with the Crown Agent in London. The Exchange Fund held a large proportion of sterling assets in its portfolio because of the Sterling Guarantee Scheme, 1971–75. After the termination of that scheme in 1975, the portfolio was diversified into other currencies, particularly the US dollar. Prior to 1975, the sterling exchange standard was virtually a variant of the Currency Board system in Singapore and Malaya and other British colonies. This 100 per cent foreign-exchange cover imposed an effective constraint on the increase in bank notes and money supply.

Between 1972 and 1974, the Hong Kong dollar was pegged to the US dollar. However, after 1972, the note-issuing system was somewhat modified. Instead of crediting the Exchange Fund's London account with sterling, the two banks credited the Fund's accounts in Hong Kong dollars with the amount of new issue in Hong Kong dollars. The Fund then had two alternative ways to use the proceeds. The first was to acquire a variety of foreign currencies, mainly US dollars, in the foreign-exchange market as and when the Fund thought fit; and the second was to deposit the Hong Kong dollar balance temporarily in the domestic banking system. The purchase of foreign exchange in the foreign-exchange market had a great effect on the exchange rate and the Fund was anxious not to depress further the exchange rate when it was falling. If the Fund chose to deposit the Hong Kong dollar balance in the second alternative, it would accelerate the increase in money and credit because the banking system would use the new deposits to expand credit, thus causing a double wave of inflation.

One more inflationary factor in this system is the lack of effective banking regulation. Apparently, the law requires banks to maintain a cash reserve of 25 per cent of deposit liabilities. But some banks manage to maintain a 'phoney reserve' by arranging with close overseas associates in Singapore, for example, to exchange deposits of equal amounts, so that in the balance sheet as presented to the Board of Monetary Affairs, there is a reserve deposit of the exchanged amount. In other words, a bank receiving $100 deposit can lend out the whole $100 without any reserve. The resulting ease of credit expansion would certainly lead to inflation.[11]

POLITICAL SHOCK AND THE IMPORTANCE OF CONFIDENCE FOR STABILISATION

As a consequence the progressive increase in money supply, M1, M2 and M3 (Table 9.9), can be directly correlated with price increases (Figure 9.1) and the depreciation of the Hong Kong dollar in the foreign-exchange market (Figure 9.2). Inflation and exchange depreciation are two faces of the same coin, it seems, in line with the quantity theory of money.

PACIFIC GROWTH AND FINANCIAL INTERDEPENDENCE

Table 9.9 Money supply of Hong Kong in domestic and foreign currencies, 1978–83 (HK$ million)

End period	M1			M2			M3		
	HK$	FC	Total	HK$	FC	Total	HK$	FC	Total
1978	—	—	20 110	—	—	66 472	—	—	76 919
1979	—	—	20 851	—	—	75 270	—	—	99 765
1980	23 076	1 122	24 198	85 000	11 180	96 240	120 454	18 319	138 773
	(95.5)	(4.6)	(100.0)	(88.3)	(11.6)	(100.0)	(86.8)	(13.2)	(100.0)
1981	23 748	1 446	25 194	96 761	19 995	116 756	145 933	30 885	176 818
1982	26 086	1 399	27 485	120 956	85 732	206 668	149 254	102 293	251 547
	(94.9)	(5.1)	(100.0)	(58.5)	(41.5)	(100.0)	(59.3)	(40.7)	(100.0)
1983 (Sep)	27 591	2 417	30 008	126 938	126 446	253 384	148 528	150 922	299 450
	(91.9)	(8.1)	(100.0)	(50.1)	(49.9)	(100.0)	(49.6)	(50.4)	(100.0)
1983 (Dec)	28 277	2 619	30 896	138 818	118 867	257 685	168 020	143 125	311 146
	(91.5)	(8.5)	(100.0)	(53.9)	(46.1)	(100.0)	(54.0)	(46.0)	(100.0)
			Growth rate (per cent)						
1980–83	7.0	32.7	8.4	17.8	119.9	38.9	11.7	98.4	30.9
1978–83	—	—	9.0	—	—	31.1	—	—	32.2

Notes: M1—currency in active circulation plus demand deposits of commercial banks;
M2—M1 plus time and savings deposits of commercial banks;
M3—M2 plus time and savings deposits of deposit-taking companies.
Figures in parentheses are percentages.

Source: *Hong Kong Monthly Digest of Statistics* (Janaury 1984) p. 50.

Table 9.9 presents M1, M2 and M3 in both Hong Kong dollars and foreign currency. Several striking features can be noted:

1 With respect to total money (including HK dollar and foreign exchange), Hong Kong dollar only and foreign currency, the growth rates of M2 and M3 were all higher than that of M1, particularly foreign currency.[12] This provides clear evidence of the shift to foreign money. The shift is more striking for the store-of-value function of money than for the transaction function of money, as M1 denotes the transaction function, whilst M2 and M3 include the asset function as well. This can be related to an old theoretical dictum, noted by Alfred Marshall and called Greshaw's Law II by Ronald McKinnon: 'stronger fiat currencies would tend to drive out weaker ones'.[13]

2 The shift can also be illustrated by analysing the domestic and foreign money components in M1, M2 and M3.

3 The exchange crisis in September 1983 seemed to be the height of the loss of confidence and of the shift to foreign money. The exchange rate was then temporarily stabilised (compare September and December 1983 figures in Table 9.9).

4 Prices (Consumer Price Index (A)) rose faster than total M1 index but less than total M3 index (Figure 9.1). This can be interpreted by the theory that liquidity, or the broad definition of money including the time and savings deposits of DTCs, rather than the narrow definition of money, is the more important factor in determining price change.[14]

Excessive growth of money and credit, the overheating of the economy, characterised by speculation on the property and share markets, and the

Figure 9.1 Consumer price index (A) total M_1 and M_3 indexes of Hong Kong, 1974–1983

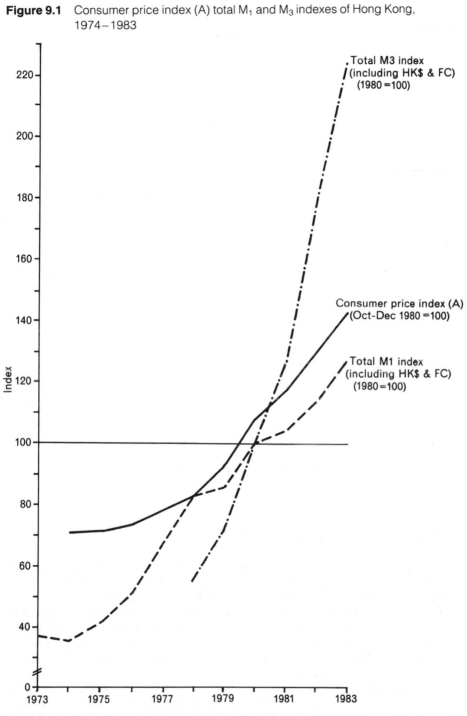

Source: *Hong Kong Monthly Digest of Statistics* and Table 9.9

Figure 9.2 Effective exchange rate index (EER) and HK$/US$ exchange rate of
Hong Kong, 1975–1983 (19.12.1971 = 100)

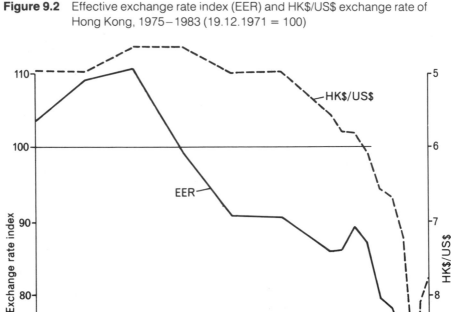

Source: Hong Kong Monthly Digest of Statistics

widening trade deficit explain the fall of the internal and external value of the
Hong Kong dollar.[15]

The falling exchange rate, high rate of inflation,[16] different domestic and
international interest rates (see Table 9.11) and higher taxation on Hong Kong
dollar deposits than on foreign-currency deposits explain the shift to foreign
money. Figure 9.2 shows that since the Smithsonian Agreement (December
1971) the trade-weighted effective exchange-rate index (EER) rose to the height
of 115.4 in January 1977. Thereafter the Hong Kong dollar became weak and
began falling. The fall seemed to be stabilising in 1979–81; in 1981–83, the fall
was precipitous and dramatic.

To make matters worse, the Hong Kong government abolished the withholding tax of 15 per cent on FC deposit interest in February 1982. At the same
time, the interest tax on Hong Kong dollar deposits was reduced from 15 per

cent to 10 per cent. Thus foreign-currency deposits would incur no income tax, whereas Hong Kong dollar deposits would attract a tax of 10 per cent. The consequence was the acceleration of the shift to foreign-currency deposits and a further fall in the exchange rate.

In 1982, the news of unsuccessful negotiations in the first few rounds between the governments of China and Britain caused political disturbance and a loss of confidence in the Hong Kong economy, culminating in the sharp drop of the exchange rate to the lowest level of HK$9.55 per US dollar in September 1983 (see Figure 9.2). After some deliberation, the Hong Kong Monetary Authority announced on 15 October 1983 the pegging of the exchange rate at HK$7.80 per US dollar, and at the same time the reversion to the former currency-issue system of before 1972. The two note-issuing banks have to offer foreign exchange to the Exchange Fund for the Certificate of Indebtedness, instead of HK dollars. Raising the interest rate as a squeeze on liquidity in the money market was conducted simultaneously with pegging the exchange rate. Important aspects are that only notes, not bank cheques, can be exchanged into US dollars at the fixed rate, thereby causing a squeeze of liquidity in the banking system, and that the exchange occurs only between the two note-issuing banks and the Fund.

The return to the pre-1972 system of currency issue has imposed a financial discipline on the economy. This variant of the Currency Board system is intrinsically equivalent to David Hume's specie flow mechanism. For the system to work, there must be political stability and wage and price flexibility, so that domestic money supply, credit and prices adjust smoothly to changes in the balance of payments. The simultaneous measures of pegging the exchange rate and operating through the money market to tighten credit and raise interest rates apparently explain the success in stabilising the exchange rate and easing the crisis. But on further thought, the success can be attributed mainly to the political factor of gradual restoration of confidence. Mrs Thatcher's subsequent concession of respecting the sovereignty of China over the whole of Hong Kong Island and New Territory after 1997 had softened the originally strong British stand and led to the closer accord in the subsequent rounds of negotiation between the Chinese and British governments, after the September 1983 crisis. The prospect of a successful negotiation has restored confidence considerably to the Hong Kong economy in general and the Hong Kong dollar in particular.

On 20 April 1984 the British Foreign Secretary, Sir Geoffrey Howe, announced that Britain would relinquish sovereignty and administrative powers to the Chinese in 1997 and that Britain and China were working towards an international agreement, preserving Hong Kong's current political freedoms of travel, press, religion, assembly and speech for 50 years after 1997. In other words, free enterprise and the capitalist system would continue and Hong Kong, being a 'Special Administrative Zone', would have much autonomy.

The consolidated balance sheets of all deposit-taking institutions (including banks and DTCs), showing the Hong Kong dollar and foreign-currency amounts, signifies an integrated financial centre (Table 9.10). Foreign-exchange amounts have a predominant share in total assets/liabilities, interbank funds,

Table 9.10 Balance sheets: all deposit-taking institutions in Hong Kong, 1980–83 (HK$ million)

	1980 (end year)			1982 (end year)			1983 (end year)		
	HK$	FC	All currencies	HK$	FC	All currencies	HK$	FC	All currencies
Total assets/liabilities	190 483 (43.8)	244 854 (56.2)	435 337 (100.0)	316 795	546 312	863 107	355 608 (31.9)	759 854 (68.1)	1 115 462 (100.0)
Assets									
Loans and advances to customers	103 878 (23.9)	80 050 (18.4)	183 927 (42.2)	182 095	149 138	331 233	197 175 (17.7)	194 117 (17.4)	391 352 (35.1)
Interbank and inter-DTC funds:									
—banks and DTCs in Hong Kong	50 863 (11.7)	35 391 (8.1)	86 253 (19.8)	83 266	83 304	166 571	96 735 (8.7)	128 155 (11.5)	224 890 (20.2)
—banks outside Hong Kong	6 514 (1.5)	96 103 (22.1)	102 617 (23.6)	9 044	238 282	247 327	14 128 (1.3)	335 699 (30.1)	349 827 (31.4)
Bank acceptances, NCDs, treasury bills, securities, commercial papers, etc.[a]	11 780 (2.7)	17 845 (4.1)	29 627 (6.8)	16 629	44 210	60 837	18 613 (1.7)	60 097 (5.4)	78 709 (7.0)
Hong Kong notes and coins	2 097 (0.5)	—	2 097 (0.5)	2 486	—	2 486	2 629 (0.2)	—	2 629 (0.2)
Other assets	15 351 (3.5)	15 465 (3.6)	30 816 (7.1)	23 275	31 378	54 653	26 328 (2.4)	41 726 (3.7)	68 055 (6.1)

Liabilities									
Deposits from customers	111 125 (25.5)	17 729 (4.1)	128 854 (29.6)	155 384	93 688	234 072	153 401 (13.8)	138 849 (12.4)	292 250 (26.2)
Interbank and inter-DTC funds:									
—banks and DTCs in Hong Kong	51 240 (11.8)	35 918 (8.2)	87 157 (20.0)	83 256	87 234	170 490	96 982 (8.7)	129 679 (11.6)	226 660 (20.3)
—banks outside Hong Kong	4 548 (1.0)	163 480 (37.6)	168 028 (38.6)	7 185	345 322	352 507	10 769 (1.0)	454 815 (40.8)	465 584 (41.7)
NCDs outstanding	1 880 (0.4)	892 (0.2)	2 772 (0.6)	5 318	6 165	11 483	5 417 (0.5)	7 877 (0.7)	13 294 (1.2)
Other liabilities, including capital funds	34 123 (7.8)	14 403 (3.3)	48 526 (11.1)	66 378	28 177	94 555	4 587 (6.7)	43 087 (3.9)	117 674 (10.5)

Notes: a   Include bank acceptances and bills of exchange; negotiable certificates of deposits; treasury bills, securities, share-holdings and interests in land and buildings; floating-rate notes and commercial papers.

        Figures in parentheses are percentages of the total balance sheet (i.e. total assets/liabilities).

Source: *Hong Kong Monthly Digest of Statistics* (January 1984) pp. 56–7.

bank acceptances. NCD and securities, whilst Hong Kong dollar amounts have a higher percentage in customer loans and deposits. The growth rate of total assets of all deposit-taking institutions was 36.8 per cent from 1980 to 1983, and 32.5 per cent from 1968 to 1983. These high growth rates of the financial institutions were greater than GDP growth, which was about 19.9 per cent from 1968 to 1983. As a comparison (see also Table 9.1), the growth rate of total assets of financial institutions in Hong Kong surpassed that of Singapore.

In 1980, the value-added in the financial, insurance, real estate and business services sector in Hong Kong amounted to HK$30 283 million, contributing about 26.8 per cent to GDP.[17] In 1980, value-added in the financial, insurance real estate and business service sector in Singapore amounted to S$4182.9 million, contributing 17.3 per cent to GDP.[18] The great boom of the Hong Kong property market in 1980 might exaggerate the Hong Kong percentage. Nevertheless, it seems that the contribution of the financial sector to GDP may be greater in Hong Kong than in Singapore.[19]

For Hong Kong, a statistical analysis of the total assets, customer loans and deposits of banks and DTCs in 1980–83 shows that: both banks and DTCs had a higher percentage of foreign currency in total assets than in Hong Kong dollars; the foreign-currency components in total assets, loans and deposits were all increasing; and the shift to foreign currency was greater in the case of DTCs than in banks.

Table 9.11 shows that the differential between domestic and international interest rates was not the major factor inducing the shift to foreign currency. The differential (Table 9.11 column 3) was greater in earlier years, 1977–80, than in 1982–83; and yet the shift to foreign currency was greatest in 1982 and 1983 in Hong Kong. The interest rate differential was greater in Singapore than in Hong Kong in 1979 and 1981–83. The appreciating Singapore dollar versus the depreciating Hong Kong dollar, the stable price level in Singapore versus the high inflation rate in Hong Kong, and consequently the higher 'real' deposit rate in Singapore than in Hong Kong explained the shift to foreign currency in Hong Kong, and the absence of such a phenomenon in Singapore.

Table 9.11   Deposit rates in Hong Kong, Singapore and the Asian dollar market

Average of year	Hong Kong 3–month deposit rate (%) (1)	US$ 3–month deposit rate (% in ADM/EDM/[a]) (2)	Difference (%) (1)–(2) (3)	Singapore 3–month deposit rate (%) (4)	Difference (%) (4)–(2) (5)
1975	—	4.83	—	4.31	−0.52
1976	—	5.64	—	3.76	−1.88
1977	1.75	6.47	−4.72	4.54	−1.93
1978	2.45	8.75	−6.30	5.29	−3.46
1979	7.61	12.06	−4.45	7.15	−4.91
1980	8.82	14.11	−5.29	11.22	−2.89
1981	13.54	16.88	−3.34	7.43	−9.45
1982	10.96	13.24	−2.28	6.16	−7.08
1983	9.00	9.65	−0.65	6.53	−3.12

Note: a   The deposit rates in the Asian dollar market and the Eurodollar market (ADM/EDM) are practically identical.

A PROPOSAL FOR MONETARY AND BANKING REFORM

As analysed above, the monetary system of Hong Kong per se is inflationary and the banking regulations are rather 'loose '; there is in effect no statutory reserve requirement for some banks. The Hong Kong and Shanghai Banking Corporation has been acting 'unofficially' as a central bank for years.[20] The argument in favour of establishing a separate central bank is that sometimes there is a conflict of interest between commercial banking and central banking, that is, between profit motive and social responsibility, and that a central bank without any commercial banking activity can command more respect from banks and financial institutions because it does not compete with them in business. Since the financial system of Hong Kong has become increasingly complex with numerous licensed banks and deposit-taking companies, perhaps a central bank or a monetary authority with fuller powers of supervision may be necessary for orderly growth in the future. There is also an urgent need to develop an orderly system for the changeover in 1997.

Perhaps for political reasons, the Hong Kong government is hesitant to set up a central bank. An alternative measure, or an easier one, is to strengthen the Exchange Fund so that all licensed banks have to maintain reserve deposits (in HK dollars) with the Exchange Fund.[21] The Exchange Fund can then regulate the volume of reserve deposits by purchase and sale of foreign exchange and HK$-denominated instruments, against the banks' reserve balance in the Exchange Fund. The cheque-clearing facility would be conducted at the Exchange Fund, instead of the Hong Kong and Shanghai Banking Corporation as at present. This would be tantamount to strengthening the Exchange Fund to act as a central bank, or monetary authority. Hong Kong could perhaps model it after the Monetary Authority of Singapore.

FUTURE PROSPECT OF HONG KONG AFTER 1997

The Chinese Government has declared that Hong Kong will be established as a Special Administrative Zone, to be administered by Hong Kong people under Hong Kong laws, with the least interference from the People's Republic of China. The existing free-enterprise system will be preserved, at least for 50 years,[22] in order to maintain the stability and prosperity of Hong Kong.

The British Government is equally sincere in desiring to maintain stability and prosperity. Apart from the agreement between the two governments on the legal and economic framework, the attitude of investors is important for the future of Hong Kong. If investors have confidence in what is called the 'Mini Constitution' and in China's pledge of political and economic autonomy, they will continue to make long-term investments. Under such circumstances, it is likely that stability and prosperity will be maintained after 1997. But can the relative position of Hong Kong as a trading and financial centre be maintained? This will depend on Hong Kong's trading and financial relations with China and Southeast Asia.

The 'Four Modernisations' of China, if successfully carried out, would certainly accelerate the growth of Hong Kong as a financial centre. In 1980, China gained about US$6.9 billion through Hong Kong; 36.5 per cent of net foreign exchange earnings came directly and indirectly from Hong Kong.[23]

Hong Kong serves effectively as an entrepot for mainland China and China supplies foodstuffs and other consumer goods to the domestic market of Hong Kong. China uses its big trade surplus with Hong Kong and Singapore to finance its trade deficits with Japan, the USA, the EEC, Canada, Australia and other countries.[24]

Secondly, Hong Kong as a financial centre has served as a window for China to international trade and finance. Hong Kong provides both short- and long-term loans and other financial facilities to China, and is a source of investment capital for China. In 1981, there were thirteen licensed banks (with 193 branches), thirteen deposit-taking companies, five insurance companies and two joint-venture merchant banks controlled by China,[25] operating within Hong Kong.

Thirdly, China gained much from Hong Kong with respect to tourist expenditure, family remittances and investment profit. Fourthly, Hong Kong is a source of investment capital for China, as Hong Kong entrepreneurs are keen to help China's modernisation by investing in hotels, real estate, residential buildings and other light industries.

For its part, China supplies cheap consumer goods, foodstuffs and crude petroleum to Hong Kong, thus helping the export-oriented industrialisation of Hong Kong. These deepseated economic ties together with historical, ethnic, cultural and geographical factors have made Hong Kong a natural entrepot for China's international trade and finance. If political stability prevails in China, and the Four Modernisations are successful, then this linkage and the extensive oil explorations in the China seas would certainly boost Hong Kong as a trading and financial centre after 1997.

Traditionally, Hong Kong has been a refuge for capital flight from neighbouring countries, such as the Philippines and Indonesia, whenever there is political disturbance. Trade and economic relations between Hong Kong and Indonesia, Singapore, Malaysia, Thailand, the Philippines, Taiwan and South Korea have become very close. As Hong Kong has had practically no exchange control, and there are free gold and commodity markets, funds flow freely in and out of Hong Kong. The crucial question is whether businessmen will have confidence in long-term investments in Hong Kong after 1997. On 28 March 1984, Jardine, Matheson & Co., an old British trading house, announced that it would shift the firm's ownership to a holding company based in Bermuda, a British colony in the West Atlantic. The stock market dropped immediately. If this were to become a trend, Hong Kong's role as a financial centre for Southeast Asia, Taiwan and South Korea may decline.

It can be argued that if Hong Kong can maintain stability and prosperity after 1997, on the basis of her close linkage with China, the beneficial effects would spill over to her relations with other countries, because China's exports and imports through Hong Kong would naturally stimulate Hong Kong's trade and economic relations with the whole region.

In fact, it has long been a practice for rich people in Hong Kong to diversify their investment in different countries, instead of 'putting all eggs in one Hong Kong basket.' Under the present circumstances, with political changes due in 1997, they may possibly 'put fewer eggs in the Hong Kong basket' with a resulting decline in long-term investment.

On balance, whether Hong Kong can maintain her relative position as a financial centre depends upon whether the economic ties with China can exert a more stimulating force than adverse factors arising from the potential lack of confidence.

MANILA AS A MINOR CENTRE: HISTORICAL REVIEW

One of the Philippines' most persistent problems has been the people's inclination to deposit their funds abroad to avoid the country's inflation, exchange depreciation, slow growth of the economy and occasional political disturbance.[26] Filipinos have tended to place their funds in Hong Kong, Singapore, London, New York and other international financial centres in time of crisis. In order to maintain funds in the Philippines, the Monetary Board created an offshore banking system in Manila, modelled on the Asian dollar market. Movement of funds in and out of the Philippines offshore banking system has been free, taxes on deposit interest and on net offshore income[27] have been exempted, and the secrecy of deposit accounts has been permitted, for the sake of establishing the system.

The offshore banking units (OBUs) commenced operation in mid-1977, with branches of foreign banks sanctioned to operate in the offshore banking system but not in the domestic banking system.

STATISTICAL ANALYSIS

Since 1976, the offshore banking system has made considerable progress. An analysis of the crucial data (Table 9.12 (a) and (b)) shows some interesting points.

1 The total number of OBUs and foreign currency deposit units (FCDUs) has increased from 55 at the end of 1979 to 73 in September 1983.

2 Total assets/liabilities, or gross resources of the offshore banking system, increased from US$6.5 billion at the end of 1979 to US$12.1 billion in September 1983, with an annual growth rate of 17.9 per cent. This should be considered as a moderate increase compared with the fast growth of the Asian dollar market in Singapore of 33.3 per cent in the same period. At the end of September 1983, total assets/liabilities of the Philippines offshore system were about 10.8 per cent of the Asian dollar market of US$112.2 billion.

3 Deposits/borrowings were increased from US$5.9 billion at the end of 1979 to US$10.6 billion in September 1983 with an annual growth rate of 16.9 per cent. Interbank deposits constituted 89.2 per cent of total deposits as in

Table 9.12(a) Offshore banking system in Manila, 1979—June 1981

	1979				1980				June 1981			
	OBUs[b]	FCDUs[a] under:		Total	OBUs	FCDUs under:		Total	OBUs	FCDUs under:		Total
		547[c]	343[d]			574	343			547	343	
Number of banks in operation	17	22	16	55	20	26	12	58	20	29	10	59
Total assets/liabilities (US$ billion)	2.9	3.2	0.4	6.5	4.1	4.8	0.4	9.3	3.8	5.0	0.4	9.2
Deposits/borrowings	2.9	2.6	0.4	5.9	3.9	3.9	0.7	8.5	3.7	4.0	0.4	8.1
Banks	2.8	2.1	0.1	5.0	3.8	3.0	0.2	7.0	3.6	3.2	0.2	7.0
Non-banks	0.1	0.5	0.3	0.9	0.1	0.9	0.5	1.5	0.1	0.8	0.2	1.1
—resident	—	0.3	0.2	0.5	—	0.7	0.2	0.9	—	0.6	0.1	0.7
—non-resident	0.1	0.2	0.1	0.4	0.1	0.2	0.3	0.6	0.1	0.2	0.1	0.4
Placements/lendings	2.9	3.1	0.4	6.4	3.9	4.6	0.4	8.6	3.7	4.7	0.4	8.8
Banks	1.9	1.2	0.3	3.4	2.6	1.8	0.2	4.6	2.5	2.2	0.2	4.9
Non-banks, of which:	1.0	1.9	0.1	3.0	1.3	2.8	0.2	4.3	1.2	2.5	0.2	3.9
—resident	0.9	1.9	0.1	2.9	1.2	2.6	0.2	4.1	1.2	2.5	0.2	3.9

Notes: a   FCDUs—expanded foreign currency deposit units.
         b   OBUs—offshore banking units, which started operation in mid-1977.
         c   547—Central Bank Circular No. 547, dated November 1976.
         d   343—Central Bank Circular No. 343, dated 24 April 1972.

Source: Unpublished data kindly supplied by the Central Bank of the Philippines.

Table 9.12(b) Offshore banking system in Manila, December 1981 – September 1983

	December 1981			December 1982			September 1983		
	OBUs[a]	FCDUs[b]	Total	OBUs	FCDUs	Total	OBUs	FCDUs	Total
Number of banks in operation	21	39	60	24	47[c]	71	26	47	73
Total assets/liabilities (US$ billion)	4 627	5 195	9 822	4 988	6 760	11 748	4 455	7 616	12 071
Deposits/borrowings	4 479	4 124	8 603	4 858	5 537	10 395	4 339	6 262	10 601
Banks	4 332	3 085	7 417	4 793	4 526	9 319	4 309	5 152	9 461
—Philippines-based banks	681	926	1 617	537	1 091	1 628	238	900	1 138
—foreign-based banks	3 651	2 159	5 815	4 256	3 435	7 691	4 071	4 252	8 323
Non-banks	147	1 039	1 186	65	1 011	1 076	30	1 110	1 140
—resident	—	838	838	—	888	888	—	1 007	1 007
—non-resident	147	201	348	65	123	188	30	103	133
Other liabilities and capital account	148	1 071	1 219	130	1 223	1 353	116	1 354	1 470
Placements/lendings	4 479	4 874	9 353	4 829	6 208	11 037	4 307	7 034	11 341
Banks	2 781	2 214	4 995	3 069	3 402	6 471	2 466	4 091	6 557
—Philippines-based banks	1 877	1 157	3 034	2 048	1 371	3 419	1 919	949	2 868
—foreign-based banks	904	1 057	1 961	1 021	2 031	3 052	547	3 142	3 689
Non-banks	1 698	2 660	4 358	1 760	2 806	4 566	1 841	2 943	4 784
—resident	1 567	2 660	4 227	1 528	2 800	4 328	1 450	2 942	4 393
—non-resident	131	—	131	232	6	238	391	1	392
Other assets	148	321	469	159	552	711	148	582	730

Notes: a OBUs—offshore banking units, which started operation in mid-1977.
  b FCDUs—expanded foreign currency deposit units.
  c There are 31 under Central Bank Circular 547 (November 1976) and 16 under Central Bank Circular 343 (24 April 1972).

September 1983. Foreign banks, mostly from Singapore and Europe, are more active in the interbank market than domestic banks. Among the non-bank customers, residents contributed 88.3 per cent of the deposits of US$1.1 billion whereas non-residents contributed 11.7 per cent. Hence the objective of the Philippines to retain the foreign-currency deposits of residents in the country has been partially achieved, but the offshore banking system has not been successful in attracting non-resident depositors as in the case of the Asian dollar market.

4   Placements/lendings were increased from US$6.4 billion at the end of 1979 to US$11.3 billion in September 1983, with an annual growth rate of 16.5 per cent. In September 1983, lending to non-bank customers took up 42.2 per cent of total lendings of US$11.3 billion, whereas lending to banks and financial institutions accounted for 57.8 per cent. This shows a higher proprotion of lending to non-bank customers, as compared with the Asian dollar market; 25.7 per cent as at end September 1983. The lending is mainly to finance the Philippines' manufacturing industry, mining industry and public utilities. Practically all the non-bank borrowers are residents; 91.8 per cent in September 1983. The offshore banking system has failed to attract non-resident borrowers, particularly the multinational companies. This point stands in sharp contrast to the Asian dollar market, where the important borrowers are multinational companies, government and government agencies, central banks, banks and financial institutions.

In short, the offshore banking system in the Philippines is domestically rather than regionally or internationally oriented. The Philippines follows the Singapore model of 1968, by separating the domestic and offshore banking systems with respect to deposits. Thus residents are not allowed to deposit in the offshore banking system unless they already have the foreign exchange and the approval of the Exchange Control Authority. However, business enterprises, particularly manufacturing and mining industries, are allowed to borrow from the offshore system to finance activities in the Philippines, subject to approval of the Monetary Board.

PROBLEMS AND PROSPECTS

The Philippines has a highly regulated economy with an inward-looking development strategy. The money and discount market is well developed, but the capital market is not; the stock exchange is rather speculative and is not effective in channelling the savings of the community into long-term investment.

The crux of the problem is that the financial infrastructure has not been developed to support the growth of the offshore banking system. There are only four foreign banks (namely, Chartered Bank, Hong Kong and Shanghai Bank, Bank of America and Citibank, N.A.) and 26 OBUs. With the small number of international financial institutions, its effectiveness in taking deposits and lending in foreign currencies, and in having direct access to the major financial centres in the world, is limited.

The second related problem is the inadequacy of the telecommunication facilities. Thirdly, the sluggish growth of the economy in 1980–84 has hindered the development of the offshore banking system. Fourthly, political disturbances and the Philippines' debt problem have retarded the growth of the economy.

Obviously all these adverse factors hamper Manila's development as a financial centre. A long-term development strategy for overcoming the shortcomings should include the liberalisation of the financial system[28] (as and when circumstances permit) by reducing the extent of the regulations, by granting more offshore licences, by allowing more international banks and Asian banks to open offices, and other measures which would strengthen the offshore system. The success of this strategy depends in part on whether the Philippines' debt crisis and political crises are resolved, enabling the development of the country's potential resources.

FOREIGN EXCHANGE MARKETS OF THE THREE CENTRES

The three developing Asian financial centres have different characteristics, which affect considerably their foreign-exchange markets.

There are formal and informal foreign-exchange markets. Our emphasis is on the predominant formal one, comprising the transactions conducted by banks and financial institutions. The informal market, comprising authorised money-changers, is subsidiary to the formal market. However, whenever there is a black market in foreign exchange arising from strict exchange control, the informal market tends to become active in black market dealings.

In the formal market, the active participants in Singapore include eight international money brokers and about 50 banks and financial institutions. The ACUs, offshore banks and financial institutions dealing with wholesale banking are particularly active. Finance companies have not yet been allowed to deal in foreign exchange.

The active participants in the forex market in Hong Kong include eleven money brokers, and about 100 banks and DTCs, although there are 134 banks 349 DTCs. In the Philippines, there are four international money-brokers, 35 commercial banks, several thrift banks, and 26 OBUs operating actively in the forex market.

In the informal market, there are 253 authorised money-changers in Singapore, 120 in Hong Kong and 567 in the Philippines.

INTERBANK TRANSACTION AND CUSTOMER TRANSACTION

Generally speaking, a forex market comprises the following components:
1 transactions including intervention, undertaken by the monetary authorities;
2 interbank transactions;

Table 9.13 Formal forex markets in six countries

	Singapore 1982	Hong Kong 1983	The Philippines 1983	Indonesia 1983	Malaysia 1982	Thailand 1983
1 Average daily turnover (US$ billion)	9	7	0.169	0.491	0.3	0.134
2 Percentage of local-currency trading/ almost third-currency trading	14/86	30/70	20/80	96/4	60/40	100/0
3 Percentage of spot transactions/ forward and swap transactions	75/25	90/10	82/18	90/10	60/40	87/13
4 Percentage of interbank transactions/ customer or merchant transactions	95/5	90/10	94/6	27/73	75/25	15/80[a]
5 Percentage of speculative transactions/ commercially based transactions	75/25	80/20	85/15	50/50	30/70	20/80
6 Percentage of transactions through brokers/direct dealing among banks	20/80	10/90	40/60	0/100	90/10	
7 Percentage of transactions inside the country/transactions outside the country	40/60	25/75	20/80	95/5	60/40	

Note: a   In addition, about 5 per cent of transactions are related to the Exchange Equalisation Fund (EEF).

Sources: Information supplied by dealers, banks, and Mr Juan Hoe of the Reserve Bank of Australia.

3 transactions between the public and banks;
4 transactions between exporters and importers, which occur only under special circumstances.

The predominance of interbank transactions over customer transactions is much more conspicuous in the three financial centres than in Malaysia, Indonesia and Thailand (Table 9.13, row 4). The importance of interbank funds with respect to deposits and lending is reflected in the importance of interbank transactions in the forex market.

The divergence between the buying and selling rates in interbank transactions is usually narrower than the divergence in customer transactions. The smaller the difference between the divergence in interbank and customer transactions, the more efficient the forex market is said to be.

VOLUME OF AVERAGE DAILY TURNOVER

Table 9.13 shows the formal forex markets in six countries, namely Singapore, Hong Kong, the Philippines, Indonesia, Malaysia and Thailand. The average turnover is about US$9 billion per working day in Singapore,[29] US$7 billion in Hong Kong and US$169 million in Manila. It seems a surprise that the volume of business was greater in Singapore than in Hong Kong, in view of the fact that Hong Kong has had a longer tradition as a financial centre. It is recognised as the world's largest financial centre and the financial system in Hong Kong is more liberalised than that in Singapore. Probably, the activity of the Asian dollar market and Asian bond market in Singapore, with many swap transactions, has boosted the forex business, particularly with respect to third-currency transactions.

The forex business in Manila is much smaller, because the financial centre is inward-looking rather than outward-looking and there are exchange controls and restrictions on banks holding foreign exchange.[30] Regulations are imposed by several bodies, including principally the Central Bank, the Securities and Exchange Commission and the Internal Revenue Commission. The forex transactions in Thailand, Malaysia and Indonesia are also small because of exchange control and various regulations.[31] It seems, therefore, that the more developed the financial centre, the greater the forex business.

LOCAL CURRENCY TRADING AND THIRD CURRENCY TRADING

Third-currency trading predominates over local-currency-trading in all the three financial centres (Table 9.13, Row 2); 86 per cent, 70 per cent and 80 per cent in Singapore, Hong Kong and the Philippines respectively. This is because speculative transactions and swap arrangements relate mainly to third-currency trading. Within the category of third-currency trading in Singapore, US$/DM and US$/£ are the most significant, in that order of importance. In recent years, sterling has declined as an international currency, whilst the Deutschmark and the Japanese yen have risen. The small percentage of local currency trading, such as S$/US$, S$/£ or S$/¥, pertains to trade and investment, shown as customer or merchant transactions in Table 9.13, Row 4.

In the Philippines, local-currency trading is very much restricted by regulations; the official exchange rate is fixed by the Monetary Authority. The only scope for forex business is to trade in a third currency outside the Philippines.

In contrast, Thailand, Indonesia and Malaysia have predominantly large proportions in local-currency trading. If ever they engage in third-currency trading, they do so through Singapore and Hong Kong. As the Thai baht is pegged to the US dollar, local-currency trading is mainly in Bt/US$. The same applies to local-currency trading in Indonesia.

SPOT TRANSACTION, AND FORWARD AND SWAP

As the forward forex markets are not yet well developed in the six Asian developing countries, spot transactions predominate over forward and swap.[32] The necessary conditions for the development of a forward forex market include an adequate volume of forex transactions and sufficient traders and investors interested in hedging their exchange risk. In Singapore, about three-quarters of forex business is in spot transactions, 20 per cent in forward transactions and 4–5 per cent in swap.

The Monetary Authority of Singapore is preparing to launch the 'Financial Futures Markets' in September 1984, dealing in currency futures and interest-rate futures. The plan is to link up with the International Monetary Market (IMM) of the Chicago Mercantile Exchange, so that Singapore as a financial centre will have a wider international connection. The crucial point for the development of a futures market is that the volume of forex transactions must be big enough, and there must be adequate liquidity in the economy.

The Gold Exchange of Singapore has been reorganised to form the Singapore International Monetary Exchange (SIMEX), which is a joint effort of the public sector (MAS) and the private-sector banks and financial institutions. The advantage of the SIMEX–IMM is that it can have 24 hours of trading capability, thus enabling dealers to hedge their position. Singapore's policy is to encourage third-currency transactions in the futures market, but to discourage local-currency transactions, in case the excessive holding and trading of the Singapore dollar outside-Singapore casues the internationalisation of the Singapore dollar. Singapore tries hard to avoid this for fear of losing control of the domestic economy. However, the development of the financial futures market would probably be constrained by this consideration.

A COMPARATIVE REVIEW OF THE THREE FINANCIAL CENTRES

The degree of integration of the domestic and offshore banking systems varies from centre to centre. Hong Kong can be said to be an integrated centre as domestic banks, international banks and joint ventures are so intermixed, deposits can be shifted flexibly between domestic currency and foreign exchange, and government regulations do not distinguish between domestic and offshore banking systems. Singapore is a more segregated centre, although the degree of integration has been increasing year after year. As shown in the above statistics, there are separable balance sheets for DBUs and OBUs as reported to the MAS, and regulations governing the two systems are separate. Manila follows the Singapore model of 1968 and is a segregated centre.

The outward-looking financial centres of Singapore and Hong Kong contrast with the inward-looking Philippine offshore banking system. In the former two centres, funds are collected outside and invested outside: an entrepot financial service. In the latter, loans and deposits of non-bank customers are mainly for residents (see Table 9.12 (a) and (b)).

One of the important problems of a financial centre is the possibility of a shift of domestic currency deposits to foreign currency deposits. In both Singapore and Hong Kong there is no exchange control. Singaopore succeeds in maintaining the domestic currency deposits by having a strong Singapore dollar[33] and a stable price level, and by conducting an appropriate interest-rate policy. Hong Kong suffered from a persistent shift of domestic currency deposits to foreign currency deposits in the 1980s because of inflation, the instability of the Hong Kong dollar and political nervousness. Capital flight has long been a problem in the Philippines. The establishment of the offshore banking system in the Philippines is an attempt to conserve the foreign exchange in the country. As exchange control is strict, domestic currency deposits cannot be shifted openly to foreign currency in the balance sheets of the banks, but a black market exchange provides a vehicle for the shift to foreign currency.

What have been the experiences in the three centres of adjusting their domestic interest rates to international influence? In the open economies of Singapore and Hong Kong, the domestic interest rates tend to follow the international ones, ceteris paribus.

However, as Singapore has a persistent capital inflow, the domestic interest rates are often lower than the international rates as shown in the Asian dollar market (New York, and London). Moreover, the government provides special credit at low interest rates for exports and for manufacturing industries to acquire capital equipment. In early 1980, interest rates in the United States and Western Europe rose sharply, and then fell equally dramatically in April/May 1980.[34] Domestic interest rates in Singapore were much lower than the rates in the Asian dollar market, following the world trend. The difference between them has become narrower since May/June 1980.[35] As a consequence, the Monetary Authority of Singapore 'persuaded' banks not to lend Singapore dollars to non-residents for arbitrage purpose, and not to cover Singapore dollar/US dollar risks for such arbitragists. Singapore discourages non-residents from borrowing Singapore dollars to swap into foreign currencies. Banks have to consult the MAS before lending S$5 million or over to non-residents. All these measures have caused the domestic interest rates to be less dependent on the world market trend.

In Hong Kong, before the September 1983 exchange crisis, domestic interest rates were much lower than the international rates. This, coupled with the differential taxation on foreign and domestic currency deposits, had caused a substantial shift of funds. The Secretary of Monetary Affairs introduced two simultaneous measures for stabilisation in October 1983; one to peg the exchange rate to the US dollar and the second to raise the domestic interest rates. Thus both money-market policy and foreign-exchange policy were used to stem the flow of funds to foreign currencies.

In the Philippines, domestic interest rates are subject to regulations, such as ceiling lending rates, deposit rates and credit quotas and do not adequately reflect market forces.[36] There is an unsatisfied demand for funds in the domestic money market and an arbitrary difference between domestic and international interest rates.

To what extent does the development of a financial centre stimulate or hamper the industrialisation of a country? The Asian dollar market and Asian bond market have attracted many international financial institutions and industrialists to invest in Singapore, have helped provide capital funds to the manufacturing industries of Singapore and have had a stimulating effect on the domestic capital market (the Stock Exchange of Singapore). However, there is a social cost in the sense that small local business and manufacturing industries sometimes find it difficult to borrow in the market, because of the high and fluctuating interest rates and the non-availability of credit in time of monetary stringency abroad. To alleviate this problem, the government has provided special funds to encourage exports and manufacturing industries.

In Hong Kong, financial centre development and growth in manufacturing industries are the consequence of free market forces. Unlike Singapore, the Hong Kong government does not take an active role in promoting those developments, except to provide good infrastructure and telecommunications. Hong Kong is traditionally the refuge for capital flight and talent flight from the neighbouring countries, such as the Philippines, Indonesia and mainland China. However, political uncertainty and the inflationary monetary system have hampered the development of Hong Kong as a trading and financial centre.

A weakness of the Hong Kong economy is that investment funds did not flow adequately into the manufacturing industries in the 1970s, but went instead into property speculation, causing a property-market boom until 1981. In this sense, financial centre development has not had the expected stimulating effect on industries.

The offshore banking system in the Philippines has not yet had much beneficial effect on the manufacturing industries. Nevertheless, the lending of foreign exchange to the manufacturing, mining, and public utility industries may have some favourable effect in the long term.

There are aspects of complementarity as well as competitiveness among the three financial centres. Singapore is principally a funding centre in the Asian dollar market and Hong Kong a lending or 'booking' centre. They compete for deposit funds and syndicated loans. But the growth of the Southeast Asian region should induce the simultaneous growth of these centres, particularly Singapore and Hong Kong. Hence, there is scope for complementary development. To use a common Chinese saying, 'hundreds of flowers bloom together.'

10 The internationalisation of Tokyo's financial markets

EISUKE SAKAKIBARA

International financial questions have recently emerged among the key issues for United States and Japanese bilateral negotiations. It is somewhat surprising that such technical questions as finance have been spotlighted as much as they have been during the past six months.

The issue, as originally perceived by the Americans, was closely related to the exchange-rate question. As the yen/dollar exchange rate continued to hover around the 240–250 mark during most of 1983, frustration among American industrialists became both widespread and deeprooted, culminating in various charges against the Japanese government of manipulating the rate.

Since there was no evidence of manipulation of the yen by the Japanese government, charges were quickly refuted by both the Japanese and US governments. However, towards the end of 1983 when President Reagan visited Tokyo, the exchange-rate issue was again raised, this time in relation to the internationalisation of the yen and deregulation of Tokyo markets.

Since disputes about individual items such as automobiles, steel and textiles had been hammered out over and over again, resulting in voluntary export controls on the part of the Japanese, American concern has shifted gradually to macro and structural issues, such as industrial targeting policy, fiscal and monetary policies and the exchange rate. With regard to the exchange rate in particular, US complaints were not necessarily directed at the Japanese market, but at the loss of competitiveness in third country markets. For example, Mr Lee Morgan, Chairman of The Caterpillar Tractor Company and Chairman of the Business Roundtable, an advisory organ for President Reagan, was reported to have said that his company was being squeezed out of third country markets by Komatsu because of the cheap yen.

According to an insider in the US government,[1] Chairman Morgan seems to have played an instrumental role in this 'campaign'. To quote, 'In late September of 1983, Lee Morgan, Chairman of Caterpillar Tractors, came to Washington. He visited the White House, Treasury and other agencies at the top levels. Wherever he went he left two gifts. The first was a copy of a new study entitled 'The Misalignment of the U.S. Dollar and the Japanese Yen: The Problem and Its Solution' by David Murchison and Ezra Solomon. The second was a toy caterpillar tractor–made in West Germany.'

According to Murchison and Solomon,[2] 'The principal cause of the imbalance [of US trade account] was a misalignment of the yen/dollar exchange rate. The yen had depreciated against the dollar due to capital outflow from Japan. The capital outflow . . . was in part the effect of a number of Japanese Government policies'.

In the words of the government insider: 'Morgan urged that the Washington policy makers progress from "benign neglect" of the dollar to a "positive exchange rate policy". The suggested remedy was a list of measures Japan would be encouraged to take to liberalise its financial markets and internationalise the yen. The ideal occasion to press the plan on the Japanese was President Reagan's upcoming trip to Japan scheduled for November'.[3]

Despite some strong opposition from within the US government, this Morgan/Solomon argument formed the basis of the US position at the time of the President's visit and thereafter.

The initial US demands on liberalisation of Japanese financial markets and internationalisation of the yen were very close to the recommended remedies of Murchison and Solomon. However, the negotiating process witnessed some subtle changes in the US position. Although the Treasury Secretary stuck to his original Morgan/Solomon proposition, negotiators and experts below cabinet level gradually shifted their position. They subsequently argued that although liberalisation had merits in itself in raising market efficiency, it may not have any immediate impact on the exchange rate. Indeed, most of the leading US experts, including Martin Feldstein, Chairman of the Council of Economic Advisers, agreed that Japanese deregulation may further weaken the yen rather than strengthen it. Since the bulk of remaining administrative guidance covers outflows of capital, the short-term effects of deregulation could very well increase the net outflow of capital from Japan, resulting in a cheaper yen.

Of course, since the exchange rate is affected by various other factors, deregulation may not have any discernible impact on the rate. Theoretically, the qualitative effect could well be a depreciating Japanese yen.

The Morgan/Solomon faction has maintained that deregulation would increase Japanese domestic interest rates, thereby inducing a net inflow of capital, which would appreciate the yen rate. There are indeed some rates in the domestic markets which are either regulated or administered, as I delineate later, and those rates may very well increases as a result of deregulation. However, there are already a sufficient number of market-determined yen instrument interest rates such as repos, CDs and bonds in the secondary market, and international arbitrage is very active. It is unlikely, therefore, that the addition of a few new market instruments such as TBs, BAs and yen-denominated deposits other than CDs, could substantially change present patterns and the volume of interest arbitrage between domestic and international markets.

The Tokyo markets are already considerably internationalised and deregulated. Although this point has often been overlooked in recent negotiations, it is crucial to recognise what is occuring in the Tokyo markets as a financial revolution.

As a matter of fact, as the year 1984 unfolds, the Japanese financial community seems to have plunged into the final stage of its structural transformation. The underlying current of change had been moving at an accelerating pace since the early seventies, and it is not impossible to continue the patchwork approach to altering the traditional financial regime. A fundamental restructuring of the present system seems due in the late 1980s and the year 1984 will be remembered as the prologue of the final stage of such revolution. 'Revolution' implies drastic solutions to very difficult problems associated with overhauling the traditional domestic financial system.

The postwar Japanese system was built around the banks as in most of continental Europe, in contrast to the Anglo-Saxon system which is characterised by the central role of open markets. The traditional system has functioned quite efficiently during the past 30 years and has contributed substantially to the successful performance of the Japanese economy as a whole.

However, deregulation of the system has reached such a stage that internationalisation after the Anglo-Saxon model is inevitable. Although this does not imply any inferiority in the traditional Japanese system, the present international norm is dominated by the Anglo-Saxon regimen, and it would be logically inconsistent to encourage internationalisation while retaining fully fledged Japanese traditions.

The Japanese assimilation of the Anglo-Saxon norm, however, is only one aspect of the ongoing 'revolution'. As in the US, the computer revolution has affected the basic modus operandi of Japanese business and is bringing about fundamental changes in the role and function of financial institutions. The rapid expansion of de facto financial operations of non-financial corporations such as department stores, supermarkets, trading firms and the financial sections of other large companies has blurred the demarcation between banks, non-banks and non-financial institutions, and rendered the established segmentation of financial business obsolete.

If this trend of permeation by non-financial institutions of financial business is left unchecked, while the activities of banks and non-bank financial institutions are being restrained, the bulk of the new financial business will fall into the hands of the former. Because of the relative underdevelopment of consumer financing, this phenomenon is particularly conspicuous in the consumer lending area. Since the institution of new regulations for non-financial corporations seems difficult, if not impossible, deregulation of financial institutions seems to be the only logical solution at this stage.

There is a similar change in the corporate sector. The growing maturity of Japanese business firms has decreased their need for one-sided dependence on banks and has made efficient asset–liability management essential. Financial consultation rather than constant provision of liquidity has become increasingly important for banks vis-à-vis corporations.

Lastly, the importance of the public sector in this process needs to be emphasised. Indeed, the fundamental premise of the traditional system was the lack of a significant amount of government securities in the market.

This characteristic disappeared in the late 1970s. The outstanding amount of government bonds totalled ¥109.7 trillion at the end of 1983, equivalent to 39.0 per cent of GNP. Including the obligations of local government and public corporations, the ratio would be as high as 58.3 per cent, far surpassing that of the United States. This is the result of large government deficits, which stood at 5.5 per cent of GNP in 1981/82, 5.4 per cent in 1982/83 and 4.7 per cent in 1983/84.

Reflecting these issues, both the size and the character of Japanese capital markets have changed very quickly. Open market transactions became the norm in the secondary markets for government bonds and repos transactions in government securities, and later in CDs, increased dramatically.

Indeed, it is in these areas of government securities and repos that fundamental changes in the Japanese financial markets began to take place. It is also expected that the appearance of large sums of near-maturity government bonds will trigger various deregulations in the short end of Japanese financial markets.

Despite the rapid transformation of traditional Japanese practices, the present state of deregulation is not satisfactory from the perspective of many foreign observers, including the US government.

In particular, the administrative controls by the Bank of Japan on call and bill transactions through the six money dealers generate negative feelings among foreign financial institutions. As the call and bill transactions are at the centre of the money markets, these guidances by the central bank, it is argued, would make other deregulation in this area insignificant. Moreover, direct bank dealing in these markets and deregulation of interbank deposit rates are more in accord with international practices.

The question here is quite fundamental, since it relates to the structure of implementation of Japanese monetary policy, including methods of money-supply control. Despite official explanations to the effect, no 'open market' operations are being conducted by Japanese authorities. What is occurring is bilateral dealing in liquidity by the authorities through the six money-market dealers who are the sole principals of transactions in the market.

Indeed, many deregulatory efforts have been made in this area in the past, and compared to ten years ago, even call and bill transactions are freer. Moreover, arbitrage between Euromarkets and such open markets in Tokyo as the *gensaki* repurchase agreement and CD markets is very active.

In addition, from the viewpoint of controlling money supply, the system has functioned quite efficiently and the performance of Japanese monetary policy so far has been relatively successful. However, the implicit quota system that results from the scheme is perceived by some participants in the market as arbitrary and unfair.

A similar type of phenomenon exists in the long-term end of the markets. Specifically, the bulk of national bonds have traditionally been underwritten by a captive syndicate consisting of almost all Japanese financial institutions. The rate and terms of issue have been determined by bilateral negotiations between the Ministry of Finance and the syndicate, resulting in an issue rate not necessarily consistent with that of the secondary market.

Private bond markets have also been dominated by four major securities companies and eight 'commissioned' banks. Although underwriting in the strict sense of the word is done by the four securities companies, the eight 'commissioned' banks advise on the amount, timing, the terms of flotation, coordinating negotiations, preparing contracts, receiving proceeds and delivering certificates. This participation of banks in the bond market is consistent with the standard procedure of securing bonds with collateral, since such practice is normal in long-term bank lending.

Some analysts have argued that bank dominance in long-term lending was due to these implicit cartelised controls on the bond market. The causality, however, is the reverse. It was possible for the banks to cartelise the market because of bank dominance in this area, through the long-term credit bank system and the semi-automatic rollover of short-term credits and so forth.

Moreover, a stable market in corporate bonds would have required the existence of a developed market in risk-free government securities, to act as a reference against which to determine appropriate corporate bond yields. The small amounts of government bonds outstanding in Japan before 1975 would have prevented the existence of such a developed government bond market, even if controls imposed on members of the government bond syndicate with regard to resale had not existed. Hence, with no frame of reference within which to set corporate bond rates, the development of a major market in long-term bonds would have been difficult until the late 1970s.

The situation, however, did change dramatically in the late 1970s and various deregulations have been implemented toward the development of government and private bond markets. The issue here again relates to the traditional role of Japanese banks which have, in reality, provided the bulk of long-term funds to industry. If open markets continue to develop and Japanese firms increase their share of funds raised there, the banks' importance, at least in this respect, would dwindle. Moreover, since the proliferation of open markets may lead to the issuance of commercial paper, the banks' function in providing short-term liquidity could also be affected.

Another sticky issue is that membership of the Tokyo Stock Exchange has been quite restrictive. Although legal barriers were lifted in May 1982, at present there are neither foreign financial institutions nor smaller Japanese securities companies represented among the standing 83 members.

Along with this issue is the fixed-commission structure for stock brokerage, stipulated by ordinance. Both of these features date back to the early 1950s, when the American Glass–Steagal practice was introduced in Japan. Since the Japanese had pursued universal banking up until that time, the need arose to protect and foster security companies as independent entities in the market. It is rather ironical that, having followed the lead of the US authorities 30 years ago in raising barriers between commercial and investment banking to foster the securities industry, Japan now finds the US government insisting on having these barriers lowered.

To summarise, although there remain some restrictive aspects in the Japanese financial markets, particularly in interbank transactions such as interbank deposits and call and bill transactions and in primary markets for government and private bonds and securities brokerage, fundamental transformations are taking place very rapidly, forcing the Japanese structure to adapt to international norms. Although the changes themselves have their primary origins in domestic factors, the pace of adaptation is being accelerated by political pressures from abroad.

In this context, it is interesting to note that the creation of an international banking facility (IBF) in Tokyo was proposed before the liberalisation–internationalisation negotiations between the two countries. According to Takashi Hosomi, President of the Overseas Economic Cooperation Fund, a Tokyo IBF was conceived prior to 1983 to implement deregulation in harmony with domestic monetary systems and policy.[4] A brief outline of the Hosomi proposal is given below.

A gradual, step-by-step internationalisation is necessary to assure the effectiveness of domestic monetary policy and to secure harmony between offshore and domestic banking systems.[5] The problem of achieving harmony with the domestic monetary system and policy involves obtaining the consent of all involved, bearing in mind the overflow effect the establishment of an IBF would have on the domestic market.

The scope of IBF activities should be restricted at first, gradually being expanded with the passage of time. The IBF system should be designed so as to allow future expansion and integration of the domestic and offshore sectors. Business tax breaks should not be offered, as the establishment of the Tokyo IBF is not aimed at simply creating an artificial offshore centre.

Financial institutions would set up special IBF accounts, separate from their existing domestic accounting procedures. These accounts would have no direct impact on the deregulation of the domestic market or on the effectiveness of domestic monetary policies, but they would promote internationalisation of the Tokyo market. IBF participants could thus be regarded in the same way as the existing overseas branches of Japanese financial institutions.

As a precaution, the maintenance of yen settlement accounts by the IBFs would be prohibited for the time being, taking into considersation possible effects on domestic M1, and negotiable CD, BA issues, and so on would be prohibited for some time, in order to segregate the IBF from domestic operations.

In accordance with Euromarket practices, interest-bearing deposits (with no restrictions on period) denominated in various currencies including the yen could be accepted as deposits. Eligible IBF depositors would be non-residents, other IBFs, overseas financial institutions and the domestic and overseas main and branch offices of financial institutions which have established IBFs (main and branch accounts). IBF deposits would be exempt from interest-rate requirements, reserve requirements, deposit-insurance requirements and withholding tax on interest.

Assets permitted to IBFs would basically consist of advances to non-residents including loans, non-residents' bonds, loans/deposits with other IBFs and overseas financial institutions, and loans/deposits with the domestic main and branch offices of financial institutions which had established IBFs.

In order for the Tokyo IBF to achieve the anticipated results, the deregulation and flexibility of administrative organs must be ensured, through reforms such as the abolition of interest-rate ceilings on deposits, exemption from reserve requirements, exclusion from deposit-insurance requirements and exemption from withholding and stamp duty taxes. Such reform is vital for establishing the confidence of depositors in the IBF.

Total foreign-currency assets and advances to non-residents, currently held in the domestic accounts of banks in Tokyo would probably shift to the Tokyo IBF. After gradually gaining popularity, the Tokyo IBF would absorb funds from overseas investors as well. Outstanding yen deposits by non-residents counterbalancing the above advances may well shift to the Tokyo IBF in the initial stages also, not to mention at least a portion of Euroyen accounts. Euroyen outstanding in the Tokyo market would steadily increase, and it is certain that the yen deposits of overseas investors would be shifted en masse to the liberalised Tokyo IBF.

In the medium-and long-term view, the founding of the Tokyo market in the Pacific Rim area, where rich investment opportunities lie and continued high growth is expected, would be beneficial to the nations in this area and to the Hong Kong and Singapore markets.

The Tokyo IBF should be designed to promote the deregulation and internationalisation of the Tokyo market without causing excessive friction to the system. The argument that even the mere idea of this proposed market will have an impact on the domestic monetary system is not an argument against the new market, but against deregulation and flexibility in the monetary system. The Tokyo IBF would be an extension of the Tokyo dollar call money market and, as far as foreign-currency transactions are concerned, would entail no great liberalisation.

The creation of the Tokyo IBF would provide an immeasurable boost to the international operations of Japanese banks, as well as help alleviate monetary friction with Europe and the US and relieve to some extent the discontent of foreign banks in Japan.

The above is a brief summary of the main points raised in the Hosomi Plan. When the Plan was published in 1983, the general reaction of Japanese financial institutions was that the pace of internationalisation of the yen and the deregulation of the Japanese financial system would be too rapid, and that a much more gradual approach was called for.

Most of the financial institutions could see no reason for a two-tier system, with domestic and offshore markets existing side by side and the same transactions being conducted in different ways in parallel markets. They felt that such a state of affairs could have an adverse effect on the existing Japanese financial system and monetary controls.

For example, at present, when a non-resident wishes to raise domestic yen, he has only the one option of accepting the long-term prime rate as the benchmark rate. However, once an offshore market is established, Euroyen floating rates may be applied, causing the long-term prime rate system in the domestic market to suffer. This is the main reason for the financial institutions' opposition to the Hosomi Plan.

The Bank of Japan's immediate objection to US-style IBFs is that the almost certain 'leakage' of Euroyen back into the domestic market would dilute the central bank's control of Japan's money supply. Furthermore, the Bank thinks the offshore yen market is already big enough. 'We have never encouraged the expansion of the Euroyen market; we have been treating it as a kind of mistress living abroad. To create the Tokyo offshore centre means that we are going to give a kind of legal charter to the Euroyen market. It means bringing that charming mistress home to live with our wife.'

Such are the reasons behind the lack of support for the Hosomi Plan amongst Japanese financial institutions, with the exception of the Ministry of Finance and the large city banks. Consequently, Mr Hosomi's Plan has been left up in the air, with no further detailed work being done on his proposal, nor other concrete proposals forthcoming.

As was described at the outset, the US government had been pushing for deregulation, originally at least, for logically untenable reasons. However, as more US experts recognise the weak link between the exchange rate and deregulation, their position gradually shifted to one of advocating deregulation for freer international financial transactions. Given the fact that services are one of America's most competitive industries on an international level, this position is understandable. Nevertheless, deregulation itself is a domestic rather than international issue. In any event, US–Japan negotiations went ahead despite the fact that the logic of the US position was not at all clear and the issues became more and more political as the Presidential election neared.

On the occasion of President Reagan's visit in November 1983, the establishment of a yen–dollar committee, a subcabinet-level ad hoc committee, was announced jointly by Finance Minister Takeshita and Secretary Regan. This working group was set the task of reporting by spring 1984.

Its first meeting took place in Tokyo in late February 1984, when paradoxically the yen had strengthened and the US dollar weakened. As a result, the original purpose of the committee, namely deregulation in order to correct the yen/dollar misalignment, gradually disappeared from the US negotiators' side and deregulation itself became the central issue within the committee.

The ad hoc committee continued to meet until May 1984, when the final report was released. Although each item may seem to cover minute technical details, these agreements do appear to have fundamental implications for the ongoing structural transformation of finance.

Firstly, deregulation of Euroyen impact loans, further liberalisation of CD-related issues and the possible creation of a TB market should have an impact on the short-term markets. The latter deregulations would have been made even in the absence of US pressure. The deregulation of interbank deposit and call and bill transactions are not mentioned in the report, as these are probably more domestic issues than the other items mentioned, and should be followed up by the Japanese themselves.

Secondly, deregulation of Euoyen bond issues should have a fundamental effect on the issue markets for domestic bonds, which have so far been somewhat restrictive. Along with the huge turnover and the new issue of government bonds expected in 1985, this liberalisation of Euroyen bonds should substantially accelerate the deregulation process in the long-term market.

Thirdly, a Japanese commitment to consider the membership issue in the Tokyo Stock Exchange should open the way for deregulation in securities broking.

Throughout the negotiations, the Japanese government's stance has been a positive one, since each of the issues raised would eventually have had to be dealt with, foreign pressure or no. There are, however, two important principles upon which this stance is based. The first is to pursue a step-by-step approach, in order to lessen the domestic impact of any deregulatory measures. The second principle is that Japan must carry out any such measures to suit Japan's own financial system and organisation, regardless of pressure from America and elsewhere.

The next and most fundamental question then is how and in what order should Japan deregulate in order to avoid unnecessary frictions, domestic or international.

First and foremost, the interbank market must be tackled. If this market is not deregulated first, the effectiveness of other measures will be limited. It is all very fine for the mutual banks to gather funds at high interest through MMCs, but what then do they do with those funds? To date, these institutions have invested the bulk of their funds in the interbank market. So, unless this market is also liberalised, deregulation of retail instruments becomes rather meaningless. Apart from Japan, there is almost no country which still regulates its interbank market interest rates.

The next step should be the wholesale market, namely the markets where large corporations and institutional investors participate. In this respect, the establishment of a TB or BA market is likely. The future liberalisation of commission fees for large stock transactions must also be considered, while forex commission is by and large already liberalised.

The establishment of a TB or BA market should lead to deregulation of interest rates for large deposits, a development which will necessitate reconsidering the present official discount rate and prime lending rate. This in turn should lead to the next stage: the liberalisation of the retail markets and small transactions. As there is no real 'retail market' as such, this issue would seem to be a matter of protecting consumer interests rather than involving market principles and rationalisation.

The last issue is the segmentation of banking business: investment versus commercial banking, trust versus commercial banking and long-term versus short-term financing.

As witnessed in US-Japan negotiations, this question could easily surface as a difficult political issue. However, this too is a domestic matter and should not be viewed as an item for the negotiating table. Nevertheless, this traditional segmentation is gradually being eroded and barriers have been lowered quite rapidly in recent years.

I have referred to this restructing of the Japanese financial system as a 'revolution'. What must be emphasised here, however, is the fact that this 'revolution' is being wrought, not by regulatory authorities, but by market forces themselves. In other words, administrative desegmentation will continue to follow, not precede, market deregulation.

11 Trade in financial services: its nature, causes, growth prospects and social effects

HERBERT G. GRUBEL

Three factors incite the interest of scholars and policy workers in the prospective growth of financial services in the Pacific region. First, there has been the spectacular growth of the financial sectors of Hong Kong and Singapore in recent years.[1] Can other countries replicate the success of these two centres and through financial sectoral growth enjoy a powerful stimulus for the rest of their economies?

Second, research has shown that in industrial countries the service sector has grown much more rapidly than the rest of the economy. In the United States especially, projections of this trend into the future have raised fears about a US economy without industrial production[2] and goods exports. Under these conditions, US imports have to be paid for by the export of services. Unfortunately, trade in services is hampered by many obstacles. To overcome these, the US government has taken a number of initiatives on the diplomatic front.[3] A better understanding of the nature and magnitude of trade in financial services will help policymakers in the Pacific rim countries deal effectively with these US initiatives.

Third, the growth of international banking went hand in hand with the growth of financial integration of most Pacific rim countries. This integration brought benefits through increased capital flows and financial efficiency. But it also caused a loss of national economic sovereignty. This loss of sovereignty is of great concern to policymakers and, to the extent that it is linked to trade in financial services, needs to be studied carefully.

In the first part of this paper I analyse the nature and likely magnitude of trade in financial services generally. The second part examines the nature of Hong Kong's and Singapore's financial business. Part three draws conclusions for policy from the preceding analysis, paying special attention to the trade-off between allocative efficiency and economic sovereignty.

THE NATURE AND MAGNITUDE OF TRADE IN FINANCIAL SERVICES

The financial service industry accomplishes two tasks. First, it clears payments among economic agents that arise from the production of goods and services, the activities of government and foreign economic relations. The cheque-clearing services of banks, foreign exchange and cash transactions are the main components of business accomplishing this task.

Second, it intermediates between ultimate savers and borrowers of funds. This task is accomplished by the use of a wide variety of debt instruments such as equities, bank deposits, fixed and variable interest securities with different maturities and security features including bills, certificates of deposit, mortgages, bonds and mutual funds. All of these may be the obligations of ultimate borrowers such as manufacturing corporations, governments or individuals that spend the proceeds on real assets, goods or services. Or they may be the obligiations of intermediaries such as banks and insurance companies that hold to themselves the obligations of ultimate borrowers. To meet the diverse needs of ultimate lenders and borrowers, modern financial industries have developed an almost bewildering variety of instruments, much as consumer goods industries have developed many varieties of basic goods.

It should be noted that the financial intermediation industry performs two distinctively different tasks. One consists of the initial sale and ultimate redemption of obligations. This is performed mainly by so-called merchant banking houses and commercial banks through loan consortia. The second task involves the brokerage of existing debt instruments in organised stock exchanges or informal kerbs on over-the-counter markets.

THE MAGNITUDE OF THE FINANCIAL SERVICE SECTOR

In principle, the size of the financial service sector can be measured in three ways. The first considers the stock of outstanding debt obligations at any moment in time. The second measures the flow of transactions per time period, that is, the total value of securities, cash and foreign exchange that changed hands. The third sums the amount of real resources used up in the provision of the sector's services during a given period. This measure is the value-added of national income accounting.

Each of these three measures has advantages and disadvantages. For the present purposes of analysis, the value-added is the most appropriate. Unfortunately, however, historic time series and data for different countries were available to me only at a level of aggregation known as 'Finance, Insurance and Real Estate', FIR for short and SIC 9 in standard national account nomenclature.

Table 11.1 presents data on the contribution of this sector to Gross Domestic Product (GDP) in countries of the Pacific rim. As can be seen, the first group of countries comprises the industrialised nations, the United States, Japan and Canada, where in 1980 the sector contributed 20.7 per cent, 15.7 per cent and 9.6 per cent of GDP, respectively. During the period 1970–80 the US and Japanese ratios grew by 13.7 per cent and 27.6 per cent, respectively, while the Canadian ratio remained unchanged.[4]

The second group consists of the developing countries, Malaysia and

Table 11.1   Finance, insurance and real estate as percentage of GDP: selected countries, 1970–80

	United States	Canada	Japan	Malaysia	Indonesia	Hong Kong	Singapore
1970	18.2	9.8	12.3	8.7	2.6	14.9	13.9
1971	18.4	10.1	13.5	8.7	2.8	18.3	14.2
1972	18.2	10.1	14.1	8.5	3.2	21.9	14.3
1973	18.0	9.9	14.2	8.3	3.3	19.1	14.7
1974	18.4	9.7	13.5	8.1	3.6	16.0	15.2
1975	18.2	10.4	14.2	8.4	3.9	15.5	15.5
1976	18.2	10.7	13.9	8.0	4.0	16.0	15.5
1977	18.9	10.8	14.1	8.0	4.5	18.3	15.3
1978	19.3	11.1	14.8	8.2	4.7	19.6	15.4
1979	19.8	10.0	15.1	8.2	4.9	20.8	15.8
1980	20.7	9.6	15.7	8.3	4.9		17.0

Source: UN Yearbook of National Account Statistics Vol. 1, Tables 1 and 10 for each country.

Indonesia. As can be seen, Malaysia's ratio was 8.3 per cent in 1980, which is much less than that of the United States and Japan, but only slightly smaller than that of Canada. Indonesia's FIR industries in 1980 contributed 4.9 per cent to GDP. Noteworthy is the fact that Indonesia's ratio nearly doubled and Malaysia's dropped slightly during the period 1970–80.

The data for Hong Kong and Singapore show that the FIR sector in these countries is comparable to that of the industrial countries. Of interest is the great volatility of the data for Hong Kong: from 14.9 per cent in 1970 the figure jumped to 22.6 per cent in 1972, dropped to 15.5 per cent in 1975 and reached 20.8 per cent again only in 1979. Singapore, on the other hand, showed a relatively steady growth from 13.9 per cent in 1970 to 17.0 per cent in 1980. This difference may well be due to the greater volatility of Hong Kong housing prices during the period.

The data in Table 11.1 confirm conventional wisdom regarding the importance of FIR in industrial countries, the sector's smaller role in developing countries and its growth and significance in Hong Kong and Singapore. We may conclude confidently that industrialisation of the LDCs in the Pacific Basin will bring relatively rapid growth in the FIR sector.

RELATION TO OTHER SECTOR GROWTH

However, Table 11.2 shows that during the 1960s in Singapore, the trade and finance sector grew only at roughly the same rate as GDP. The leading growth sectors during this period were construction, manufacturing and utilities. During the 1970s, on the other hand, trade and finance had the second largest growth rate after transportation and communications, but utilities and manufacturing grew at nearly the same pace.

It is interesting to note the similar experience of Canada. During the 1960s trade and finance grew exactly at the rate of GDP. During the 1970s this sector retained the growth rate of the preceding decade while that of GDP was lowered significantly by the reduced growth of all of the goods-producing industries.

Figure 11.1   The growth of service- and goods-producing industries in Canada, 1935–84

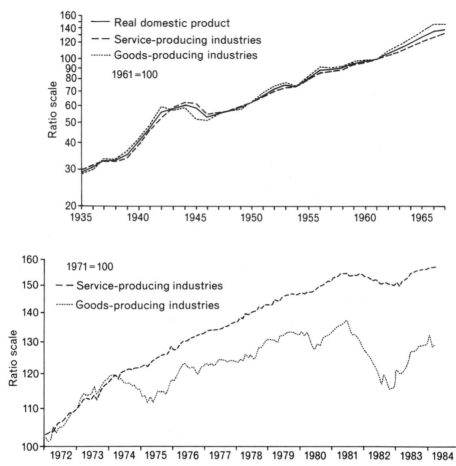

Source: Statistics Canada *Real Domestic Product by Industry* Cat. 61–213.

The data in Table 11.2 suggest that the trade and finance sectors grew in proportion to GDP during the prosperous 1960s and were a source of stability and stimulus to growth during the 1970s when the energy crisis, inflation and recessions slowed output growth in the goods-producing sectors.

FINANCE IN PERSPECTIVE TO INSURANCE AND REAL ESTATE

Table 11.3 shows the contributions to GDP which are made by the individual components of the class Finance, Insurance and Real Estate in Canada during the period 1971–81.[5]

Table 11.2 Trade and finance growth rates in perspective: Singapore and Canada

	Canada		Singapore	
	1960–70	1970–81	1960–70	1970–81
	Average annual growth rates at constant factor costs			
Agriculture	2.5	1.8	5.0	1.7
Mining	6.5	−0.2	9.0	8.8
Manufacturing	6.8	3.2	13.0	9.7
Construction	4.5	2.2	12.3	5.8
Electricity, gas and water	7.9	6.3	10.6	10.0
Transport and communications	6.6	5.3	7.8	14.0
Trade and finance	5.6	5.3	9.0	10.1
GDP at market prices	5.6	3.8	8.8	8.6

Source: IBRD *World Tables* 3rd edn, 1983.

Table 11.3 Finance compared with insurance and real estate: Canada, 1971–81 (industries as percentage of GDP)

Year	Finance industries SIC 901	Insurance carriers SIC 902	Insurance agencies and real estate industries SIC 903	Imputed rent	Banks and other depositories SIC 701	Security brokers and dealers SIC 705
1971	2.28	0.92	3.87	3.89	1.52	0.21
1972	2.34	0.86	3.64	3.71	1.53	0.23
1973	2.35	0.72	3.76	3.39	1.57	0.23
1974	2.38	0.58	3.79	3.20	1.61	0.17
1975	2.64	0.66	3.70	3.19	1.82	0.17
1976	2.57	0.90	3.77	3.27	1.78	0.16
1977	2.58	0.89	3.91	3.53	1.70	0.15
1978	2.54	0.88	4.06	3.61	1.80	0.19
1979	2.37	0.70	4.03	3.55	1.61	0.23
1980	2.44	0.60	4.10	3.69	1.57	0.34
1981	2.28	0.57	4.24	4.23	1.50	0.26

Source: Statistics Canada *Real Domestic Product by Industry* (April 1984) Cat. 61–213.

As can be seen, the Finance Industries, SIC 901, contributed only 2.28 per cent to Canadian GDP in 1971 and 1980. The contribution of insurance carriers, SIC 902, fluctuated between a high of 0.92 per cent in 1971 and a low of 0.57 per cent in 1981. In 1981, insurance agencies, the real estate industry and imputed rent made up 70.8 per cent of the total of the FIR sector. A similar relationship existed in other years.

In Table 11.3 the contributions of banks and other deposit-accepting institutions (SIC 701) and of security brokers and dealers (SIC 705) are shown separately. The data suggest that these two industries represent the bulk of the category finance industries.

We may conclude from the data in Table 11.3 that the contribution to GDP of finance industries proper is relatively small in Canada. If this relationship also holds for LDCs and Singapore and Hong Kong, the data in Table 11.3 have important implications for the future growth in trade in financial services.

TRADE IN FINANCIAL SERVICES—RETURNS ON CAPITAL

Services generally are produced as a flow from stocks of physical, human, knowledge and financial capital. For example, aeroplanes and ships yield transportation services; the human capital of physicians produces medical services; the knowledge capital of computer firms underlies the sale of computer services; security portfolios bring investment income. Financial services draw on all four types of capital brought together in financial intermediary firms.

In the analysis of trade in financial services, it is important to distinguish between the trade in capital assets and the services proper. The flow of finance capital is recorded in the capital accounts of the balance of payments. The income from foreign-asset holdings is reflected in current trade on services accounts.[6]

Income and payments on capital have attracted the attention of analysis frequently in the past, mainly as part of the study of balance-of-payments structure and trends and the welfare effects of capital flows.[7] National balance-of-payments statistics show prominently data on trade in capital services. To avoid confusion, this type of international financial service trade will here be referred to as international factor service trade. It is not the main focus of this chapter. Other chapters in this volume deal with the balance-of-payments and financial interdependence aspects of international capital and factor service flows.

TRADE IN FINANCIAL SERVICES PROPER

National balance-of-payments statistics do not routinely publish statistics on trade in services that have as their domestic counterpart the value-added of FIR noted above. The main reason for this state of affairs is that, historically, financial services have been either intermediate inputs into exportables, or they have been non-tradable.

Financial services required in the production of exported goods and services are part of the final price of these exports. As such, they are reflected in balance-of-payments statistics, but just like other intermediate inputs, they are not shown separately.

The services provided by financial intermediaries to consumers typically involve close personal relationships. Bank lending and borrowing, pension and trust management and trade in securities with private wealthholders draw heavily on personal knowledge of the creditworthiness and character of transactors. In the production and maintenance of this essential knowledge in the past, physical proximity has been so essential that for all practical purposes the sevices were non-tradable. Historically, therefore, balance-of-payments accounts on financial services have been zero or negligibly small.

However, in recent years changes in communications and transportation technologies and different regulation of financial sectors in different countries have encouraged the spread of multinational banks and enterprises and increased travel. As a by-product of these developments, financial services have ceased to be non-tradables. In the next section the nature and likely growth of this new financial trade will be analysed in detail.

Before we turn to this task it is useful to note that current practices used in the construction of national accounts are based on the assumption that bank services are non-tradable.[8] Thus, national income accountants apportion the value-added of banks and other such institutions into intermediate inputs and consumption according to the proportion of the banks' liabilities owned by firms and private individuals respectively. There is no provision for the fact that in recent times some proportion of the firms and individuals may be foreigners.

As a result of this practice the level and growth of national income and of the financial sector are biased downward. This may be seen by considering the allocation of $1 million of bank services to the domestic manufacturing sector under present practices. That sector's value-added and therefore contribution to GDP is lowered by $1 million, as financial services along with other intermediate inputs are deducted from final sales. Now assume that in fact the $1 million bank services did not go to a domestic but to a foreign firm with all its manufacturing facilities abroad. Under these conditions, the sale of financial services should be treated as an export. As such, it would raise GDP by the full $1 million and would not diminish the value-added of domestic manufacture.

The bias from the disregard of the export of financial services in national accounting practices has been negligible historically and probably still is for relatively closed economies. However, for small, open countries and especially those specialising in financial service production, like Singapore, Hong Kong and Luxembourg, the existing practices may involve a serious bias.[9]

DIRECT TRADE IN FINANCIAL SERVICES

Direct trade in financial services takes place between financial intermediaries in one country and residents of another. It is useful to distinguish four types of such financial business.

Traditional Capital Flows Intermediation

International capital flows are the end of a long chain of interregional flows mediated by the financial industry. Thus, banks in small towns attempt to bring together local lenders and borrowers. Local imbalances are passed on to regional centres and remaining imbalances reach national centres. Groups of countries often have regional supra-national centres, with New York serving as the world centre of finance. Imbalances within national centres give rise to international capital flows.[10]

Singapore and Hong Kong are regional, supra-national centres that attract loan and deposit business from within their territories and neighbouring countries. This regional business was fostered by the comparative advantage which the local communities developed during their colonial status, when English banking skills were the best in the world and dominated international capital markets. Their comparative advantage also results from the central location of these countries and the deliberate support which government policy provided for its advance. Human capital, good communications systems and a favourable regulatory environment are essential ingredients in the development of this business.

But Singapore and Hong Kong also serve as centres through which the region is linked to other parts of the world. As such, they are members of a small club of centres that includes London, New York, Tokyo, Luxembourg, Bahrain and Panama. These centres provided the expertise that put together the very large loans of the 1970s, which in the final analysis brought together as ultimate lenders and borrowers the OPEC surplus countries and the LDCs with ambitious development plans.

There is little doubt that the regional, supra-national intermediation role of Singapore and Hong Kong will continue to grow in the future along with the growth of income and wealth in the Pacific region. The intermediation business derived from OPEC surpluses has diminished and is likely to give little further stimulus. On the other hand, traditional capital flows from industrial countries to Pacific region LDCs should increase further and add to the business of the two centres as the entire region enjoys rapid development.

It is easy to overestimate the value-added that is involved in the business giving rise to international capital flows. The principal sums may be large, but value-added consists merely of the spread between lending and borrowing rates and some placement fees. The lower cost of information caused by the electronics revolution will probably put further pressure on these spreads in the future. To the extent that the spread reflects risk, increasing international diversification of lenders serves to reduce risk and therefore narrow the spreads. Growth reduction will also be caused by policies of neighbouring countries designed to develop their own financial sectors.

Diverted Trade

Analysts of Euro and Asian currency markets are in almost unanimous agreement that the growth of these markets since the mid-1960s is largely due to trade diversion caused by taxation and regulation in the industrial countries. In chapter 8, Hewson showed how the Singapore government carefully and deliberately deregulated and removed taxes on international banks in order to encourage them to take up residence there. The absence of reserve requirements on commercial bank deposits denominated in foreign currencies undoubtedly represents the greatest single stimulus for the growth of the Asian currency business of Hong Kong and Singapore.[11]

The Asian currency business basically involves lending and borrowing by firms and individuals who, in the absence of differential taxation, would do their lending and borrowing in locations more suitable to their basic business. For example, the corporate headquarters of Exxon and IBM are in New York, where they do most of their banking transactions. In the past, they would also lend and borrow short-term and meet long-term financing needs in this centre. However, because of the differential rate of taxation on intermediation business, these firms can obtain both higher rates on their deposits and lower costs on their borrowing abroad than they could in New York. Often, they do this business abroad with branches of their New York banks.

There is no doubt that a substantial part of the Singapore and Hong Kong financial business is due to this locational diversion.[12] Unfortunately, it is not possible to quantify exact amounts. However, in the assessment of the future growth of trade in financial services, it is important to note that this type of business may well cease to grow and may even shrink, as many industrial countries deregulate their financial sectors, reserve requirements are reduced and nominal interest rates drop. Lower nominal interest rates reduce the implicit effective tax rate of given reserve requirements. The withdrawal of several foreign banks from London, Singapore and Hong Kong in recent years shows the effects of recent developments in the field. Working in the opposite direction and increasing incentives for locational diversion are the expected further reductions in communications costs, which lower the costs and risks of international branch banking.

Global Money Market Business

The US federal funds market has for several decades permitted banks to lend and borrow very short-term funds. Through this market, US banks have been able to use a given high-powered money base to generate a greater money supply than was possible previously.

In recent years, a worldwide equivalent of the US federal funds market has developed. It arbitrages between very short-term national money markets and takes advantage of global time-zone differences. Singapore and Hong Kong banks participate in this business, aided by their favourable time-zone location and the existence of efficient communications and banking systems.

Unfortunately, it is not possible to document the magnitude of the value-added in these banking operations. However, it is known that all of these operations are between banks and take place at extremely thin margins. The value-added is probably very small relative to the other business under discussion, though nearly all of it represents direct trade with other countries. This trade is likely to grow with the real growth of the world economy.

Direct Financial Service and Retail Business

The electronic revolution and deregulation have permitted the financial sectors of industrial countries to expand the menu of differentiated payments and investment services. Charge cards, automated tellers, money market funds, travellers cheques, Euro-credit cheque systems and others have made it easier, more convenient or cheaper to make payments. Mutual funds, futures markets for securities, commodities and currencies, credit-card systems operated by banks and retailers have raised returns to lending and lowered the risks and cost of borrowing and lending.

It is not clear whether and by how much this product differentiation of the financial service industries has raised their value-added. On the one hand, the new services may have met some previously hidden needs and there has probably been some increased value-added through linkages with other services. An analogy may be useful here. The product differentiation in the automobile industry and the sale of built-in music systems may have induced an increased consumption of automobile services as a proportion of GDP.

On the other hand, the electronics revolution and deregulation also have lowered costs of production and raised efficiency. This could have resulted in reduced overall spending on financial services, just as the lower cost of cars can encourage less spending on transportation.

Conditions in Hong Kong and Singapore

Hong Kong's and Singapore's financial service industries have similarly expanded the menu of differentiated financial services. However, it is likely that observed growth in this field reflects primarily the income elasticity of demand for these services. In the future, this elasticity will continue to lead to growth of the industry.

International trade in financial service and retail business generally is small because all of it requires, or benefits from, the physical proximity of customers and agents. Local banks and securities dealers are infinitely more convenient for business than are their foreign counterparts, in spite of the low costs of telephone communications.

Tourist Business

There exist some financial services that are useful mostly for tourists and international business travel, such as credit cards and travellers' cheques systems. Clearly, in this field, global integration gives rise to significant economies of scale. The provision of these services to travellers and licence fees to Visa, American Express and similar firms result in international transactions on financial service accounts. Unfortunately, no data are available on the magnitude of this business. It should be noted, however, that margins in these activities cannot be large since electronics keep costs low and rents from product differentiation are limited by the relative ease of entry. Nevertheless, the value of this tourist-related trade should continue to grow together with the expected increase in international travel.

Differentiated Services and Product Cycles in the Financial Service Trade

Differentiated financial services, developed by intermediaries in the industrial countries, are unlikely to give rise to intra-industry trade[13] in the way product differentiation has in consumer goods. The reason for this is that differentiation in the service field is easy to imitate and adapt to local conditions. For example, economies of scale in providing NOW accounts are negligible relative to those encountered in the production of automobiles and video recorders. The special ingredients of success that underlie the worldwide franchising of retailers in the fast-food, hotel, clothing and car-rental business, appear to be present in the financial service business to a much smaller degree. However, even if there is a significant expansion of global branches of the American Express Company and Merill Lynch serving local consumers, the amount of international trade in financial services due to it is likely to be small. After all, most of the business is with locals and most employees are recruited locally. The essential foreign input that gives rise to foreign payments consists of some top-level managerial input, product know-how and the economies of linkage to a global information and advertising network.

In this context it is worth noting that one of the most dynamic innovators in the financial service field in the United States has been Chicago's International Money Market. This institution is the offspring of the well-known Chicago Mercantile Exchange and it pioneered successfully trade in foreign exchange futures, among other financial instruments. For some time, Asians wishing to invest in such futures had to do business with the Chicago institution. The result was trade in financial services. However, recently there was an announcement that the Singapore Money Exchange (SIMEX) would be established and offer much the same services as the Chicago IMM. While cooperation between the two centres can be expected to be high, international trade in financial services should drop, much as the US export of cars drops when General Motors opens a manufacturing plant abroad.

Vernon has shown that US manufacturing firms have been able to maintain exports in spite of foreign imitation of product differentiation. They produce a constant flow of innovations.[14] The resultant product cycle trade reflects the comparative advantage of the United States in human- and knowledge-capital endowment.

The possible existence of a similar service cycle trade in finance is potentially important for Singapore and Hong Kong. These centres appear to be at a stage of development where available skills are more suited for imitation than innovation. However, the differentiated financial services available in these centres may well serve the entire region.

THE BENEFICIAL EFFECTS OF TRADE IN FINANCIAL SERVICES: THE EXPERIENCE OF HONG KONG AND SINGAPORE

The development of human- and knowledge-capital resources rather than the availability of basic, low-cost labour provide the basis of exploitable comparative advantage in Hong Kong and Singapore. Statistics show that Hong Kong and Singapore have financial industries that are large in comparison with those of other developing countries in the region. This fact reflects the successful development of the human and knowledge capital, which is partly the outcome of historical traditions and partly the result of deliberate government policies, especially in Singapore. Because of their locations and the characteristics of the neighbouring countries, a significant proportion of the value-added in financial service industries in Hong Kong and Singapore is due to exports.

The decision to concentrate human- and knowledge-capital formation on these industries appears to be rational and intelligent, given the basic original factor endowments of these two small countries. The growth of the financial service industries has undoubtedly contributed significantly to the countries' increased productivity. Further human- and knowledge-capital formation in this industry is likely to yield similar positive results.

The development of the financial service industries of Hong Kong and Singapore has also increased the efficiency of the capital markets of these countries and of other countries in the region. This has resulted in better use of scarce capital resources, lowered transaction costs and increased capital inflows from abroad.

These benefits accrue to the two countries and the region largely in the form of externalities. They are nevertheless very important and may become even more so in the future. The entire literature on financial repression discussed in other chapters in this volume stands in support of this proposition.[15]

It is well known that the benefits of financial development and integration with world markets are acquired at the cost of reduced national economic sovereignty. The free, rapid and massive movement of capital between countries should make it impossible to have interest rates, exchange rates, or both, that are optimal for the pursuit of Keynesian employment policies, especially the choice of an optimal inflation–unemployment trade-off. However, the conventional wisdom on economic sovereignty in the Keynesian sense has been challenged by monetarist theories and empirical evidence during the 1970s. The opportunity for a longer run trade-off betweem inflation and unemployment seems largely illusory.

Instead, theory and empirical evidence have shown that the true costs of integrating nations into the global capital market is greater susceptibility to cyclical and random disturbances. The inflations and recessions of the 1970s were worldwide to an extent unknown before the integration of the world's capital markets.

The experiences of Hong Kong and Singapore during the 1970s and early 1980s are, by and large, consistent with this world wide experience. However, while most industrial countries and the LDCs of Africa and South America went through periods of absolute, real declines of GNP, Hong Kong, Singapore and their close neighbours only experienced slowdowns in growth rates.

These facts may be explained by two characteristics. Singapore and Hong Kong have always insisted on a strict separation between Asian-currency and related business on the one hand and their domestic financial development on the other. While this separation has not been entirely successful—Singapore residents can now make deposits and take out loans in the Asian currency business—it has been tight enough to prevent the excesses that caused the overexpansion and debt crisis in so many other countries during the 1970s. And, with some exceptions, governments of the region kept realistic perspectives on both the alleged energy crisis and the seemingly very low cost of foreign capital. These experiences suggest that the development of financial sectors and trade in financial services will bring potential loss of economic sovereignty and may increase economic instability. But they also show that intelligent management can deal effectively with these costs of financial development. Under these conditions, the benefits from this development in the form of capital market efficiency and higher factor productivity clearly outweigh the costs.

In preceding sections the analysis suggested that the growth of Singapore's Asian currency business owed its success largely to selective deregulation in a surrounding sea of regulation. This fact has one important social implication if deregulation becomes more general. In the extreme, it could lead to a severe shrinking of this business in Singapore. Under these conditions, office space, communications facilities and human skills employed by the industry would have to find alternative uses. The adjustment costs would be a real social burden. It remains to be seen whether and when they arise, and how large they would be, but policymakers should be aware of the potential problem.

The attribution of the growth of the Asian currency business to selective deregulation also has important implications for other countries. It is highly unlikely that other centres can repeat Singapore's success by initiative and selective deregulation. There simply is not enough business to be diverted, little to be created, and 'learning by doing' economies have given Singapore a very significant productivity advantage. This, of course, does not mean that countries cannot develop strong, productivity-increasing domestic financial sectors. The limitation concerns trade in international financial services that is based on selective deregulation.

SUMMARY AND CONCLUSIONS

International trade in financial services, as contrasted with international capital flows and Asian currency markets, is a neglected field of study. The basic reason for this state of affairs is that in the past financial services required heavy local inputs, which made the services non-tradable except as intermediate inputs into conventional traded goods and services.

The falling costs of communication, heavy regulation of the financial sector and product differentiation through the application of computers have opened the possibility of increased trade in financial services. The rapid growth of Hong Kong's and Singapore's financial sectors in recent years appears to have been strongly influenced by opportunities for international trade.

Statistics on value-added by financial intermediaries suggest that, compared with more traditional export-oriented industries, the potential for trade in financial services is quite limited. In industrial Canada, the contribution of the financial sector to GDP is only about 2 or 3 per cent.

In the future, Singapore's export of financial services is likely to continue to grow as it performs its role as a regional, supra-national centre, serving its neighbours and linking the region to the world's capital markets. The growth of the Asian-currency business is more uncertain, as the government-created stimuli for its past development diminish with deregulation and lower interest rates. Future trade in differentiated payments and investment services is uncertain. In this field, locational advantages dominate over proprietary, product-differentiation characteristics, though there is a potential for short-lived service cycle trade and international franchising.

Trade in financial services in the Pacific and elsewhere is likely to have its main social effects not through the exploitation of comparative advantage. Instead, trade in financial services has its main social effects through its influence on the efficiency of national and regional capital markets. Foreign competition is a powerful antidote to financial repression by government policies. But trade in financial services also increases the level and volatility of international capital flows, and through them reduces national economic sovereignty. The social effects of this loss of sovereignty are, to a considerable degree, dependent upon the wisdom with which governments handle the opportunities and dangers, as recent history has shown.

Part IV Financial Interdependence and Macro Management

12 Recent US–Japan financial interactions under flexible exchange rates

MASARU YOSHITOMI

This chapter addresses the following four issues: the characteristics of recent misaligned dollar–yen exchange rates and the new dilemma facing Japanese macropolicies; US–Japan financial interdependence under flexible exchange rates; the nature and persistency of the current-account surplus of Japan; and the role of the Japanese financial market in world economic development. By highlighting these four issues, we reach the conclusion that Japan as a capital exporter could contribute better to the development of the world economy, if macroeconomic policies were coordinated more effectively between the two largest countries in the Pacific region.

CHARACTERISTICS OF RECENT MISALIGNED DOLLAR–YEN EXCHANGE RATES AND THE NEW DILEMMA FACING JAPANESE MACROPOLICIES

Misaligned dollar–yen exchange rates have remained a key financial issue in US–Japan economic relations over the recent few years. This is not only because Japan's current-account surplus will run to more than US$31 billion in 1984, according to the latest OECD Economic Outlook, or nearly 3 per cent of GNP. It is also because the Bank of Japan has been unable to be independent of such external development for its conduct of domestic monetary policy, causing high real interest rates in Japanese financial markets.

The growing surplus in Japan's current account includes an intolerably large bilateral trade imbalance, intolerable particularly to US politicians in a presidential election year, causing strong protectionist sentiment among industries beaten by weaker international competitiveness. This time, however, such weakened international competitiveness of US industries can be accounted for by the half-completed supplyside fiscal policy in the United States. Supplysiders rightly wanted to stimulate private savings, not private demand, since the US saves so little. For this purpose, they prevailed on the government to reduce marginal personal tax rates by about 25 per cent and introduced both accelerated depreciation measures and extended investment tax credits. To be successful in stimulating private savings, the large government deficit resultant from such income tax reductions should be contained by substantially cutting down overexpanded defence spending and social security benefits and raising indirect non-income taxes in accordance with the supplyside ideas. The November 1984 presidential election made it difficult to complete this policy package, however.

As a result, large non-cyclical structural budget deficits, as compared with the savings available, have had two unintended simultaneous effects. One is the rapid US domestic recovery since early 1983, and the other is the continued overvaluation of the US dollar, caused at least partly by high real dollar interest rates. These consequences easily explain the growing large US current-account deficit. It is no wonder that the US current-account deficit will amount to US$81 billion in 1984 and reach more than US$100 billion in 1985, according to the latest OECD Economic Outlook. These figures suggest that the richest country will suck in world savings to the extent of nearly 3 per cent of its large GNP, a historically unprecedented phenomenon.

The large US external deficit thus generated should find its counterpart in the rest of the world. Hence, Japan's larger current-account surplus in 1983–84 is largely a reflection of the US twin deficits, that is, the budget deficit and consequent external deficit. Many Japanese economists, particularly Keynesians, however, attribute Japan's large current-account surplus to weaker domestic demand. They believe that the recent larger current-account surplus has been a result of an excess supply of Japanese goods being pushed out of domestic markets due to weak internal demand, and not an excess demand for Japanese goods in the US markets, due to the demand-cum-strong dollar force attributable to the incomplete implementation of the supplyside fiscal policy package. In view of the abnormally large surplus on the current account of Japan in 1983–84, it is sometimes suggested that the Japanese government should undertake discretionary and expansionary Keynesian policy measures to reduce Japan's external surplus.

This suggestion is, however, very risky for two reasons. First, in principle, an expansionary fiscal policy should be aimed at achieving domestic, not external, equilibrium, that is, high employment without accelerating underlying inflationary expectations. This is because an expansionary fiscal policy may overshoot the target of domestic equilibrium, if such a policy is undertaken only for the purpose of reducing external surplus without taking into consideration the domestic deflationary gap. This is particularly important because the latest recession in 1981–1982 was very mild, and the deflationary gap has remained rather small in Japan. Thus, the present combination or coexistence of the large current-account surplus and the near-high employment provide the Japanese economy with a new dilemma under flexible exchange rates. If we were under fixed exchange rates, expansionary macroeconomic policies combined with revaluation of the yen would be most desirable in order to remedy this typical dilemma, and simultaneously to achieve domestic and external equilibrium. Under the floating exchange-rate regime, however, exchange rates are market determined, and so long as dollar–yen exchange rates continue to be misaligned due to the incomplete supplyside fiscal policy in the US, it would be almost impossible for Japan to conduct the switching policy aimed at appreciating the exchange of the yen. The introduction of the interest-rate equalisation tax, aimed at an appreciation of the yen, could be suggested together with, say, the introduction of investment credit tax. Apart from the question about its effectiveness, however, the interest-rate equalisation tax may generate even higher interest rates in the US, through reducing net capital outflow from Japan.

Second, an expansionary fiscal policy is risky because it would further boost the already high level of real interest rates. This is because, in the integrated international bond markets, under near-perfect substitutability between home and foreign bonds as discussed above, larger aggregate government deficits of both the United States and Japan would simply cause higher interest rates with unchanged private savings. A prerequisite for sustained economic growth is a reasonable level of interest rates. Today, as we are all aware, interest rates are too high in the sense that long-term nominal interest rates are higher than the expected growth rate of nominal GNP in most countries. Even in Japan, interest rates at the long end are around 7.5 per cent a year against an expected growth rate of about 6–6.5 per cent for nominal GNP in the medium run (4–4.5 per cent for real GNP and 2 per cent for GNP deflator). Larger aggregate deficits with the resultant higher interest rates would run counter to the prerequisite for sustained growth.

US–JAPAN FINANCIAL INTERDEPENDENCE UNDER FLEXIBLE EXCHANGE RATES

More than twenty years ago, Mundell-Fleming[1] clearly demonstrated that once international capital movements are introduced, there would be no mechanism of perfect insulation from foreign economic disturbances, even under flexible exchange rates. Theoretically, however, it cannot be predetermined whether an expansionary fiscal policy at home causes the exchange rate of the home currency to appreciate or depreciate. This is because it is not theoretically known whether the current-account deficit, induced by such expansionary fiscal policy, will outweigh the capital-account surplus, that is, the net capital inflow induced by higher interest rates, which are in turn caused by unaccommodated expansionary fiscal policy.

The world econometric model, developed by the Economic Planning Agency (EPA), can shed some light on this issue.[2] The EPA model is one of the first attempts in the academic world to endogenise exchange-rate movements through thorough modelling of the financial and balance-of-payments sectors of nine countries (summit seven, Australia and Korea), and to link them via an international trade linkage submodel. Individual country models are basically Keynesian so that the IS curve, the LM curve and the BP (balance-of-payments) curve could be generated for each country model through dynamic simulations. For determining the exchange rate, the structural balance-of-payments approach is adopted in such a way that credits and debits in the balance of payments, including the authorities' intervention in the foreign-exchange market, should be equalised for each quarter through exchange-rate movements within the given quarter. While the trade account is determined in flow terms by export and import functions under the explicit constraint of the international trade linkage submodel, where total world exports must be equal to total world imports, the capital account is determined in stock terms based on a portfolio approach to the asset-markets equilibrium. The remaining world economy, after subtracting nine individual countries, still accounts for around 40 per cent of the whole world GNP and trade. This is divided into six regions: Latin America, Asia (excluding South Korea), the Middle East, Western Europe (excluding West Germany, France, the United Kingdom and Italy), socialist countries, and the rest of the world. Each regional model is very simple, carrying basically only two behavioural equations of import demand and export prices. Since the EPA model thus grasps the whole world economy, exogenous variables are limited essentially to macropolicy variables (monetary and fiscal) of nine individual countries and export prices of the Middle East, essentially petroleum prices. By simulating the EPA multi-country model, the economic interdependence under flexible exchange rates, specifically the insulation and transmission mechanisms, can be analysed.

Let us summarise the essential features of the impact on the world economy of an expansionary fiscal policy in the United States by the use of multiplier simulations of the EPA model (see Table 12.1).

First, the effective exchange rate of the US dollar appreciates; that is, the exchange rate of non-US currency depreciates vis-à-vis the dollar when US fiscal policy becomes expansive. This impact on its own exchange rate of an expansionary US fiscal policy makes a sharp contrast to that of the same policy in other countries, where expansionary fiscal policies cause depreciations of their own currencies. This important asymmetry in the world economy is generated for the following reason. The LM curve of the United States is steeper than those of other countries. Interest rates are very sensitive to demand shocks in the goods market. The higher interest rates generated thus attract net capital inflow into the US, outweighing the worsening of the current account caused by the expansionary fiscal policy. In the case of expansionary fiscal policy undertaken by other countries, the response of interest rates to such demand shock and the resultant capital inflow are too small to offset the worsened current account.

Second, the effect of an expansionary US fiscal policy is transmitted to real GNP of other countries with greater force under flexible than under fixed exchange rates. In particular, the impact on real GNP in West Germany is much greater under the present floating regime, reflecting a large amount of capital outflow and the resultant large depreciations of the Deutschmark. Thus, the transmission effect is intensified under flexible exchange rates in the case of an expansionary fiscal policy undertaken by the United States.

The greater transmission effect arises largely from a stronger increase in net imports of other countries in real terms due to depreciations of their currencies vis-à-vis the dollar. In contrast, however, the effect of expansionary fiscal

Table 12.1 Effects of sustained increase in real government expenditure of the US by 1 per cent of real GNP (per cent, deviations from the standard solution)

Country	Year	Spot exchange rate		Real GNP		Absorption deflator		Short-term interest rate[a]		Current account[b]		Official settlement[b]	
		Fix	Flex	Fix	Flex	Fix	Flex	Fix	Flex	Fix	Flex	Fix	Flex
US	1	0	-0.59	2.02	2.01	0.61	0.57	1.05	1.02	-1.61	-1.47	-1.52	-2.46
	2	0	-0.71	2.01	2.03	1.45	1.38	1.40	1.38	-4.53	-4.52	-3.49	-4.17
	3	0	-0.29	1.81	1.84	2.16	2.12	1.69	1.70	-5.53	-5.07	-4.29	-3.38
JA	1	0	0.66	0.14	0.17	0.04	0.11	0.09	0.08	440	241	-589	25
	2	0	0.95	0.51	0.56	0.17	0.36	0.14	0.13	1864	1685	194	305
	3	0	0.78	0.79	0.88	0.32	0.59	0.14	0.12	3702	3804	117	483
GE	1	0	0.89	0.09	0.17	0.01	0.04	0.05	0.03	0.31	0.17	-1.31	-0.70
	2	0	2.25	0.36	0.59	0.05	0.20	0.15	0.07	1.24	1.48	-1.83	-0.62
	3	0	2.67	0.54	0.98	0.13	0.44	0.26	0.10	2.31	3.26	-2.48	-0.19
UK	1	0	0.32	0.08	0.11	0.04	0.06	0.36	0.35	135	138	-34	-6
	2	0	0.11	0.53	0.56	0.26	0.25	0.66	0.64	281	320	-20	-6
	3	0	0.33	0.76	1.01	0.65	0.76	0.82	0.81	507	437	-123	-42
AL	1	0	0.09	0.02	0.04	0.02	0.02	0.20	0.18	49	67	73	-51
	2	0	-1.15	0.13	0.02	0.13	-0.07	0.49	0.46	151	150	72	-90
	3	0	-2.09	0.11	-0.08	0.28	-0.16	0.75	0.77	201	167	173	-142
KR	1	0	0	0.67	0.61	0.11	0.06	0.00	0.00	94	83	57	49
	2	0	0	2.17	2.16	0.65	0.53	0.02	0.02	192	193	120	121
	3	0	0	2.95	3.06	1.44	1.42	0.04	0.04	33	69	107	126

Notes: a Percentage points.
b Units for balance-of-payments items are as follows: US—US$ billion; JA—US$ million; GE—DM billion; UK—£ million; AL—ALS million; KR—US$ million.

Source: The EPA World Econometric Model of February 1984.

policies undertaken by other countries is transmitted to other countries not necessarily with greater force under flexible exchange rates. This is mainly because the currencies of other countries appreciate vis-à-vis the currency of the transmitting country, offsetting expansive income effects exerted by the expansionary fiscal policy in the transmitting country.

Third, higher interest rates of the United States brought about by her expansionary fiscal policy are transmitted to other countries to a much lesser extent under flexible than under fixed exchange rates. This is because under the flexible rate regime the depreciation of other currencies greatly reduces the amount of necessary intervention by the authorities in the foreign-exchange market, resulting in a much smaller decline in the high-powered money in transmitted countries.

From the above observations, economists may welcome the more favourable impact under flexible exchange rates of the expansionary US fiscal policy on real GNP in other transmitted countries, and the lesser transmission effect of high US interest rates on financial markets in other countries. It is indeed true that the floating exchange-rate regime transmits the impact of the expansionary fiscal policy more favourably to other countries in terms of real GNP and interest rates. The real issue of today is, however, the trade-off relationship in other countries between real GNP on the one hand and price inflation and external trade imbalance on the other. For example, West Germany confronts the trade-off relationship between higher GNP and higher inflation rates, both of which are induced by the currency depreciation of the Deutschmark in the face of the expansionary US fiscal policy. In fact, the multiplier simulation exercises of the EPA world model demonstrate that the trade-off relation between real GNP and domestic price inflation, measured by an increase in real GNP per domestic price inflation, worsens twice as much under flexible exchange rates (Table 12.2). In the case of Japan, it confronts the trade-off relationship between higher GNP and higher net real exports, since the latter causes a stronger protectionistic attitude in the United States.

Once they do confront such trade-off relations, the independence of macropo-

Table 12.2 Trade-off between real GNP and inflation in West Germany under an expansionary US fiscal policy[a] (per cent, deviations from the standard solution)

	Fix[b]			Flex[b]			
	Real GNP	Inflation	Trade-off ratio	DM exchange rate per dollar	Real GNP	Inflation	Trade-off ratio
1st	0.09	0.01	9.0	0.89	0.17	0.04	4.3
2nd	0.36	0.05	6.2	2.25	0.59	0.20	3.0
3rd	0.54	0.13	4.2	2.67	0.98	0.44	2.2

Notes: a   Based on multipliers for a sustained increase in real non-wage government expenditure in the United States by 1 per cent of GNP. Multipliers in the table indicate the impact of an expansionary US fiscal policy upon economic variables in West Germany.
b   Fix—fixed exchange rates; flex—flexible exchange rates.

Source: Masaru Yoshitomi and the EPA World Model Group *The Insulation and Transmission Mechanisms of Floating Exchange Rates Analyzed by the EPA World Econometric Model* March 1984 licies in West Germany and Japan is greatly reduced. In a broad sense, monetary policies become targeted at the exchange-rate movement for the purpose of preventing further depreciations of their currencies. A consequence is the hesitation of the monetary authorities to reduce the official discount rate with resultant high real interest rates in both West Germany and Japan.

Figure 12.1 shows how real interest rates at the long end in major industrial countries tend to converge to levels in the United States. There are two reasons for such convergence of high long-term interest rates in real terms. One is the authorities' hesitation to reduce domestic short-term interest rates in the face of the currency depreciations, as discussed above. The authorities in both West Germany and Japan could have reduced the official discount rate in correspondence with lower domestic inflation rates in 1981–1984. For example, while Japan's inflation rate measured by the consumer price index declined by more than 2.5 percentage points during the period from the fourth quarter of 1981 to the first quarter of 1983 (from around 4.5 per cent down to about 2 per cent),

Figure 12.1   Movements of real long-term interest rates in major countries

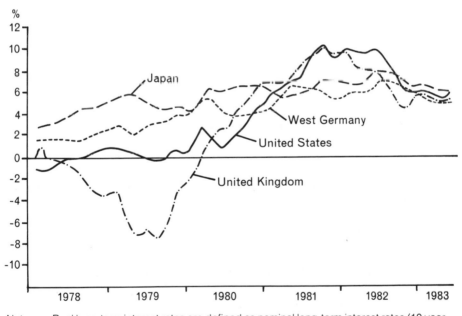

Note: Real long-term interest rates are defined as nominal long-term interest rates (10 year national bonds) minus expected inflation rates (GNP deflator). Expected inflation rates are one year lead actual inflation rates, and recent expected inflation rates are based on OECD projections.

Source: Taken from the Research Department Economic Planning Agency, *The Present Condition of the Japanese Economy*, December 1983.
          Japan: Bank of Japan, *Economic Statistics Monthly*.
          US: Fed., *Federal Reserve Bulletin*.
          W. Germany: Bundes Bank, *Monthly Report*.
          UK: Central Bureau of Statistics, *Financial Statistics*.

the Bank of Japan reduced the official discount rate by only 0.5 percentage points during the same period. Higher short-term interest rates tend to generate higher long-term interest rates. The other is the increasingly near-perfect substitutability between home-currency-denominated bonds and dollar-denominated bonds, reflecting the rather rapid liberalisation of the Japanese financial markets, to which we will return in some detail in the next section. If long-run inflationary expectations affect long-term nominal interest rates and if international differences in underlying inflationary expectation between countries correspondingly affect the expected rate of depreciation of a currency in the long-run, then the expected rate of return on home bonds in real terms tends to be equal to that on dollar bonds. This is because higher real interest rates in the US continue to attract capital from Japan so long as there remains as international difference in the expected rate of return in favour of dollar bonds.[3]

How Japanese long-term interest rates are influenced by domestic nominal short-term interest rates and the expected rate of return on dollar-denominated long-term assets is vividly demonstrated by the following estimated monthly equation for the period from March 1979 to September 1983.[4]

Japan's long-term interest rate = 21.593
                                  (5.809)
+ 0.068   (Japan's short-term interest rate)
  (1.292)
+ 0.204   (expected rate of return on dollar assets)
  (3.548)
+ 0.196   (expected rate of return on dollar assets)$_{-1}$
  (2.751)
+ 0.038   (expected rate of return on dollar assets)$_{-2}$
  (0.606)
− 0.544   (coupon rate on domestic bonds)
  (−4.652)
− 0.135   (national bonds outstanding in proportion to total private financial
  (−2.700)   assets)
$R^2 = 0.838$,   DW = 1.787,   SE = 0.166.

THE NATURE AND PERSISTENCY OF JAPAN'S CURRENT-ACCOUNT SURPLUS

It is indeed true that the current-account imbalance of both Japan and the United States will be abnormally large in 1984–85 at about 3 per cent of GNP in each country. But Japan has had a persistent current-account surplus since 1965, a surprisingly early date. In other words, Japan has been a natural international creditor, with a chronic current-account surplus for nearly a decade and a half. The issue today is the magnitude of Japan's current-account surplus, not its existence. Under the normal circumstances of exchange rates and the world business cycle, Japan's surplus would account for about 1.5 per cent of GNP (see Table 12.3), equivalent to around US$1.8 billion in 1983–85. If the current account substantially rises above or declines below this level, some anomaly should be sought for in the areas of exchange rates, including J-curve effects, oil shocks, or the international mismatch of business cycles.

Since Japan began to register a current account surplus at about 1.5 per cent of GNP in 1965–70, there have been three abnormal periods. The first was in 1970–71, when the surplus was greater because of the unrealistic yen exchange rate under the Bretton Woods fixed exchange-rate regime. After the first oil crisis, Japan's surplus rose in 1977–78 because of very weak domestic demand, caused by a decline in private fixed capital formation while private savings remained high. The third occurred in 1983–84, when the incomplete supply-side fiscal policy became a major cause of another anomaly.

While these were the cases for the abnormally large surpluses, the two oil crises in 1973–74 and 1979–80 caused even deficits, or smaller surpluses only in the current account of Japan. Oil deficits, the incrementals of oil bills, accounted for more than 4 per cent of GNP on each occasion. How did Japan remain an international creditor despite such large current-account oil deficits in the 1970s? It was possible only by offsetting the oil deficits by exporting more goods and services. Such expansion of net exports from Japan accounted for 9 per cent of GNP during the period from 1973 to 1982. It is no wonder that such an extraordinary increase in net exports at constant prices (in real terms) caused trade conflicts between Japan and her partner countries.

Japan's progression to the position of an international creditor in the 1970s has been accompanied by: a reduction in the rate of increase in the capital stock

Table 12.3 Japan: current account imbalance in 1965–84

Calendar year	Current account (US$ million, on a balance-of-payments basis)	Proportion of the external current imbalance to nominal GNP (percentage, on a national-account basis)
1965	932	1.1
1966	1 254	1.3
1967	−190	−0.0
1968	1 048	0.8
1969	2 119	1.3
1970	1 970	1.1
1971	5 797	2.6
1972	6 624	2.3
1973	−136	0.0
1974	−4 693	−0.9
1975	−682	−0.1
1976	3 680	0.7
1977	10 918	1.6
1978	16 534	1.8
1979	−8 754	−0.8
1980	−10 746	−0.9
1981	4 770	0.6
1982	6 850	0.8
1983[e]	22 550	1.9
1984[e]	31 250	2.5

Note: e estimates (from the most recent OECD *Economic Outlook*).
Sources: OECD *Economic Outlook*; Economic Planning Agency *Annual Report on National Accounts*.

in Japan while its domestic saving rate has remained high; a shift toward large government budget deficits; and a steady shift toward the production of knowledge-intensive, as well as high value-added products. In other words, even while the Japanese economy sustains high employment, the budget of the central government remains in a deficit, while the current account remains in a surplus. This is because the extra private savings, generated by the reduced rate of increase in the capital stock in the early 1970s, have been absorbed both by government deficits and by the current-account surpluses. The enhancement of Japan's industrial structure fits this stage of Japanese economic development as a capital exporter, in the form of direct investment and transfer of technology and management skills.

THE ROLE OF THE JAPANESE FINANCIAL MARKET IN WORLD ECONOMIC DEVELOPMENT

Within the basic function of providing savings to the world economy based on the chronic current-account surplus, Japan, as an international financial intermediary, will borrow short and lend long.

Borrowing short means that non-residents can make investments in yen-denominated short-term assets holding international liquidity. For this, treasury bills are the best financial investment. Japan, however, lacks free markets for its treasury bills, primarily because subscribers' yields on newly issued treasury bills are regulated at levels lower than the official discount rate. As a result, the Bank of Japan has been the sole buyer of new treasury bills and the open market for treasury bills is underdeveloped. Since the massive issue of ten-year maturity national bonds started in 1975, the remaining maturity of the outstanding national bonds has recently shortened, and the Ministry of Finance will have to smoothly redeem and refinance matured national bonds without disturbing the markets. Given these new circumstances, the Ministry of Finance will be under mounting pressure to liberalise treasury bill rates in order to raise short-run bridging funds in the financial markets. By satisfying such domestic financial requirements, the Ministry of Finance would also satisfy the international financial requirement of non-residents to hold international liquidity in the form of yen-denominated short-term assets.

Japan is also in a position to provide long-term capital, including direct investment, portfolio investment, syndicated loans and foreign aid. There are two issues involved here. One is an allocation of net capital outflow among direct investment, portfolio investment, syndicated loans and foreign aid, which will briefly be touched upon because of limited space. The other is the liberalisation and internationalisation of the Japanese financial market which plays a role as an international financial intermediary.

Table 12.4 indicates the broad direction of Japan's long-term capital movements and official transfer by major areas in 1982, as follows. Firstly, Japan is a large exporter of long-term capital in the form of direct investments, loans

Table 12.4 Japan: long-term capital movements by form and by area, 1982 (US$ billion)

	Total		OECD countries						Communist countries		Other countries		International organisations	
			USA		EC		Other							
	A	L	A	L	A	L	A	L	A	L	A	L	A	L
Direct investments	-4.5	0.4	-0.6	0.2	-0.6	n	-0.6	0.2	n	—	-1.7	n	—	—
Trade credits	-3.2	0.0	-0.8	—	-0.2	n	0.2	—	-0.5	—	-1.6	—	—	—
Loans	-7.9	-0.2	-0.1	-0.1	-0.9	n	-1.1	n	-1.0	—	-3.8	n	-1.1	n
Securities	-9.7	7.6	-0.6	1.4	-4.5	4.5	-3.2	-0.2	n	n	-0.3	1.8	-0.9	n
External bonds	—	4.3	—	0.4	—	0.4	—	3.3	—	—	—	0.1	—	—
Other	-2.0	0.3	-0.5	n	-0.2	n	n	n	—	n	-0.7	0.3	-0.5	—
Total long-term capital	-27.4	12.4	-3.6	1.9	-6.3	5.0	-5.0	3.3	-1.5	n	-8.1	2.3	-2.4	n
Official transfer	-1.4	n	n	n	n	n	n	n	n	n	-0.9	n	-0.4	n

Notes: A—changes in assets, with negative sign indicating capital outflows;
L—changes in liabilities.
n—negligible (less than US$100 million).

Source: Bank of Japan *Balance of Payments Monthly* April 1983.

(including trade credits), and securities, whereas official transfer is relatively small. In passing, the calendar year 1982 registered a current-account surplus of only US$6.1 billion. Secondly, while Japan's direct investment is diversified among the US, the EC countries and other, mainly developing, countries, loans and trade credits concentrate on developing countries, small OECD countries and international organisations. Thirdly, capital movements in the form of securities, including external bonds, are two-way transactions, and both outflows and inflows centre on OECD countries. At the time of writing, data are not available for 1983 on long-term capital movements by area. However, there are indications that in 1983, international securities transactions were attracted to the US financial markets.

The coexistence of high employment, the budget deficit and the current-account surplus has necessitated the liberalisation and internationalisation of the Japanese financial market. As a result, the Japanese financial system is rapidly shifting from administratively determined interest rates combined with extensive control over international capital transactions, toward market determination of interest rates together with free international capital movements. This rapid shift reflects the following important developments of the Japanese financial market in both its domestic and its international aspects.

Domestically, the most important aspect is the substantial accumulation of national bonds as a result of the combination of high employment with a government deficit since 1974. The central government's deficits have accounted for 4–6 per cent of GNP in each year since 1975, reflecting both cyclical and non-cyclical factors. By the end of 1983, the outstanding national bonds amounted to 40 per cent of GNP, one of the largest ratios among advanced countries, and they will keep on growing in relation to GNP in the next several years. The growth of public holdings of national bonds has exerted great market pressure toward the liberalisation of regulated interest rates on national bonds in the secondary market. This is because financial institutions, forced to subscribe to newly issued national bonds at higher prices than in the markets, have wanted to transact their national bonds freely in the secondary market, for the purpose of obtaining freer portfolio management. This reflects the growing proportion of national bonds in the total assets held by financial institutions. Interest rates on national bonds became market-determined in the secondary market in 1977, when financial institutions were allowed to sell national bonds after the required minimum holding time of one year, subsequently reduced to three months in 1981. The increasing difficulties facing the Ministry of Finance in selling new national bonds smoothly, if subscribers' yields in the primary market remain too low compared with interest rates in the secondary market, resulted in yields on newly issued bonds becoming more flexible. Since national bonds were the last domestic bonds with regulated interest rates in the secondary market, all interest rates have been market-determined since 1977. It is the secondary market rather than the primary market that matters for international capital transactions, although it is indispensable for the internationalisation of the yen to liberalise interest rates on treasury bills in the primary market, as mentioned earlier. There is a close substitutability between short-term securites in the secondary market; including national bonds close to date of redemption, CDs, *gensaki* (repurchase agreements), and foreign-currency deposits on the one hand, and commercial bank deposits on the other. It is now almost a matter only of time before the deregulation of interest rates on commercial bank deposits, in particular large deposits, occurs.

Another important domestic aspect of the liberalisation of the Japanese financial market is the weakening of the detailed segmentation among various financial institutions. The roles of various financial institutions such as commercial banks, security houses, long-term credit banks and trust banks have been highly compartmentalised. Recent financial innovations, however, have blurred the distinction between financial assets to be provided for consumers and enterprises by commercial banks and security houses, since both financial institutions can now provide similar market-interest-bearing short-term assets. What is unique about the segmentation in the Japanese financial market is the distinction between commercial banks and long-term credit banks. While commercial banks can obtain loanable funds through deposits and short-term CDs, only long-term credit banks (together with the Bank of Tokyo) are allowed to issue bank debentures. As to asset management, long-term credit banks extend essentially long-term loans beyond one year, while commercial banks extend short-term loans, though very often on a revolving basis.

One of the most important aspects of the internationalisation of Japanese financial markets was the de facto decontrol of foreign-exchange regulations in 1977, which became de jure with the introduction of the new foreign-exchange act in December 1980, when formal exchange controls were almost fully dropped. In April 1984, the principle that forward exchange-market contracts should be made only on the basis of actual transactions was abolished, contributing to freer activities of speculators in the foreign-exchange market.

Another significant aspect of the liberalisation of the Japanese financial market is the greater access to the Euroyen markets for both non-residents and residents. However, raising funds in yen through the issuance of Euroyen bonds is controlled, though this has become more flexible in recent months, and Euroyen loans beyond one-year maturity are controlled. These regulations reflect the requirement of backing domestic corporate bonds by collateral and the aforementioned domestic compartmentalisation between commercial banks and long-term credit banks. Further rapid liberalisation of Euroyen bonds and long-term loans would be confronted with the vested interest of long-term credit banks, which have been protected by the segmentation. Raising funds in yen by non-residents through issuing yen-denominated foreign bonds in Japan, called samurai bonds, is controlled by the Ministry of Finance, but will reportedly be liberalised soon.

CONCLUSIONS

The liberalisation and internationalisation of the Japanese financial market are necessitated by the combination of high employment, the budget deficit and the current-account surplus of Japan. The rapid integration of the Japanese financial market with international markets, of course, enhances the opportunity for investors to enjoy better portfolio selection, hopefully improving resource allocation and thus contributing to world economic development. At the same time, however, such deeper international integration ensures that domestic interest rates and the conduct of monetary policy in Japan will be more influenced by external financial environments, particularly the United States. Already, domestic economic management and development have been disturbed and frustrated. Recent examples are the misaligned US dollar–yen exchange rates, due to the incomplete supplyside fiscal policy in the United States, and the convergence of real interest rates in Japan toward the too-high real interest rates in the United States. A new form of international monetary and fiscal coordination must be sought, but that issue is beyond the scope of this chapter.

13 Trade and financial interdependence under flexible exchange rates: the Pacific area

JORGE BRAGA DE MACEDO

The performance of the world economy in the last ten years has been very uneven. In industrial countries, growth was much slower than expected; it fell from 5 per cent per annum in 1960–73 to about 2 per cent in 1973–82. The slowdown was less brutal in developing countries, where the rate fell from 6 per cent to 4.5 per cent between the two periods. Among the developing countries, those in the Pacific area managed to sustain an annual rate of growth of 7.5 per cent, close to the high rate of 8 per cent they recorded in the previous period. Nevertheless, if policies in industrial countries continue to be contractionary, or if major exchange rates continue to be volatile, it will be harder to sustain Pacific growth without a substantial increase in trade and financial interdependence among the middle-income countries of the region.[1]

Expectations of self-sustained, fast and stable growth in the OECD area were formed during the so-called postwar 'belle epoque'. For 25 years, macroeconomic policies preserved full employment and reasonable price inflation at home while allowing for a rapid expansion of international trade and capital movements. Judged by this standard, the performance of the last decade has generated the belief that Atlantic prosperity is over. In the process, scepticism about the effectiveness of national macroeconomic policies in restoring full employment without inflation, or in reducing inflation without unemployment, became widespread.

The volatile policy environment of recent years reflects this scepticism: high trade and financial interdependence implies conflicts between national policy objectives and gives rise to potentially inefficient strategic behaviour by national actors. In the 1970s, these conflicts were exacerbated by the oil shocks. In the early 1980s, the rise of the dollar also caused a global shock. Moreover, when there are shared instruments, such as the exchange rate, which are very sensitive to expectations about the future, signals of the lack of credibility of a particular macroeconomic policy package become evident in the foreign-exchange market. To offset these signals requires a high degree of international policy coordination.

In the absence of conflicts among national policy objectives, expectations about the future would be less volatile. International policy coordination would then become possible and, as a consequence, a fixed exchange-rate regime, such

277

as the one which prevailed during the postwar 'belle epoque', could be enforced. If the exchange rate between major currencies were fixed, macroeconomic policy in smaller countries might also be facilitated.

Even though international policy coordination would support a fixed-exchange-rate system, there is no incentive to coordinate. Because each country would be better off if the other country initiated monetary expansion, an explicit agreement, monitored by an international organisation, would be required to enforce the coordinated expansion in both countries. The task would clearly be more difficult if the coordination was to be achieved among a large number of countries.

The design and implementation of a comprehensive recovery program among industrial countries would also have to be based on the expectation that future changes in exchange rates would settle at some 'equilibrium' value. Otherwise if expectations remained volatile, so would exchange rates and competitiveness. Credible government intervention in the foreign-exchange market to limit exchange-rate volatility would surely be desirable. However, it would involve operations on a scale which does not seem viable under the present international order. The degree of international monitoring required may even raise fundamental value judgments about the sovereignty of nation-states.

The slowdown of inflation cannot induce a worldwide recovery of private economic activity which is expected to last, as it did during the postwar 'belle epoque', until macroeconomic policies of major countries are better coordinated, both internally and internationally.[2] Furthermore, the substantial fiscal imbalance between the United States and other OECD countries is likely to call for serious macroeconomic adjustment in the years to come, and this will be reflected in the world value of the dollar.

In the meantime, the scepticism about the effectiveness of central bank intervention policies need not be a reason for undue pessimism about the sustainability of world economic recovery. Indeed, the rise of stock-market prices in major industrial countries in early 1983, the concerted steps to deal with the 'external debt problem' without a major financial crisis, and the strong recovery of the United States allow for some optimism.

This chapter is organised into two sections. First, a theoretical assessment of the different outcomes of a policy interdependence game between two similar industrial countries, linked by international trade and high capital mobility, is presented. The results are expressed as deviations from a long-run equilibrium where expectations are fully realised. They are followed by a quantitative explanation of the world value of the US dollar in the last ten years, which gives large weight to the volatility of expectations about the long-run international competitiveness of US products.

The implications of the contractionary bias implied by strategic behaviour in industrial countries, and of the volatility in major exchange rates for the middle-income countries in the Pacific area are assessed in the second section. Exchange-rate policies in several of these countries reveal a benign pegging to the US dollar, which contrasts both with the fervent experimentation prevailing in the southern cone of America and with the tradition of currency unions encountered in West Africa. This neglect of the volatility of the dollar explains why, in the last few years, some countries changed the peg by means of sharp devaluations. These devaluations have hindered regional trade and financial interdependence, thereby increasing the vulnerability of the Pacific area to policy games played elsewhere. The consequences of policy coordination in the area along the lines of a 'joint float' are taken up in the conclusion.

POLICY INTERDEPENDENCE UNDER FLEXIBLE RATES

The idea that macroeconomic policies would become increasingly ineffective if they did not recognise the increased interdependence among nation-states was put forth in the late 1960s, in the context of the North Atlantic area. It has been widely discussed among economists and political scientists since then, and the word 'interdependence' has also been prominent in national and international policy debates.[3] Furthermore, historians have used the notion of a 'world-system' in discussions not only of the 19th century but also of earlier periods. A 'world-system' is based on a network of channels of trade and financial interdependence among countries and implies reciprocal constraints on the attainment of their domestic macroeconomic policy objectives. These constraints, which might be codified into explicit international rules or agreements, also apply to the periphery of the system where the reciprocity of interdependence is absent.

The very popularity of the term interdependence suggests several meanings. The most relevant for macroeconomic policy pertains to the effects abroad of a particular measure. One country's policy has repercussions on another country, which in turn has implications for the first country. If interdependence increases, the effect of the policy on the output of the initiating country tends to be smaller and the output effect abroad tends to be larger.[4]

When prices are allowed to vary, macroeconomic disturbances will change not only output but also the terms of trade. Since these refer both to the competitiveness of domestic versus foreign goods, measured by the real exchange rate, and to the relative price of consumption and saving, measured by the real interest rate, trade and financial interdependence crucially affect the transmission mechanism. Capital flows ensure that the return on foreign assets (in domestic currency) equals the return on domestic assets, at least in the absence of exchange controls as well as of risk-aversion on the part of international investors. By assuming that this arbitrage condition holds, we overstate the constraints implied by financial interdependence. This is appropriate for a discussion of Atlantic policy interdependence, where financial flows are hardly controlled, but should be qualified in discussing the Pacific. In any event, the relative strength of the effects of monetary policy on exchange rates and interest rates is crucial for the outcome of the policy game analysed below.

In the late 1960s, international economists were virtually unanimous in claiming that exchange-rate flexibility would insulate national economies from each other, thus allowing greater macroeconomic control of interdependence.

With volatility of major exchange rates becoming a central feature of world financial markets in the last ten years, unanimity has disappeared. Certainly, volatility has not been as detrimental to international trade and payments as some feared but, because of slower adjustment in goods markets, it has generated far more variation in the relative price of national outputs than would be called for by underlying demand and supply disturbances.

The prevailing scepticism about the effectiveness of central bank intervention in large, well-organised foreign-exchange markets suggests that exchange-rate volatility in the last ten years has derived from problems of credibility of national government policy.[5] The stance of the United States administration, on the other hand, may be related to the special role of the US dollar in the international monetary system.

Strategic Behaviour in Industrial Countries

Even in a theoretical world of two symmetric interdependent economies, conflicts of national policy objectives imply a flexible-exchange-rate system. The reason is that these conflicts tend to be solved by non-cooperative methods.[6] If the monetary authorities were to cooperate, they would jointly try to reduce inflation and unemployment and the solution would be efficient for both countries. Because there is no reason for either country to believe that the other country will cooperate, this solution will not arise spontaneously. An acceptable rule or agreement monitored by an international agency will be necessary to enforce cooperation. If the two countries are identical, this cooperative solution will support a fixed exchange rate.

In the absence of an international monitoring agency, the two monetary authorities will not behave cooperatively. Instead, each will try to attain the domestic objective, based on an anticipation of the other country's policy response. This outcome will be inferior to the cooperative outcome, as it involves a social loss arising from the inefficient allocation of resources.

However, if only one country, the leader, correctly anticipates the other country's response, the outcome will be asymmetric. Even if the two countries gain, the leader gains proportionately less than the follower. Furthermore, if the two countries are identical, there is no economic reason for either one to act as leader and therefore the spontaneous outcome will be the symmetric non-cooperative solution, where both countries are worse off. These theoretical possibilities are consistent with the observed reluctance of major industrial countries to act as leaders, or 'locomotives', even though they advocate cooperation.

To illustrate the framework, consider the case where the price of domestic output is rigid in both countries. Then the cooperative solution succeeds in eliminating unemployment, while monetary expansion sustains a fixed exchange rate and the same inflation in both countries. If each country tries to lower inflation by appreciating the currency, neither succeeds in eliminating unemployment. This outcome hinges on the dominance of interest-rate effects on money demand rather than on investment, as well as on large trade elasticities. It is therefore the appropriate one to focus on when the consequences of trade and financial interdependence must be assessed. Furthermore, in this setup, the leader will overexpand knowing that the follower will appreciate the currency. This appreciation lowers inflation while the leader's expansion reduces unemployment, so that the gains of the follower are greater than the gains of the leader. Therefore, both will be reluctant to take the initiative and remain at the relatively less desirable symmetric non-cooperative point.

This example is illustrated in Figure 13.1. Taking the log-linear two-country macromodel described in Appendix 13A and assuming that the authorities are minimising the deviations of output and the price level from their steady-state values, we can define the loss contours in the space of the single instrument available in each country, the money stock, M and M∗.

Figure 13.1 Strategic responses to a price rigidity

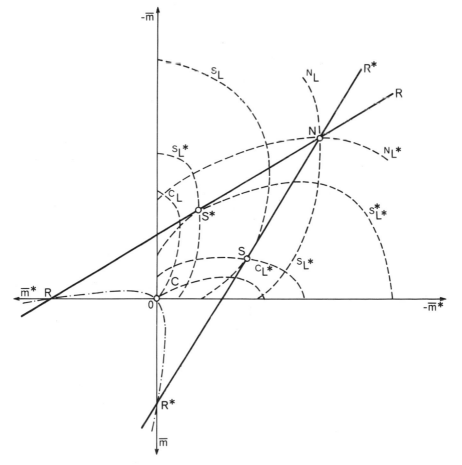

By normalisation, we choose as the origin the cooperative solution where the monetary expansion accommodates the price rigidity (point C in Figure 13.1). This yields a common loss $^CL = {}^CL^*$. Since all other solutions shown involve lower money stock, the direction of the axis is reversed. The straight lines RR and R*R* are the loci of the reaction functions of the home and foreign country, respectively. Their intersection denotes the non-cooperative outcome, labelled N, where loss is greatest $^NL = {}^NL^*$. At that point, though, the money stocks remain equal so that the exchange rate does not move. If the home country acts as a leader, the outcome is preferable for both $^SL > L$ and $^SL^* > {}^NL^*$. However, the home country would prefer to be a follower since $^SL > {}^{S*}L^*$ similarly for the foreign country $^{S*}L^* > {}^SL^*$.

A fixed-exchange-rate agreement, forcing the solution to be on the 45° line, would prevent the two countries from reaching N or, for that matter, S for S*, since at those points the exchange rate will have to change. The problem is how to make a commitment to fix the exchange rate credibly, since there would be incentives for each country to wait for the other country to expand and be the 'locomotive'. An international agreement such as the one underlying the Bretton-Woods system, monitored by an international organisation, would be needed to solve the problem, even in a two-country world. Even if such agreement existed, though, the mere expectation of exchange-rate changes would generate incentives to depreciate or appreciate the currency and under-mine the credibility of the system.

Note finally that the unemployment which is associated with the non-cooperative solution would, in the absence of other shocks, imply over time a lower rate of inflation so that, in the long run, it might be preferable to the more inflationary cooperative solution.[7] This is related to the neglect of internal cooperation, and requires a dynamic analysis where expectations adjust, like the one underlying the discussion to follow.

Nevertheless, it can be said that the qualitative analysis of the prospects for world recovery based on the strategic interaction of two symmetric economies is consistent with the protracted stagflation in the OECD area, to the extent that the interest-rate effects of monetary policy have dominated. This has con-strained recovery in industrial countries and, as mentioned, a sustainable OECD recovery is necessary, but perhaps not sufficient, for sustainable growth in the Pacific as well as for economic recovery in the world at large.

The Volatility of Expectations and the World Value of the Dollar

As shown in Table 13.1 below, the dollar exchange rates of major currencies have been quite volatile. To obtain an indicator of the world value of the dollar, we average major bilateral exchange rates in proportion to the country's gross domestic product in dollars (multilateral weights).[8] In the last ten years, this indicator shows a phase of relative stability prevailing from 1973 to early 1976; a phase of devaluation extending until mid-1980; and a phase of steep apprecia-tion continuing until the present.

Table 13.1 Volatility of dollar exchange rates (per cent per annum)

	Mean	Coefficient of variation	Range
Major currencies			
Canada	2.2	4	38
France	4.7	5	99
West Germany	−1.0	26	113
Italy	9.5	2	119
Japan	−0.6	37	99
Pacific floaters			
Malaysia	−0.5	27	72
Singapore	−1.5	8	66
Pacific peggers			
Indonesia	6.3	5	204
South Korea	6.9	3	86
The Philippines	3.2	2	31
Thailand	1.0	6	48
Taiwan	0.5	10	38

Note: Exchange rates are defined as US dollars per unit of currency of country in stub at end of quarter from 1973(2) to 1984(2) (positive number indicates depreciation against the dollar).

Sources: IMF *International Financial Statistics*; Central Bank of China *Financial Statistics* (for Taiwan).

Due to the stability of relative inflation rates, the variations in the nominal effective exchange rate of the US dollar have been matched almost exactly by variations in its real exchange rate. Goods-price arbitrage was therefore very weak.

In a large well-organised speculative market, asset-price or intertemporal arbitrage ensures that actual exchange rates equal their discounted expected equilibrium values. For example, in the presence of inflationary expectations, a positive real differential of 5 per cent per annum in the United States will be associated with an equal expected real appreciation of the dollar. Unlike relative goods prices, real interest differentials do seem to be correlated with the exchange rate. Nevertheless, only one-fourth of the quarterly volatility of the nominal exchange rate of the dollar, from 1973 to 1982, can be explained by intertemporal arbitrage.

In sum, the real exchange rate today will differ from the real exchange rate yesterday due to the change in the real interest differential and to the change in expectations about the equilibrium real exchange rate. If these are taken as given, exchange-rate movements can be captured by arbitrage conditions.[9]

But expectations about the equilibrium real exchange rate cannot be taken as given. Information on which they are based varies, sometimes dramatically, from day to day. These changes are not only due to changes in the fundamental determinants, but also to the existence, recognised by market participants, of some probability of a sudden return to the equilibrium value. Similarly, the belief in a change in policy regime, even if it is erroneous, can be a source of changes in expectations, which will be all the more important in an unstable environment.[10] A rough way of embodying the influences of changes in expectations, or 'news', about the long-run equilibrium real exchange rate is to take the residuals from an equilibrium model of the real exchange rate. This is conditional upon specifying the correct equilibrium model.

With the financial markets of major industrial countries highly integrated, capital is free to move across different currencies. If international investors compare risk and return characteristics of assets, so that they exhibit risk-aversion, equilibrium exchange rates will be influenced by portfolio considerations.[11] Take a simplified setting, in which the change in the equilibrium real exchange rate can be expressed as a function of current account, the accumulation of foreign-currency deposits by US residents, and of velocity, being the relative monetary and growth conditions in the United States and abroad. An empirical application of this equilibrium model over the floating period shows that, on average, a unit fall in the normalised relative current-account surplus of the US induces a depreciation of the real effective exchange rate of the dollar by one-fourth, whereas the average effect of a fall in velocity is a one-to-one real depreciation.[12] Changes in fundamentals explain 40 per cent of the actual volatility of the real exchange rate.

The difference between actual changes and equilibrium changes is then used as a proxy for 'news'. The explanation of the changes in the nominal exchange rate also includes the arbitrage variables; relative inflation rates and changes in real interest differentials. A special effect due to a change in the US administration is allowed for. All variables except the 'news' become insignificant and the regression explains over 60 per cent of the variance of the nominal exchange rate.[13]

The importance of 'news' shows the difficulty in anticipating exchange-rate changes. This also reduces the ability of central banks to dampen volatility by intervention. Bearing in mind the simplicity of the estimation methods used, the results confirm the advantage of relying on a portfolio equilibrium framework, rather than exclusively on arbitrage conditions. Since it only allows for currency diversiffication, this simplified equilibrium model cannot capture the US fiscal–monetary mix after 1982. Renewed expectations of a fiscal deficit raising US real interest rates are required for the equilibrium real exchange rate to continue appreciating, in spite of a widening current-account deficit.

PACIFIC TRADE AND FINANCIAL INTERDEPENDENCE

Rather than attempting to estimate the measures of trade and financial interdependence emphasised earlier, we assess interdependence among the middle-income countries of the Pacific area by an investigation of their exchange-rate regimes, an analysis of regional trade patterns, and an overview of trade in relative prices (as measured by trade-weighted effective exchange rates, deflated by relative consumer prices). It will become apparent that trade and financial interdependence is channelled through the two entrepots of the region, Singapore and Hong Kong. Furthermore, the analysis in the first section is relevant to Singapore and Malaysia, where most of the ingredients of trade and financial interdependence can be found.

Nevertheless, as stated in the conclusion, trade and financial interdependence in the middle-income countries of the Pacific as a group is still quite low by North Atlantic standards.

Exchange-rate regimes in Pacific middle-income countries

As mentioned, both the nominal and the real effective exchange rates of the US dollar depreciated from 1977 to 1980 and have appreciated since then. This remarkable medium-term swing followed a period of relative stability, with a mild depreciation in 1975. As a rule, the Pacific middle-income countries followed this pattern closely. Except for 1983, when they let the dollar appreciate in nominal and real terms, the trade-weighted exchange rates of most Pacific middle-income countries have depreciated and appreciated with the dollar, in what may be called an exchange policy of 'benign neglect'. While a distinction can be made between 'peggers' and 'floaters', it does not necessarily coincide with the official exchange-rate regime, as described, say, in the International Monetary Fund's *Annual Report on Exchange Restrictions*.

Indeed, no country is explicitly pegged to the US dollar. Rather the peg is an undisclosed basket of trading partners' currencies. On the other side, the two floaters, Malaysia and Singapore, are to a large extent bilaterally pegged despite the absence of a formal commitment to that effect.

Consider the five unofficial dollar peggers. During 1975–82, their effective exchange rates followed the dollar's, with some anticipating it. Thus the Philippines and Korea depreciated in 1976 and 1982, while Indonesia and Thailand appreciated in 1979 and the Philippines in 1980. Changes in effective exchange rates were also brought about by discrete devaluations against the dollar. This was the case in 1983 for Indonesia and the Philippines (both by about 150 per cent), in 1982 for Taiwan (13 per cent), in 1981 for Thailand and Taiwan (38 per cent and 17 per cent respectively), in 1980 for Korea (about 120 per cent), in 1978 for Indonesia (200 per cent), in 1975 for the Philippines (30 per cent) and in 1974 for Korea (85 per cent). Singapore and Malaysia also let their currencies depreciate against the dollar in 1975, by 50 per cent and 30 per cent respectively.

Since these devaluations are not synchronised, the correlation between the end-of-period dollar rates of the peggers is very weak from the second quarter of 1973 to the second quarter of 1984. Indeed, the only value higher than 0.5 is between Thailand and Taiwan. In contrast, among the main industrial partners of the United States except Canada, the correlation among dollar rates is generally higher than 0.5, the only lower values being 0.4, between Japan and the United Kingdom and Italy. The correlation of the dollar rates of the Pacific peggers with the yen–dollar rate is also quite weak, the highest being Taiwan (0.32).

The two joint floaters, however, exhibit a correlation of about 0.9 between themselves and also with the Mark–dollar rate. The correlation with the yen–dollar rate is about 0.5, slightly lower than the one between the yen–dollar and the mark–dollar rates. Table 13.1 shows the variability of the Pacific peggers relative to the floaters, and to the currencies used in the computation of the effective rate of the dollar described above. Despite the crude measures used, it is clear that variability is lowest for the dollar peggers.

To analyse the trends in trade-weighted exchange rates, some indication of trade shares and elasticities is needed. Since trade elasticity estimates which discriminate between the imports of various origins are not easily available, the network of trade interdependence has to rely on measures of average openness.[14] But, in the model in the first section, a large multiplier or a high elasticity substantially increases the degree of trade interdependence and leads to a strong negative feedback of monetary policy. A merchandise trade matrix, while it neglects invisibles and smuggling, provides a rough approximation to the trade channel of structural interdependence. In Table 13.2, the Pacific middle-income countries are arranged as the four NICs and the so-called new NICs, which include the ASEAN countries except Singapore. To make the role of the overlapping country more apparent, shares less than 1.5 per cent were set to zero. As a consequence, rows and columns do not add up to the numbers reported under total. The last row and column refer to the share of the country's trade accounted for by other Pacific middle-income countries. The largest values are for Singapore, Malaysia and Indonesia, even though Thailand on the export side and Hong Kong on the import side are also above the average of 19 per cent.

Using the set of trade weights reported in Appendix 13A (Tables 1 and 2), nominal and effective exchange rates for our seven Pacific countries were computed (see Appendix 13A, Tables 3–9). The real rates presented are very crude approximations for relative traded goods prices, due to the existence of several export incentives, but they give an idea of the evolution of the purchasing power of the domestic currency over a foreign basket of goods in relation to a domestic one.[15] We will focus on their annual average value using import weights. These tend to overstate the weight of the United States and Japan because the European Community is not aggregated. Better estimates of the weights of the EC are thus reported in the last row. Similarly, trade of Singapore and Indonesia is not reflected in the table. Using the Indonesian export shares from Table 13.2, the 'other' category is as reported in parentheses in Appendix 13A (Table 1). This figure was used to compute a set of import weights for Singapore which may be a better approximation of reality.

According to Table 13.3, the nominal effective exchange rate of the dollar peggers did not, on average, change by more under floating than it had during most of the Bretton-Woods period. The opposite is true of the floaters. Again, a decline in the absolute value of the mean rate of change, from the fixed to the flexible rate period, is evident in virtually all countries. The exception is the rate of Singapore when some imports from Indonesia are allowed for. There is a real appreciation instead of a depreciation and its magnitude increases with the sharp devaluations of the Indonesian currency since 1978. The coefficients of variation, the standard deviation over mean, convey the same message.

We observed in the first section that the nominal and real effective exchange rates of the US dollar, using multilateral weights, were almost perfectly

Table 13.2 Pacific trade matrix, 1979 (per cent)

Exporter	Importer									
	Taiwan	South Korea	Hong Kong	Singapore	Malaysia	Thailand	The Philippines	Indonesia	Total	% world
Taiwan	—	*	6	2	*	*	*	2	15	16
South Korea	*	—	3	*	*	*	*	*	8	9
Hong Kong	*	*	—	2	*	*	*	*	5	7
Singapore	*	*	6	—	12	3	*	3	27	33
Malaysia	*	*	*	11	—	*	*	*	17	27
Thailand	*	*	*	2	*	—	*	*	7	24
The Philippines	2	2	*	11	*	*	—	*	3	12
Indonesia	*	2	*	*	*	*	*	—	18	20
Total	7	7	19	30	15	7	6	9	100	
% World	9	7	20	31	33	17	15	22		

Note: *—less than $260 million (1.5 per cent of total).

Source: Computed from data in I. Yamazawa 'Japan and her Asian Neighbours in a Dynamic Perspective' in The Global Implications of the Trade Patterns of East and Southeast Asia Kuala Lumpur: NBER, 1984.

Table 13.3   Nominal and real import-weighted effective exchange rates: correlations
(per cent per annum)

	Nominal		Real			
	Mean		Mean		Coefficient of variation	
	1958–72	1973–83	1958–72	1973–83	1958–72	1973–83
Singapore	−0.2	−1.1	1.5	0.2	1	50
SG[a]	−1.3	−2.4	−1.0	−3.5	5	3
Malaysia	−0.0	−0.8	2.4	1.0	1	5
Indonesia	9.4	10.3	—[b]	0.8	1	17
Thailand	0.6	2.6	1.9	0.7	2	8
The Philippines	10.9	6.3	8.2	1.8	3	5
South Korea	17.6	8.1	8.8	1.9	3	4
Taiwan	2.4	1.4	1.3	−0.5	20	21

Notes: Weights as in Table 1 of Appendix 13.1.
  a   Includes imports from Indonesia.
  b   Because of the hyperinflation of the early 1960s comparable figures are not available.

Sources: Consumer prices from IMF *International Financial Statistics* and Central Bank of China *Financial Statistics* (for Taiwan).

Table 13.4   Prices and import-weighted exchange rates: correlations

	Nominal and real effective exchange rates (EER)		Nominal EER and relative consumer prices (P*/P)		Real EER and relative consumer prices	
	1958–72	1973–83	1958–72	1973–83	1958–72	1973–83
Singapore	0.7	0.7	*	0.5	0.8	1.0
SG[a]	1.0	0.8	0.9	0.6	1.0	1.0
Malaysia	0.5	0.8	0.2	*	0.9	0.6
Indonesia	—[b]	0.9	—[b]	−0.2	—[b]	0.1
Thailand	0.5	0.6	−0.2	−0.1	0.8	0.7
The Philippines	1.0	0.8	−0.3	*	−0.2	0.6
South Korea	1.0	0.6	−0.3	−0.4	*	5.0
Taiwan	0.6	0.6	−0.2	0.3	0.6	0.9

Notes: a   Includes imports from Indonesia.
  b   Because of the hyperinflation of the early 1960s comparable figures are not available.
  *—less than 0.05 in absolute value.
  The figures represent average annual changes, with statistics rounded to the nearest decimal point.

Sources: Consumer prices from IMF *International Financial Statistics* and Central Bank of China *Financial Statistics* (for Taiwan).

correlated during the floating rate period. This is not the case in the Pacific middle-income countries, as seen in Table 13.4: the highest correlation, 0.9, is for Indonesia, where the policy was one of sharp nominal devaluations. Interestingly, over the longer period, the Philippines and Korea are the ones closer to relative purchasing-power parity (1 and 0.9 respectively from 1958 to 1983). Relative inflation rates are very weakly correlated with nominal exchange-rate changes. The correlation is higher with real exchange rates precisely because of the lower variability of nominal exchange rates: the lowest values are for devaluation-prone Indonesia and Korea.[16]

The cross-country correlations shown in Table 13.5 confirm the pattern of

Table 13.5 Cross-country correlations, 1973–83

	Indonesia	Malaysia	Singapore	SG[a]	The Philippines	Thailand	Taiwan
Malaysia	−0.1						
	(0.1)						
Singapore	*	0.7					
	(*)	(0.8)					
SG[a]	−0.6	0.6					
	(−0.3)	(0.8)					
The Philippines	0.6	0.1	0.2	−0.2			
	(0.4)	(0.4)	(0.4)	(0.3)			
Thailand	0.2	0.4	0.2	0.1	0.2		
	(0.2)	(0.5)	(0.3)	(0.3)	(0.7)		
South Korea	−0.2	0.3	0.2	*	0.2	0.2	
	(−0.1)	(0.1)	(−0.2)	(−0.1)	(0.6)	(0.5)	
Taiwan	0.2	0.6	0.6	0.3	0.5	0.8	0.2
	(0.4)	(0.4)	(0.4)	(0.3)	(0.8)	(0.9)	(0.5)

Notes: a   Includes imports from Indonesia.
  *—Less than 0.05 in absolute value.
  Numbers refer to percentage changes in annual averages of nominal effective exchange rates, rounded to nearest digit. (Numbers in parentheses refer to real EERs.)

Sources: Consumer prices from IMF *International Financial Statistics* and Central Bank of China *Financial Statistics* (for Taiwan).

dollar rates discussed above: low correlations of nominal and real effective rates for most pairs of countries. Taiwan does display high real correlation with the Philippines and Thailand, and the same is true between the two joint floaters, to which we now turn.

A Singapore–Malaysia Joint Float

The development of Singapore as an entrepot for international trade and finance has been a major factor in the trade and financial interdependence of the middle-income countries of the Pacific. The economic proximity to Malaysia, with which it once was federated, has also been noted. It is possible to recast the policy games of the first section in a broader setup which allows two small countries to act on their money stocks given domestic shocks and the outcome of the policy game of large countries, as captured by their bilateral exchange rate.[17] If there are no differences in the trade pattern of the small countries with the large ones, the bilateral rate of the small countries will be fixed, unless one of them acts as a leader. Otherwise, the bilateral rate of the small countries may move in the cooperative solution.

If the most relevant policy game of industrial countries is between the United States and Japan, trade patterns of Malaysia and Singapore are roughly symmetric. If, instead, the game is between the United States and Europe, Malaysia would be more sensitive to European shocks, given the weights in Appendix 13A (Tables 1 and 2).

Even in the case of a symmetric sensitivity, the bilateral rate between Malaysia and Singapore could move if one of the countries acted as a leader. Due to its role as a financial centre, Singapore may have performed that role in the early 1980s, thereby allowing Malaysia to be less contractionary. Needless to say, a cooperative agreement between Singapore and Malaysia would be less contractionary still.[18]

Recalling that interest-rate movements are an important channel of policy interdependence, some evidence on the deposit-rate differentials between Singapore and Malaysia is shown in Table 13.6.[19] While annual averages hide a lot of information and should be used with caution, the volatility of expectations about the world value of the US dollar can certainly account for the observed variations in the realised real interest differential. It seems therefore consistent with the expectation of a Singapore–Malaysia joint float.[20]

Table 13.6 Realised interest-rate differentials between Singapore and Malaysia (per cent per annum)

	3-month deposit rate (period average)		Consumer prices		Real differential (+ in favour of Singapore)
	Singapore (1)	Malaysia (2)	Singapore (3)	Malaysia (4)	(1) − (3) − (2) + (4) (5)
1975	4.3	5.7	3.3	5.1	0.4
1976	3.8	5.0	−2.4	2.4	3.6
1977	4.5	5.0	3.3	4.8	1.0
1978	5.3	5.0	4.7	4.5	0.1
1979	7.2	6.2	4.5	3.6	0.1
1980	11.2	8.8	7.9	7.0	1.5
1981	7.4	10.5	8.7	9.8	−2.0
1982	6.2	10.5	3.7	6.0	−2.0
1983	6.5	8.8	1.2	3.4	−0.1

Sources: Item 1—Lee op. cit. p. 43, Table 2.5.
Item 2—Bank Negara Malaysia Money and Banking in Malaysia Kuala Lumpur, 1984, pp. 464, 968 (end of period averaged using quarterly averages of interbank rates).
Items 3 and 4—IMF International Financial Statistics.

CONCLUSION

Over the last ten years, flexible exchange rates among industrial countries generated an erratic pattern in relative prices and made basic signals of resource allocation very noisy. Growth declined worldwide, but mostly in industrial countries. In the Pacific area, exchange rates were not as volatile and growth continued. Policy interdependence under flexible exchange rates may thus be partly responsible for the slowdown of growth.

Due to the erratic pattern of real exchange rates, it is very difficult to assess, let alone correct, the misalignment of the major world currencies. The preferred explanation of exchange-rate volatility stressed changes in the fundamental determinants of the real exchange rate, identified as monetary velocities and current accounts. National governments can stabilise expectations about fundamentals by designing credible macroeconomic policies. The overwhelming influence of 'news', and the size of world financial markets relative to central bank reserves, strains the credibility of uncoordinated intervention in the foreign-exchange market.

The realisation that, even when the analysis is restricted to major industrial countries, intervention in foreign-exchange markets cannot reduce volatility, has generated proposals designed to lessen trade and financial interdependence among the major industrial countries. The large size and efficient organisation of the foreign-exchange market makes the effectiveness of trade and exchange restrictions temporary at best.

An international monetary system where greater stability in exchange rates could again be expected requires a credible commitment to coordinated macroeconomic policies, and therefore the existence of incentives for policy coordination. Given the contractionary bias of the flexible-exchange-rate system, additional monetary expansion in the US and other industrial countries could rekindle inflationary expectations and hurt the ongoing recovery.

In the absence of incentives for coordination among industrial countries, higher trade and financial interdependence among the middle-income countries of the Pacific could help preserve the growth potential of the region. The widespread policy of pegging to the US dollar, while making exchange rates less volatile, has often been accompanied by sharp devaluation against the numeraire. An alternative, which requires higher Pacific interdependence than the one prevailing during the last decade, would be a joint float along the lines of the policies seemingly pursued by Malaysia and Singapore. To manage this float, monetary policy would adjust to accommodate changes in import-weighted exchange rates, such as the ones presented in this paper. As financial interdependence increases, the indicators for the change in this basket peg become the fundamental determinants of the equilibrium real exchange rate, as discussed in connection with the world value of the dollar.

14 External shocks, policy responses and external debt of Asian developing countries

SEIJI NAYA
AND WILLIAM JAMES

The world debt problem that has emerged in recent years has its origins in the period of the 1970s, when substantial structural changes in the world economy were brought about by a number of major events, not least of which was the 'oil price revolution'. The debt problem now appears to centre on the developing nations and their ability to successfully carry through the structural adjustment process. In what follows, an overview of the debt situation and the macroeconomic picture is given, with emphasis on the position of the developing countries in Asia.

Between the first oil shock of 1973 and the present, there has been a quantum jump in the external debt of oil-importing developing countries (OIDCs). There has also been a large expansion in the external debt of oil-exporting developing nations in Latin America, Asia and sub-Saharan Africa. The trend towards greater external borrowing was also apparent in Asia, though at a rate below the average for all developing countries. Disbursed debt outstanding increased by more than 500 per cent between 1973 and 1983 in the OIDCs, as Table 14.1 shows. Significantly, debt-service payments have risen even more sharply, absolutely, and in relation to exports and GNP. The composition of external debt has also changed, with private sources, mainly commercial banks, dominating official sources both in absolute figures and in terms of growth (Table 14.2). Over the past two years (not shown in Table 14.2) there has been such a marked slowdown in new commercial bank lending that OIDCs' debt-service payments have begun to exceed new borrowings so that there is a negative net capital inflow to these capital-short nations.

The heavy buildup of debt following the first oil price shock was a rational response by policymakers in the developing world to the severe burdens imposed by higher oil prices and periodic contractions in economic activity in the industrialised nations. Following the steep recession of 1974–75, the banks had high levels of liquidity, economic growth and trade expansion were moderate and the cost of funds appeared cheap, as inflation rates were often in excess of lending rates. Borrowing allowed many OIDCs to accelerate investment programs, despite enlarged current-account deficits, so that developmental progress could continue. This was the case for the developing countries of Asia. This grouping came through the first oil-shock–recession sequence

Table 14.1 Public and private debt of non-oil developing countries[a] (US$ billion)

	1973	1974	1975	1976	1977	1978	1979	1980	1981	1982	1983
Total outstanding debt of non-oil developing countries	130.1	160.8	190.8	228.0	278.5	336.3	369.9	474.0	555.0	612.4	664.3
Short-term debt	18.4	22.7	27.3	33.2	42.5	49.7	58.8	85.5	102.2	112.7	92.4
Long-term debt	111.8	138.1	163.5	194.9	235.9	286.6	338.1	388.5	452.8	499.6	571.6
By type of creditor											
—official sources	51.0	60.1	70.3	82.4	98.7	117.5	133.0	152.9	172.4	193.2	218.7
—private guaranteed sources	31.5	42.0	52.4	66.6	85.3	112.7	137.8	158.1	183.7	202.2	239.3
—private unguaranteed sources	29.3	36.0	40.8	45.9	51.4	56.4	67.3	77.5	96.7	103.9	113.7
By analytical group											
—net oil exporters[b]	20.4	26.0	34.1	42.4	53.5	61.2	70.5	79.4	96.5	108.1	129.0
—net oil importers	91.4	112.1	129.4	152.5	182.7	225.4	267.6	309.1	356.2	391.5	442.6
By area											
—Africa	14.2	17.7	21.9	26.9	35.0	42.1	49.6	55.1	60.5	67.1	75.0
—Asia	30.0	34.6	39.8	46.4	57.9	67.4	76.1	88.4	100.8	115.1	131.7
—Middle East	8.7	10.3	13.3	16.1	20.3	24.7	28.4	32.9	35.4	39.3	43.7
—Western Hemisphere	44.4	58.2	68.6	82.0	94.0	114.3	135.1	154.7	192.6	208.9	247.4
Total debt service	17.9	22.1	25.1	27.8	34.7	50.3	65.0	76.2	94.7	107.1	93.2
Debt-service ratio[c]	15.9	14.4	16.1	15.3	15.4	19.0	19.0	17.6	20.4	23.9	19.3

Notes: a The countries covered under the heading 'oil-exporting countries' are Algeria, Indonesia, Iran, Iraq, Kuwait, Libyan Arab Jamahiriya, Nigeria, Oman, Qatar, Saudi Arabia, the United Arab Emirates, and Venezuela. They include those whose oil exports are at least 100 million barrels a year and account for at least two-thirds of the country's total exports (1978 averages).
b The countries classified in the subgroup 'net oil exporters' are Bahrain, Bolivia, the Congo, Ecuador, Egypt, Gabon, Malaysia, Mexico, Peru, the Syrian Arab Republic, Trinidad and Tobago, and Tunisia.
c Payments as a percentage of exports of goods and services.

Source: IMF *World Economic Outlook* Occasional Paper 21, Washington, D.C., May 1983, pp.200, 204.

Table 14.2 Non-oil developing countries: current account positions and aspects of their financing, 1973–83[a] (US$ billion)

	1973	1974	1975	1976	1977	1978	1979	1980	1981	1982	1983
Current account deficit[b] (net)	−11.3	−37.0	−46.3	−32.6	−28.9	−41.3	−61.0	−89.0	−107.7	−86.8	−67.8
Use of reserves	−10.4	−2.7	1.6	−13.0	−12.5	−17.4	−12.6	−4.5	−2.1	7.1	−7.2
Total financing requirement	−21.7	−39.7	−44.7	−45.6	−41.4	−58.7	−73.6	−93.5	−109.8	−79.7	−75.0
Non-debt-creating flow (net)[c]	10.3	14.6	11.8	12.6	14.4	17.9	23.9	24.1	28.0	25.1	24.2
Long-term borrowing from official sources (net)	4.9	6.8[d]	11.7	10.5	11.4	13.8	13.3	17.6	23.0	19.5	23.8
Use of reserve-related credit facilities[e]	0.2	1.6	2.4	4.6	0.4	0.3	0.4	1.8	5.9	10.7	10.8
Other borrowing (net)[f]	6.3	16.7	18.7	17.9	15.2	26.7	36.0	50.0	52.9	24.4	16.1
Memorandum items											
Borrowing in bond markets, net of repayment	1.0	1.0	1.0	2.0	3.0	4.0	3.0	2.0	3.0	3.0	
Borrowing from banks, net of payment[g]	9.8	18.6	23.2	21.5	14.7	25.6	35.9	53.3	52.5		

Notes:
a Excludes data for China before 1977.
b Net total of balances on goods, services and private transfers.
c Official transfers, SDR allocations, gold monetisation, valuation adjustments, and direct investment flows (net).
d Excludes the effect of a revision of the terms of the disposition of economic assistance loans made by the United States to India and repayable in rupees, and of rupees already acquired by the US government in repayment of such loans. The revision has the effect of increasing government transfers by about $2 billion, with an offset in net official loans.
e Comprises use of fund credit and short-term borrowing by monetary authorities from other monetary authorities.
f Includes net long-term borrowing from private sources, other short-term borrowing (net), including errors and omissions.
g Approximated by the sum of long-term borrowing from financing institutions (net), exceptional financing and other short-term borrowing (net), which is broadly consistent with natural balance-of-payments statistics of total net borrowing (long-term and short-term) from private banks.

Source: IMF *World Economic Outlook* Occasional Paper 21, Washington, D.C., May 1983, p.194, *Annual Report 1983* p.78.

remarkably well compared with other developing regions. Higher real GDP growth and export growth rates, combined with lower-than-average inflation rates) were indicative of the sound economic management that generally characterised these countries.

Between 1976 and 1979 OIDCs' external public medium- and long-term debt rose at the fastest rate for the period of 1971–83 as a whole. Fairly healthy growth in world trade during these years (averaging about 6.5 per cent per annum; see Table 14.3) helped allay fears of a general debt crisis at that time, even though structural changes in energy use, trade patterns and the industrial sector remained incomplete. The second oil shock of 1979–80 upset the structural adjustment process under way in the OIDCs. It quickly forced the more prosperous, but unemployment-, deficit- and inflation-ridden industrial nations to adopt strict austerity measures. The resulting recession, unlike that following the first oil shock, was to be a prolonged and painful event. The widespread adoption of deflationary policies, particularly in the areas of monetary and incomes policies was necessary in order to lay the basis for a sustainable recovery. This created very difficult financial conditions in world capital markets. Nominal interest rates rose to very high levels and persisted despite gradual declines in the rate of inflation. This resulted in record high real interest rates and the alarming rise in the debt-servicing burdens of OIDCs. At the same time, some of the larger oil-exporting developing countries continued to expand borrowings for ambitious development programs, based on their expectations of rising oil revenues.

Simultaneously, protectionist pressures increased in the industrial nations, due to severe structural unemployment and large-scale business failures. World trade growth fell in 1980 and collapsed in 1981–82. The recession led to declines in the export receipts of OIDCs and, combined with harsh financial conditions, resulted in a growth slowdown. The severe recession and energy-saving by OECD nations led to moderation in oil prices. While this had good effects on oil-importers, it led to serious adjustment problems in large oil-exporting developing countries, particularly Mexico. While many countries in developing Latin America and Africa suffered declines in real GDP and exports almost immediately after the second oil price shock in 1980–81, the countries in developing Asia for the most part continued to grow. It was only in 1982 that Asia was hit hard by the recession, as real growth rates tumbled to half of what they were on average between 1973 and 1981. Indonesia and Malaysia, developing Asia's major oil-exporting countries, had sharp reductions in real growth in 1982 that continued into 1983 despite the beginnings of world recovery. A major factor was the virtual halt in export growth in 1982. The 1983 recovery saw OIDCs in Asia record improved growth rates, but these were still far below their previous decade-long average. The Philippines recorded its lowest growth rate on record.

Like the recession, the external debt crisis came to Asia after a time-lag. By the early 1980s, debt problems had forced reschedulings in large debtor nations in Latin America and Eastern Europe. This led to a tightening of lending policies by commercial banks and even stretched the resources of the interna-

Table 14.3 Growth of world production and trade, 1963–82 (average annual percentage change in volume)

	1963–73	1973–82	1974	1975	1976	1977	1978	1979	1980	1981	1982
World commodity output	6.0	2.0	2.5	–1.0	7.0	4.5	4.0	4.0	1.0	1.0	–2.0
World export total	8.0	3.0	3.5	–3.0	11.0	4.5	5.5	6.0	1.5	0.0	–2.0
Agricultural products	4.0	4.0	–3.5	5.0	9.5	2.0	9.0	7.0	5.0	3.0	1.0
Minerals[a]	7.0	–2.5	–2.5	–7.5	4.5	2.0	1.5	5.0	–6.0	–12.0	–7.0
Manufactures	11.0	4.5	8.0	–4.5	13.0	5.0	5.0	5.0	5.0	3.5	–1.5

Notes: a Includes fuels and non-ferrous metals.

Source: GATT *International Trade 1982–1983* Geneva, 1983, p.1.

tional financial institutions, which found their resources constrained by aid-fatigue in the developed countries. Asia experienced its first real brush with the debt crisis in late 1983, when the Philippines had to seek rescheduling of a portion of its relatively large external debt.

At the same time that the Philippine crisis was attracting attention, other large Asian borrowers found they had to carefully reexamine their own situations and adopt stringent measures to reduce current-account deficits and put off new commitments. This was certainly the case for Indonesia where the oil glut and recession called for bold measures. These included: 1) reduction of domestic subsidies on fuel, food and fertiliser consumption; 2) austerity measures in current spending of government; 3) delay or cancellation of large public-sector investment projects; 4) devaluation; 5) renewed emphasis on non-oil exports; 6) liberalisation of financial markets in order to increase domestic saving and more efficiently allocate scarce investment resources. Malaysia, to a lesser extent, was also obliged to adopt some similar measures. Thus, oil-exporting and oil-importing developing countries alike have been adversely affected by recession and harsh financial conditions.

The worldwide economic recovery has picked up steam in 1984, led by the strong resurgence of the United States economy. Other major OECD nations have also experienced higher real growth rates with continued moderation of inflation. From a zero base in 1982, real GNP growth in the industrial market economies has exceeded 3 per cent for the past eighteen months or so. The recovery has been welcome news for the Asian developing countries and for other developing nations that rely on trade expansion to improve output growth.

Already the four newly industrialising countries (NICs) of Hong Kong, Taiwan, Korea and Singapore have seen average export growth in 1983 of 10.7 per cent and, as a consequence, real GDP has grown at an average of around 7 per cent. The Southeast Asian countries have also experienced improved external conditions as commodity prices have rebounded. However, foreign exchange shortages and supply bottlenecks have prevented the Philippines from achieving export expansion. Indonesia has found that declines in oil earnings are difficult to replace, as not enough emphasis had been put on other sources of foreign-exchange earnings in the past. The failure of exports to grow rapidly in South Asia is symptomatic of deeper structural problems that cannot be rapidly resolved.

There is legitimate concern that external debt problems of developing nations could stifle world economic recovery before sustained growth can resume. The reasoning is that if country after country with debt-servicing difficulties adopts strict austerity measures to avoid default, world demand will contract and recession will again result. Alternatively, there is the possibility of financial crisis in the event of defaults by large debtors, as overcommitted commercial banks are themselves unable to meet commitments to depositors. While the latter scenario is improbable given the existing international institutions and central bank supervision, the intricacies of international interdependence make it imperative to take preventive measures before such crises arise.

It is equally important to have a proper understanding of the origin and nature of the debt problem. The issue must be studied in the context of the external shocks and policy responses of the past decade. The next section assesses the magnitude of the external shocks and their impacts on the balance of payments of twelve Asian developing countries (ADCs). It also examines the policy responses to the shocks. The penultimate section of the paper seeks to ascertain the long-term capability of Asian countries to meet their debt-servicing obligations while continuing to develop. The emphasis is on the relationship between domestic efforts to mobilise and efficiently allocate investment resources and debt-servicing capacity. This highlights the role of domestic economic management and development policy. In the conclusion, some comments are made on the requirements for a more favourable external economic environment.

EXTERNAL SHOCKS AND POLICY RESPONSES IN TWELVE ASIAN DEVELOPING COUNTRIES: ESTIMATING THE IMPACT OF EXTERNAL SHOCKS

World inflation, the two oil price increases, and the subsequent recessions in the industrial countries were the sources of the external shocks[1] that affected the Asian developing economies over the past ten years.[2] In the case of the non-oil developing countries, the balance-of-payments effects of the external shocks can be classified into two categories. The first consists of losses due to terms-of-trade deterioration. These include not only the impact of higher oil prices on the import bill, but also the relative downward price inflexibility of manufactured and capital goods exported by industrial nations. On the export side, one must include the downward flexible prices of primary commodities, and these are especially significant in South and Southeast Asian countries.[3] The second category includes losses due to recession, largely reflected in falling export volume due to the declining aggregate demand and incomes of the industrial nations. The recessions also added to protectionist pressures that had already begun in the mid-1970s in most industrialised nations. These led to secondary reductions in the demand for exports of the developing Asian countries, as trade restrictions on certain types of goods, especially labour-intensive manufactures, began to proliferate.

The quantitative impact of these effects on the Asian developing countries can be assessed using a similar methodology to that originally applied by Balassa.[4] The countries under consideration are classified into three groups according to their levels of development, as indicated by per capita incomes and the extent of industrial development, and 'openness' to the international economy indicated by trade/GDP ratios.

The first group consists of the four newly industrialising countries (NICs), with the highest average per capita GDP, the greatest (average) trade/GDP ratio and the most significant level of industrialisation. The second group is composed of the four middle-income and natural-resource-rich Southeast Asian countries, which for analytical purposes must be further subdivided between the two net oil importers (the Philippines and Thailand) and the two net oil exporters (Malaysia and Indonesia).[5] The third group consists of the lower income, agrarian, and generally 'inward-looking' South Asian countries, Burma, India, Pakistan and Sri Lanka. It should be noted that Burma is basically self-sufficient in oil, and while sometimes a marginal net exporter it also has to import some refined oil products. Also, Sri Lanka is relatively 'open', especially since 1977 when trade liberalisation policies were implemented. Tables 14.4 and 14.5 provide data on the various indicators used for the classification of countries.

The impact of the external shocks on Asian developing countries as a whole, on the various subgroups, and on individual countries can be measured in various ways. The magnitude of external shocks can be seen by measuring the total balance-of-payments impact in relation to total output or GNP as is done in the second column of Table 14.6. The net oil importers had adverse effects, the simple average of which equalled 17.5 per cent of GNP between 1974 and 1982. Note that the effects are larger in percentage terms for the smaller, more open countries such as Singapore, Hong Kong and Sri Lanka and smaller for the larger or relatively closed economies such as Burma and India.[6] The magnitude of positive effects in relation to GNP on the two oil exporters can also be seen in Table 14.6; note that the favourable effect on Indonesia, which is much more dependent on oil revenues than Malaysia, was comparable in magnitude to the adverse effects on the more open oil importers.

This broad measure of external shocks as a percentage of the size of an economy's total output provides one gauge for indicating the size of adverse effects beyond the control of economic managers. However, the measure underestimates the aggregate impact for countries, such as the Philippines and Korea, which have borrowed heavily from commercial banks at variable rates of interest, since the monetary policies of developed nations and, therefore, the real interest rates in major capital markets are outside the purview of their economic management.[7] The analysis does not include the period of declining nominal oil prices, due to data limitations. Hence, the negative effects on oil exporters and the positive effects on oil importers of the oil price cuts in 1983 are not included. Preliminary calculations indicate these effects were much smaller than the previous oil shocks, however, in absolute terms and relative to GNP.

In order to divide the impact of external shocks into their two components (terms-of-trade and export-volume effects), it was necessary to make some assumptions regarding the possible economic trends in the absence of external shocks. It is assumed that average real economic growth rates during the period before the first oil shock would have continued and that market shares of exports and relative prices of exports and imports would have more or less remained unchanged during the subsequent period, 1974–82.[8]

Adverse terms-of-trade effects were estimated by contrasting base-year values with changes that occurred in the relative prices of a country's exports and imports. In the case of exports, this was due to world prices rising faster from the 1971–73 base than the price index of a country's exports; and, in the case of imports, of rises in a country's import prices at a more rapid rate than world

Table 14.4 Selected economic indicators of Asian developing countries

Country	Real GDP per capita 1982^a ($)	Manufacturing (1982)		Exports/GDP				Imports/GDP			
		Share in GDP (%)	Share in employment (%)	1963	1972	1977	1982	1963	1972	1977	1982
Newly industrialising											
Hong Kong	5 330	25.1^b	37.3	69.4^e	75.0	75.2	80.8	92.7	84.2	81.7	90.8
South Korea	1 760	32.8	21.1	2.3	15.8	28.4	32.1	15.0	24.5	30.6	35.6
Singapore	5 900	21.5	29.7	123.3	75.4	125.8	141.9	151.8	116.9	159.8	192.2
Taiwan	2 540	42.4	31.6	16.7	37.1	43.5	47.2	15.4	32.1	39.6	41.3
Southeast Asia											
Indonesia	580	15.4	8.0^c	8.2	16.2	23.7	26.0^c	6.2	14.2	13.6	15.5^c
Malaysia	1 840	17.9	15.7	51.2	34.1	46.3	46.6	49.3	33.0	34.5	48.2
The Philippines	820	24.8	15.0^c	7.7	13.9	15.0	12.6	6.5	16.9	20.5	20.7
Thailand	800	21.0	7.1^c	14.2	13.7	18.1	18.6	18.8	18.8	24.0	22.9
South Asia											
Burma	190	10.3	8.0	17.0	5.6	5.6	7.3	14.7	7.4	6.6	14.7
India	250	15.8^c	26.8^d	3.8	4.1	6.0	5.3^c	5.5	3.5	6.4	9.2^c
Pakistan	380	16.1	14.5	5.1	6.3	7.7	8.2	14.4	11.0	16.2	18.3
Sri Lanka	320	19.4	29.9^b	23.3	12.4	18.0	24.6	25.5	14.4	16.6	41.3^c

Notes: a 1980–82 base period, using methodology in *World Bank Atlas*.
  b 1980.
  c 1981.
  d Organised sector only.
  e 1966.

Table 14.5 Indicators of dependence on oil imports (percentages)

	Oil imports/ GNP		Oil imports/ imports		Oil imports/ exports		Commercial energy imports[a]/ consumption	
	1972	1982	1972	1982	1972	1982	1972	1982
Newly industrialising								
Hong Kong	2.4	6.7	3.0	7.4	3.3	8.3	100.9	100.0
South Korea	2.1	9.2	8.6	26.0	13.4	27.9	67.1	85.6
Singapore	17.1	60.3	14.5	34.0	22.5	46.0	259.0[b]	210.7[b]
Taiwan	2.2	9.4	6.8	23.2	5.9	19.8	72.7	98.5
Southeast Asia[c]								
Malaysia	2.2	—	6.6	—	6.4	—	13.2	—
The Philippines	2.2	5.6	12.9	26.9	16.6	42.0	96.0	95.4
Thailand	1.9	7.3	10.1	30.8	13.9	38.8	106.9[b]	103.0[b]
South Asia								
Burma	..	0.1[d]	11.5	2.1[d]	..	1.8[d]	11.0	9.6
India	0.4	3.9[d]	11.5	43.1	7.4	76.2	26.0	22.1
Pakistan	0.3	5.7	4.4	30.0	4.3	64.6	43.8	36.5
Sri Lanka	0.3	10.5	1.6	28.5	1.8	54.4	116.8[b]	107.4[b]

Notes: a   Refers to net imports (imports less exports and bunkers).
b   The ratios of commercial energy imports to commercial energy consumption in Singapore, Thailand and Sri Lanka sometimes exceed 100 per cent because of some exports of petroleum and refined petroleum products.
c   Indonesia was a net oil exporter, and so was Malaysia from 1980.
d   1981.

Table 14.6 Size of external shocks and the ratio of external shocks to gross national product (average of 1974–82)

Country	External shocks ($ million)	Ratio of external shocks to GNP (%)
Newly industrialising	−2 833.7	−24.8
Hong Kong	−2 800.1	−26.7
South Korea	−3 668.2	−13.3
Singapore	−2 506.1	−46.3
Taiwan	−2 360.4	−12.7
Southeast Asia[a]	−2 462.9	−14.9
Indonesia	7 740.9	23.6
Malaysia	696.9	6.4
The Philippines	−2 531.8	−14.5
Thailand	−2 394.0	−15.2
South Asia	−1 885.2	−14.2
Burma	−50.8	−1.8
India	−3 808.7	−4.6
Pakistan	−3 152.9	−26.8
Sri Lanka	−528.5	−23.5

Note: a Average for the Philippines and Thailand only.

prices. Trend values for export demand were compared with hypothetical values, derived for each country by considering what would have happened if exports had grown in line with world demand after 1971–73, the difference comprising the export-volume effect. Actual balance-of-payments situations were then compared with the trend and hypothetical imports and exports in order to assess the policy responses.[9] The results that emerge are quite interesting. First, let us examine the balance-of-payments effects of terms-of-trade losses, which reflect in part the large increases in oil prices relative to export-volume effects, which in turn reflect the impact of the severe recessions. From Table 14.7, it can be seen that the terms-of-trade effect on the balance of payments was generally stronger than the export-volume effect, except for two of the NICs and Pakistan. This is prima facie evidence that oil prices had more severe immediate consequences than did the world recessions for the balance of payments[10] in most of these countries. The two effects add up to 100 per cent of the balance-of-payments impact of external shocks, and it can very roughly be said that 75–80 per cent of the effects were due to terms-of-trade losses and the remainder due to export-volume declines.

The next issue that must be addressed is the process of adjustment each subgroup and country made to the adverse (or favourable) external shocks. The policy responses and economic management related directly to the ability of countries in Asia to maintain their development progress. It is in the adjustment to external shocks that the differences between the resilient Asian economies and other developing regions come to the fore. Moreover, it is in economic management that differences within the Asian developing countries in the subgroups stand out most clearly, though individual country experiences also

Table 14.7 External shocks and adjustment responses (percentages)

	Balance-of-payment effects					Direct adjustment		
	Terms of trade (1)	Export volume (2)	Total external shocks (3)	Export market penetration (4)	Import substitution (5)	Import reduction through lower GNP growth (6)	Total (4)+(5)+(6) (7)	Net external finance (8)
Newly industrialising								
Hong Kong	-35.6	-64.4	100.0	85.2	-2.2	13.6	96.6	3.4
South Korea	-83.2	-16.8	100.0	104.5	17.1	4.6	126.2	-26.2
Singapore	-98.1	-1.9	100.0	67.0	-41.8	17.5	42.7	57.2
Taiwan	-43.8	-56.2	100.0	132.9	16.3	13.5	162.7	-62.7
Southeast Asia								
Indonesia	83.6	16.4	100.0	2.3	-1.1	0.5	1.7	-101.7
Malaysia	71.6	28.4	100.0	39.9	-25.4	4.3	18.8	-118.8
The Philippines	-75.1	-24.9	100.0	17.5	2.3	-2.6	17.2	82.9
Thailand	-90.1	-9.9	100.0	25.5	8.6	2.6	36.7	63.4
South Asia								
Burma	-158.5	58.5	100.0	-153.9	-0.8	111.4	-43.3	143.3
India	-72.8	-27.2	100.0	3.3	-2.3	2.2	8.2	91.9
Pakistan	-46.7	-53.3	100.0	-3.1	0.8	-5.6	-12.9	112.9
Sri Lanka	-76.5	-23.5	100.0	-3.6	14.8	-17.5	-11.3	111.3

Note: Figures are averages of 1974–82.

Sources: IMF *International Financial Statistics* (various issues); *Balance of Payments Yearbook* (various issues); UN *Yearbook of International Trade Statistics* (various issues); *Key Indicators of Developing Member Countries of ADB* (various issues).

provide for some interesting comparisons. Herein the concern is mainly with medium- to long-term structural changes and policies rather than with very short-term changes.

Adjustments to balance-of-payments disturbances are unavoidable. However, there can be significant differences in the social costs of various forms of adjustment. There are available means, initially at least, to delay adjustment to adverse external shocks, but this type of response is not costless and may, under some conditions, be even more expensive than more direct forms of adjustment.

In Table 14.7 are set out four types of economic adjustment to external shocks (see columns 4–8).[11] One path to adjustment is for a country to simply export more to pay for the higher import bill. To do this, it is necessary to increase its share of world export markets either by diversifying exports and trade partners or by successfully competing against other producers in established markets. This approach is compatible with sustained income growth but it implies reduced domestic absorption (consumption plus investment).[12]

Here, a country may run against protectionist measures designed to limit market penetration by foreign firms. One can see from column 4 of Table 14.7 that 'increase in export market share' was the predominant form of adjustment response by the NICs. Korea and Taiwan had export drives that were so successful that they outweighed the external shocks (exceeded 100 per cent)! The two other NICs were highly successful as well.

Export-market shares of the two oil-importing Southeast Asian countries increased to a much smaller, yet still significant extent, with Thailand doing better than the Philippines. There were very large differences between export-market penetration among the oil-exporting Southeast Asian nations. Indonesia showed a very small increase, whereas Malaysia had the largest gain outside of the NICs. Export shares and the competitiveness of South Asian countries actually declined, except for India, which alone showed a modest increase over the hypothetical value.[13]

Closely related to increased competitiveness, as evidenced by gains in export-market shares, was success in import substitution (column 5 of Table 14.7).[14] The two larger NICs (Taiwan and Korea) were able to replace a significant amount of imports with domestic production while they were expanding exports. For the two city-states, Hong Kong and Singapore, import substitution is simply not a viable option. In Southeast Asia, Thailand did better than the Philippines in import substitution, while Indonesia and Malaysia had negative values. Indonesia's figure was insignificant and while Malaysia's was quite large, it was still well below the increase in the export-market-penetration value. The countries most associated with import substitution industrialisation policies in South Asia (Burma, India, Pakistan) had fairly low or even negative figures.[15]

The low values for import substitution possibly indicate that by the mid-1970s, much of the scope for further cutting imports by substituting domestic production had been used up. The types of imports remaining were essential intermediate inputs and unavailable capital equipment. The financial constraints imposed by external shocks and various bottlenecks may also have limited scope for expansion into capital goods production.

A further means of adjustment is to lower the trend growth rate, at least temporarily, thus reducing aggregate demand. Give the income elasticity of import demand, a decline in aggregate demand will result in a fall in import expenditure. This belt-tightening type of adjustment could not be entirely avoided by most oil-importing countries, nor even by the oil exporters during recession years. Moderation of average real GNP growth below trend values was a significant form of adjustment in three of the NICs, though it was less so for Korea, as well as Thailand and India.[16]

In the Philippines, as well as Pakistan and Sri Lanka, hypothetical growth rose above the trend value, indicating that higher growth rates occurred in spite of balance-of-payments deficits. In the Philippines case this was rather small, but in the other countries it was quite significant.

The extent of adjustment by means of increased export-market shares, import substitution and import savings, through lower growth in relationship to the external shock effect on the balance of payments determines the degree to which net external borrowing is adopted. Net external financing (column 8 in Table 14.7) is simply set equal to the difference between the actual resource gap (actual imports minus exports, adjusted for world prices) and the trend resource gap (trend imports minus exports at 1971–73 prices).[17]

It must be recognised that the first three measures of policy responses are not solely or even predominantly functions of domestic policymaking. Export market shares depend on a number of things often beyong a country's control. Nor are the effects neatly independent and separable in all cases. For example, 'internal shocks', such as harvest failures due to poor weather, could have significant impact on the accuracy of measurement of import savings effects. With such qualifications in mind we may now examine the final response measure in Table 14.7, the resort to additional net external finance.

The larger countries of East Asia and the two Southeast Asian oil exporters were, in effect, net creditors as far as the residual resource gap measure is concerned.[18] All the other countries (except for Hong Kong) relied to a varying but significant degree on net external finance.

The relative size of this type of policy response among oil importers is smallest for the NICs, ranging from high negative values for Taiwan (−63 per cent) to a fairly high positive value (+57 per cent) for Singapore. Net external finance figured prominently in the adjustment process of the Philippines and Thailand, but again the results show that this policy response in the Philippines substantially exceeded that of Thailand (83 per cent as against 63 per cent). In South Asia, net borrowing actually exceeded 100 per cent of the effects of the external shocks in three of the four countries, and was by far the predominant mode of adjustment.

The policy responses to adverse external shocks show a distinct pattern in the country subgroups. The NICs relied mainly on increased export market penetration and secondarily on import savings and import substitution. Only Singapore had much recourse to net external finance in the sense we are discussing. The Southeast Asian oil importers to some extent increased export market shares but, in the main, had recourse to net external finance. Thailand performed better than the Philippines and to some extent adjusted by means of import substitution and import savings. The South Asian countries overwhelmingly opted for borrowing, a course that only India kept to under 100 per cent of external shocks. For the net oil exporters, the challenge posed by positive external shocks was quite different. They faced admittedly less gruesome trade-offs than did the oil importers, but still had tough decisions to make.

On balance Malaysia and Indonesia were positively affected by the external shock of oil-induced terms-of-trade effects compared to negative, recession-induced export-volume effects. (This, it must be stressed, leads to the hypothetical improvement in the net external accounts of these two countries that appear in the final column of Table 14.7). In reality, of course, both countries expanded their external borrowings to fuel larger government current budget outlays, and to build up infrastructure and other investment programs. Hence, actual external debt positions were built up quite a bit, in both Malaysia and Indonesia, especially after the second oil shock of 1979. To the extent that the oil boom increased the reserves and perceived earning power of the two oil exporters, their international credit standing was enhanced. However, as will be seen in the following section, the efficiency with which external funds were used has a major impact on long-term debt-servicing capacity that can swamp the favourable impact of greater oil earnings. The potential adverse impact of oil wealth on non-oil tradables production, due to exchange-rate movements, can cause problems even before the resource bonanza comes to an end. Income distribution may turn against smallholders in the agricultural sector unless countermeasures are taken. The inflationary effect of a boom in oil revenue and the temptation to boost expenditures through subsidies are also potentially powerful. The nature of the policy responses in both oil-exporting and oil-importing countries thus has had an important influence on the problem of external debt that has emerged in Asia over the past year.

EXTERNAL DEBT PROBLEMS AND CAPACITY TO REPAY IN ADCS: A CRITICAL INTEREST-RATE APPROACH

The 'debt explosion' since 1973 has placed many developing countries in difficult straits, and though the nature of the difficulties varies from country to country, there is both a short-term problem of balance-of-payments adjustment and a longer term problem of structural adjustment.[19] In Asia, most debt accumulation has been due to the need for additional finance for basically sound investments in development projects. However, external conditions have called for even more reliance on domestic resource mobilisation and greater efficiency in resource allocation.

External debt is composed of public debt and private debt, part of which is often guaranteed by governments of borrowing countries. External debt also varies according to term to maturity; fixed versus flexible rates of interest;

commercial or official sources; and for official sources, 'soft' versus less concessional loans. Information on short-term and private non-guaranteed debt is scanty; therefore most of the discussion that follows focuses on long-term public or publicly guaranteed private debt.

The external debt of the Asian developing countries increased less rapidly since 1972 than the total for all OIDCs, even though the annual rate of change was about 16 per cent in Asia between 1973 and 1983 (see Table 14.1). The debt in Asia has been of high productivity as it resulted from, in the main, investments in domestic energy development, agriculture and industrialisation efforts. However, the continued debt buildup in some Asian countries during the early 1980s at the time of a severe recession (for example, in Malaysia, the Philippines, Indonesia and Korea) and growing government budget deficits has caused concern that less efficient uses of externally borrowed funds were being made. This is strikingly apparent for Malaysia and Indonesia, where publicly guaranteed external debt continued to grow at an average annual rate of over 15 per cent between 1980 and 1983, which was three times as high as the rate for the oil-importing developing countries in Asia.

The emergence of debt problems can be traced to two basic causes. First is the unexpected deterioration in external conditions, including the decline of world trade, sharp drops in commodity export prices, and the tightening of lending terms and conditions. The terms and conditions of new loans to Asian developing countries became, in general, increasingly harsh since the end of the 1970s, though with sharp differences among countries and subgroups. Lending for South Asia continued to be highly concessional and adverse changes were far less there than in East and Southeast Asia. The average real interest rates on new borrowings in 1981 by the NICs and Southeast Asian countries were twice those of 1970, while the average grace and maturity periods decreased greatly. The number of fixed-interest-rate loans dropped relative to variable-rate borrowings. Consequently, the proportion of concessional loans in outstanding public debt fell to only 15 per cent for the NICs and to 35 per cent in Southeast Asia, while it remained close to 90 per cent in South Asia. The worsening of conditions for borrowers caused a much faster rate of increase in debt-servicing payments than in total external public debt in the newly industrialising and Southeast Asian groups.

In addition to the deterioration in lending terms faced in financial markets, the emergence of 'aid-fatigue' in donor nations has resulted in further difficulties. India has been adversely affected by this and will shortly have to seek commercial sources of loans as its share in soft loans from the World Bank has been reduced. The collapse of export growth in 1981–82, increasing protectionist measures against manufacturing exports from Asia in industrial nations, and doubt about the sustainability of economic recovery have caused commercial lenders to be much more circumspect about extending new credit, and even in rolling over short-term trade credits. These are all largely factors external to the Asian developing countries. They are indicative of hard times but are not sufficient to identify, much less to predict, which specific countries will have serious debt problems.

Table 14.8 Macroeconomic trend indicators (percentages)

Country	Growth rate of GNP		Domestic saving ratio		Gross domestic investment ratio		Resource gap	
	1964–73	1974–82	1964–73	1974–82	1964–73	1974–82	1964–73	1974–82
Newly industrialising								
Hong Kong	..	8.8	..	25.5	..	26.7	..	1.2
South Korea	9.7	7.2	14.5	22.4	22.6	27.4	8.1	5.0
Singapore	12.0[a]	8.1	18.8[a]	30.0	30.9[a]	40.9	12.1	10.9
Taiwan	11.2	7.3	25.0	35.5	24.7	30.3	-0.3	5.2
Southeast Asia								
Indonesia	..	7.0	6.4[a]	22.9	12.2[a]	21.2	5.8	-1.7
Malaysia	..	6.8	19.2	26.8	18.5	28.7	0.3	1.9
The Philippines	5.3	5.5	17.4	24.0	21.0	29.9	3.6	5.9
Thailand	7.7	6.4	21.6	22.9	23.4	26.2	1.8	3.3
South Asia								
Burma	-0.2	5.1	6.2	11.7	12.3	19.2	6.1	7.5
India	3.3	3.8	13.8	19.6[b]	18.3	22.5	4.5	2.9
Pakistan	0.8	1.4	11.7	12.6	15.4	15.9	3.7	3.3
Sri Lanka	4.7	7.0	10.0	5.3[b]	16.5	22.8	6.5	17.5

Notes: a 1965–73 average.
b 1974–81 average.

Various measures can be used to assess the dimensions of external debt, to indicate whether a problem exists and to help determine in advance likely cases of near-default and the need for rescheduling. The buildup of external debt closely tracks the investment-saving or resource gap (Table 14.8) and is reflected in the current-account gap (Table 14.9). One may contrast the experiences of the Philippines and Thailand in this regard. The continued wide resource gap and the increase in the deficit on current account relative to GNP following the second oil shock in the Philippines foreshadowed the debt crisis of 1983.

Other indicators such as the debt-service to export ratio, the debt-service to GNP ratio, and the reserves to import ratio, are also commonly used. Generally these indicators tell one that the debt-servicing capacities of the NICs and Southeast Asian countries, like those elsewhere, diminished during the period since the first oil shock (Table 14.1). However, the debt-servicing burden in developing Asia is still quite a bit lower than for major debtors in Africa and Latin America (Table 14.10). Debt indicators alone may not accurately represent the complete picture and, therefore, may be misleading in predicting which countries may require rescheduling. Inability to repay debt frequently occurs in countries that do not appear to be heavy borrowers or to have particularly serious resource gaps. They may simply have a very narrow export base and thus be highly susceptible to terms-of-trade losses or shortfalls, due to events such as harvest failures. Long-term capacity to meet debt obligations depends on the borrowing nation's ability to generate production and exports out of externally financed investments. This, in turn, is greatly influenced by domestic economic policies. One useful methodology for the purpose of evaluating long-term debt-servicing capacity is the derivation of the critical interest rate.[20]

The critical interest rate (CIR) indicates the level of real interest rate on the

Table 14.9 Current account deficits as a percentage of GNP

Country	1980	1981	1982	Average 1974–82
Newly industrialising				
Hong Kong	..	..	..	..
South Korea	−9.1	−7.2	−3.9	−5.6
Singapore	−13.8	−10.3	−8.7	−10.7
Taiwan	−2.4	1.1	4.7	0.5
Southeast Asia				
Indonesia	4.0	−0.8	−6.8	−0.9
Malaysia	−0.8	−9.2	−13.3	−2.3
The Philippines	−6.8	−5.9	−8.4	−5.3
Thailand	−6.2	−7.1	−2.7	−4.7
South Asia				
Burma	−5.9	−5.3	−9.5	−4.3[a]
India	−1.1	−1.4	..	−0.7[b]
Pakistan	−4.6	−2.6	−4.2	−5.4
Sri Lanka	−16.1	−10.4	−12.3	−5.7

Notes: a Average 1975–81.
       b Average 1974–81.

Table 14.10   External debt of major borrowers and their debt–service ratios

	External debt at end 1982, including short-term debt (US$ billion)	Debt–service ratio (%) in 1983 (estimate)	Debt–service ratio (%) excluding short-term debt
Latin America			
Argentina	38.0	154	88
Brazil	85.5	117	67
Chile	17.2	104	54
Colombia	10.3	95	38
Ecuador	6.6	102	58
Mexico	80.1	126	59
Peru	11.5	79	47
Venezuela	29.5	101	25
Subtotal	278.1	117	56
Asia			
Indonesia	25.4	28	14
South Korea	36.0	49	17
Malaysia	10.4	15	7
The Philippines	16.6	79	33
Taiwan	9.3	19	6
Thailand	11.0	50	19
Subtotal	108.8	36	14
Middle East and Africa			
Algeria	16.3	35	30
Egypt	19.2	46	16
Israel	26.7	126	26
Ivory Coast	9.2	76	34
Morocco	10.3	65	36
Nigeria	9.3	28	14
Turkey	22.8	65	20
Subtotal	113.8	58	16
Total	501.1	71	30

Source: Morgan Guaranty Trust Co. *World Financial Market* March 1983.

external debt of a country under which its external debt will grow at the same rate as its GDP. In other words, the CIR is the maximum interest rate that can be paid on external debt without increasing the ratio of debt outstanding to GDP. If the average interest rate on external debt exceeds the CIR for a long period of time, the ratio of debt outstanding to GDP will continue to increase, leading to an unbearable burden. Thus, a comparison of the CIR with actual average interest rates on external debt provides a measure of the long-run debt-servicing capacity of a borrowing country.

The CIR can also be used to identify the factors which affect a country's debt-servicing capacity. It is determined by three indicators of domestic economic performance: the GDP growth rate, the incremental capital–output ratio (ICOR) and the marginal saving rate. It shows basically that the efficiency with which capital is used and the extent to which domestic savings are mobilised are major determinants of the long-run debt-servicing capacity of a country. The CIR, thus, can be viewed as a bridge that connects a country's external debt problem to the management of the domestic economy.

The CIRs for eleven of the dozen Asian developing countries were calculated for the two periods 1966–75 and 1976–82.[21] The former period includes the first oil shock and the latter includes the second oil shock. The CIRs for each country and country group are shown in Table 14.11.

The ICORs were estimated from country data and, due to differences in procedures for estimating capital-formation, cross-country comparisons must be made with great caution. The ICOR estimates for Pakistan, Indonesia and Sri Lanka appear to be quite low. This is most likely due to underestimation of investment, as is noted in an ADB study.[22] For the CIR analysis, the rise in the ICOR, not its initial or end-period value, is what matters. The country data confirm that there has been a decline in the productivity of capital to some extent. However, the rise in the ICOR would also reflect changing structure of investment, including the capital-intensive development of domestic energy resources in countries such as India and the Philippines.

During 1976–82 the CIR of the newly industrialising countries (NIC) group slightly decreased compared to that of 1966–75 (from 9.3 to 8.3). Although the marginal saving rate (MSR) has increased significantly from 27 per cent to 32 per cent, the percentage rise in the ICOR was even greater than the rise in the MSR. It increased from 3.0 in 1966–75 to 3.8 in 1976–82. As far as the NIC group as a whole is concerned, it was the deteriorating efficiency of investment capital that reduced its debt-servicing capacity.

Disaggregating between the NICs, the CIRs of Korea and Taiwan have somewhat decreased due to their higher ICORs, while those of the two 'city-states' slightly improved. The increase in the CIR for Singapore was mainly caused by the spectacular savings performance. On the other hand, the

Table 14.11 Critical interest rates[a] of Asian developing countries

	Growth rate of real GDP (%)		Incremental capital–output ratio		Marginal saving rate (%)		Critical interest rate (%)	
	1966–75	1976–82	1966–75	1976–82	1966–75	1976–82	1966–75	1976–82
NICs	9.5	9.2	2.9	3.8	27.1	31.9	9.3	8.3
Hong Kong	7.4	10.9	2.8	2.5	24.3	24.6	9.1	9.6
South Korea	10.0	9.1	2.7	4.3	24.6	31.2	8.9	7.0
Singapore	11.2	8.6	3.2	4.3	33.8	48.2	10.5	11.6
Taiwan	9.3	8.6	3.0	3.8	29.1	31.9	9.8	8.4
Southeast Asia								
Indonesia[b]	7.5	7.9	2.2	3.3	18.0	22.6	8.5	6.6
Malaysia	6.6	7.7	3.2	3.7	24.6	26.0	8.0	6.9
The Philippines	5.6	5.4	3.3	4.7	26.5	21.8	8.9	4.5
Thailand	7.7	6.9	3.3	3.7	24.2	21.8	7.2	5.7
South Asia	4.0	4.1	4.1	4.3	18.6	20.0	4.9	5.0
India[b]	3.8	3.8	4.4	4.7	20.2	21.8	4.9	5.0
Pakistan	5.3	5.9	2.6	2.2	9.0	5.5	2.4	4.2
Sri Lanka	5.8	5.5	2.5	3.4	8.5	10.7	2.1	2.8

Notes: a The critical interest rate is calculated using the following formula:

$$CIR = r(S_1 - S_0) / (k - r - S_{0i})$$

where CIR is the critical interest rate, r is the rate of growth of real GDP, S_1 is the marginal saving rate, S_0 is the initial saving rate (assumed to be 5 per cent), and k is the incremental capital–output ratio.

b The data cover only the years up to 1981.

improved CIR for Hong Kong is largely attributable to the enhanced efficiency in its investment.

The CIR for the Southeast Asian group was somewhat lower than that for the NIC group during the period 1966–75. Furthermore, it declined rapidly from 8.2 per cent in 1966–75 to 5.9 per cent in 1976–82. The main contributing factor for this decline was the increase in the group ICOR. Although the MSR of the Southeast Asian group slightly increased, this was not sufficient to offest the adverse effect of an increased ICOR.

Among the Southeast Asian countries, the Philippines experienced the most drastic decline in its CIR. It had the highest ICOR of any country except India and the rise in the ICOR has been quite steep in the Philippines. Other Southeast Asian countries also experienced a decline in their CIR, mainly due to their increasing ICOR.

Compared with the NIC and the Southeast Asian groups, the CIR for South Asia was low, being around 5 per cent. The reasons for the low CIRs are again two fold: high ICOR and low MSR. India is mostly responsible for the high ICOR for the South Asian group and Pakistan and Sri Lanka have shown relatively poor performances in their savings mobilisation. The CIR of the South Asian group has, however, slightly increased during 1976–82. This is a good sign since to some extent all these countries will have to rely more on commercial or less soft official sources of external finance in the future.

The CIR analysis shows that the long-run debt-servicing capacities of the Asian developing countries have, on average, deteriorated. The CIRs of countries experiencing declines fell mainly because of the decreased efficiency of their invested capital. At the same time, average interest rates on foreign loans have risen sharply. The debt-servicing capacities were therefore adversely affected by both domestic and external conditions.

Nonetheless, the CIR results reveal that the Asian countries continue to be highly productive in the use of external finance. The CIR estimates further indicate that the debt problem is not at all insurmountable provided external conditions improve so that the policy efforts to come to grips with payments imbalances and, in the longer term, to make structural adjustments can be successfully implemented.

The deterioration in the efficiency of capital in the NICs and Southeast Asian groups is mainly a reflection of the prolonged worldwide recession. But it is also due to some inappropriate industrialisation policies adopted by these countries. The unfavourable changes in the ICOR suggest that there must be some adjustments in the industrialisation policies of three of the four NICs, in order to enhance debt-servicing capacity.

The single major factor which distinguished the relative performance of each country group was the marginal saving rate.[23] The continued better performance of the NIC group in terms of the level of the CIR was mainly due to high and increasing MSRs during the period under consideration. This shows the importance of domestic resource mobilisation in meeting external debt problems.

The CIR analysis complements to a large degree the results in the second section of the paper dealing with external shocks and adjustment responses. The more open, outward-looking countries are generally much stronger in debt-servicing capacity than the inward-looking nations. Sound domestic economic policies have been a major reason why Asian developing countries have attained more rapid rates of real growth and export expansion with lower inflation than have developing countries in other regions. It is interesting to note that the Philippines, with the lowest trade–GDP ratio in ASEAN and the most protectionist tariff structure as well, has been the only country to date in Asia to require debt rescheduling during the present crisis. It is only the Philippines that has experienced a decline in its exports-to-income ratio since 1979 among the countries included in the study. Though the causes of the Philippine crisis are more complex than the trade regimen, one cannot easily reject the view that ill-advised, inward-looking policies were a strong contributing factor.

There has been concern in Asia that the debt crisis may spread or that problems in one country may make lenders tougher on others. There is also the perception that there appears to be no solution to the debt problem that meets the twin criteria of achieving good results and being politically acceptable.

CONCLUSION

This chapter has provided a quantitative assessment of the impact of the external shocks of oil price changes and world recessions on the developing Asian countries. It has also examined the nature of the adjustment process from a long-term perspective. The critical interest-rate measure was used to determine the debt-servicing capability of these countries, also from a long-term viewpoint. The results indicate developing Asian countries do have a strong capacity to meet debt-servicing obligations while continuing to grow and develop. This, however, assumes that short-term macroeconomic policies will succeed and that the external economic climate will improve.

The task for short-term macroeconomic manangement in developing countries with problems in debt-servicing is to bring about balance-of-payments improvements through reduced import demand and improved foreign-exchange earnings. Aggregate-demand management and exchange-rate adjustment are the two necessary policy elements that must be adopted, so that a sustainable balance-of-payments position can be achieved. Stabilisation measures to reduce import demand, reallocate resources in favour of tradable goods and especially exports require some time and a non-inflationary environment to succeed. Government budget deficits need to be pared down as part of the process.

Short-term austerity programs are unpopular and require a fair degree of social stability to be implemented successfully. Care must be taken to insure that vulnerable low-income households do not bear a disproportionate share of the burdens of adjustment. The implementation of policies aimed at promoting structural change that provide incentives to agricultural and manufacturing enterprises producing for export, in a manner that creates substantial new employment opportunities, is one way to lessen the hardships imposed.

Initiatives to liberalise trade and financial markets, encourage domestic savings, increase investment efficiency, reduce distortions in factor and goods markets, cut down public-sector waste and upgrade the skills, health and education of the labour force are all necessary. Changes of this nature require more than simple policy declaration; they require substantial improvement in the capabilities of policymakers as well as better understanding of institutional aspects of development.

Sustained growth can resume once external balance is attained and structural change is under way. For the transition from 'short-term' stabilisation to 'long-term' structural change to be made successfully, not only must appropriate domestic policies be consistently followed in the developing countries; it is also necessary that a more favourable world economic environment be created. In this context, several issues stand out. These include the 'new protectionism', the danger of rising expectations of inflation and high real interest rates, and the problem of reduced capital inflows to the developing countries.

Protectionism by the industrial economies has undoubtedly increased in recent years. However, the direct effects on trade with the developing countries have probably been somewhat exaggerated. It is likely that indirect effects of protectionist threats and measures on the pattern of investment in developing countries such as those in Asia have been more significant. The impetus to shift policies in the developing nations to a more outward-looking basis may have been reduced. This deserves more study, but it is still obvious that resistance to protectionism must continue and be strengthened in all countries.

The persistence of high real interest rates in world capital markets reflects, in the present recovery period, the effects of increased demand for funds as well as expectations that inflation rates may themselves rise with world demand. The large deficits in government budgets, particularly in the United States, Japan and some EEC countries, have made it far more difficult to reduce inflationary expectations about the future than would otherwise be the case. This problem demonstrates that macroeconomic policies in the more developed countries have a very important impact on the debt problem in the developing nations. Improved fiscal discipline would reduce the strain on monetary managers and increase confidence that the current recovery will be sustained without rekindling inflation. No doubt this would help ease upward pressure on interest rates. Declines in real rates of interest would greately ease the debt-servicing burden on developing nations and expedite their adjustment process.

The persistence of high real interest rates in world capital markets reflects, in the present recovery period, the effects of increased demand for funds as well as expectations that inflation rates may themselves rise with world demand. The large deficits in government budgets, particularly in the United States, Japan and some EEC countries, have made it far more difficult to reduce inflationary expectations about the future than would otherwise be the case. This problem demonstrates that macroeconomic policies in the more developed countries have a very important impact on the debt problem in the developing nations. Improved fiscal discipline would reduce the strain on monetary managers and increase confidence that the current recovery will be sustained without rekindling inflation. No doubt this would help ease upward pressure on interest rates. Declines in real rates of interest would greatly ease the debt-servicing burden on developing nations and expedite their adjustment process.

The state of flows of financial resources is alarming from the standpoint of development. At a time when commercial banks are being very cautious, aid-fatigue has reduced the availability of official development assistance (ODA). That ODA which is available has also become less concessional. Clearly, increased reliance on debt financing is not desirable at this stage. Developing countries may consider improving the environment for direct foreign investment and increased equity participation by outside investors. However, it is most unlikely inflows from these sources will grow rapidly enough to meet the requirements of development. It is therefore of great importance that various ways to maintain adequate financing through commercial sources, as well as bilateral and multilateral government agencies, be found. Again, this is essential if progress on the long-term debt problem is to be made. In this context, consideration should be given to various proposals for international monetary reform.

The debt situation in Asia cannot be completely separated from that of Latin America or Africa. To some degree private commercial banks may have to engage in lending to heavily indebted Latin American countries as part of debt-restructuring agreements, as in the recent Mexican rescheduling. This means less funds may be available for lending to more creditworthy Asian countries than otherwise. In addition, it should be noted that solutions to the debt situation must be linked to the issues of trade liberalisation and finance for development. Maintainance of an open world trade system will offer encouragement to liberalisation efforts in developing countries. The nature of the adjustment process is such that degrees of dislocation, unemployment and business failure are almost unavoidable. However, these should be held to a minimum through judicious continued allocation of development assistance funds, as in the World Bank's structural adjustment lending, and by use of expenditure switching and supplyside policies rather than depending solely on harsh expenditure-reduction programs. In this matter the burden of adjustment will be less onerous and can be shared more evenly across income groups.

The Asian developing countries have achieved a remarkable record of growth, trade expansion and low inflation. They met the challenges of the external shocks of oil prices and world recessions in the past decade. More than other developing regions, countries in East and Southeast Asia adopted policies that made them a significant source of dynamism in the world economy from which other regions have benefitted. To some degree, here as elsewhere, too much reliance was placed on external borrowings. Yet it also must be stressed that the savings performance of Asian countries has been excellent. The resilience of Asian economies has been confirmed and the long-term prospects appear to be great for renewed dynamism. The CIR analysis indicates the Asian countries have strong debt-servicing capacity as well. If the world economic environment can be improved there is reason for continued optimism regarding Asia and this, in turn, is a hopeful sign to developed and developing nations everywhere.

Part V   Overview

15 Issues and perspectives: an overview of banking regulation and monetary control

RONALD I. MCKINNON

The first part of this review focuses on financial policy at the national level: on what we have learnt about the process of financial repression; on what happens during liberalisation, taking the Pacific rim countries as illustrations. Does domestic interest-rate policy significantly affect economic development?

The second part, which considers the system as a whole, is more international in scope. The stability of the exchange-rate mechanism among the principal convertible currency countries is analysed, focusing particulary on monetary interactions between Japan and the United States. Then the origins of the banking crisis, which is associated with the debt problems of less developed countries (LDCs) and with the growth of unregulation offshore financial centres, are examined. How should the regulation of the large commercial banks be internationally coordinated?

FINANCIAL CONTROL IN INDIVIDUAL LDCS

The problems of financial repression and liberalisation in individual countries have been thoughtfully analysed in the chapters by Cole and Patrick and by Cole, Chunanuntathum and Loohawenchit. It is obvious that the absence of government deficits that are financed by taxing the domestic monetary system is a necessary condition for successful financial liberalisation. The following discussion of financial strategies for liberalising economies simply assumes that this politically difficult fiscal control problem has been satisfactorily resolved.

Real rates of interest and economic growth

What lessons have been learnt? Both the chapters cited provide evidence that countries which have maintained high real rates of interest generally have had higher rates of real financial growth. In turn, the success of the private sector in accumulating financial assets in real terms is associated with higher real economic growth. Hugh Patrick is a pioneer in this kind of analysis. Back in the 1960s he investigated the question of whether postwar Japanese financial growth led the development process or simply followed real growth which had other causes. He concluded that Japan's economic growth was, in part, finance-led.

Some data on private holdings of 'broad' money throw light on these issues. Table 15.1 presents ratios of the broad money supply (M2) to gross national product (GNP).[1] One noticeable characteristic is that even the slower growing Asian countries (shown in the lower panel) tend to be more financially developed than typical Latin American countries (shown in the upper panel). However, both groups of slowly growing economies have fairly low ratios of M2 to GNP, averaging about 0.22.

In contrast, Table 15.2 shows financial development in the really rapid-growth economies of West Germany, Japan, South Korea, Taiwan and Singapore. A high M2/GNP ratio and its rapid growth both indicate a large real flow of loanable funds through the organised financial sector. By and large, the capital market in most of these economies was dominated by the banking system, so that ratios of M2 to GNP encompass the main domestic flow of loanable funds in the system. By 1980, Japan, Taiwan and Singapore had M2/GNP ratios of 0.75 or more. Only South Korea had a much lower ratio of M2 to GNP (0.34) and had to make up for this shortage of domestic loanable funds by borrowing heavily abroad. The other countries shown in Table 15.2 are now net international creditors.

Table 15.1 Bank loanable funds in typical semi-industrial LDCs (ratio of M2 to GNP)

	1960	1965	1970	1975	1980	Mean 1960–80
Argentina	0.245	0.209	0.267	0.168	0.234	0.225
Brazil	0.148	0.156	0.205	0.164	0.175	0.170
Chile	0.123	0.130	0.183	0.099	0.208	0.149
Colombia	0.191	0.204	0.235	—	0.222	0.210
Mean ratio of M2 to GNP for four Latin American countries						**0.184**
India	0.283	0.262	0.264	0.295	0.382	0.297
The Philippines	0.186	0.214	0.235	0.186	0.219	0.208
Sri Lanka	0.284	0.330	0.275	0.255	0.317	0.291
Turkey	0.202	0.223	0.237	0.222	0.136	0.204
Mean ratio of M2 to GNP for four Asian countries						**0.247**

Source: IMF *International Financial Statistics* (various issues)

Table 15.2 Bank loanable funds in rapidly growing economies (ratio of M2 to GNP)

	1955	1960	1965	1970	1975	1980
West Germany[a]	0.331	0.294	0.448	0.583	0.727	0.913
Japan	0.554[b]	0.737[b]	0.701[b]	0.863	1.026	1.390
South Korea	0.069	0.114	0.102	0.325	0.323	0.337
Taiwan	0.115	0.166	0.331	0.462	0.588	0.750
Singapore	—	—	0.542[b]	0.701	0.668	0.826

Notes: a As well as deposits and currency, the German series includes bank bonds sold directly to the public.
b The bias is downward because deposit information on specialised credit institutions was not collected.

Source: IMF *International Financial Statistics* (various issues).

Although a higher rate of financial growth is positively correlated with successful real growth, Patrick's problem remains unresolved: what is the cause and what is the effect? To disentangle these issues, Table 15.3 presents some data from a recent study on interest-rate policies in developing countries.[2] Pure data availability and membership of the IMF were the criteria on which countries were selected.

For any one country over time, the real interest rate can vary a great deal, even from positive to negative or vice versa. For the period 1971 to 1980, the IMF calculated an average real interest rate for each country on a fairly common asset, usually a thirty-day deposit. Countries were then classified according to whether their average real interest rate was positive, mildly negative or highly negative. Because most of these countries have fragmented interest-rate structures, a representative interest rate is not easy to select. Nevertheless, the IMF, with its massive resources, somehow managed to devise the three-way classification shown in Table 15.3.

In Figure 15.1, real financial growth (which is not the same as measured personal saving) is shown to be positively correlated with real GDP growth. The left-hand panel of Figure 15.2 shows that those countries which maintain positive real rates of interest have higher growth in real financial assets, as might

Table 15.3 Selected developing countries grouped according to interest-rate policies: growth of real financial assets and real GDP, 1971–80 (compound growth rates; per cent per annum)

	Financial assets[a]	GDP
1 Countries with positive real interest rates		
Malaysia	13.8	8.0
South Korea	11.1	8.6
Sri Lanka	10.1	4.7
Nepal	9.6	2.0
Singapore	7.6	9.1
The Philippines	5.6	6.2
2 Countries with moderately negative real interest rates		
Pakistan[b]	9.9	5.4
Thailand	8.5	6.9
Morocco	8.2	5.5
Colombia	5.5	5.8
Greece	5.4	4.7
South Africa	4.3	3.7
Kenya	3.6	5.7
Burma	3.5	4.3
Portugal	1.8	4.7
Zambia	−1.1	0.8
3 Countries with severely negative real interest rates		
Peru	3.2	3.4
Turkey	2.2	5.1
Jamaica	−1.9	−0.7
Zaire	−6.8	0.1
Ghana	−7.6	−0.1

Notes: a Measured as the sum of monetary and quasi-monetary deposits with the banking sector, corrected for changes in the consumer price index.
  b The period covered is 1974–80.

Source: IMF *International Financial Statistics* and staff estimates.

Figure 15.1 Selected developing countries: growth of real GDP and real financial assets, 1971–80

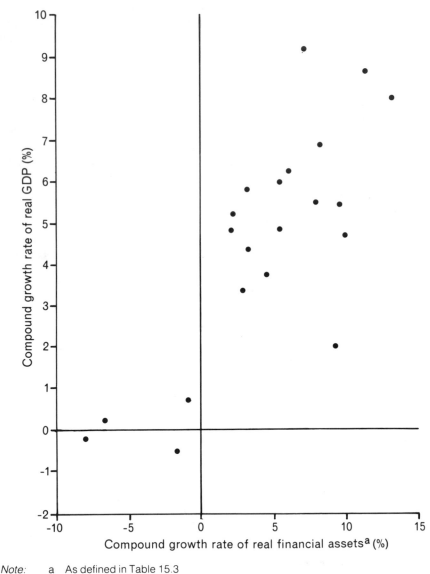

Note: a   As defined in Table 15.3

Source: IMF, *International Financial Statistics*

be expected. Most importantly, the right-hand panel of Figure 15.2 shows a significant positive correlation between real rates of interest and real growth in GDP.[3] This positive correlation is worked out in more detail in the IMF's statistical regressions reproduced in Table 15.4.

Figure 15.2 Selected developing countries grouped according to interest-rate policy: growth of real financial assets and real GDP, 1971–80

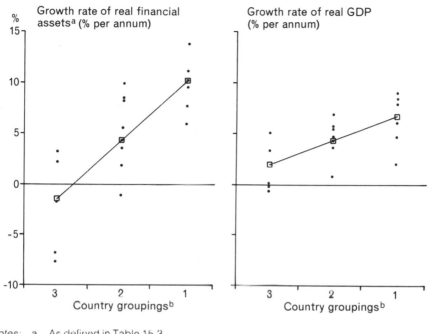

Notes: a As defined in Table 15.3
b See Table 15.3 for specifications of these groupings

With this kind of regression analysis, care must be taken in deciding which variables are exogenous and which endogenous. Positive correlations between growth in financial assets and growth in GDP do not show which way the causality operates. However, a case can be made for treating the real rate of interest as exogenous for the purposes of portfolio choice by individual investors. Governments frequently intervene to set ceilings on nominal rates of interest, and at the same time they determine the aggregate rate of price inflation; the real rate of interest, therefore, is very much determined by public policy. The statistical analysis in Figure 15.2 and Table 15.4, then, shows that higher real rates of interest seem to 'cause' higher rates of real economic growth. But this is not to deny that there may be some reverse causation.

Any positive link between real rates of interest and personal saving, as measured in the GNP accounts, is much less apparent. The results of cross-country statistical studies linking inflation rates to levels of personal saving have been quite ambiguous.

In an economy with high inflation, real rates of interest on financial assets are usually negative. Because of the high inflation, however, the private sector is forced to abstain from current consumption. Individuals must keep adding to their nominal money balances in order to prevent their real balances from

Table 15.4 Summary of estimated regressions

Dependent variables	Independent variables[a]						F-statistic[g]	R-square
	Constant	R[b]	M[c]	Y[d]	RM[e]	RY[f]		
1 Y	4.30 (9.12)	2.40 (2.64)					13.3 (1.19)	0.41
2 Y	2.66 (5.26)		0.39 (5.50)				30.3 (1.19)	0.61
3 Y	4.35 (11.0)	2.40 (4.40)			0.36 (3.11)		14.5 (2.18)	0.62
4 M	4.35 (5.55)	5.86 (4.42)					29.4 (1.19)	0.61
5 M	-2.41 (1.61)			1.57 (5.50)			30.3 (1.19)	0.61
6 M	4.35 (6.70)	5.86 (6.54)				0.97 (3.11)	26.2 (2.19)	0.74
7 M-Y	3.46 (4.07)						16.6 (1.20)	0.45

Notes:
a   t-statistics are given in parentheses.
b   Interest-rate-policy indicator: it is one for countries in group 1, zero for countries in group 2, and minus one for countries in group 3. (Country groupings are as shown in Table 15.3.)
c   Rate of growth of real broad money over the decade 1971–80.
d   Rate of growth of GDP over the decade 1971–80.
e   Residuals from the regression on line 4. This component represents the part of M that is uncorrelated with interest-rate policy.
f   Residuals from the regression on line 1. This component represents the part of Y that is uncorrelated with interest-rate policy.
g   Degrees of freedom are given in parentheses.

Source: IMF staff estimates based on data presented in Table 15.3

declining. This inflation 'tax', which is being extracted by the government, is classified in the GNP accounts as if it were saving. However, real personal financial assets are not accumulating, and the flow of loanable funds to the private sector may be quite low.

Typically, therefore, systematic relationships cannot be derived from cross-sectional data between personal saving and real rates of interest, or between personal saving and inflation. Fortunately, correlating real interest rates with real growth, while ignoring nominal saving, seems to give satisfactory results. Taiwan offers the best case of sustained financial liberalisation and high real interest rates in recent times, but Taiwan is omitted from the IMF's analysis.

A revisionist view of the Japanese financial experience has recently been provided by Horiuchi.[4] By international standards, Japan experienced very robust financial growth in the 1950s and 1960s, with a high and rising ratio of M2 to GNP (see Table 15.2), but the Japan of that era was widely considered to have a repressed financial system. Horiuchi demonstrates that this was not true, in the sense that real rates of interest were above international levels. Nominal interest rates in Japan were higher than those in the United States or West Germany; moreover, increases in the Japanese wholesale (tradable goods) price index in the 1950s and 1960s were almost zero. Horiuchi (correctly) uses the wholesale price index to calculate real from nominal rates of interest, and concludes that Japan's real interest rates were above national levels. (Use of the more rapidly inflating Japanese consumer price index, which I believe is inappropriate, would show a much lower Japanese real rate of interest.[5])

During the 1950s and 1960s, the Japanese government was far less successful than is commonly believed in influencing the domestic flow of capital. The relatively small flow of government-directed cheap credit was largely allocated to 'sunset' or declining industries. Internationally competitive firms had no trouble bidding for funds at close to the market rate of interest. Horiuchi's argument that Japan maintained a non-repressed financial system as a basis for high real economic growth carries conviction.

According to the chapter by Cole and Patrick, South Korea has pursued more erratic financial policies, sometimes being more repressed than at other times, occasionally moving from negative to positive real rates of interest. Korean financial policy and inflation rates have followed a cyclic pattern. Fortunately, a vigorous informal credit market has systematically kept the opportunity cost of capital quite high. This characteristic, of course, does not emerge from the formal data, but the case of Korea does not seem so exceptional when the informal credit market is taken into account.

Financial liberalisation without an equities market: some regulatory problems

This correlation between a positive real rate of interest and successful economic growth fits the theme elaborated by the author in 1973: the importance of eliminating financial repression.[6] From the vantage point of a dozen years later, monetary stability seems even more important as a necessary condition for successful economic development.

However, the problems of maintaining financial control during the movement from a highly repressed financial structure to a more liberalised one is much more difficult than my 1973 analysis suggested. Bringing down price inflation without undue reliance on foreign capital, while simultaneously preventing bank failures and financial stress, is technically quite difficult. Financial failures in Chile and Argentina in the early 1980s offer unfortunate examples of the need for caution in promoting financial liberalisation. And the question may well be asked what the ideal degree of deregulation of the domestic banking system might be.

Successful liberalisation is not simply a question of removing all regulations, despite what Herbert Grubel seems to suggest in his chapter. The peculiar importance of stabilising the monetary system makes some government regulation inevitable. In order to encourage small-scale savers to acquire monetary assets, the government must explicitly or implicitly insure bank deposits used as a means of payment. There are too many externalities involved in the use of money for the government not to insure the main part of the monetary system, perhaps (but not necessarily) in the form of deposit insurance. In addition, official reserve requirements against bank deposits are often necessary to secure monetary control.

But at the same time, as Peter Drake pointed out in his chapter, a substantial equities market is difficult to organise in most LDCs. It is quite expensive to establish the economies of scale necessary for stock trading. Closely held family enterprises in Asia are very secretive, and the last thing they want is to go public. The South Korean government has tried various draconian measures to force firms to go public, as Wontack Hong and Yung Chue Park noted. But equity markets remain thin and volatile with insider trading; the Taiwan market has been characterised as a 'gambling casino'; and investors have still not recovered from the collapse of the Thai stock market in 1979. When the flow of accounting information about business is limited, an information problem that is aggravated when price inflation is high and variable, a broadly based equities market is hard to develop.

In such an economy, without an adequate, organised market for risk-taking, the government must be very cautious about what banks are allowed to do. If total deregulation permits private banks to do anything they want, they become in effect a source of risk capital. Then, when lending rates of interest are increased to balance the risk, adverse risk selection is the result: only risky borrowers will come forward.[7] Extraordinarily high interest rates in the free market for bank loans and deposits, such as the 30–40 per cent real yields in Chile and Argentina in the late 1970s, may be a signal of financial disaster to come.

Banks may or may not engage in this risky lending, depending on the prudential regulations they face. When banks are effectively unregulated in choosing their loan portfolios, there is a kind of unfair bet involved if the government, either de facto or de jure, insures their deposit base. If the banks undertake risky lending, shareholders and owners of the banks, if they are privately owned, will take the majority of any profits that might be made when such risk-taking is successful; the government does not share in extraordinary profits. In contrast, if a financial bust occurs, owners may lose their equity but otherwise walk away while the public insurance agency or the central bank picks up the pieces. Given the unavoidable insurance of deposits in the monetary system, fairly conservative regulation of banks, in order to reduce the riskiness of their portfolios, is mandatory.

However, the objective of allowing the banks to operate fairly competitively while paying substantial real interest rates on deposits remains important. How can this objective be reconciled with conservative regulation of the banks, which effectively puts a ceiling on the nominal interest rates that the banks may charge or offer?

In reconciling these conflicting goals, the highly successful experience of Taiwan since 1960 is well worth examining. The Central Bank of China has maintained a very stable price level (since 1960), except when the economy experienced unexpected international shocks. Banks are owned and controlled by the government, with standard lending and deposit rates that are very substantial in real terms, ranging between 9 per cent and 14 per cent since 1960. The banks sometimes use compensatory deposits and so forth to charge a little more than the standard rate on loans. Consequently, these controlled interest rates have been kept close to market-clearing levels, at least for fairly 'safe' borrowers. The high real deposit rate of 8–9 per cent led to the rapid real financial growth shown in Table 15.2. Although Taiwan did not have a completely free market in domestic loans and deposits, price stability made effective financial liberalisation much easier to achieve.

Consider the regulation of financial institutions other than banks, such as finance companies, which accept term deposits or issue notes in order to make loans. Clearly, if the banks are regulated towards conservatism in their portfolio selection and in the interest rates they pay or charge, a group of completely unregulated finance companies cannot be allowed to emerge to issue deposits—money or near-monies—that are very competitive with what the banks can offer. Such companies can divert resources from the organised banking system and cause sudden disintermediation, as happened in Chile in 1975–76, when the savings and loans system actually collapsed.

Thailand also experienced a financial collapse because finance companies were inadequately monitored. Once finance companies are officially sanctioned, the impression arises that the government will stand by them if something goes wrong. A more uniform treatment of the deposit-taking institutions is required; a completely unregulated fringe (with some government sanction) cannot be allowed to displace an inner core of commercial banks that are tightly regulated or even heavily taxed. There has to be a balance in this respect.

But even if such a balance were struck, the economy could still be left with inadequate sources of risk capital; hence the importance of encouraging the development of non-bank open markets for primary securities, both stocks and bonds, to supplement the risk capital provided by individual proprietors. Japan, which up to ten years ago had a largely bank-based capital market, now has a robust stock market that is an important source of risk capital for both new and established Japanese firms. There has also been rapid growth in primary securities trading in Taiwan and, to a lesser extent, in South Korea (although primary securities issued in Korea are still largely guaranteed by banks because the flow of accounting information from business remains inadequate). In addition, a stable price level is necessary for trade to develop in longer term primary securities.

Once a vigorous primary securities market exists independently of the banking system, the dilemma of how to regulate deposit-taking banks is more easily resolved. Regulation may be very conservative, as befits a system with implicit or explicit government insurance for deposits, to ensure the safety of the monetary system and the stability of the price level. The commercial banking system may then be expected to shrink relative to the rest of the capital market as economic and financial development proceed.

Inflows of foreign capital and overborrowing

How should foreign capital inflows be treated? Fiscal control should come first, and the government can then liberalise the domestic financial system by raising real rates of interest, reducing reserve requirements and so on. Equally important is the removal of all or most protective quotas and tariffs on the current account of the balance of trade. Finally, at the last stage of the liberalisation process, restrictions on foreign capital inflows or outflows can be eased.

Several examples have now been given of countries that overborrowed in the attempted transition to a more liberalised economic structure. Typically, an initial period of successful liberalisation induced large and unexpected inflows of foreign capital, which subsequently posed severe problems in financial management. International agencies such as the World Bank may even have aggravated this problem in so far as they tried to 'bribe' countries into liberalising by injecting capital while liberalisation was occurring.

It is my impression that the Koreans were somewhat surprised and disturbed in the mid-1960s, after their very successful reforms, when a huge amount of private foreign capital flowed into South Korea. The newly acquired stability in the Korean price level was upset because this inflow of foreign capital caused the government to loss control of the monetary base. Korea, of course, survived this and adjusted to it, but it remains true that there was a large and unexpected inflow of capital into the country. Something similar apparently happened in Sri Lanka, which absorbed a lot of foreign capital when it embarked on liberalisation in the late 1970s and now has an almost unmanageable debt problem.

However, the most spectacular example was Chile. Chile seemed to do most things right, but its one obvious mistake was to overborrow grossly as it reduced tariffs in foreign trade and raised domestic interest rates. Given the nature of

Chile's economy, this overborrowing was more extreme than any step taken by Korea.

Why does the market fail to take properly into account what is going to happen to the liberalising economy? Is there some sort of market failure in the movement of foreign capital at the moment when liberalisation occurs? Liberalisation is a one-shot experiment for most participants: both for the locals, who are going through a major liberalisation for the first time in their lives, and for international bankers, who do not seem to learn much from the experience of other countries. Consequently, the theory of rational expectations, where everybody understands what is likely to happen, simply does not apply.

Take the case of a successful trade and financial liberalisation, where the real exchange rate is set at an internationally competitive level and real interest rates are raised to give the desired rate of domestic financial growth. In such circumstances, there could well be a discrete portfolio shift on the part of international lenders in favour of that country. Chile was treated as a pariah in the international capital market from about 1972 to 1976, and could not borrow a cent when it needed to. Suddenly, however, Chile undertook a series of reforms that seemed to be paying off, leading to widespread rosy projections about the future. External lenders all changed their minds simultaneously, and there was a once-and-for-all shift of their portfolio preferences in favour of Chile.

A great inflow of capital like this poses a dilemma for the monetary authorities regarding the real exchange rate. If the exchange rate is floating, it will appreciate immediately and the nascent export activities will be pushed down. On the other hand, if the exchange rate is fixed, as it was in Korea in the mid-1960s and Chile in the late 1970s, the inflow of capital will cause them to lose control of the monetary base so that domestic inflation will return, or at least will not slow down as fast as initially intended. Massive capital inflows create this dilemma under any exchange-rate regime. By 1980, Chile had become grossly overvalued in the foreign exchanges, and its tradable goods sector became quite uncompetitive just when it was eliminating protectionist tariffs and quotas.

This natural tendency towards overborrowing can be greatly aggravated if the host government guarantees foreign credits and goes out of its way to solicit foreign capital. In addition, mercantilist agencies like the export–import banks of the United States, Japan and Europe stand willing to give credits with no questions asked. In these circumstances, individual private borrowers in LDCs do not perceive the normal, upward-sloping supply curve of finance: they believe they can borrow at what is, from their myopic perspective, an essentially flat rate of interest. Clearly, these government interventions in the international flow of capital can make overborrowing much worse.

In conclusion, a case can be made for governments to place strict limitations on inflows of foreign capital during the liberalisation process because the market will not necessarily work correctly in response to such a sharp change in public policy. The government should strive for a balance between imports and exports, and should not allow imports to grow rapidly relative to exports, the real counterpart of a large inflow of foreign capital. Certainly, the real exchange rate must be kept at an internationally competitive level if liberalisation is to succeed.

POLICY COORDINATION AMONG INDUSTRIAL ECONOMIES

This section analyses macroeconomic instability at the international level: the problem of coordinating macroeconomic policy among the principal industrial countries, including Japan and the United States. I find Jorge de Macedo's model in chapter 13 a little unsatisfying because it portrays the two countries as if they were symmetrically placed and does not recognise the hard fact that the international economy is based on the US dollar. The United States has an asymmetrical relationship with other countries. The US Federal Reserve Bank does not typically intervene in the foreign-exchange market as other central banks do; international indebtedness is in dollar terms, exchange reserves are largely in dollars, and so forth. In order to acquire a proper macroeconomic overview of how the system works, this asymmetry must be explicitly recognised. It is strange that very few writers in the professional journals take the dollar standard seriously.

American benign neglect: the 1950s and 1960s

Elsewhere, I have suggested how American monetary policy might best be internationalised in the context of the world dollar standard.[8] According to Kong-Yam Tan, during the 1950s and 1960s, under a strong dollar standard and fixed exchange rates, the Federal Reserve Bank could rely on domestic monetary indicators to stabilise American and international price levels in dollar terms, while following a policy of benign neglect with respect to other countries. This strategy benefited the rest of the world provided that the United States used its freedom to stabilise the dollar's international purchasing power.[9]

In the 1950s and 1960s, stable price-level and exchange-rate expectations meant that the Federal Reserve Bank could safely use the domestic dollar rate of interest as a short-run indicator for monetary policy. In the intermediate run, a Friedman-type monetary rule based on American money growth alone would have worked reasonably well. In those days, American officials did not have to worry about money growth in other countries, nor was there much systematic pressure for or against the US dollar in the foreign-exchange market. Alternative 'reserve' currencies, which now compete with the US dollar as a significant asset in international portfolios, did not then exist. Purely domestic monetary indicators were sufficient, in these two decades, for the Federal Reserve Bank to stabilise the international monetary systems unilaterally.

Knowing that the American authorities were successfully stabilising the international purchasing power of the dollar, other industrial countries could fix their dollar exchange rates and follow purely dependent monetary policies. For example, Japan maintained the exchange rate of 360 yen to the US dollar for twenty years, from 1950 to 1970. If net international payments tended towards surplus, the Bank of Japan expanded its monetary supply; and monetary policy became tight when Japan's balance of payments was in deficit. This foreign-exchange-based monetary policy worked well throughout the 1950s to the late 1960s, Japan's era of very rapid economic growth.

The need to coordinate monetary policies in the 1980s

What constituted an adequate strategy for the 1950s and the 1960s, however, has proved inadequate in the 1970s and the early 1980s. The empirical characteristics of both the American economy and the world economy have changed. No longer are there expectations of stability in the average US dollar exchange rate; there are other convertible currencies which, at the margin, compete as an international store of value. Investors no longer automatically put all their international reserves into United States Treasury bonds or bills. For example, the Monetary Authority of Singapore diversifies its exchange reserves into other convertible currencies. During the 1970s and the 1980s, continual shifts in these international portfolio preferences can and did destabilise the American monetary system.[10]

The key to stabilising the American price level (and that of the industrial world) is therefore to internationalise United States monetary policy. Acting in the best interests of the United States, the Federal Reserve system should establish itself as the world's monetary balance wheel by:

allowing growth in the United States money base to deviate from its norm in order to stabilise the dollar exchange rate with hard currency trading partners; and compensating for excesses or shortfalls in money growth in these same partner countries, so as to smooth growth in 'world' money.

Fortunately, these two requirements need not conflict if the other principal central banks, say the Bundesbank and the Bank of Japan, were to cooperate with the Federal Reserve Bank. Indeed, if each of these three banks were to fix its rate of domestic credit expansion but vary the 'foreign' component of the national monetary base symmetrically so as to stabilise the dollar/Mark or dollar/yen exchange rate, both requirements would be automatically satisfied. When one country's money supply was expanding, the other(s) would be contracting in an offsetting fashion. How such coordination could evolve in stages, in order to be both technically and politically feasible, I have dealt with in detail elsewhere.[11]

With the liberalisation of the Japanese capital market, discussed in chapter 10 by Sakakibara, the Japanese monetary authorities now have a much more immediate interest in monetary coordination with the United States. Because of the capital-account restrictions previously in place, the Japanese monetary system used to be somewhat insulated from the American. The Japanese authorities had some limited scope to manipulate domestic monetary policy with purely domestic goals in mind, although the international economy could not be ignored. That degree of freedom has now been eroded. Previously, the Bank of Japan did have a degree of internal control and could stabilise the yen/dollar exchange rate by sterilised intervention or by telling the commercial banks how much they could borrow or lend in international markets. Such non-monetary methods of stabilising the exchange rate will no longer work. In the mid-1980s, therefore, the case is even stronger for the Bank of Japan and the US Federal Reserve Bank to manage their money supplies jointly, in order to stabilise the yen/dollar exchange rate and the 'world' price level more effectively.

My reading of the situation in November 1984 is that a certain amount of (implicit) monetary coordination occurred in 1982–83. Fortunately for the world economy, the Federal Reserve Bank undertook an extraordinary monetary expansion measured on a two-year basis, the main expansion being from mid-1982 to mid-1983. The purpose of the expansion was to pull the US (and world) economy out of the depression of 1982. Monetary expansion in the United States was warranted because the dollar was (and is) very high in the world exchange markets: international demand has shifted towards the dollar. The Japanese also played the game correctly by having a fairly tight monetary policy, beginning in September 1982 and continuing to the present time, in response to the shifting of international demand away from yen assets.

These mutual adjustments in national monetary policies have permitted some realignment of the US dollar exchange rate from 270 yen to about 240 yen. However, a rate of 200 yen to the dollar would be even better by any reasonable criterion of purchasing-power parity. Nevertheless, this modest degree of implicit coordination in 1982–83, while insufficient, was still advantageous for the system as a whole.

In 1984, however, the US Federal Reserve Bank again allowed American money growth to slow unduly in the face of a sharp increase in the foreign-exchange value of the dollar. To avoid more protectionist pressure in the United States, the German and Japanese central banks responded more or less correctly by reducing their money growth to protect their currencies from depreciating even further. The unfortunate outcome is that aggregate money growth in the major industrial countries—the United States, Japan and Europe—fell well below its normal non-inflationary growth path. The result in 1985 could be an unnecessary and unplanned economic downturn. The failure to properly internationalise American monetary policy can be costly indeed!

Fiscal policy and real interest rates

The other aspect of the coordination problem is fiscal policy. It is my view that monetary policies should be geared towards stabilising exchange rates almost independently of what happens in the fiscal sphere. However, the huge United States fiscal deficit is the prime cause of the high real interest rates in the world economy, making life unnecessarily difficult for the LDCs and putting great strain on the international banking system.

One pessimistic scenario suggests that the highly indebted LDCs are insolvent if real rates of interest remain above 10 per cent. Nominal interest rates on dollar loans are now closer to 11–12 per cent, plus the margin that poor countries must pay above LIBOR (the London Interbank Offer Rate). Given a stable international price level for tradable goods (primary commodities), current real interest rates are well above the 10 per cent critical level.

The implication is that the United States authorities must cut back their massive fiscal deficits if a major international default and banking crisis is to be avoided. Nor should countries like Japan, and those in Europe, become more 'expansionary' in the Keynesian fiscal sense. The pool of saving in the world is too small, and worldwide interest rates too high, for other industrial countries to engage in further deficit spending.

Unfortunately, a number of economists have suggested that European countries and Japan should run bigger fiscal deficits. A recent issue of the *Economist* (19 May 1984) reviewed the Dornbusch–Buiter proposal to do exactly that; to promote a big increase in government expenditure in European countries in order to reduce unemployment. Furthermore, the United States has pressured Japan to increase its fiscal deficit as a way of reducing the Japanese trade surplus. In my view, this pressure is entirely inappropriate.

Small improvements in the budgetary positions of Japan and West Germany, coupled with a massive improvement in the United States, constitute the preferred strategy. Without some adjustment of this sort, the ensuing banking crisis will probably be very hard to deal with.

Regulation and the banking crisis

This brings the discussion back to banking regulation and offshore markets. To what extent can the present debt crisis of the LDCs be associated with the Eurocurrency system in general and the Asian dollar market in particular? If the domestic financial system is regulated and distorted, and then transactions by non-residents in offshore centres are made completely free, it cannot be known a priori whether welfare within the system as a whole will improve or deteriorate. The theory of the second-best suggests that the result must be evaluated empirically.

Consider the original development of the Euromarket in London in the 1960s. My own view is that the initial net effect on the world economy was positive. The international financial system had been constipated by exchange controls and unduly low ceilings on domestic interest rates in most industrial countries. Even the United States had its interest-equalisation tax and 'voluntary' restraints on bank lending abroad, and rates of interest on domestic deposits were subject to restrictive ceilings. Without the Euromarket, trade finance and the normal hedging–covering service provided by the banks to international traders would have been much less efficient. In addition, competition from the Euromarket enforced considerable liberalisation within national money markets. So the rapid development of the Euromarket as an unregulated intermediary competing with regulated ones was a net gain to the system as a whole in the 1960s—a big net gain.

That said, what might be called the negative aspects of unregulated Euromarkets began to emerge in the 1970s: highly risky long-term bank loans to LDCs, with few or no loan-loss provisions. This is not the kind of lending traditionally associated with monetary intermediaries that are supposed to be regulated towards conservatism in order to protect the payments mechanism. But there is a great deal of ambiguity about who is responsible for the Eurobanks—for supervising them and bailing them out. Irresponsible lending practices could therefore develop more readily.

The dual system of regulation has become quite unbalanced. Take the case of a large American bank which is regulated towards conservatism in its national lending operations. It must meet reserve requirements (ratios of outstanding loans to capital) and faces substantial restraints on what may be included in its domestic loan portfolio. If a window of opportunity is suddenly opened for the bank to operate in a relatively regulation-free environment, it will begin to take more risks in this deregulated area than it would have done if the whole portfolio were deregulated. The willingness of individual banks to take very great risks in their international portfolios through the Euromarkets reflected the fact that their domestic portfolios were primarily regulated towards safety.

This incentive for undue risk-taking was further aggravated by deposit insurance in domestic markets, and by the known commitment of the central banks to come in and bail out domestic depositors if any threatening bank crash occurred. In the case of the American banks, the United States government is a silent partner putting up risk capital. The shareholders of the Bank of America, or Wells Fargo, can undertake risky foreign loans in the knowledge that, if the whole system collapses, the most they can lose is their invested capital. On the other hand, if the system holds together, the banks stand to make quite large profits. Ex ante, the shareholders get the upper tail of the distribution of profits, in which the American government does not share, but the government must cover a disproportionate share of any massive losses. The bottom line here is that commercial banks are the wrong institutions to be engaged in long-term international lending on a large scale.

In the 19th century, the instruments of international finance were better matched to the term structure and riskiness of the loans. A huge long-term bond market was centred in London, but trading in equities was also important. So when Russia defaulted on the Czarist bonds, the banking system as a whole was not threatened. According to the 'real bills' doctrine, commercial banks were confined to providing short-term trade credit, which was supposed to be fully collateralised. In those days, the commercial banks were not the principle source of international risk capital.

Contemporary students tend to think that the international capital market is bank-based by nature because they observe little else. But, of course, it is regulatory imbalance, rather than superior efficiency, that has caused insured commercial banks to dominate the international capital market. A long-term international bond market cannot thrive in the face of such heavily subsidised competition; this bias in favour of banks also exists in the (unregulated) international market. However, it should also be noted that a long-term capital market operates best when international price levels and exchange rates are fairly stable—as they were under the 19th-century gold standard.

A new regulatory approach

The present international debt burden poses a very acute threat to the solvency of the banking system. Nevertheless, ignoring the present debt crisis for the moment, what form would an ideal regulatory system take? If the conditions of twenty years ago, before the development of this indebtedness, could be re-created, how should the domestic and international lending operations of the commercial banks be properly restricted?

One promising development was the Glass–Steagall (GS) Act of 1934, to which Eisuke Sakakibara referred in chapter 10. In the United States, the GS Act requires the separation of merchant banks and securities houses from commercial banks, with only the former providing risk capital. In the late 1940s, the Americans imposed a similar requirement on the Japanese capital market, which allowed Japanese securities houses to evolve independently of the banking system. In the 1980s, paradoxically, the United States government is advising Japan to eliminate the artificial separation of commercial banks and securities houses!

Until very recently, the GS Act probably encouraged regulators to repress deposit rates of interest in the commercial banking systems of both countries with undue rigour. This should definitely be avoided, but a case can be made for restoring the essential distinction between monetary institutions—where the safety-first rule is paramount—and the 'risk-taking' capital market. Some version of the GS principle should apply in a balanced fashion at both the domestic and international levels. This would encourage a more appropriate development of the international capital market, based mainly on bonds and equities. Merchant banks and securities houses, which are not insured by their governments, would again become the main actors in long-term international borrowing and lending.

This new regulatory approach would somewhat undermine the status of offshore centres, such as the Asian dollar market, that have thrived in the existing state of regulatory imbalance. What is being suggested is at least a partial closing of the regulatory loopholes that encourage 'Euro' trading in the major convertible currencies. The industrial countries should combine to consolidate their offshore banking subsidiaries with the parent banks and formulate a common set of rules, GS-type rules, for governing these consolidated banking entities.

These rules would apply in a balanced fashion to international and domestic lending and be fairly uniform across Europe, Japan and the United States, so that there would be no mercantilist advantage to be secured by a bank incorporating in one country rather than another. These rules would also tend to restrict the role of commercial banks in highly risky lending operations and, on the positive side, encourage merchant banks, mutual funds and so forth to develop bond and equity trading in the international capital market. The commercial banks would be confined to their traditional role of providing short-term trade credit, clearing international payments and providing hedging services on a short-term basis. In other words, commercial banks would continue to be the principal dealers in the short-term foreign-exchange market.

In the 1980s, those few countries that are not classified as being in crisis are continually being pressured by bankers to increase their outstanding indebtedness. Under this new regulatory approach, they could be visited by bond salesmen or merchant bankers, but not by pin-striped representatives of the commercial banks.

In conclusion, the flows of goods and finance have become more completely internationalised in the 1980s. Therefore, no industrial country can run a satisfactory monetary policy on a purely national basis, ignoring its exchange rate and paying no attention to money growth elsewhere. Nor should bank rules and regulations, whether for offshore centres or 'onshore' domestic finance, be decided by individual countries without reference to what their trading partners are doing. The institutions of the international capital market should be designed to reflect much more accurately the risks involved in cross-country and cross-currency lending, while the payments mechanism should be carefully regulated to be safe.

APPENDIXES

2A The financial structures of Pacific Basin economies

The financial structure of Australia (year-end 1982)

	Head offices	Total offices	Total assets[a] ($A million)	Percentage of total assets
Central bank				
Reserve Bank of Australia*	1	na	14 350	—
Deposit money banks				
Trading banks	**12**	**5 108**[b]	**39 429**	**25.7**
—major trading banks[c]	6	4 738	34 008	22.2
—other trading banks	6	370	5 421	3.5
Savings institutions				
Savings banks	**15**	**5 678**[b]	**28 625**	**18.6**
Long-term credit institutions				
Development institutions			**2 449**	**1.6**
—Australian Resources Development Bank*		1	870	0.6
—Commonwealth Development Bank*		1	682	0.4
—Primary Industry Bank of Australia*		1	529	0.3
—Australian Industry Development Corporation*		1	386[d]	0.2
			64 310	**41.9**
Registered building societies	6 751[e]	6 751	14 861	9.7
Credit cooperatives	648[b]	648	3 201	2.1
Authorised money market dealers	9	9	1 659	1.1
Money market corporations	52	52	12 814	8.3
Finance companies	102	102	27 077	17.6
General financiers	94	94	2 890	1.9
Intragroup financiers	12	12	1 458	0.9
Other non-bank financial corporations	8	8	350	0.2
Rural credit institutions				
Pastoral finance companies	**15**	**15**	**1 868**	**1.2**
Insurance and pension institutions				
Life insurance companies	**48**	**48**	**16 840**	**11.0**
Total assets (excluding central bank)			**153 521**	

Notes: a   Total assets in Australia only.
         b   1981 figure.
         c   'Major trading banks' are five large private trading banks together with the state-owned Commonwealth Trading Bank; 'other trading banks' comprise one local, two overseas and three state-owned banks.
         d   Operational loans and investments outstanding as of June 1980.
         e   Of the 6751 registered building societies, 139 are listed as 'permanent'.
         *   Government financial institution.
         na Not available.

Sources: ABS *Monthly Summary of Statistics* December 1983, and *Yearbook Australia 1982*; Reserve Bank of Australia *Bulletin* May 1983.

The financial structure of Canada (year-end 1980)

	Head offices	Total offices	Total assets (Can$ million)	Percentage of total assets
Central bank				
Bank of Canada*	1	16	17313	—
Deposit money bank				
Charter banks			**291523**	**50.2**
—domestic	11	7414	281244	48.4
—foreign affiliates	na	50–100	10279	1.8
Savings institutions			**6112**	**1.0**
Government savings banks*	1	na	2446	0.4
Quebec Savings Bank	1	na	1747	0.3
Province of Ontario Savings Bank	1	22	504[a]	—
Montreal City & District Savings Bank	1	na	1415[b]	0.2
Long-term credit institutions			**137124**	**23.6**
Trust companies	na	na	38968	6.7
Credit unions	na	3926[c]	31610	5.4
Sales finance and consumer loan companies	na	na	14295	2.5
Investment dealers	na	na	6673	1.1
Mutual funds and investment companies	na	na	5166	0.9
Mortgage loan companies	na	na	16075	2.8
Small loans companies	4	4	na	na
Licensed money lenders	33	33	na	na
Other private intermediaries	na	na	24337	4.2
			38251	**6.6**
Federal Business Development Bank	1	110	2001	0.3
Province of Alberta Treasury branches*	1	102	1496[c]	0.3
Other government intermediaries	na	na	34754	6.0
Insurance and pension institutions			**107443**	**18.5**
Life insurance companies	153	153	37629	6.5
Other insurance companies	357	357	20091	3.5
Pension funds	na	na	49723	8.6
Total assets (excluding central bank)			**580453**	

Notes: a   Figure represents total deposits in 1979.
      b   1978 figure.
      c   1977 figure.
      *   Government financial institution.
     na Not available.

Sources: Department of Finance *Economic Review 1982*: Ronald Shearer et al. *Macroeconomics of the Canadian Financial System*: Statistics Canada *Canadian Statistical Review.*

The financial structure of Hong Kong (year-end 1980)

	Head offices	Total offices	Total assets (HK$ million)	Percentage of total assets
Central bank				
None	—	—	—	—
Deposit money banks				
Licensed banks	**113**	**1 078**	**294 979**	**67.4**
—domestic banks	34	na	na[a]	32.7
—foreign banks	79	na	na	34.7
Deposit-taking companies[b]	**302**	**na**	**140 358**	**32.1**
—domestic	na	na	na[c]	na
—foreign	na	na	na	na
Representative offices of foreign banks	104	—	na	na
Long-term credit institutions				
Development Loan Credit Fund	1	—	1 566.5[d]	0.4
Home Ownership Fund	1	—	989.5[d]	0.2
Lotteries Fund	1	—	na	na
Hong Kong Building and Loan Agency	1	—	na	na
Hong Kong Credit Insurance Corporation	1	—	na	na
Hong Kong Fintracon	1	—	na	na
Insurance institutions				
Retirement or pension funds	1 731[d]	—	na	na
Insurance companies				
—domestic	209[d]	—	na	na
—foreign	234[d]	—	na	na
Total assets			**437 890**	

Notes: a Foreign banks accounted for 51.5 per cent of total assets of the licensed banks in 1979.
        b Deposit-taking companies (DTCs) includes registered merchant banks and finance companies.
        c Foreign-owned DTCs accounted for 53.2 per cent of total assets of all DTCs in 1979.
        d 1979 figure.

Source: Hong Kong Census and Statistics Department Hong Kong Annual Digest of Statistics, 1983.

The financial structure of Indonesia (at March 1982)

	Head offices	Total offices	Total assets (Rp billion)	Percentage of total assets
Central bank				
Bank Indonesia*	1	36	11 561	—
Deposit money banks				
Commercial banks	**87**	**1 030**	**13 149**	**84.2**
—state banks*	5	712	10 857[a]	69.5
—national private banks	71	298	1 356	8.7
—foreign/joint-venture banks	11	20	936	6.0
Development banks	**28**	**194**	**1 115[b]**	**7.1**
—State Development Bank (Bapindo)*	1	19	na	na
—local development banks	26	174	488	3.1
—private development bank	1	1	na	na
Savings institutions			**396**	**2.5**
State Savings Bank (BTN)*	1	12	396[c]	
Private savings bank	2	2	na	
Long-term credit institutions			**611**	**3.9**
Investment finance companies	9	—	504	3.2
Development finance companies	3	—	107	0.7
Other finance companies	2	—	na	na
Rural credit institutions			**53.4[d]**	**0.3**
Village banks	3 256	—	10.6	0.1
Paddy banks	1 737	—	0.6	—
Petty traders' banks	164	—	na	na
Employees' banks	1	—	na	na
Government pawnshops	469	—	42.3	0.3
Credit cooperatives	13 000	—	na	na
Insurance institutions				
Insurance companies	75	—	**293[e]**	**1.9**
Total assets (excluding central bank)			**15 617.5**	

Notes:
a   Assets of the State Development Bank (Bapindo) are included in the figure for state banks.
b   Figure includes assets of Bapindo, 26 local development banks, and one private development bank.
c   Figure represents total savings outstanding from the two government savings schemes, Tabanas and Taska.
d   Figure represents credit outstanding.
e   Figure represents total investments, 1980.
*   Government financial institution.
na   Not available.

Sources: Bank Indonesia Report for the Financial Year 1981/1982 pp. 33–43; Indonesian Financial Statistics January 1984, pp. 14–89; Lee and Jao Financial Structures and Monetary Policies in Southeast Asia.

The financial structure of Japan (year-end 1982)

	Head offices	Total offices	Total assets (¥1000 million)	Percentage of total assets
Central bank				
The Bank of Japan	1	na	263 999	—
Deposit money banks				
Commercial banks	**86**	**8 367**	**2 833 489**	**35.4**
—city banks	13	2 634	1 419 032	17.7
—regional banks	63	5 361	819 998	10.2
—trust banks	7	318	166 641	2.1
—long-term credit banks	3	54	318 454	4.0
—foreign banks	75	75	109 364	1.4

The financial structure of Japan (year-end 1982) (cont'd)

	Head offices	Total offices	Total assets (¥1000 million)	Percentage of total assets
Small business banks			**1 145 075**	**14.3**
—Sogo banks	71	na	382 861	4.8
—Zenshinren Bank	1	—	41 546	0.5
—Shinkin banks	456	na	479 388	6.0
—Shoko Chukin Bank	1	na	71 250	0.9
—National Federation of Credit Cooperatives	na	na	12 090	0.2
—Credit cooperatives	468	—	112 351	1.4
—National Federation of Labor Credit Associations	na	na	7 836	0.1
—Labor credit associations	47	—	37 753	0.5
Postal savings			**740 301**[a]	**9.2**
Postal savings*	na	na	740 301	9.2
Long-term credit institutions				
Financial institutions for small businesses			**126 002**	**1.6**
—Finance Corporation of Local Public Enterprise*	1	—	70 086	0.9
—Small Business Credit Insurance Corporation	1	—	3 146	—
—Small Business Finance Corporation	1	—	52 770	0.7
Securities finance institutions			**77 871**	**1.0**
—securities finance companies	3	—	9 698	0.1
—securities companies	218	—	68 173	0.9
Government financial institutions			**379 290**	**4.7**
—Japan Development Bank*	1	na	63 230	0.8
—Hokkaido and Tohoku Development Corporation*	1	—	8 433	0.1
—Okinawa Development Finance Corporation*	1	—	6 864	0.1
—Export–Import Bank of Japan*	1	na	60 080	0.7
—People's Finance Corporation*	1	—	47 500	0.6
—Housing Loan Corporation*	1	—	178 658	2.2
—Medical Care Facilities Finance Corporation*	1	—	0 010	0.1
—Environmental Sanitation Business Finance Corporation*	1	—	7 919	0.1
Rural credit institutions			**866 651**	**10.8**
Norinchukin Bank	1	na	157 744	2.0
Agricultural cooperatives	4 352	—	331 716	4.1
Credit federations of agricultural cooperatives	47	—	222 246	2.8
Fishery cooperatives	1 751	—	22 764	0.3
Credit federations of fishery cooperatives	35	—	14 324	0.2
Agriculture, Forestry and Fisheries Finance Corporation*	1	—	45 568	0.6
National Mutual Insurance Federation of Agricultural Cooperatives	na	na	na	na
Mutual insurance federations of agricultural cooperatives	47	—	72 289	0.9
Insurance institutions			**607 771**	**7.6**
Postal Life Insurance and Postal Annuity*	1	na	195 021	2.4
Life insurance companies	23	—	327 206	4.1
Non-life-insurance companies	22	—	85 544	1.1
Other non-bank financial institutions			**1 237 187**	**15.4**
Trust Fund Bureau of the Ministry of Finance*	1	na	1 237 187	15.4
Total assets (excluding central bank)			**8 013 637**	

Notes: a Figure represents total savings.
　　　　* Government financial institution.
　　　　na Not available.

Sources: Bank of Japan, Research and Statistics Department *Economic Statistics Monthly* 42, January 1984; Federation of Bankers' Associations of Japan *Banking Systems in Japan* 1982.

The financial structure of South Korea (year-end 1982)

	Head offices	Total offices	Total assets (W billion)	Percentage of total assets
Central bank				
The Bank of Korea*	1	na	9 766.1	—
Deposit money banks				
Commercial banks	**62**	**1 091**	**40 384.3**	**44.9**
—nationwide banks	7	679	31 337.9	34.8
—local banks	11	368	4 128.7	4.6
—foreign banks	44	44	4 917.7	5.5
Savings institutions			**5 968.4**	**6.6**
Mutual savings and finance companies	na	na	1 211.3	1.3
Trust accounts of banks	na	na	4 757.1	5.3
Postal savings*	na	na	na	na
Long-term credit institutions				
Specialised banks			**18 885.3**	**21.0**
—Korea Exchange Bank*	1	—	11 918.5	13.1
—Medium Industry Bank	1	—	2 477.4	2.8
—Citizens' National Bank	1	—	2 790.2	3.1
—Korea Housing Bank*	1	—	1 699.2	1.9
Investment companies			**5 734.6**	**6.4**
—merchant banking companies	6	—	1 105.4	1.2
—investment and finance companies	32	—	2 150.2	2.4
—investment trust companies	3	—	2 479.0	2.8
Development institutions			**12 520.9**	**13.9**
—Korea Development Bank*	1	—	10 072.8	11.2
—Export–Import Bank of Korea*	1	—	1 665.8	1.9
—Korea Long-Term Credit Bank	1	—	782.3	0.9
Rural credit institutions			**4 144.7**	**4.6**
Agricultural cooperatives	na	na	3 713.6	4.1
Fisheries cooperatives	na	na	431.1	0.5
Insurance institutions			**2 287.3**	**2.5**
Life insurance companies	5	—	na	na
Daehan Educational Insurance Company	1	—	na	na
Total assets (excluding central bank)			**89 925.5**	

Notes: *   Government financial institution.
        na   Not available.

Source: Bank of Korea *Annual Report. 1982.* and *Monthly Statistical Bulletin* 38. 2. 1984.

The financial structure of Malaysia (year-end 1982)

	Head offices	Total offices	Total assets (M$ million)	Percentage of total assets
Central bank				
Bank Negara Malaysia*	1	na	13 813.2	—
Deposit money banks				
Commercial banks	**38**	**608**	**48 946.2**	**55.3**
—national private banks	22	462	34 029.3	38.5
—foreign banks	16	146	14 916.9	16.8
Savings institutions				
National Savings Bank			1 263.5[a]	1 4
—regional and public offices	21	—	na	na
—post office savings	709	—	na	na
Long-term credit institutions				
Development institutions			**2 176.9**	**2.5**
—Development Bank of Malaysia*	1	—	381.0	0.4
—Malaysian Industrial Development Finance Berhad*	1	—	478.1	0.5
—Industrial Development Bank of Malaysia*	1	—	174.3	0.2
—Borneo Development Corporation*	1	—	75.9	0.1
—Sabah Development Bank*	1	—	1 067.6	1.2
State economic development corporations*	11	—	na	na
Credit institutions			**972.2**	**1.0**
—Credit Guarantee Corporation	1	—	519.2	0.6
—Malaysia Export Credit Insurance Company	1	—	408.0	0.5
Housing credit institutions	3	—	**1 631.9**	**1.8**
—Malaysia Building Society Berhad*	1	—	1 117.7	1.3
—Borneo Housing Mortgage Finance Berhad*	1	—	378.2	0.4
—Sabah Credit Corporation	1	—	136.0	0.1
			12 959.1	**14.6**
Merchant banks	12	15	3 593.8	4.1
Finance companies	40	248	9 106.0	10.3
Cooperative central banks	15	—	259.3	0.3
Rural credit institutions			**1 424.8**	**1.6**
Agricultural Bank of Malaysia	1	48	953.2	1.1
Federal Land Development Authority*	1	na	na	na
Bank Rakyat*	1	20	408.6	0.5
Rural cooperative societies	1 100	—	na	na
Farmers' Organization Authority	1	218	63.0	0.1
Insurance and pension institutions				
Insurance companies	**64**	—	**2 203.4**	**2.5**
Provident and pension funds	**na**	—	**16 972.8**	**19.2**
—Employees' Provident Fund	1	—	14 479.3	16.4
—Social Security Organisation	1	—	470.9	0.5
—Teachers' Provident Fund	1	—	149.4	0.2
—Armed Forces' Fund	1	—	910.5	1.0
—other provident and pension funds	na	—	962.7	1.1
Other non-bank financial institutions				
Discount houses	5	—	—	—
Total assets (excluding central bank)			**88 505.8**	

Notes: a Figure represents total deposits.
      b Figure represents loans guaranteed.
      * Government financial institution.
      na Not available.

Source: Bank Negara Malaysia *Annual Report 1982* and *Quarterly Economic Bulletin* 16, 1/2 March–June 1983.

The financial structure of New Zealand (mid-1982)

	Head offices	Total offices	Total assets ($NZ million)	Percentage of total assets
Central bank				
Reserve Bank of New Zealand*	1	na	2 886.2	—
Deposit money banks				
Trading banks	**4**	**1 000**	**7 860.4**[a]	**36.2**
—Bank of New Zealand*	1	236	na	na
—other trading banks	3	na	na	na
Foreign banks	—	—	—	—
Savings institutions	**17**	**na**	**5 546.9**	**25.6**
Post Office Savings Bank*	1	1 156	2 002.1[b]	9.2
Private savings banks	4	na	1 120.7	5.2
Trustee savings banks	12	na	2 424.1	11.2
Long-term credit institutions	**51**	**51**	**4 125.2**	**19.0**
Stock and station agents	25	25	643.0	3.0
Finance companies	26	26	2 439.1[c]	11.2
Building societies	na	na	1 043.1	4.8
Merchant banks	na	na	na	na
Insurance and pension institutions			**4 169.9**	**19.2**
Life insurance offices	na	na	4 169.9	
Total assets (excluding central bank)			**21 702.4**	

Notes: a   Excludes assets of the savings bank subsidiaries of the four trading banks.
           b   Year-end 1981.
           c   Assets of only those finance companies reporting loans and advances outstanding over $NZ5 million; in 1971
                these accounted for 90 per cent total assets of all finance companies.
           *   Government financial institution.
           na   Not available.

Sources: Reserve Bank of New Zealand *Annual Report 1983*, and *Reserve Bank Bulletin* May 1983; Department of Statistics
           New Zealand Official Yearbook 1983.

The financial structure of the Philippines (year-end 1980)

	Head offices	Total offices	Total assets (pesos million)	Percentage of total assets
Central bank				
Central Bank of the Philippines*	1	na	na	—
Deposit money banks				
Commercial banks	**32**	**1 501**	**144 401.0**	**49.7**
—state banks	2	na	41 395.0	14.3
—private banks: domestic	26	na	84 275.1	29.0
: foreign	4	na	18 730.9	6.4
Savings institutions			**8 928.8**	**3.0**
Savings and mortgage banks	10	266	7 352.6	2.5
Stock savings and loan associations	91	251	1 576.2	0.5
Long-term credit institutions			**63 250.5**	**21.8**
Development banks				
—private development banks	43	154	1 618.3	0.6
—Development Bank of the Philippines*	1	na	33 099.9	11.4
Investment houses	12	62	8 607.3	3.0
Finance companies	342	531	11 920.1	4.1
Investment companies	62	—	4 979.7	1.7
Securities dealers/brokers	141	—	1 035.5	0.4
Fund managers	12	12	1 658.1	0.6
Lending investors	57	61	50.2	—
Non-stock savings and loan associations	7	7	292.4	0.1
Rural credit institutions			**32 612.2**	**11.2**
Rural banks	1 030	1 155	5 524.2	1.9
Land Bank of the Philippines*	1	42[a]	27 088.0	9.3
Insurance and pension institutions			**17 484.9**	**6.0**
Government service insurance system*	1	—	9 245.5	3.2
Social security system*	1	—	8 220.7	2.8
Private insurance companies	7	—	18.7	—
Other non-bank financial institutions				
Philippine Amanah Bank*	1	9[a]	6 056.0	2.1
Pawnshops	544	598	290.5	0.1
Other government financial institutions (ACA and NIDC)*	2	—	17 466.2	6.0
Total assets (excluding central bank)			**290 490.1**	

Notes: a 1981 figure.
            * Government financial institution.
            na Not available.

Sources: IMF–World Bank Mission, 1979; *Central Bank Fact Book* 1980; Philippine Statistical Yearbook 1981.

The financial structure of Singapore (year-end 1982)

	Head offices	Total offices	Total assets (S$ million)	Percentage of total assets
Central banks				
Monetary Authority of Singapore*	1	na	15 744.4	—
Singapore Currency Board*	1	na	na	—
Deposit money banks	**118**	**357**	**48 537.2**	**48.3**
Commercial banks				
—domestic: fully licensed	13	181	na	na
—foreign: fully licensed	24	na	na	na[a]
: restricted	13	na	na	na[a]
Offshore banks	68	na	na	na
Savings institutions			**5 058.4**	**5.1**
Post Office Savings Bank*	1	107	5 058.4[b]	5.1
Long-term credit institutions			**27 377.8**	**27.2**
Finance companies	35	132	5 357.4	5.3
Merchant banks	47	na	22 020.4[c]	21.9
Development Bank of Singapore	1	na	na	na
Insurance institutions			**17 465.7**	**17.4**
Central Provident Fund*	1	na	15 655.5[b]	15.6
Insurance companies	80	—	**1 810.2**	**1.8**
—Singapore Life Insurance Fund	1	—	1 001.7	1.0
—Singapore General Insurance Fund	1	—	808.5	0.8
Other financial institutions			**2 050.5**	**2.0**
Discount houses	4	—	2 050.5	2.0
International money brokers	9	—	na	na
Pawnshops	na	—	na	na
Total assets (excluding central banks)			**100 489.6**	

Notes: a   Foreign fully licensed and restricted banks accounted for 73.2 per cent of the total assets of commercial banks at the end of 1978.

        b   Figure represents total deposits.

        c   Domestic unit opertions of merchant banks accounted for 12.5 per cent of merchant bank total assets in 1982.

        *   Government financial institution.

        na   Not available.

Source: Monetary Authority of Singapore Annual Report 1982/83. Monthly Statistical Bulletin December 1983. and Monthly Digest of Statistics January 1984.

The financial structure of Taiwan (year-end 1982)

	Head offices	Total offices	Total assets (NT$ million)	Percentage of total assets
Central bank				
Central Bank of China*	1	na	618 208	—
Deposit money banks				
Commercial banks	**51**	**734**	**1 490 261**	**68.0**
—domestic banks	24	734	1 373 094	62.6
—local branches of foreign banks	27	—	117 167	5.3
Savings banks				
Postal savings system*	**1 536**	—	**260 126**	**11.9**
—post offices	1 067	—	na	na
—postal agencies	469	—	na	na
Long-term credit institutions			**203 928**	**9.3**
Medium business banks	8	189	104 301	4.8
Investment and trust companies	8	24	93 199	4.3
Bills finance companies	3	—	3 236	0.1
Fuh-Wha Securities Finance Company	1	—	3 192	0.1
Rural credit institutions			**189 067**	**8.6**
Credit cooperative associations	75	—	104 635	4.8
Farmers' associations	282	—	84 432	3.9
Fisheries associations	12	—	na	na
Insurance institutions			**49 289**	**2.2**
Life insurance companies	9	—	39 271	1.8
Fire and marine insurance companies	14	—	10 018	0.5
Total assets (excluding central bank)			**2 192 671**	

Notes: *   Government financial institution.
          na   Not available.

Source: Central Bank of China *Financial Statistics Monthly. Taiwan District* December 1983, and *Statistical Yearbook of the Republic of China. 1983.*

The financial structure of Thailand (year-end 1981)

	Head offices	Total offices	Total assets (B million)	Percentage of total assets
Central bank				
Bank of Thailand*	1	na	157 183.5	—
Deposit money banks				
Commercial banks	**30**	**1 556**	**358 309.1**	**67.7**
—domestic banks	16	na	na	na[a]
—foreign banks	14	na	na	na
Savings institutions			**34 256.1**	**6.5**
Government Savings Bank*	1	415	31 173.2	5.9
Savings cooperatives	353[b]	353	3 082.9[c]	0.6
Long-term credit institutions			**100 535.5**	**19.0**
Industrial Finance Corporation*	1	3[c]	5 532.1	1.0
Small Industrial Finance Office*	1	na	56.2[c]	—
Government Housing Bank*	1	na	11 742.0	2.2
Security companies	15	15	1 352.8	0.3
Finance companies	112	112[b]	76 896.7	14.5
Credit financier companies	33	33	4 955.4	0.9
Rural credit institutions			**25 116.7**	**4.7**
Bank for Agriculture and Agricultural Cooperatives (BAAC)*	1	60	19 336.3	3.7
Agricultural cooperatives	906	906	5 780.4[c]	1.1
Insurance institutions			**7 980.0**	**1.5**
Insurance companies	12	527	7 980.0	1.5
Other non-bank financial institutions				
Government-approved pawnshops	325	325	**2 908.7**	**0.5**
—government	23	23	323.3	0.1
—private	192	192	2 382.7	0.5
—others	110	110	202.7	—
Total assets (excluding central bank)			**529 106.1**	

Notes:
a Domestic banks accounted for 97 per cent of deposits and 93.5 per cent of total loans in 1979.
b Year-end 1980 figure.
c Year-end 1979 figure.
* Government financial institution.
na Not available.

Source: Bank of Thailand Annual Report 1981, Annual Report 1982, Quarterly Bulletin 23, 3, September 1983, and 'Financial Institutions in Thailand' Quarterly Bulletin 21, 1, March 1981.

The financial structure of the United States (year-end 1982)

	Head offices	Total offices	Total assets (US$ million)	Percentage of total assets
Central bank				
Federal Reserve Bank*	12	38	190 128	—
Deposit money banks				
Commercial banks	**14 936**	**39 914**	**2 027 807**	**43.8**
—domestic banks	14 435	na	1 820 100	39.3
—foreign banks	279[a]	672	207 707	4.5
Savings institutions	**5 070**	**20 389**	**880 242**	**19.0**
Savings and loan associations	4 652	17 705	706 045	15.2
Mutual savings banks	418	2 684	174 197	3.8
Long-term credit institutions			**455 804**	**9.8**
Credit unions	17 498	17 498	69 572	1.5
Domestic finance companies	na	na	179 500	3.9
Investment companies	na	na	76 741	1.7
Domestic money market funds	na	na	76 862	1.7
Security brokers and dealers	na	na	33 500[b]	0.7
Housing and real estate	**15**	**42**	**19 629**	**0.4**
—real estate investment trusts	na	na	5 800[b]	0.1
—Government National Mortgage Association*	1	1	6 868	0.1
—Federal National Mortgage Association*	1	8	5 600	0.1
—Federal Home Loan Mortgage Corporation*	1	21	1 300	—
—Federal Home Loan Bank Board	12	12	61	—
Rural credit institutions	**2**	**46**	**19 390**	**0.4**
Farm Credit Administration*	1	na	14 300	0.3
Farmers' Home Administration	1	46	5 090	0.1
Insurance and pension institutions			**1 249 311**	**27.0**
Life insurance companies	na	na	584 311	12.6
Other insurance companies	na	na	180 100[b]	3.9
Pension funds	na	na	286 800[b]	6.9
Government employee retirement funds	na	na	198 100[b]	4.3
Total assets (excluding central bank)			**4 632 554**	

Notes: a 1983 figure.
b 1980 figure.
* Government financial institution.
na Not available.

Sources: Board of Governors of the Federal Reserve System *Annual Statistical Digest, 1982, Federal Reserve Bulletin* various issues, and *Flow of Funds Accounts, Assets and Liabilities Outstanding, 1957–80*; US Department of the Treasury *Treasury Bulletin*; US League of Savings Association *1981 Savings and Loan Sourcebook, The US Savings and Loan Directory 1982*, and *Statistical Information on the Financial Services Industry*.

6A Regression analysis methodology

The data used for the regression analysis cover twenty-one years, from 1960 to 1981, and eight Asian countries. Standard international statistics from the IMF and World Bank were used to estimate the constants of the following model:

$$M\ Two_t = \alpha + \beta \cdot YDPC_t + \gamma \cdot DP_t + \hat{\varepsilon}_t$$

where M Two = Ratio of M2 to GDP
YDPC = GDP per capita in thousands of 1980 US dollars
DP = Per cent change in the GDP deflator during the previous year (a proxy for price expectations).

Regression results using ordinary least squares exhibited positive serial correlation in the error terms, rendering inference testing unreliable for each of the eight countries. Correction for first-order autocorrelation (AR(1)) was made using a maximum likelihood iterative procedure after Beach and McKinnon ('A Maximum Likelihood Procedure for Regression with Autocorrelated Errors' *Econometrica* 46, 1978, pp. 51–58) and the results are reported in Appendix 6B, Table 1. Note that the R-squared statistics are no longer meaningful indicators of explanatory power due to constraints on the intercept arising from the AR(1) transformation. However, estimation of the covariance terms is unbiased and consistent, and hence inference tests can be applied.

To estimate the trend coefficients used in country comparisons, the data were pooled after using the estimated rho coefficients generated by the procedure mentioned above. Transformation of each country's observations followed the Prais–Winsten approach, that is, each observation from 1961 to 1981 was transformed by the following:

$$M\ TWO_t - \hat{\rho}_i M\ TWO_{t-1} = \alpha\ (1-\hat{\rho}_i) + \beta\ (YPC_t - \hat{\rho}_i YPC_{t-1}) + \gamma\ (INF_t - \hat{\rho}_i INF_{t-1}) + \varepsilon_t$$

where $\hat{\rho}_i$ = the estimated first-order correlation coefficient for country i.

The first observation for each country (1960) was transformed by multiplying the variables by $(1 - \rho_i^2)$. Ordinary least squares estimation was then used with the pooled sample and dummy variables by country were included to constrain the sample to a common slope while allowing for individual country intercepts. The results of this regression (see Table 6B.2) provide the basis for comparison of different country slope coefficients generated from the initial country estimates adjusted for the AR(1) process. Intercepts were also compared using a simple average across the sample as a trend indicator. Alternative weighting schemes to place less emphasis on outlying panels or observations (e.g., robust estimation techniques) may be a useful extension, given the diversity of the sample, but have not been pursued here.

6B Regression tables

Table 6B.1 Country regressions with AR(1) corrections[a]

	α	β	γ	R^{2b}	$F_{2,18}$	DW	$\hat{\rho}^c$
Hong Kong	0.494	0.181	−0.381	0.87	13.8	2.0	0.55
	(7.46)	(6.18)**	(−2.35)*				(2.66)*
Indonesia	0.003	0.330	−0.002	0.81	13.5	1.5	0.71
	(0.08)	(3.39)**	(−1.75)				(4.08)**
Korea	0.093	0.135	−0.026	0.62	15.0	1.05	0.87
	(1.39)	(2.42)*	(−0.35)				(9.43)**
Malaysia	0.020	0.279	−0.23	0.97	115.4	1.86	0.41
	(0.98)	(16.2)**	(−4.07)**				(1.97)
Philippines	0.228	−0.057	−0.056	0.51	36.99	1.27	0.72
	(6.76)	(−0.97)	(−1.62)				(4.98)**
Taiwan	0.134	0.221	−0.228	0.97	18.8	1.27	0.82
	(3.62)	(9.37)	(4.29)**				(6.17)**
Thailand	0.165	0.256	−0.099	0.85	17.2	1.42	0.74
	(5.70)	(4.61)**	(−1.80)				(4.96)**
Singapore	−0.036	0.374	0.234	0.72	20.39	1.4	0.86
	(−0.22)	(7.59)**	(1.09)				(8.26)**

Notes: a t-statistics in parentheses, where
  * = significant at 5 per cent
  ** = significant at 1 per cent
  b R-squared coefficients are reported from the untransformed data due to inconsistencies introduced in AR (1).
   R-squares by the Prais–Winsten first-observation transformation.
  c $\hat{\rho}_1$ = Estimated first-order autocorrelation coefficient.

Table 6B.2 Results of the pooled data regression

Variable	Coefficient Values	t-statistic	$\hat{\beta}_i - \hat{\beta}\rho^*$
YPC ($\hat{\beta}\rho$)	0.228	(12.63)	—
INFLAT ($\hat{\gamma}\rho$)	−0.003	(−0.78)	—
Country Intercepts			
Hong Kong	0.279	(8.0)	−0.047
Indonesia	0.027	(7.3)	0.102
Korea	0.016	(8.1)	−0.093
Malaysia	0.166	(8.3)	0.051
Philippines	0.039	(7.4)	−0.285
Taiwan	0.061	(7.6)	−0.007
Thailand	0.075	(5.6)	0.032
Singapore	0.180	(5.9)	0.146

Note: * $\hat{\beta}_i - \hat{\beta}\rho$ is the value of each country YPC coefficient from Table 1 minus the pooled data coefficient on YPC, and
   presents each country's deviation from trend on a per capita income slope parameter.

7A Variables and sources used in analysis

Variables (all are deflated by capital goods prices of WPI (1975 = 100) and are in billion won)

I:	Investment.
ΔK^*:	Change in desired capital stock.
ΔKDB:	Change in the volume of loans extended by Korea Development Bank (KDB).
ΔDMB:	Change in the volume of loans extended by deposit money banks (DMB).
ΔFL:	Change in the volume of foreign loans.
ΔKFL:	$\Delta KDB + \Delta FL$.
ΔDFL:	$\Delta DMB + \Delta FL$.
ΔKML:	$\Delta KDB + \Delta DMB + \Delta FL$.
K:	Actual capital stock.
NI:	Net investment.

Industrial sectors

I:	Clothing and footwear—miscellaneous manufactures.
II:	Textiles—wood products.
III:	Metal products—electrical machinery.
IV:	Iron and steel—cement.
V:	Pulp and paper—non-ferrous metal.
VI:	Industrial chemicals—rubber tyres.
VII:	Machinery—transport equipment.

2	KDB	(KDB loans):	BOK *Economic Statistics Yearbook* various issues.
3	DMB	(DMB loans):	BOK *Economic Statistics Yearbook* various issues.
4	FL	(foreign loans):	EPB *Economic Indicators of Korea* March 1984.
5	K	(capital stock):	H.C. Choo, Y.S. Kim and J.H. Yun 'Estimates of Capital Stock in Korean Industries, 1966–77' *Research Report 82–06*, Korea Development Institute, 1982.

7B Data description and sources

Dependent variable

I   Investment (1975 constant prices).
Bank of Korea (BOK) *National Income in Korea* 1982; Economic Planning Board (EPB) *Report on Mining and Manufacturing Census* various issues, and *Report on Mining and Manufacturing Survey* various issues.

Independent variables

K^* (desired capital stock $= \alpha V^n/q \, (r + \delta - \dot{q}^E)$.

α (capital share) $= 1 - $ (compensation to employee) $\times$ (paid workers + unpaid workers) / (paid workers) $\div$ (total value-added) $-$ (net indirect tax).
BOK *Input–Output Tables* various issues; EPB *Report on Mining and Manufacturing Census* various issues, and *Report on Mining and Manufacturing Survey* various issues.

V^n (nominal value-added).
BOK *National Income in Korea* 1982.

q (capital goods price index, 1975 $= 1.00$).
BOK *Price Statistics* 1983.

δ (economic depreciation rate).
BOK *Financial Statements Analysis* various issues.

$\dot{q}^E$: $(\dot{q}_{-1} + \dot{q} + \dot{q}_{+1})/3$.

r (kerb market interest rate).
Data provided by BOK.

13A Effective exchange rates of selected Southeast Asian nations

Table 13A.1 1980 import weights

	SG(SGa)	ML	ID	TL	PL	KR	TW
Singapore	—	12	9	6	*	*	*
Malaysia	14	—	*	*	*	*	*
Indonesia	* (11)	*	—	*	*	*	*
Japan	18	23	13	21	20	26	28
Australia	*	5	5	*	*	*	*
United States	14	15	31	14	24	22	22
Saudi Arabia	12	6	9	9	10	15	8
Germany	*	5	6	4	4	*	*
United Kingdom	*	5	*	*	*	*	*
Other	42 (31)	29	32	46	42	37	39
Momo: EC9	11	20	13	9	12	13	8

Note: * Neglected.

Source: IMF *Direction of Trade. Trade Statistics of the Republic of China* (for Taiwan).

Memo item
Singapore: from C. Wong 'Trends and Patterns of Singapore's Trade in Manufactures' NBER, 1984.
Malaysia: from Lin, chapter 5 'Western Europe', average 1975–80.
Indonesia: from R. Beals 'Trade Patterns and Trends in Indonesia' NBER, 1984.
Thailand: from J. Ajanant 'Trade Patterns and Trends in Indonesia' NBER, 1984.
The Philippines: UK and Germany only.
South Korea: Germany, UK and France only.
Taiwan: from C. Schive 'Trade Patterns and Trends in Taiwan' NBER, 1984.

Note: NBER. Proceedings of a conference on *The Global Implications of the Trade Patterns of East and South-East Asia* Kuala Lumpur, January 1984.

Table 13A.2 1980 export weights

	SG	ML	ID	TL	PL	KR	TW
Singapore	—	19	11	8	*	*	*
Malaysia	15	—	*	*	*	*	*
Thailand	4	*	*	—	*	*	*
Japan	8	23	20	15	17	17	11
Australia	4	*	*	*	*	*	*
United States	13	16	49	13	28	26	36
Saudi Arabia	*	*	*	*	*	5	3
Germany	*	*	*	4	4	5	4
Netherlands	*	*	*	13	6	*	*
United Kingdom	*	*	*	*	*	3	*
Other	56	36	20	47	35	44	46
Memo EC9	12	20	6	19	12	13	13

Note: * Neglected.

Source: Same as for Table 13A.1.

Table 13A.3 Indonesia: effective exchange rates

| | Nominal | | Real | |
	Export	Import	Export	Import
1958	0.302	0.303	2 800.5	2 973.2
1959	0.302	0.303	2 493.0	2 657.0
1960	0.302	0.296	2 133.7	2 209.3
1961	0.302	0.297	1 132.5	1 174.6
1962	0.302	0.297	462.0	475.8
1963	0.302	0.297	212.8	217.0
1964	0.302	0.297	92.9	94.8
1965	0.302	0.297	14.0	14.2
1966	0.302	0.297	2.4	2.4
1967	0.302	0.297	0.721	0.924
1968	0.589	0.580	0.820	0.816
1969	0.640	0.631	0.807	0.803
1970	0.717	0.711	0.853	0.846
1971	0.787	0.781	0.942	0.931
1972	0.917	0.906	1.071	1.054
1973	1.000	1.000	1.000	1.000
1974	0.957	0.976	0.822	0.831
1975	0.951	0.978	0.754	0.785
1976	0.946	0.970	0.669	0.710
1977	1.007	1.025	0.686	0.723
1978	1.259	1.255	0.831	0.851
1979	1.742	1.764	0.995	1.028
1980	1.720	1.755	0.907	0.934
1981	1.766	1.754	0.885	0.883
1982	1.713	1.719	0.813	0.819
1983	2.429	2.406	1.052	1.046

Table 13A.4 Korea: effective exchange rates

| | Nominal | | Real | |
	Export	Import	Export	Import
1958	0.112	0.111	0.346	0.335
1959	0.112	0.111	0.339	0.329
1960	0.140	0.136	0.393	0.373
1961	0.281	0.272	0.749	0.713
1962	0.286	0.277	0.738	0.702
1963	0.286	0.277	0.637	0.608
1964	0.471	0.456	0.828	0.794
1965	0.586	0.568	0.937	0.899
1966	0.598	0.579	0.884	0.845
1967	0.595	0.577	0.818	0.785
1968	0.604	0.590	0.778	0.750
1969	0.630	0.615	0.759	0.735
1970	0.683	0.662	0.749	0.717
1971	0.777	0.752	0.789	0.752
1972	0.931	0.918	0.881	0.852
1973	1.000	1.000	1.000	1.000
1974	0.988	0.985	0.920	0.944
1975	1.190	1.185	0.998	1.050
1976	1.174	1.185	0.934	1.026
1977	1.216	1.235	0.946	1.051
1978	1.338	1.379	0.957	1.066
1979	1.341	1.360	0.871	0.938
1980	1.677	1.686	0.935	0.985
1981	1.843	1.095	0.911	0.974
1982	1.878	1.939	0.906	0.957
1983	1.995	2.094	0.956	1.022

Table 13A.5 Malaysia: effective exchange rates

	Nominal		Real	
	Export	Import	Export	Import
1958	1.030	1.058	0.721	0.744
1959	1.030	1.058	0.742	0.769
1960	1.030	1.042	0.756	0.772
1961	1.034	1.045	0.777	0.798
1962	1.035	1.046	0.801	0.821
1963	1.035	1.046	0.808	0.824
1964	1.035	1.046	0.831	0.848
1965	1.035	1.046	0.860	0.876
1966	1.035	1.046	0.883	0.897
1967	1.035	1.045	0.874	0.886
1968	1.035	1.034	0.906	0.907
1969	1.035	1.035	0.945	0.949
1970	1.035	1.041	0.970	0.981
1971	1.048	1.054	1.011	1.027
1972	1.051	1.052	1.019	1.033
1973	1.000	1.000	1.000	1.000
1974	0.965	0.966	0.976	0.974
1975	0.970	0.957	1.018	1.036
1976	1.010	0.984	1.098	1.128
1977	1.025	0.982	1.113	1.158
1978	1.086	1.034	1.180	1.218
1979	1.032	0.984	1.145	1.190
1980	1.020	0.981	1.160	1.217
1981	1.072	1.021	1.193	1.238
1982	1.030	0.967	1.129	1.162
1983	1.039	0.955	1.121	1.137

Table 13A.6 The Philippines: effective exchange rates

	Nominal		Real	
	Export	Import	Export	Import
1958	0.248	0.259	0.335	0.367
1959	0.248	0.259	0.342	0.377
1960	0.250	0.253	0.339	0.359
1961	0.252	0.255	0.347	0.368
1962	0.479	0.483	0.643	0.677
1963	0.489	0.493	0.649	0.678
1964	0.489	0.493	0.617	0.643
1965	0.489	0.493	0.627	0.648
1966	0.488	0.492	0.616	0.631
1967	0.488	0.492	0.599	0.612
1968	0.488	0.492	0.612	0.622
1969	0.488	0.492	0.632	0.642
1970	0.743	0.750	0.897	0.903
1971	0.825	0.828	0.911	0.908
1972	0.920	0.921	0.965	0.953
1973	1.000	1.000	1.000	1.000
1974	0.981	0.989	0.851	0.967
1975	1.051	1.051	0.929	0.975
1976	1.073	1.082	0.972	1.042
1977	1.126	1.121	0.997	1.077
1978	1.266	1.234	1.098	1.151
1979	1.264	1.229	0.986	1.025
1980	1.271	1.240	0.925	0.959
1981	1.303	1.232	0.900	0.942
1982	1.325	1.329	0.862	0.909
1983	1.740	1.750	1.048	1.105

Table 13A.7 Singapore: effective exchange rates

	Nominal			Real		
	Export	Import	Import[a]	Export	Import	Import[a]
1958	1.076	1.087	1.304	10.25	0.965	1.472
1959	1.075	1.087	1.304	1.017	0.972	1.481
1960	1.075	1.045	1.263	1.031	0.949	1.452
1961	1.076	1.045	1.263	1.051	0.972	1.480
1962	1.077	1.045	1.263	1.067	0.990	1.502
1963	1.077	1.045	1.263	1.072	1.000	1.508
1964	1.077	1.045	1.263	1.069	1.007	1.515
1965	1.077	1.045	1.263	1.086	1.027	1.539
1966	1.077	1.045	1.263	1.096	1.033	1.541
1967	1.077	1.045	1.263	1.101	1.037	1.539
1968	1.077	1.045	1.134	1.120	1.056	1.259
1969	1.077	1.045	1.119	1.155	1.103	1.272
1970	1.077	1.045	1.099	1.199	1.147	1.267
1971	1.080	1.052	1.091	1.210	1.176	1.258
1972	1.055	1.049	1.065	1.214	1.192	1.231
1973	1.000	1.000	1.000	1.000	1.000	1.000
1974	0.991	0.988	0.989	0.949	0.960	0.935
1975	0.954	0.959	0.961	0.963	1.032	0.985
1976	0.969	0.985	0.990	1.056	1.200	1.130
1977	0.977	1.011	1.009	1.100	1.283	1.186
1978	0.975	1.038	1.010	1.113	1.307	1.159
1979	0.941	0.996	0.916	1.102	1.264	0.995
1980	0.924	0.974	0.896	1.101	1.233	0.958
1981	0.894	0.952	0.877	1.076	1.190	0.914
1982	0.867	0.924	0.850	1.062	1.156	0.876
1983	0.856	0.926	0.807	1.075	1.173	0.796

Note: a Including imports from Indonesia.

Table 13A.8   Taiwan: effective exchange rates

	Nominal		Real	
	Export	Import	Export	Import
1958	0.837	0.788	1.050	0.898
1959	0.941	0.887	1.078	0.924
1960	0.939	0.870	0.924	0.784
1961	0.949	0.879	0.884	0.758
1962	0.949	0.879	0.884	0.767
1963	0.949	0.879	0.888	0.781
1964	0.949	0.879	0.906	0.804
1965	0.949	0.879	0.930	0.833
1966	0.949	0.879	0.943	0.846
1967	0.949	0.879	0.941	0.847
1968	0.949	0.879	0.907	0.817
1969	0.950	0.879	0.910	0.820
1970	0.955	0.822	0.933	0.839
1971	0.964	0.897	0.960	0.872
1972	1.004	0.972	1.006	0.953
1973	1.000	1.000	1.000	1.000
1974	0.983	0.968	0.758	0.776
1975	0.984	0.965	0.798	0.833
1976	0.982	0.964	0.835	0.896
1977	1.008	1.012	0.856	0.948
1978	1.047	1.115	0.891	1.032
1979	1.026	1.071	0.856	0.956
1980	1.010	1.056	0.795	0.866
1981	1.023	1.081	0.751	0.811
1982	1.055	1.080	0.789	0.818
1983	1.084	1.126	0.824	0.861

Table 13A.9   Thailand: effective exchange rates

	Nominal		Real	
	Export	Import	Export	Import
1958	0.812	0.859	0.647	0.695
1959	0.819	0.866	0.692	0.748
1960	0.820	0.840	0.712	0.745
1961	0.826	0.838	0.681	0.714
1962	0.821	0.831	0.671	0.703
1963	0.819	0.829	0.696	0.728
1964	0.818	0.828	0.722	0.752
1965	0.818	0.828	0.750	0.774
1966	0.818	0.828	0.751	0.767
1967	0.818	0.828	0.745	0.762
1968	0.818	0.828	0.758	0.773
1969	0.819	0.829	0.775	0.789
1970	0.824	0.834	0.816	0.831
1971	0.841	0.848	0.875	0.879
1972	0.913	0.921	0.949	0.946
1973	1.000	1.000	1.000	1.000
1974	0.980	0.971	0.911	0.928
1975	0.999	0.974	0.960	0.998
1976	0.981	0.968	0.998	1.046
1977	1.037	1.013	1.004	1.092
1978	1.169	1.137	1.101	1.182
1979	1.199	1.140	1.084	1.133
1980	1.197	1.133	0.984	1.023
1981	1.196	1.198	0.936	1.020
1982	1.188	1.195	0.925	1.003
1983	1.182	1.212	0.909	1.001

13B A two-country model of policy interdependence

1

The analysis of policy interdependence described in the text is based on a conventional two-country macro model, with several features borrowed from P. Kouri and S. Macedo 'Exchange Rates and the International Adjustment Process'. We use a log-linear formulation, where variables are measured relative to their steady-state values. The two IS curves are given by:

$$y = a\Theta - b'r - b''r* \tag{1}$$
$$Y* = -a\Theta - b''r - b'r* \tag{2}$$

where y ($y*$) is (the log of) domestic (foreign) real output;

   r ($r*$) is the domestic (foreign) real interest rate;

   $\Theta = e + w* - w$ is (the log of the) real exchange rate;

   e is the (log of the) domestic currency price of foreign currency;

   w ($w*$) is (the log of) the price of domestic (foreign) goods

   a is the elasticity of output relative to the real exchange rate;

   b' (b'') is the intertemporal substitution semi-elasticity relative to the domestic (foreign) real interest rate.

As shown in Macedo 'Exchange Rate Volatility in an Interdependent World Economy', equations (1) and (2) are derived from the open-economy income identity in the two countries, where domestic absorption is a function of domestic output and (through investment) of the domestic real interest rate, and the current account is a function of domestic and foreign outputs and the terms of trade (inverse of the real exchange rate). Thus the parameter a is given by the average propensity to import evaluated at the steady-state, the open-economy multiplier with repercussion and the sum of the trade elasticities subtracted from one. Similarly, the parameter b' is given by the investment share in output evaluated at the steady-state, the multiplier and the real interest elasticity of domestic investment divided by the real domestic interest rate. The parameter b'' is given by the share of the domestic-currency value of investment abroad in domestic output times the multiplier times the foreign elasticity divided by the foreign real rate. To illustrate, suppose the values for the savings and import propensities are, respectively, 0.1 and 0.5, so that the multipliers of domestic and foreign expenditure are as in note 3 in the text. They are now to be applied

362

to changes in domestic investment induced by changes in the domestic and foreign real interest rates. Domestic and foreign investment as shares of domestic output are 20 per cent and interest elasticities are 0.1 at home and abroad. Then, at interest rates of 10 per cent, the semi-elasticities of aggregate demand will be $b' = 1.1$ and $b'' = 0.9$. Under these conditions, the foreign trade multiplier will be 0.9. If the average propensity to import is also 20 per cent and the trade elasticities are unity, we will get $a = 0.18$.

The two LM curves are given by:

$$m - p = \zeta (y + w - p) - c\,i \tag{3}$$
$$m* - p* = \zeta (y* + w* - p*)\,c\,i* \tag{4}$$

where m ($m*$) is the (log of the) domestic (foreign) money stock;
i ($i*$) is the domestic (foreign) nominal interest rate;
p ($p*$) is the domestic (foreign) price levels;
ζ is the income elasticity of money demand
c is the interest semi-elasticity of money demand.

Equations (3) and (4) are obtained from a variable-velocity money-demand function, where the level of the exchange rate enters through the price index used to deflate money balances and transactions demand is a function of national income rather than output. Also, exchange-rate depreciation raises money demand by less, unlike the one-to-one effect implied by purchasing-power parity, but the size is given by the share of the foreign good in consumption rather than by the share of foreign assets in wealth. This is clear from the definition of the price indexes.

$$p = (1 - \beta)w + \beta (w* + e) = w + \beta\Theta \tag{3'}$$
$$p* = (1 - \beta*) w* + \beta* (w - e) = w* - \beta*\Theta \tag{4'}$$

Price and exchange-rate expectations are introuded by three crucial arbitrage conditions, which, under perfect foresight, are written as:

$$i = i* + \dot{e} \tag{5}$$
$$r = i* - \dot{p} \tag{6}$$
$$r* = i* - \dot{p}*. \tag{7}$$

While there is substantial evidence against the risk-neutral behavior underlying (5), we use it to keep the model tractable. On the other hand, nominal interest rates are deflated by the price index used to deflate nominal money balances, so that terms of trade changes also have a less than one-to-one effect on the real interest differential. Taking as a benchmark the case where $\beta = \beta*$, we see that, if consumption is biased toward the domestic good ($\beta < \frac{1}{2}$), a faster real depreciation will raise the real interest-rate differential:

$$r = r* + (1 - 2\beta)\dot{\Theta}. \tag{8}$$

This is the channel through which changes in the real exchange rate have an effect on relative outputs, with sign depending on the consumption bias. Subtracting (2) from (1) and using (8), we can express the cyclical position of the two countries in terms of the real exchange rate and its rate of change:

$$y - y* = 2a\Theta - (b' - b'')(1 - 2\beta)\dot{e}. \tag{9}$$

On the other hand, subtracting (4) from (3) and using (5), we see that the nominal exchange rate will change so as to offset changes in the relative velocities of money. These can be expressed in terms of relative real money balances (deflated by domestic prices), the real exchange rate and the cyclical position of the two countries:

$$\dot{e} = -\frac{1}{C}[\bar{m} - \bar{m}* - 2(1 - \zeta)\beta\Theta - \zeta(y - y*)] \tag{10}$$

where $\bar{m} = m - w$
and $\bar{m}* = m* - w*$

Suppose that the prices of domestic output are exogenously fixed at $w = w* = \bar{w}$. Then $\Theta = e$ and the dynamics of the system reduce to:

$$[c + (b' - b'')\zeta(1 - 2\beta)]\dot{e} = 2[a\underset{\cdot}{\zeta} + \beta(1 - \zeta)]e - (m - m*). \tag{11}$$

In steady-state, the exchange rate is proportional to relative money balances:

$$e = \frac{1}{2}\frac{m - m*}{a\zeta + \beta(1 - \zeta)}. \tag{12}$$

The role of the parameter β hinges on the existence of a terms-of-trade effect on money demand and it vanishes when $\zeta = 1$.

Substituting for the interest rate in (3) from (1), we get another steady-state relationship:

$$y = \frac{1}{\zeta + p}[\bar{m} + a(\bar{p} - \beta)e] \tag{13}$$

where $p = c/(b' + b'')$
and $\bar{\beta} = \beta(1 - \zeta)/a$.

A similar expression holds for foreign output. While the effect of own expansionary monetary policy is always positive, the effect of depreciation—and, via (12), of contractionary monetary policy abroad—on domestic output will hinge on the relative sizes of p and $\bar{\beta}$. A low interest-rate elasticity of aggregate demand, or an income elasticity of money demand equal to or larger than unity, implies $p > \bar{\beta}$, and the effect will be positive.

For concreteness, suppose that the nominal interest-elasticity of money demand is 0.1. Then, at nominal interest rates of 10 per cent, the semi-elasticity of money demand will be one. Using the values indicated earlier, we get $b' + b'' = 2$, so that the ratio will be $p = 0.5$. Note that, as long as there is no expected inflation, the level of interest rates cancels, so that p would not decrease at higher interest rates. On the other hand, a nominal elasticity of 0.4 will make $p = 2$.

Suppose now that the share of foreign goods in the consumer price index and the income elasticity are both one half. Then we will have $\bar{\beta} = 1.4$ so that it will be less than p. If the trade elasticities double, we get $\bar{\beta} = 0.46$, less than the first value of p. With unit trade elasticities and $\zeta = 0.82$, we get $\tilde{\beta} = 0.5$, so that it exactly equals p.

2

To analyse strategic behavior in response to the fixed price $\bar{w}$, it is convenient to work with the real money stocks in both countries, e.g., $\tilde{m} = m - \bar{w}$. We will henceforth drop the bar from the real money stocks, to avoid cluttering. Substituting (12) into (13) and (3'), we express the two targets in the home country as:

$$y = \mu m - \mu* m \qquad (14)$$
$$p = \bar{w} + \nu (m - m*) \qquad (15)$$

where $\quad \mu = \dfrac{2\zeta + p + \tilde{\beta}}{2 (\zeta + \tilde{\beta}) (\zeta + p)}$

$\mu* = \dfrac{p - \beta}{2 (\zeta + \tilde{\beta}) (\zeta + p)}$

and $\quad \nu = \dfrac{\beta/a}{2 (\zeta + \tilde{\beta})}$

Note that $1 > \mu > \mu*$ and that $\mu > \nu > 0$ while the sign of $\mu*$ hinges on the relative sizes of p and $\tilde{\beta}$. When $\mu* > 0$, we will have $\mu* > \nu$ as long as $\beta < a$, since the condition $p > (\beta/a)/(1 - \beta/a)$ is then weaker than $p > \tilde{\beta}$. The expressions for foreign output and the foreign price level are like (14) and (15), with the instruments reversed.

Suppose now the monetary authorities in both countries wish to minimise a quadratic loss function expressed in terms of y and p, the deviation of output and the consumer price index from their steady-state values:

$$L = y^2 + np^2 \qquad (16)$$

where n is the weight attached to the price objective.

We will focus here on the case where $\mu* > 0$, so that an expansionary monetary policy abroad creates unemployment at home. We can see from equations (14) and (15) that, if both countries jointly set $m = m* = 0$, that is, if they increase their money stock in proportion to the given change in the price of their domestic output, then $y = y* = 0$ and $p = p* = \bar{w}$. This cooperative solution yields a loss given by:

$$^cL = {}^cL^* = nw^{-2} \qquad (17)$$

Each country may try to increase the money stock by less, however, in order to appreciate its currency and reduce inflation. If both try to do so, in the mistaken belief that the other country does not react against the corresponding depreciation, we will have a non-cooperative solution. To characterise it, substitute from (14) and (15) into (16), to obtain the loss function in terms of the instruments. It defines the loss contours as the ellipses shown by broken lines in Figure 13.1 in the text. Then differentiate totally and set to zero, to yield:

$$gm - g*m* + n\nu\bar{w} + (\tilde{g}m* - g*m - n\nu w)\frac{dm*}{dm} = 0 \qquad (18)$$

$$gm* - g*m + \mu\nu\bar{w} + (\bar{g}m - g*m* - n\nu w)\frac{dm*}{dm} = 0 \qquad (18')$$

where $g = \mu^2 + n\nu^2$
        $\bar{g} = \mu*^2 + n\nu^2$
        $g* = \mu\mu* + n\nu^2.$

To find the Cournot–Nash solution, set both conjectural variations to zero, to yield:

$$gm - g*m* = -n\nu\bar{w} \qquad (19)$$
$$gm* - g*m = -n\nu\bar{w}. \qquad (19')$$

Solving, the Cournot–Nash solution is again given by equal money stocks but a lower level of output and less inflation than at the cooperative point:

$${}^N m = {}^N m* = -n\frac{(\nu/\mu)}{\mu - \mu*}\bar{w}. \qquad (20)$$

Substituting from (19) into (14) and (15), and then into (16), we get the (common) loss. Using (17), we express it as a proportion of the cooperative solution:

$${}^N L = [1 + n\,(\nu/\mu)^2]^C L. \qquad (21)$$

If the home country assumes that the foreign country will play the non-cooperative solution just described and minimises loss subject to the other country's Cournot reaction function, then, if this assumption is correct, we will have a Stackelberger solution, where the conjectural variations will be dm*/dm* = g*/g and dm/dm* = 0.

Using these results in (18) and (18'), we get a real money stock that is higher than at N, even though it is still negative:

$${}^S m = {}^{S*} m* = {}^N m\,A \qquad (22)$$
$${}^S m* = {}^{S*} m = {}^N m\,A* \qquad (22')$$

where $A = (g^2 - g*\tilde{g})/\Delta$
        $A* = (g^2 - 2g*^2 + gg*)/\Delta$
        $\Delta = g\,(g + g*) - g*^2[(g - \tilde{g})/(g - g*)].$

It can be shown that $1 > A* > A$, so that the Stackelberger solution is less contractionary than the Nash, and less contractionary for the follower than for the leader.

Finally, the locus of efficient points is given by the tangency of the loss contours. Equating the slopes from (18) and (18'), we get:

$$g*(m^2 + m*^2) - (g + \tilde{g})\,mm* - n\nu\bar{w}(m + m*) = 0. \qquad (23)$$

This is an hyperbola going through the origin and through the intersection of the axes and the Cournot reaction functions, as shown by the dotted line in Figure 13.1 in the text.

Consider now the case where $\mu* < 0$. As shown in the second numerical example given earlier, it requires a low elasticity of money demand. It is clear from (20) that the size of the contractionary bias is smaller in that case but, as seen in (21), this does not affect loss in the Cournot–Nash solution.

From the definition of $g*$ after (18), we see that, in order for $g* < 0$, given that $\mu* < 0$, it is also necessary that the weight on the price level target be low:

$$n < \frac{(p - \tilde{\beta})(2\zeta + p + \tilde{\beta})}{(\beta/a)^2(\zeta + p)^2}. \tag{24}$$

Note that the bias in the Stackelberger solution becomes smaller for the leader if condition (24) is satisfied because in that case $A > A^*$. Also, the numberical example would give $g* < 0$ if $n < 1$. This case can be illustrated in Figure 13.1, with downward-sloping reaction functions.

Notes

Chapter 1

1   The authors of the comments included in this chapter were the discussants of the papers presented at the Fourteenth PAFTAD Conference. These papers comprise the chapters of this volume. The discussants were: for chapter 2, Sir Frank Holmes and Professor Augustine H.H. Tan; chapter 4, Professor Philip Anisan; chapter 7, Dr Mohammad Ariff and Dr Peter Drysdale; chapter 8, Dr David Schulze, Professor Richard Cooper, Dr Chia Siow Yue and Professor Augustine H.H. Tan; chapter 9, Dr Kiyoshi Kojima and Dr Ralph C. Bryant; chapter 10, Dr Robert Chia, Mr Zenta Nakajima, Dr Lawrence Krause, Professor Richard Cooper and Professor Shinichi Ichimura; chapter 11, Professor Richard Cooper, Professor H. Edward English and Professor Heinz Arndt; chapter 12, Dr Daniel Kane, Mr Francis Chan and Professor Ronald McKinnon; chapter 13, Professor Richard Cooper; chapter 14, Dr Mukul G. Asher and Professor Luo Yuanzheng.

The precis of the discussants' comments were prepared by the authors of this chapter and editors of the volume, Augustine Tan and Basant Kapur.

2   See chapter 2.
3   ibid.
4   ibid.
5   ibid.
6   E.S. Shaw *Financial Deepening in Economic Development* London: Oxford University Press, 1973; R.I. McKinnon *Money and Capital in Economic Development* Washington, D.C.: The Brookings Institution, 1973.
7   See chapter 4.
8   McKinnon *Financial Deepening in Economic Development* chapter 12.
9   See chapter 5.

Chapter 2

We thank Mark Sundberg, Andrew Bernard, and Robert Uriu for research assistance, Larry Meissner for editorial suggestions, and Lance Taylor and Michael Roemer for their comments.

1   This process had been documented and analysed, among other places, in the thirteen Pacific Trade and Development conferences held since 1968, and is recorded in the published Papers and Proceedings for each conference.
2   Brunei and Papua New Guinea are excluded from the sample due to their newness of independent status and lack of data. The financial characteristics, policies and

problems of the Latin American Pacific rim nations are substantially different, hence they are excluded from consideration here.

3 See William Byrd *China's Financial System—The Changing Role of Banks* Boulder: Westview Press, 1983.

4 See David C. Cole and Park Yung Chul *Financial Development in Korea, 1945–1978* Cambridge: Harvard University Council on East Asian Studies, 1983.

5 cf Akira Kohsaka, The High Interest Rate Policy in Economic Development, mimeo, Institute of Developing Economies, Tokyo, March 1984.

6 Robert Summers and Alan Heston 'Improved International Comparisons of Real Produce and its Composition: 1950–1980' *Review of Income and Wealth* June 1984.

7 Warren L. Coats and Deena R. Khatkhate, Monetary Policy in Less-Developed Countries: Main Issues, mimeo, Institute of Developing Economies, Tokyo, March 1984.

8 This is not the place to review the general theoretical and empirical literature on the role of finance in development. However, important references include: Hugh T. Patrick 'Financial Development and Economic Growth in Underdeveloped Countries' *Economic Development and Cultural Change* January 1966; John G. Gurley and Edward S. Shaw 'Financial Development and Economic Development' *Economic Development and Cultural Change* April 1967; Raymond W. Goldsmith *Financial Structure and Development* New Haven: Yale University Press, 1969; Edward S. Shaw *Financial Deepening in Economic Development* New York: Oxford University Press, 1973; Ronald I. McKinnon *Money and Capital in Economic Growth and Development* Washington: The Brookings Institution, 1973; R.I. McKinnon (ed.) *Money and Finance in Economic Growth and Development*, New York: Marcel Dekker, 1976; Warren L. Coats Jr and Deena R. Khatkhate (eds) *Money and Monetary Policy in Less Developed Countries: A Survey of Issues and Evidence* Oxford: Pergamon Press, 1980; and J.D. Von Pischke et al. *Rural Financial Markets in Developing Countries* Baltimore: Johns Hopkins University Press, 1983.

9 The major country studies include: for Korea, Cole and Park *Financial Development in Korea*; for Malaysia and Singapore, Drake *Financial Development in Malaysia and Singapore*; for Japan, Hugh T. Patrick 'Japan', in Rondo Cameron et al. *Banking in the Early States of Industrialization* New York: Oxford University Press, 1967, and 'Japanese Financial Development in Historical Perspective, 1868–1980', in Gustav Ranis et al. *Comparative Development Perspectives* Boulder: Westview Press, 1984; and for the Philippines, Hugh T. Patrick and Honorata A. Moreno 'Philippine Private Domestic Commercial Banking, 1946–1980, in Light of Japanese Historical Experience' in Gustav Ranis and Kuzashi Ohkawa *Japan and The Developing Countries* Oxford: Basil Blackwell, 1984.

The important cross-country studies include: Asian Development Bank, Economics Office *Domestic Resource Mobilization through Financial Development* Manila, February 1984; Cheng Hang-Sheng 'Financial Deepening in Pacific Basin Countries', Federal Reserve Bank of San Francisco *Economic Review*, Summer 1980; Robert F. Emery *The Financial Institutions of Southeast Asia* New York: Praeger, 1970; Maxwell J. Fry, Financial Structure, Monetary Policy and Economic Growth in Hong Kong, Singapore, Taiwan and Korea, 1960–1981, mimeo, University of California, May 1983, and 'Inflation and Economic Growth in Pacific Basin Developing Economies' Federal Reserve Bank of San Francisco *Economic Review* Fall 1981; Lee Sheng-Yi and Y.C. Jao *Financial Structures and Monetary Policies in Southeast Asia* New York: St Martins Press, 1982; and George J. Vishkins *Financial Deepening in ASEAN Countries* Honolulu: Pacific Forum, 1980.

10 As previously stressed, the real rate of financial development is overestimated, perhaps substantially. The analogous difficulty has been to incorporate subsistence production in national accounts; similar adjustments are not made in financial data.

Since all production must be financed, in low-income countries much depends on a mixture of unrecorded internal finance and unrecorded 'traditional' external finance; while development external finance increasingly goes through recorded channels, and the proportion of internal finance probably declines.

11   Asian Development Bank *Domestic Resource Mobilization through Financial Development* Vol. 1, p. 18.

12   The most extensive empirical research on these relationships, including the Asian Development Bank study, has been done by Maxwell Fry (see bibliography). Cheng 'Financial Deepening in Pacific Basin Countries' adduces a positive relationship between financial deepening measured by the financial interrelations ratio and the real deposit rate in the Pacific Basin countries.

13   Heinz W. Arndt 'Financial Development in Asia' *Asian Development Review* (ADB) 1, 1, 1983.

14   Gurley and Shaw 'Financial Development and Economic Development'.

15   Lee and Jao *Financial Structures and Monetary Policies in Southeast Asia* Tables 2.5 and 8.4.

16   We are indebted to Maxwell Fry for providing basic data for regression estimations.

17   A useful but dated description of the financial systems of Southeast Asian nations is provided by Emery *The Financial Institutions of Southeast Asia*. More current evaluations, descriptions and data for the financial systems of Hong Kong, Indonesia, Malaysia, the Philippines, Singapore and Thailand appear in Lee and Jao *Financial Structures and Monetary Policies in Southeast Asia*; whilst for Korea see Cole and Park *Financial Development in Korea*; and for Taiwan see Eric Lundberg 'Fiscal and Monetary Policies' in Walter Galenson (ed.) *Economic Growth and Structural Change in Taiwan* Ithica: Cornell University Press, 1979. The publications of the monetary authorities in each country are a basic reference source.

18   See Patrick 'Japan' in Cameron et al. *Banking in the Early Stages of Industrialization*, and Patrick 'Japanese Financial Development in Historical Perspective' in Ranis et al. *Comparative Development Perspectives*.

19   Asian Development Bank *Domestic Resource Mobilization Through Financial Development* Vol. 2.

20   For a comparative discussion of development finance banks (companies) which have been created in Korea, Taiwan, the Philippines and Singapore see David L. Gordon 'Development Finance Companies, State and Privately Owned' World Bank Staff Working Paper No. 578, 1983.

21   Patrick 'Financial Development and Economic Growth in Underdeveloped Countries' *Economic Development and Cultural Change*.

22   ibid.

23   U Tun Wai and Hugh T. Patrick 'Stock and Bond Issues and Capital Markets in Less Developed Countries' *IMF Staff Papers* July 1973.

24   Cole and Park *Financial Development in Korea*.

25   For a criticism of the supply-leading approach see Panitchpadki Supachai 'Financial Structure; Segmentation and Development' Bank of Thailand *Quarterly Bulletin* 21, 1, March 1981.

26   Leroy P. Jones and Il Sakong *Government, Business and Entrepreneurship in Economic Development: The Korean Case* Cambridge: Harvard University Council on East Asian Studies, 1980.

27   Cole and Park *Financial Development in Korea*.

28   Patrick and Moreno 'Philippine Private Domestic Commercial Banking, 1946–1980'.

29   Wu Yuan Li and Wu Chun-hsi *Economic Development in Southeast Asia—The Chinese Dimension* Stanford: Hoover Institution Press, 1980, p. 96.

30   Rotating credit associations in various institutional forms have been pervasive

throughout Asia and Africa. On occasion, they have appeared also in contemporary European-based societies, such as the 'suit clubs' in Melbourne in the 1930s for financing the purchase of a new suit of clothes; see Peter J. Drake *Money for Finance and Development* New York: John Wiley & Sons, 1980, p. 135.

31 This interplay over time between 'traditional' and 'modern' financial sectors is analysed in case studies on Japan by Patrick 'Japanese Financial Development in Historical Perspective, 1868–1980'; on Korea by Cole and Park *Financial Development in Korea*; and on Indonesia by Ross H. McLeod, Financial Entrepreneurship in the Small Business Sector in Indonesia, PhD dissertation, Australian National University, 1982.

32 For models and analyses of the relationship between regulated and unregulated markets, see Cole and Park *Financial Development in Korea*; Kohsaka 'The High Interest Rate Policy in Economic Development'; and S. Van Wijnberger 'Interest Rate Management in LDCs' *Journal of Monetary Economics* 12, 2, September 1983.

33 See Patrick and Moreno 'Philippine Private Domestic Commercial Banking, 1946–1980'.

34 Von Pischke et al. *Rural Financial Markets in Developing Countries* provides many micro studies on rural finance but most empirical evidence is for Africa and India with little from the Pacific Basin economies.

35 See Cole and Park *Financial Development in Korea*.

36 Asian Development Bank *Domestic Resource Mobilization through Financial Development* Vol. 2, Table 8, p. 268.

37 R.J.G. Wells 'The Rural Credit Market in Peninsular Malaysia: A Focus on Informal Lenders' *Asian Economics* 31, December 1979.

38 Cole and Park *Financial Development in Korea* Table 30, pp.131–2.

39 Central bank of China, Economic Research Department *A Supplement to Financial Statistics Monthly, Taiwan District, Republic of China* 2nd edn, Taipei: October 1983, Table 24C.

40 See Patrick and Moreno 'Philippine Private Domestic Commercial Banking'.

41 Van Wijnberger 'Interest Rate Management in LDCs' *Journal of Monetary Economics* has developed a Keynesian model of the relationship between the regulated and the unregulated sectors (banks and kerb market), in which an increase in the regulated time-deposit interest rate can have an adverse impact on inflation rates and real growth. The results depend on important implicit as well as explicit assumptions. Notably, an increase in the deposit rate attracts funds to banks from the kerb market and, because of positive reserve requirements, the total supply of loanable funds to business decreases. Such a contractionary policy would be an unwise part of an interest-rate reform package; the monetary authorities would properly offset this contraction in loanable funds. His model does not take into account the effect of more efficient investment allocation resulting from a market-determined system of interest rates and elimination of the rents accruing under credit rationing. A similar, more comprehensive modelling approach and discussion appears in Lance Taylor *Structuralist Macroeconomics: Applicable Models for the Third World* New York: Basic Books, 1983.

42 Banks used other mechanisms to evade deposit and loan interest-rate ceilings, and corporations encouraged employees' deposits at interest rates above those allowed in the regulated sector; Hugh T. Patrick 'Interest Rates and the Grey Financial Market in Japan' *Pacific Affairs* Winter 1965–1966.

43 See Cheng Hang-Sheng 'Financial Reform in Australia and New Zealand' Federal Reserve Bank of San Francisco *Economic Review* 1, Winter 1983.

44 See chapter 10 by Eisuke Sakakibara and chapter 12 by Masuru Yoshitomi in this volume.

45 See Ronald A. Shearer, John F. Chant and David E. Bond *The Economics of the*

Canadian Financial System: Theory, Policy and Institutions 2nd edn, Scarborough, Ontario: Prentice Hall, 1983.

46   Cheng 'Financial Reform in Australia and New Zealand' Federal Reserve Bank of San Francisco *Economic Review*.

47   See Park Yung Chul, Recent Developments in the Financial Sector of the Korean Economy, mimeo, September 1982; and Lee Dukhoon 'Recent Developments in Korea's Financial Sector' Discussion Paper No.30, Economic Research Institute, Economic Planning Agency, Tokyo, March 1984.

48   Patrick and Moreno 'Philippine Private Domestic Banking'.

49   See David C. Cole and Park Yung Chul, Interest Rate Policy in Sri Lanka, mimeo, Harvard Institute for International Development, November 1982.

50   Patrick and Moreno 'Philippine Private Domestic Banking'.

Chapter 3

1   For example, see Edward K.Y. Chen 'Economic Interdependence in the Western Pacific Basin: A Hong Kong Perspective' Discussion Paper, Institute for Developing Economies Workshop, Tokyo, December 1983; and John Wong 'The Integration of China into the Western Pacific Basin Economy: Implications for ASEAN' report submitted to the Institute for Developing Economies, Tokyo, 1983.

2   Some writers refer to the area as the Asian–Pacific region, for example, Richard W. Moxon et al. 'International Business and the Century of the Pacific' *Research in International Business and Finance* Vol. 4, Part A, pp. 1–27. The People's Republic of China has been excluded because of scarcity of data, except in the discussion on foreign investment in the third section.

3   This question has to some extent been discussed by Hal Hill and Brian Johns in their forthcoming article 'The Role of Direct Foreign Investment in Developing East Asian Countries' for *Das Weltwirtschaftliches Archiv*. The *World Development Report, 1984* has as its focus the role of capital flows.

4   Almost all the flows discussed in this paper (except for the bank data) are recorded annually. Data are not available regarding the maturity structure of these flows.

5   The developed countries included comprise the member countries of the Development Assistance Committee (DAC) of the OECD. Apart from the PB5, the other countries are in Europe; a list of the European DAC members can be found in Table 3.17.

6   Net private-sector flows by source country are derived as net total flows less net ODA, less net OOF.

7   There was a large jump in private-sector flows in 1981—this could be due to the significant increase in bank lending in that year, which was subsequently cut back when debt crises, such as that of Poland, began to occur.

8   Public debt includes borrowings by governments as well as publicly guaranteed debt.

9   'All sources' refers to the DAC countries, multilateral institutions and OPEC.

10   Consider the following cases:
1   T1/T increases over time and x/T2 increases by the same amount;
2   T1/T increases over time and x/T2 increases by more;
3   T1/T increases over time and x/T2 decreases, but by less;
4   T1/T decreases over time and x/T2 also decreases, but by less.

The flows from the PB5 to the PB8 are considered to have increased in relative importance in cases 2 and 3. Note that x/T2 increases in cases 1, 2 and 3.

11   The ratios for private-sector flows to the PB8 for 1977 show an unusually small volume originating from the PB5 relative to the European countries. The data reveal that there were abnormally large negative private-sector flows from the US to

Indonesia and Malaysia in that year.

12 These exceptions are OOF in 1978, 1981 and 1982, and private-sector flows in 1977.

13 These exceptions are OOF in 1982 and private-sector flows in 1977.

14 Total flows originating from Australia, Canada and New Zealand comprised less than 5 per cent of the total in both periods. This percentage is, however, higher for ODA (Australia's share increased from 3.7 per cent to 7 per cent) and OOF (Canada's share was 13 per cent in 1980–82).

15 The figures in Table 3.8 for foreign investment in Indonesia are for approvals and, moreover, exclude the oil and financial sectors. Once the oil sector is included the ratio for American investment increases substantially; see Hal Hill 'Survey of Recent Developments' and Thee Kan Wie 'Japanese Direct Investment in Indonesian Manufacturing' *Bulletin of Indonesian Economic Studies* 20, 2, August 1984, pp. 1–38 and pp. 90–106 respectively. Also, not all approved investments are realised. Similar matrices of foreign investment by host and home country can be found in Sueo Seiguchi 'Direct Investment in the Pacific Basin: Interim Report' Direct Investment Task Force, Japan Center for International Exchange, Tokyo 1983 (for the years 1976 and 1980); ESCAP Secretariat 'ASEAN Foreign Investment from Pacific Forces' *ASEAN and Pacific Economic Cooperation* Development Papers No. 2, 1983, pp.179–230; and Mari Pangetsu 'Japanese and Other Foreign Investment in the ASEAN Countries' Australia–Japan Research Centre, Research Paper No. 73, 1980.

16 Foreign investment in the People's Republic of China is as yet only a minor proportion of the country's use of foreign capital; loans have been much more important, although the reverse was true in 1983. See Lin Jian-Hai, Issues in Debt Management: the China Perspective, mimeo, 1983.

17 In fact Asia was the most important region for Japanese investment until the early 1980s. In Table 3.11 two definitions of US foreign investment are used. The difference is that the 1966–77 definition considers the total assets of affiliates that are 25 per cent or more owned by US parent companies. The definition for the 1982 data is restricted in terms of ownership to the US parent company's claims only.

18 See, among others, Sueo Seiguchi and Lawrence B. Krause 'Direct Foreign Investment in ASEAN by Japan and the United States' in Ross Garnaut (ed.) *ASEAN in a Changing Pacific and World Economy* Canberra: ANU Press, 1980, pp. 421–46; ESCAP Secretariat 'ASEAN Foreign Investments from Pacific Sources'; and Hill and Johns 'The Role of Direct Foreign Investment in Developing East Asian Countries'.

19 Another factor for both Japanese and US investment would be the move to less-developed countries to take advantage of the Generalised System of Preferences available to them.

20 Heinz W. Arndt 'Financial Development in Asia' *Asian Development Review* 1, 1, 1983, pp. 86–100.

21 Chen 'Economic Interdependence in the Western Pacific Basin: a Hong Kong Perspective'.

22 Foreign investment from Asian developing countries is well discussed by Louis T. Wells jr 'Multinationals from Asian Developing Countries' *Research in International Business and Finance* Vol. 4, Part A, 1984, pp. 127–43 and Donald J. Lecraw 'Comments on Wells' in the same volume, pp. 149–51, as well as in Krishna Kumar and Maxwell C. McLeod (eds) *Multinationals from Developing Countries* Lexington: Lexington Books, 1981.

23 In the 1980s there have been significant flows of Korean and Taiwanese investments into the US, so that the US constitutes the most important region for those investments today. From the point of view of the US, however, foreign investment

by the Asian NICs is still a minuscule percentage of total foreign investment in the country.

24   This trend is described by Nicholas C. Hope and David W. McMurray, Loan Capital in Development Finance, the Role of Banks and Some Implications for Managing Debt, mimeo, 1983; and Jeffrey A. Katz 'Capital Flows and Developing Country Debt', World Bank Staff Working Paper No.352, 1979.

25   This trend is also evident in OECD data. See Table 3.2 for the composition of official flows to the PB8 countries.

26   OECD *OECD Development Co-operation* Paris: OECD Publications, 1983.

27   The shortness of the time-series available is a severe constraint in this case. The comparison of the early 1970s with the early 1980s could well indicate a decline in this ratio.

28   Park Yun S. 'A Comparison of Hong Kong and Singapore as Asian Financial Centres' in Philip D. Grub et al. *East Asia: Dimensions of International Business* Australia: Prentice Hall, 1982, pp. 21–28.

29   More detailed data from the US Treasury *Bulletin* reveal that Singapore held large deposits for Treasury bills with the US banks. This is consistent with the report that about 90 per cent of GSIC's assets were in US Treasury bills and gold while the remainder was in blue-chip stocks and debentures in the US, Japan, Australia and Europe, and in American real estate (*Fortune* 21 March 1983, pp. 148–52). It was also disclosed that the GSIC managed the then about US$15 billion of the foreign-exchange assets of the country.

30   Attempts were made to obtain unpublished data on Japanese banks' net claims by country. These attempts, however, did not succeed. It is very likely that Japanese bank lending to the PB9 countries has increased substantially, although the total volume of lending is still less than that of the US banks.

Chapter 4

In preparing this chapter for publication, I have been glad to incorporate valuable contributions made at the PAFTAD Conference by Philip Anisan, Liang Kuo-Shu and H.W. Arndt. I am most grateful to Hans Kunnen for allowing me access to material on Fiji which he gathered in the course of research for a MEc degree in the University of New England; to Professor Liang Kuo-Shu, for the original draft of which my section on Taiwan is a condensed version; and to Philip Anisan, for his valuable comments upon the chapter's penultimate section.

1   Edward J. Kane 'Policy Implications of Structural Change in Financial Markets' *American Economic Review* 73, May 1983, p. 97.

2   C.P. Kindleberger 'International Financial Intermediation for Developing Countries' in R.I. McKinnon (ed.) *Money and Finance in Economic Growth and Development* New York: Marcel Dekker, 1976.

3   See for example Andrea Calamanti 'The Stock Exchange and Securities Market in Morocco' *Savings and Development* IV, 1980, pp. 226–302.

4   J.M. Samuels and N. Yacout 'Stock Exchanges in Developing Countries' *Savings and Development* V, 1981, pp. 217–32.

5   Robert B. Dickie 'Development of Third World Securities Markets: An Analysis of General Principles and a Case Study of the Indonesian Market' *Law and Policy in International Business* 13, 1981, pp. 177–223.

6   See for example U Tun Wai and Hugh Patrick 'Stock and Bond Issues and Capital Markets in Less Developed Countries' *International Monetary Fund Staff Papers* July 1973.

7   Samuels and Yacout 'Stock Exchanges'.

8   P.J. Drake *Money, Finance and Development* Oxford: Martin Robertson, 1980,

pp. 213–15, 225–27.

9 Dickie 'Development of Third World Securities Markets' p. 188.

10 D.W. Stammer 'Financial Development and Economic Growth in Underdeveloped Countries: Comment' *Economic Development and Cultural Change* 20, January 1972.

11 Dickie 'Development of Third World Securities Markets' pp. 190–91.

12 On all these points see G.C. Maniotis 'Reliability of the Equities Market to Finance Industrial Development in Greece' *Economic Development and Cultural Change* 19, July 1971, pp. 660–62; U Tun Wai and Patrick 'Stock and Bond Issues and Capital Markets' pp. 260, 288; Andrea Calamanti 'The Tunisia Stock Exchange' *Savings and Development* III, 199, pp. 157–84. Calamanti also notes that taxation systems sometimes favour capital increases by way of capitalisation of reserves.

13 Dickie 'Development of Third World Securities Markets' pp. 201–2.

14 S.W. Nam and Y.C. Park 'Financial Institutions and Markets in South Korea' in M.T. Skully (ed.) *Financial Institutions and Markets in the Far East* London: Macmillan, 1982.

15 Nam and Park 'Financial Institutions' p. 161; Dickie 'Development of Third World Securities Markets' p. 183.

16 See David C. Cole and Yung Chul Park *Financial Development in Korea 1945–1978* Cambridge, Mass.: Harvard University Press, 1983, p. 87.

17 ibid p. 91.

18 Dickie 'Development of Third World Securities Markets' p. 183; Cole and Park *Financial Development* pp. 91–92.

19 ibid p. 89.

20 Nam and Park 'Financial Institutions' p. 161.

21 ibid p. 162.

22 Cole and Park *Financial Development* p. 109.

23 S.Y. Lee and Y.C. Jao *Financial Structures and Monetary Policy in Southeast Asia* London: Macmillan, 1982, p. 160.

24 Dickie 'Development of Third World Securities Markets' p. 183.

25 P.J. Drake 'The New Issue Boom in Malaya and Singapore' *Economic and Cultural Change* 18, October 1969, pp. 73–91.

26 Bank Negara Malaysia *Money and Banking in Malaysia* (Kuala Lumpur) 1979, p. 316; 1981, p. 85.

27 ibid 1979, p. 325.

28 Monetary Authority of Singapore *Annual Report 1978/79* Singapore, 1979, pp. 39–40.

29 P.J. Drake *Financial Development in Malaya and Singapore* Canberra: Australian National University Press, 1969; *Money and Banking in Malaysia* 1979, pp. 321–26.

30 ibid p. 323.

31 M.T. Skully *Financial Institutions and Markets in Southeast Asia* London: Macmillan, forthcoming.

32 M.T. Skully 'Financial Institutions and Markets in Hong Kong' in Skully (ed.) *Financial Institutions and Markets in the Far East* London: Macmillan, 1982, pp. 66–67.

33 Y.C. Jao *Banking and Currency in Hong Kong: A study of Postwar Financial Development* London: Macmillan, pp. 78–81.

34 ibid p. 130.

35 Lee and Jao *Financial Structures* p. 18.

36 Skully 'Financial Institutions' p. 62.

37 Lee and Jao *Financial Structures* pp. 18–307.

38 ibid p. 19.

39 Skully 'Financial Institutions' pp. 65–66.

40 Kane 'Policy Implications' p. 99.

Chapter 5

1   H. Patrick 'Financial Development and Economic Growth in Developing Countries' *Economic Development and Cultural Change* 14, 2, 1966.
2   J.G. Gurley and E.S. Shaw 'Financial Structure and Development' *Economic Development and Cultural Change* 15, 3, 1967.
3   R.W. Goldsmith *Financial Structure and Development* New Haven and London: Yale University Press 1969.
4   E.S. Shaw *Financial Deepening in Economic Development* New York: Oxford University Press, 1973.
5   Y.K. Wang 'Monetary Interdependence Among ASEAN Countries' United Nations, ECAFE *ASEAN and Pacific Economic Co-operation Development Papers* 2, 1983.
6   Kano 'Interdependence in the ASEAN Region' Paper for a research committee of the Institute of Developing Economies, 1980.

Further relevant reading
Association of South-East Asian Nations *10 years ASEAN* 1978; R.C. Bryant *Money and Monetary Policy in Interdependent Nations* Washington, D.C.: The Brookings Institution, 1980; R.C. Bryant 'Financial Interdependence and Variability in Exchange Rates' Staff Paper, The Brookings Institution, Washington, D.C., 1980; M. Long 'A Note on Financial Theory and Economic Development', in J.D. Von Pischke et al. (eds) *Rural Financial Markets in Developing Countries* World Bank EDI Series in Economic Development, Johns Hopkins University Press, 1983; S. Matsumoto 'The Structure of Interdependence in South-East Asia and the Future of the ASEAN States' in Hagiwara *Asia in the 1980s: Interdependence, Peace and Development* Institute of Developing Economies Symposium Proceedings, 7, 1982; P.B. Rana *ASEAN Exchange Rates: Policies and Trade Effects* Singapore: ASEAN Economics Research Unit, Institute of Southeast Asian Studies, 1981; A.K. Swoboda 'Exchange Rate Regimes and US–European Policy Interdependence' *IMF Staff Papers* 30, 1, March 1983; United Nations *Economic Co-operation for ASEAN* Report of a United Nations Team, 1972; G.J. Vishkins *Financial Deepening in ASEAN Countries* Pacific Forum, 1980.

Chapter 6

1   Many finance companies were directly involved in making this artificial boom, in which several stock prices were manipulated and bidden up to an extraordinary level as compared to their intrinsic value. One stock price company, Raja Finance, was driven up to more than twenty times its initially issued price. The public as a whole lost, and with many inexperienced individual participants losing heavily in the stock-market crash there has been a drastic setback for the young capital market in Thailand.
2   There are no taxes collected on interest earned from savings deposits.
3   The finance company interest rate used in this study is not net of tax since this formulation seems to yield slightly better results. Furthermore, if it is to be used as a proxy for the interest rate in the unregulated market, taxes should not be subtracted.

Chapter 7

1   Long-term loans are not tied to export sales but have been extended since 1973 in a discretionary manner to industries specialising in exports.
2   The system has also several defects. See Y.C. Park 'Export-Led Growth and

Industrial Transformation in Korea, 1970–80' Institute of Economic Development Discussion Paper No. 7, Korea University, 1983.

3   This can be seen more clearly when the export financing scheme is compared with a real depreciation designed to encourage exports. A real depreciation, like interest subsidies, would favour export sales but does not necessarily improve exporters' accessibility to bank financing.

4   They amounted to only about 12 per cent of total loans in 1962–66 and about 19 per cent in 1967–71.

5   W. Hong 'Export-Oriented Growth and Trade Patterns of Korea' Paper presented at NBER Conference *The Global Implications of the Trade Pattern of East and Southeast Asia* Kuala Lumpur, January 1984.

6   W. Hong *Trade, Distortions and Employment Growth in Korea* Seoul: Korea Development Institute, 1979, p. 201.

7   Since 1980, there were significant devaluations and worldwide high interest rates which effectively terminated the era of low-cost foreign borrowing for Korean businessmen.

8   The weighted average real interest rate on entire loans provided by all banking institutions in Korea amounted to −14.4 per cent per annum in 1962–64, 4.1 per cent in 1965–71 and −6.2 per cent in 1972–76. The real interest rate applied to discounts of commercial bills amounted to −7.1 per cent, 0.5 per cent and −2.5 per cent in each period. This implies that the rates on discounts of commercial bills overestimate the real interest rates on total bank loans by 4–7 per cent. See Hong *Trade, Distortions and Employment Growth in Korea* pp. 162–201.

9   The 'gross' rate of return on capital is defined as the ratio of non-labour share of value-added to capital stock. Capital stock consists of physical assets and net working capital. The gross rates of return and L/VA ratios presented in Table 7.2 represent the average annual figures for the periods 1971–73, 1974–79 and 1980–82 respectively.

10 Shipbuilding, automobiles and parts, large-scale machinery manufacturing and industrial chemical sectors revealed above-average rates of return during the high growth period of 1974–79.

11 The synethic fibre yarn sector has also maintained above-average L/VA ratios and achieved significant factor substitutions but may be exceptional in the sense that this sector could maintain very high gross rates of return. Sugar refining, rubbertrees, and pulp and paper products sectors maintained below-average L/VA ratios and yet these sectors revealed very high rates of return and achieved significant factor substitutions and output expansions. The high rates of return revealed in these sectors might be explained by the high rates of protection accorded to them, but all these sectors achieved substantial increases in export shares. Petroleum refining, which has been the most capital-intensive manufacturing sector in Korea, did not maintain very high L/VA ratios. The refineries were mostly financed by direct foreign investments. This sector revealed very low rates of output expansion, factor substitution and export increase.

12 This measure required 1217 large firms to report their holdings of land and buildings, classified into those used for business operations and others presumably held for real estate speculation.

13 Developed by D.W. Jorgenson 'The Theory of Investment Behaviour' in R. Ferber (ed.) *Determinants of Investment Behaviour* New York: NBER, 1967, and extended by T. Kwack, Investment Allocation in a CCE Model for Korea, mimeo, Korea Development Institute, 1983.

14 ibid.

15 ibid.

16 By pooling the data, we are implicitly assuming that the paired sectors have similar

lag structures in investment behaviour. Although this assumption is not realistic, it is likely that sectors with comparable factor intensities have similar lag structures.

17 See chapter 4 of D.C. Cole and Yung Chul Park *Financial Development in Korea, 1945–78* Studies in the Modernisation of the Republic of Korea: 1945–75, Council on East Asian Studies, Harvard University, 1983.

18 The non-monetary financial institutions (excluding KDB and EXIMB), such as investment companies, savings institutions, life insurance companies and the Korea Long-Term Credit Bank, are almost entirely owned and controlled by this selected group of entrepreneurs.

Chapter 8

This chapter is a revised edition of a paper delivered at the Fourteenth PAFTAD conference. It has been revised to cover recent developments in the internationalisation of the Australian banking system.

1 For a summary of available data, see OECD *The Internationalisation of Banking—The Policy Issues* Paris, 1983; also Tables 8.1–8.5.

2 The essential elements of this framework have been developed in J. Hewson and E. Sakakibara *The Eurocurrency Markets and their Implications—A 'New View' of International Monetary Problems and Monetary Reform* Lexington: D.C. Heath Lexington Books, 1975; J. Hewson *Liquidity Creating and Distribution in the Eurocurrency Markets* Lexington: D.C. Heath Lexington Books, 1975; and J. Niehans and J. Hewson 'The Eurodollar Market and Monetary Theory' *Journal of Money, Credit and Banking* August 1976.

3 For a more detailed discussion and analysis of the development of Singapore as a financial centre, see J. Hewson 'Offshore Banking in Australia' chapter 4 in *Australian Financial System Inquiry: Commissioned Studies and Selected Papers* Part 2 (Macroeconomic Policy: External Policy) Canberra: AGPS, 1982; and J. Hewson 'The Asia-Dollar Market and Monetary Policy' chapter 9 in *MAS Papers on Monetary Economics* 1981.

4 Additional details are available in Reserve Bank of Australia 'Overseas Operations of Australian Banks' *Statistical Bulletin* February 1982 and March 1983.

5 The case is assessed in more detail in Government of New South Wales *Whitlam Report* 1984.

Chapter 9

I am grateful to the Central Bank of the Philippines and the Monetary Authority of Singapore, which have supplied unpublished data. I have learned much from discussion with Mr Juan Hoe of the Reserve Bank of Australia and Dr Ralph C. Bryant, a Research Fellow of the Institute of Southeast Asian Studies. In particular, Mr Hoe has provided me with much information on the foreign-exchange markets.

1 See Jack Revelli 'Financial Centres, Financial Institutions and Economic Change' in Harry Y. Johnson (ed.) *The New Mercantilism: Some Problems in International Trade, Money and Investment* Oxford: Basil Blackwell, 1974, pp. 74–89; and Revelli 'International Financial Centres' Paper read at the University of Pavia, 10 June 1983. For a discussion of the three financial centres in Britain, Singapore and the US and their problems of monetary control, see Ronald I. McKinnon 'Offshore Markets in Foreign Currencies and Monetary Control: Britain, Singapore and the United States' in MAS *Papers on Monetary Economics* Singapore University Press, 1981.

2 Japan has not been in favour of developing Tokyo as a financial centre because interest rates would be likely to rise and fluctuate with the world movement, hindering Japan's industries. It is possible however that the Japanese government might reconsider its opposition.

3 See E.S. Shaw *Financial Deepening in Economic Development* New York: Oxford University Press, 1973; R.I. McKinnon *Money and Capital in Economic Development* Washington, D.C.: The Brookings Institution, 1973; and McKinnon (ed.) *Money and Finance in Economic Growth and Development* New York: Marcel Dekker, 1976.

4 By definition, Asian curency units operate in foreign exchange.

5 Since July 1975, banks have been free to set their own lending and deposit rates. Moreover, from September 1981 banks were permitted to fix their own rates for large domestic transactions of $40 000 or over, such as letters of credit, loans and overdrafts, securities transactions and mail and telegraphic transfer. This partially removed the regulated charges of the Association of Banks in Singapore.

6 For detailed statistics and discussion, see Lee Sheng-Yi 'The Role of Singapore as a Financial Centre' Paper presented to the Seventh Conference of the ASEAN Economic Association, held in Denpasar, Indonesia, November 1982.

7 For a detailed statistical analysis see Lee Sheng-Yi 'Recent Development in the Asian Currency Market and the Asian Bond Market' Occasional Paper No. 32, Institute of Economics and Business Studies, Nanyang University, April 1979, pp. 17–18, Table 3.

8 On September 27 1983, in a break with tradition, the Hong Kong Government took over Hong Lung Bank in an emergency rescue action.

9 The exchange fund was established in 1935, when Hong Kong followed China's lead in abandoning the silver standard.

10 Coins and $1 notes are issued by the Hong Kong government and are fully backed by the Coin Security Fund, which has now been merged with the Exchange Fund.

11 For a criticism of the monetary system of Hong Kong, see Lee Sheng-Yi 'Inflation and Monetary and Banking System of Hong Kong' *Economic Report Hong Kong* (in Chinese), 15 March 1983, pp. 10, 14.

12 It should be noted that with the rapid depreciation of the exchange rate, the expansion of the money supply with respect to foreign currency components (Table 9.9) is exaggerated, because one US dollar deposit in one period would automatically increase in the next period. Nevertheless, no matter what adjustments are made, monetary growth (M2 and M3) was substantial in the period 1980–83.

13 See A. Marshall *Money, Credit and Commerce* London: Macmillan, 1922, pp. 61–2; and R.I. McKinnon 'Two Concepts of International Currency Substitution' Paper delivered to the Fourteenth PAFTAD Conference, Sinagpore, 1984.

14 See for example the Radcliffe Report, 1959; and Milton Friedman 'The Quantity Theory of Money—a Restatement' in Milton Friedman (ed.) *Studies in the Quantity Theory of Money* University of Chicago Press, 1956.

15 For a discussion, see *Hong Kong: Economic Prospects to 1987* London: Economist Intelligence Unit, November 1983, pp. 26–28.

16 Annual inflation rate (per cent), 1977–83:

1977	5.5	1981	14.9
1978	5.8	1982	10.9
1979	11.9	1983	10.0
1980	15.1		

Note: The rate is estimated from the weighted average of three consumer price indexes, and the Hong Kong index for different income groups.

Source: Hong Kong Monthly Digest of Statistics

17　See Census and Statistics Department *Estimates of Gross Domestic Product, 1966– 1983, Hong Kong* 1983.

18　See Department of Statistics *Survey of Service: Singapore* 1980.

19　This observation is made with reservations, because the differences between the systems and definitions used by the two financial centres make a realistic comparison difficult.

20　See S.Y. Lee 'The Asian Dollar Market, Asian Bond Market and the Hong Kong Bank Group in Frank H.H. King (ed.) *Eastern Banking: Essays in the History of the Hong Kong and Shanghai Banking Corporation* London: Athlone Press, 1983, pp. 594–5; and Y.C. Jao 'Financing Hong Kong's Early Postwar Industrialization: The Role of the Hong Kong and Shanghai Banking Corporation' in King, ibid. pp. 545–67.

21　This proposal was advanced in the *Asian Monetary Monitor* September/October 1983.

22　China amended the Constitution so that the Special Administrative Zone, including Hong Kong, Macao and Taiwan, would have a high degree of autonomy.

23　The estimate of Y.C. Jao. See his paper 'Hong Kong's Role in Financing China's Modernization' in A.J. Youngson (ed.) *China and Hong Kong: The Economic Nexus* Hong Kong: Oxford University Press, 1983, pp. 58–9; and *Hong Kong: Economic Prospects to 1987* London: Economist Intelligence Unit, November 1983, pp. 42–52.

24　The surplus has increased progressively from HK$10 billion in 1978 to HK$18.5 billion in 1981—see Jao 'Hong Kong's Role in Financing China's Modernization' p. 15. For the general pattern of China's trade see Lee Sheng-Yi 'Asean Trade with China' in Saw Swee-Hock and Hong Hai (eds) *Growth and Direction of Asean Trade* Singapore: University Press, 1982, pp. 45–9.

25　Data source: Hong Kong Banking Commissioner's Office and Registrar-General's Department, quoted in Jao, ibid p. 31.

26　The proclamation of Martial Law by President Marcos in 1972 caused a reduction in strikes, riots and political disturbances, until the assassination of Opposition Leader Benigno Aquino brought to a head the mounting discontent and sparked off continuing political turmoil.

27　Presidential Decree No. 1773, 16 January 1981, abolished the 5 per cent tax on net offshore income, which had been effective since December 1976.

28　For a discussion of the importance of financial liberalisation and deepening, see Shaw *Financial Deepening in Economic Development* and McKinnon *Money and Capital in Economic Development*.

29　Singapore's Minister for Finance, Mr Lee Yock Suan, stated that by February 1984, the average turnover of forex transactions in Singapore had increased to about US$11 billion per working day.

30　During the current political turmoil (1984), the Philippines government ordered banks to surrender all their foreign exchange to the Monetary Authority, except what was necessary to maintain a working balance.

31　The Bank of Thailand limits the foreign exchange held by the banks to not more than 10 per cent of their capital funds.

32　The forward market is practically non-existent in Indonesia, except for swap facilities for customers with offshore loans.

33　From the Smithsonian Agreement of December 1971 to the present, the trade-weighted exchange-rate index for the Singapore dollar has risen continuously by about 29 per cent. See Lee Sheng-Yi 'Foreign Exchange Management in Singapore' *Asia Pacific Journal of Management* National University of Singapore, August 1984.

34　For a discussion of the problem caused by the dramatic rise in world interest rates, see John R. Hewson 'The Asian Dollar Market and Monetary Policy' in MAS *Papers on Monetary Economics* Singapore: University Press, 1981, pp. 188–92.

35   In the 1980 episode, the outflow of funds due to the interest differential depreciated the Singapore dollar against the US dollar.

36   For a discussion of the financial system and interest rates in the Philippines see Lee Sheng-Yi and Y.C. Jao *Financial Structures and Monetary Policies in Southeast Asia* New York: St Martins Press, 1982, pp. 189–91.

Chapter 10

1   Jeffrey A. Frenkel 'The 1984 Campaign for Liberalisation of Japanese Capital Markets' Paper presented at the Symposium on Current Issues in Changes in Socio-economic Structure and The International Implications, Tokyo, August 1984.

2   David Murchison and Ezra Solomon 'Misalignment of the US Dollar and the Japanese Yen: The Problem and Its Solution' (no publication details) 19 September 1983.

3   Frenkel 'The 1984 Campaign for Liberalisation of Japanese Capital Markets'.

4   Takashi Hosomi 'A Draft Plan for the Establishment of an International Banking Facility in Tokyo' in the Institute for Financial Affairs Newsletter *Money and Finance* February 1983.

5   E. Sakakibara and A. Kondoh 'Study on the Internationalisation of Tokyo's Money Markets' Japan Center for International Finance *Policy Study Series* No. 1, June 1984.

Chapter 11

1   See Z. Hodjera 'The Asian Currency Market: Singapore as a Regional Financial Centre' *IMF Staff Papers* 25, 2, June 1978; J.R. Hewson 'Offshore Banking in Australia' *Australian Financial System Inquiry, Commissioned Studies and Selected Papers, Part 2* Canberra: AGPS, 1981; and J. Wong 'ASEAN Economies: Growth and Adjustment' *The Studies of Business and Industry* March 1984.

2   For influential US arguments about the decline of US manufacturing, see B. Bluestone and B. Harrison *The Deindustrialization of America: Plant Closings, Community Abandonment and the Dismantling of Basic Industries* New York: Basic Books, 1982; and R.B. Reich *The Next American Frontier* New York: Times Books, 1983.

     T.J. Dilorenzo criticises the deindustrialisation hypothesis in 'The Myth of America's Manufacturing Sector' *The Heritage Foundation Backgrounder* 321, January 1984.

     In Figure 11.1, I present Canadian data on the growth of the services and goods-producing industries between 1935 and 1984. Until 1973, both sectors grew at practically identical rates. They did so again from 1975 to the middle of 1981 and during 1983. Sharp declines in goods production during the recessions of 1974 and 1981–82 opened up a performance gap that has been narrowed, but not closed, during the 1983 recovery. These data show that the growth of goods production tends to be cyclic, and that the relative growth of the service industries is a very recent phenomenon.

3   For a review, see F.C. Bergsten and W.R. Cline (eds) *Trade Policy in the Eighties* Washington, D.C.: Institute for International Economics, 1983, especially chapter 17.

4 As noted above, this growth in the US may well be due to the relative decline of goods-producing industries following the 1976 recession. However, it may also be due to the general deregulation of US industry, which took place simultaneously. For reasons that I have been unable to unravel, the UN statistics on FIR for Canada are smaller than those shown in Canadian Department of Finance and Statistics *Economic Review* April 1978 and April 1983, according to which Canada's FIR sector contributed the following to GDP:

Year	1950	1960	1970	1980
Percentage	12.25	12.33	11.54	12.85

5 The sum of SIC 901–903 in Table 11.3 does not add up to the value of SIC 9, as shown in the same source from which the data of Table 11.3 were taken. Adding imputed rent, which has no SIC code, results in a sum only marginally different from SIC 9. However, adding SIC 701 and 705 to SIC 901–903 plus imputed rent gives a number greater than SIC 9. Presumably, SIC 701 and 705 are components of SIC 901.

6 The following analogy may be useful. The export of US aeroplanes is recorded in the merchandise account. When US citizens use these foreign-owned planes they give rise to a US import of travel services.

7 See G. Hufbauer and M. Adler *Overseas Manufacturing Investment and the US Balance of Payments* Washinton, D.C.: US Treasury Department, 1968.

8 For a more detailed analysis of this point see H.W. Arndt 'Measuring Trade in Financial Services' Banca Nazionale del Lavoro *Quarterly Review* 1984.

9 The issue of this bias was the subject of a recent annual meeting of the Association for Research in Income and Wealth.

10 For a development of these arguments, see C.P. Kindelberger *The Formation of Financial Centers* Princeton, N.J.: Princeton University Press, 1974.

11 Consider a bank receiving a deposit of $100 on which it pays $8 interest. It lends out the full amount and earns $10. Assume that under these conditions the average $2 value added per $100 deposit is the normal return to banking in all countries.

Now consider that one small country imposes a reserve requirement of 10 per cent on deposits and that it pays no interest on these reserves. In this small country lending and borrowing rates are unchanged. The only effect of the tax is that banks can lend out $90 and earn only $9 on every $100 deposit, leaving a value-added spread of $1. The reserve requirement has in fact imposed a tax of 50 per cent on the free-market value added of banks. Under these conditions, banks have strong incentives to open branches abroad and encourage their traditional customers to do business there. For an elaboration of this point, see H.G. Grubel 'Interest Payments on Required Reserves to Control Euro-Currency Banking' in Machlup et al. *Reflections on a Troubled World Economy. Essays in Honour of Herbert Giersch* London: Macmillan, 1982.

12 It probably constitutes the main reason for the existence of branches of foreign banks in Singapore, though they also perform minor service functions for their national enterprises and for tourists. For a fuller discussion, and further references see Grubel, ibid.; 'The New International Banking' Banca Nazionale del Lavoro *Quarterly Review* 1983; and 'Towards a Theory of Free Economic Zones' *Weltwirtschaftliches Archiv* 118, 1, 1982.

13 ibid.

14 R. Vernon 'International Investment and International Trade in the Product Cycle' *Quarterly Journal of Economics* May 1966.

15 A standard reference on the subject is R.I. McKinnon *Money and Capital in Economic Development* Washington, D.C.: The Brookings Institution, 1973.

Chapter 12

1   M. Fleming 'Domestic Financial Policies under Fixed and Floating Exchange Rates' *IMF Staff Papers* November 1962, pp. 369–80.
2   Economic Planning Agency *World Econometric Model* Tokyo: March 1984.
3   For the long-term asset market equilibrium, $i = e + i^*$, where i is the home nominal interest rate, i^* is the dollar nominal interest rate and e is the expected rate of appreciation of the home currency vis-à-vis the dollar. As noted in the text, if $i = r + p$, and $i^* = p^* + p^*$ and if $e = p - p^*$, where r and r^* denote home and dollar real interest rate respectively, and p and p^* denote home and US inflation rate, respectively, then the equilibrium condition should be that $r - p = (p - p^*) + (r^* + p^*)$; that is, $r = r^*$.

Chapter 13

1   W. Branson classifies the Pacific middle-income countries into the Asian industrialising countries (Hong Kong, Korea and Singapore) and the NICs (Indonesia, Malaysia, Thailand and the Philippines) in his chapter on 'Monetary Stability and Exchange Rate Objectives in Singapore' in Monetary Authority of Singapore *Papers on Monetary Economics* Singapore University Press, 1981. Like B. Aghelvi ('Experiences of Asian Countries with Various Exchange Rate Policies' in J. Williamson (ed.) *Exchange Rate Rules* London: Macmillan, 1981), Branson includes India as a low-income NIC. I exclude India, include Taiwan as the fourth Asian industrialising country and make passing reference to Hong Kong.
2   The interaction of internal and external coordination weakens the case for cooperation among central banks, as recently shown by R. Rogoff 'Productive and Counter-Productive Cooperative Monetary Policies' International Finance Discussion Paper No. 233, Federal Reserve Board, 1983. I do not incorporate these issues in the analysis, even though they are an important element in the scepticism about macroeconomic policies mentioned at the outset. In fact, when the incentive for central banks to inflate is somehow ruled out, the presumption for cooperation re-emerges. We thus come back to the direct link between the lack of credibility of macroeconomic policies and the volatility of expectations.
3   The debate between economists and political scientists is discussed in R. Cooper 'Economic Interdependence and Coordination of Economic Policies' in R. Jones and P. Kenen (eds) *Handbook in International Economics* North Holland, 1984. A. Bressand (ed.) *RAMSES, The State of the World Economy* Ballinger, 1982 claims that 'economic security' has been declining: an idea similar to the link between vulnerability and interdependence put forward by political scientists, but also consistent with the volatility of expectations stressed below in the text.
4   For example, consider a world economy composed of two identical countries where prices are fixed. If the common marginal propensity to save is 10 per cent, we know that a unit increase in world autonomous expenditure will increase world output by ten. Assume now a marginal propensity to import of 0.5 by both countries. A unit increase in expenditure in one of them will increase domestic output by a multiplier of 5.5, and foreign output by a multiplier of 4.5. If the marginal propensities to import increase to 75 per cent, however, the domestic effect will decrease to 53 per cent of the world output increase of ten units, and the foreign effect will increase to 47 per cent. Higher propensities would, of course, reduce the multiplier.
5   See M. Feldstein 'The Dollar and Exchange Market Intervention' draft paper, Paris, 1983.

6   Simple game-theoretic macromodels can be found in K. Hamada 'Macroeconomic Strategy and Co-ordination under Alternative Exchange Rates' in R. Dornbusch and J. Frenkel (eds) *International Economic Policy* Johns Hopkins University Press, 1979; and in M. Canzoneri and J. Gray 'Two Essays on Monetary Policy in an Interdependent World' Discussion Paper No. 219, February 1983. See also J. de Macedo 'Comment on Oudiz and Sachs' Proceedings of the NBER Conference on *The Global Implications of the Trade Patterns of East and Southeast Asia* Kuala Lumpur, January 1984.

7   The point is made by Cooper 'Economic Interdependence and Coordination of Economic Policies'.

8   A trade-weighted index, such as the one used in the second section for Asian countries, would tend to be more stable in the case of the US because it assigns a large weight to a low-variance currency, the Canadian dollar. From 1973 to 1979, for example, the bilateral index depreciated by slightly over one-half of the multilateral index (5.4 per cent as opposed to 8.6 per cent per annum).

9   See J. Frenkel 'International Liquidity and Monetary Control' in G. von Furstenberg (ed.) *International Money and Credit: The Policy Roles* International Monetary Fund, 1984.

10 A positive interest-rate differential in favour of the home country can sustain an overvaluation; the higher the probability of a crash, the larger the overvaluation is likely to be. For example, if this probability is as high as one-half, an annualised interest differential of 5 per cent will support an overvaluation of 10 per cent per annum. A similar problem (which has received more attention in the exchange-rate literature) is called the 'peso problem' and refers to the effect of an expected change in policy on the current exchange rate, thus increasing its volatility as well as the volatility of the real exchange rate. Finally, the exchange rate might move 'too much' because of facts or erroneous beliefs. To the extent that these are autocorrelated, the forecast error will be difficult to detect empirically. For further discussion, see R. Dornbusch 'Equilibrium and Disequilibrium Exchange Rates' *Zeitschrift fur Wirtschafts und Sozialwissenschaften* 6, 1982.

11 For an exposition of the so-called 'portfolio view', see J. Tobin and J. de Macedo 'The Shortrun Macroeconomics of Floating Exchange Rates: An Exposition' in J. Chipman and C. Kindelberger (eds) *Flexible Exchange Rates and the Balance of Payments* North Holland, 1981.

12 The normalised relative current account goes from a US surplus at the end of 1976 to a substantial relative US deficit in 1982. Thus, before 1982, relative deficits in the United States coincided with the depreciating dollar. We can also identify a period of increasing US velocity throughout 1978 (even though velocity had decreased in 1977), followed by a sharp ascent in 1979 and again after the second quarter of 1981. See J. de Macedo 'Exchange Rate Volatility in an Interdependent World Economy' draft paper, Princeton University, May 1983.

13 ibid. for a description of the theoretical model used in the estimation, and for the econometric results.

14 This is also true of the measure of trade interdependence used by S.Y. Lin in chapter 5 of this volume.

15 See J. Tobin and J. de Macedo 'The Shortrun Macroeconomics of Floating Exchange Rates: An Exposition' for an interpretation along these lines.

16 This point was noted by Aghelvi 'Experiences of Asian Countries with Various Exchange Rate Policies' for the period of the weak dollar, 1973–78.

17 The model can be found in J. de Macedo 'Small Countries in Monetary Union: A Two-Tier Model' draft paper, Princeton University, April 1984.

18 Essential differences with the Currency Board experience are, of course, monetary sovereignty and 'generalised floating'. See Bank Negara Malaysia *Money and*

Banking in Malaysia Kuala Lumpur, 1984, p. 31. Nevertheless, the tradition of the Straits dollar or the Malayan dollar cannot be altogether ignored. Lin, in chapter 5, mentions a 'striking ... close relationship ... throughout the period 1965–82'.

19 M. Khan 'The Dynamics of Money and Prices and the Role of Monetary Policies in SEACEN Countries' Southeast Asian Central Banks Research and Training Centre, Occasional Paper No. 1, 1980 warns of the likely important role of interest rates in the money demand functions of Southeast Asian countries. Lin, in chapter 5, gives lending rates in these countries for selected years and notes their lack of simultaneity.

20 Whether it is joint or not, the float of the Singapore currency will certainly be managed, to an extent that makes it difficult to distinguish from a passive crawling peg. Branson ('Monetary Stability and Exchange Rate Objectives in Singapore') proposes an import-weighted basket adjusted with roughly equal weights to current account and reserve targets. As in the models in the first section, monetary policy adjusts to accommodate that exchange rate. Higher financial interdependence would make the indicators close to their fundamental determinants in the models in the first section.

Chapter 14

The authors thank D.H. Kim and J.S. Lee of the Asian Development Bank for their inputs into this chapter. Any errors or omissions are the responsibility of the authors.

1 This section of the paper draws heavily from Seiji Naya 'Effects of External Shocks on the Balance of Payments, Policy Responses and Debt Problems of Asian Developing Countries' *Philippine Economic Journal* 23, 1, 1984 Technical discussion of the methodology has been kept to a minimum herein and one may refer to the appendix of the publication cited here for a more detailed account.

2 In a number of countries, particularly the agrarian economies of South and Southeast Asia, internal shocks were very significant throughout this period as well. This point will be returned to later in examining the experiences of some of these countries.

3 Note that the terms of trade of oil exporters like Malaysia and Indonesia are favourably affected by oil price increases.

4 Bela Balassa 'The Newly-Industrializing Developing Countries After the Oil Crises' World Bank Staff Working Paper No. 437, Washington, D.C., October 1980.

5 These countries, in addition to Singapore and Brunei, comprise the Association of Southeast Asian Nations (ASEAN). Herein, Singapore is included among the NICs, while Brunei is excluded. Also, it should be noted that Malaysia only emerged as a net oil exporter in 1976. While Indonesia is an OPEC member, Malaysia is not.

6 Recall that Burma was not so much affected by oil prices since it is nearly self-sufficient. Pakistan experienced significant adverse effects, out of proportion to its relatively low trade/GDP ratio, due to its heavy dependence on oil imports and sharp declines to below trend values in its exports.

7 The margin above prime interest rates paid in London or New York by sovereign borrowers and the size of the debt outstanding are largely subject to economic management. This point will be returned to later in the chapter.

8 In the case of the terms of trade, the average for the period 1971–73 was used as the base year. For export volumes, it was assumed that the trend growth of 1963–73 would have continued.

9 Details are available from the authors on request.

10 This corresponds to Balassa's findings also (Balassa 'The Newly-Industrializing

Developing Countries After the Oil Crises'). In the case of the oil exporters, it should also be noted that the hypothetical rise in oil exports above trend values was offset somewhat by declines in their hypothetical volumes of non-oil exports, thus reducing the export-volume effect measure.

11   In Table 14.7, the positive numbers for oil-exporters in columns 1 and 2 correspond to the positive effects on the balance of payments of these countries shown in Table 14.6. The figures in columns 4 to 8 have the interpretation as for the oil-importers. For this reason, the sum of the final two columns will total −100 per cent for oil-exporters, indicating positive external shocks, while those of oil-importers equal +100 per cent, indicating negative external shocks.

12   Of course, if one can increase domestic savings while raising the efficency of investment, and/or attract greater direct foreign investment, the investment share in gross output need not fall, and can even rise. This may have occurred in some cases, as will be seen in Table 14.8.

13   Burma's huge percentage slide in export-market share should be viewed in the context of the very small size of external shocks to GNP.

14   This effect is measured by the difference between hypothetical imports, calculated for the actual GNP growth of a country, assuming constant import-demand elasticities based on 1963–73 values, and actual imports during 1974–82. Greater efficiency of domestic firms producing tradables, increased use of domestic energy as a share of total energy, and/or restrictions on imports, could account for positive import substitution.

15   Sri Lanka had fairly high import substitution and it was the one country in South Asia that extensively liberalised imports, albeit only in 1977.

16   Burma's case appears to be anamalous. Table 14.8 shows that actual GNP growth rose substantially between 1974 and 1983, yet Table 14.7 gives a reduced growth rate below the trend value as a large source of adjustment. The apparent contradiction is partly because of the very small size of external shocks relative to GNP in Burma, and partly due to the sensitivity of the measures used in Table 14.7 to changes induced by 'internal shocks'.

17   Note that the 'resource gap' measures include only merchandise trade and exclude non-factor services and transfers.

18   It is important to stress that the measure made herein reflects only that the actual, but still positive, resource gap turned out to be smaller than the indicated trend resource gap. As will be seen in the case of Korea, itse actual current-accounts deficits have been substantial and have led it to become the largest actual borrower among the Asian developing countries.

19   This section makes use of computations provided by J.S. Lee in his article 'The External Debt-Servicing Capacity of Asian Developing Countries' *Asian Development Review* 1, 2, 1983, pp. 66–82. This article also provides more details on the methodology.

20   See Table 14.11 for the CIR formula.

21   Burma was excluded because of data limitations.

22   See Asian Development Bank, Economics Office *Domestic Resource Mobilization Through Financial Development* Vols I and II, Manila, February 1984.

23   ibid. This study provides a wealth of material on the determinants of savings rates and the efficiency of the financial sector in a number of developing Asian countries.

Chapter 15

1   These ratios are taken from IMF *International Financial Statistics* (various issues). The IMF defines M2 as money plus quasi-money plus deposits outside commercial

banks. M2 is a stock tabulated at 30 June for each calendar year; GNP is the flow of output for the year.

2   IMF 'Interest Rate Policies in Developing Countries' Occasional Paper No. 22, October 1983.

3   A similar result was obtained by M. Fry 'Money and Capital or Financial Deepening in Economic Development' *Journal of Money, Credit and Banking* 10, 4, 1978.

4   A. Horiuchi 'Economic Growth and Financial Allocation in Post War Japan' Working Paper, University of Tokyo, 1984.

5   R.I. McKinnon *Money and Capital in Economic Development* Washington, D.C.: The Brookings Institution, 1973, pp. 96–97.

6   ibid.

7   J.E. Stiglitz and A. Weiss 'Credit Rationing in Markets with Imperfect Information' *American Economic Review* June 1981.

8   R.I. McKinnon *An International Standard for Monetary Stabilization* Washington, D.C.: Institute for International Economics, 1984.

9   Tan Kong-Yam, Flexible Exchange Rates and Interdependence: Empirical Implications for US Monetary Policy, PhD dissertation, Standford University, California.

10 McKinnon *An International Standard.*

11 ibid. chapter 5.

Bibliography

Andersson, Thomas and Rudengren, Jan 'External Capital Flows: The Case of the Five ASEAN Countries' *Ekonomiska For sKningsinstitutet vid Handelshogskolan* No. 1, Stockholm: 1984.

Arndt, Heinz W. 'Financial Development in Asia' *Asian Development Review* 1, 1, 1983.

—— 'Measuring Trade in Financial Services' in Banca Nazionale del Laboro *Quarterly Review*, 1984.

Asian Development Bank, Economics Office *Domestic Resource Mobilisation Through Financial Development* Vols I and II, Manila: 1984.

Asian Monetary Monitor September/October, 1983.

Association of Southeast Asian Nations *10 Years ASEAN* 1978.

Australian Financial System Inquiry *Commissioned Studies and Selected Papers* Part II, Canberra: Australian Government Printing Service, 1984.

Ayre, P.C.I. (ed.) *Finance in Developing Countries* London: Frank Cass and Co., 1977.

Balassa, Bela 'The Newly-Industrialising Developing Countries after the Oil Crisis'. World Bank Staff Working Paper No. 437, October 1980.

Bank Negara Malaysia *Money and Banking in Malaysia* Kuala Lumpur: 1979.

—— *Annual Report* Kuala Lumpur: 1979.

Bank of Thailand, Department of Economic Research 'Financial Institutions in Thailand' *Quarterly Bulletin* 21, 1, 1981.

Bergsten, Fred C. and Cline, William R. (eds) *Trade Policy in the Eighties* Washington, D.C.: Institute for International Economics, 1983.

Bluestone, Barry and Harrison, Bennet *The Deindustrialisation of America: Plant Closings. Community Abandonment and the Dismantling of Basic Industries* New York: Basic Books, 1982.

Bressand, A. (ed.) *Ramses, the State of the World Economy* Ballinger, 1982.

Bryant, Ralph C. *Money and Monetary Policy in Interdependent Nations* Washington, D.C.: The Brookings Institution, 1980.

—— 'Financial Interdependence and Variability in Exchange Rates' The Brookings Institution Staff Paper, 1980.

Byrd, William *China's Financial System—The Changing Role of the Banks* Boulder: Westview Press, 1983.

Calamanti, Andrea 'The Tunis Stock Exchange' *Savings and Development* Vol. 3, 1979.

—— 'The Abidjan Stock Exchange' *Savings and Development* Vol. 4, 1980.

—— 'The Stock Exchange and Securities Market in Morocco' *Savings and Development* Vol. 4, 1980.

Cameron, Rondo et al. *Banking in the Early Stages of Industrialisation* New York: Oxford University Press, 1967.

Canzoneri, M. and Gray, J. 'Two Essays on Monetary Policy in an Interdependent

World' Federal Reserve Board, International Finance Discussion Paper No. 219, February 1983.

Central Bank of China, Economic Research Department *A Supplement to Financial Statistics Monthly. Taiwan District, Republic of China* 2nd edn, Taipei: 1983.

Chen, Edward K.Y. 'Economic Interdependence in the Western Pacific Basin: A Hong Kong Perspective' Institute of Developing Economies Workshop Discussion Paper, Tokyo: December 1983.

Cheng, Hang-Sheng 'Financial Deepening in Pacific Basin Countries' in Federal Reserve Bank of San Francisco *Economic Review* Summer, 1980.

Cheng, Hang-Sheng 'Financial Reform in Australia and New Zealand' in Federal Reserve Bank of San Francisco *Economic Review* Winter 1983.

Chipman, J. and Kindleberger, C. (eds) *Flexible Exchange Rates and the Balance of Payments* Amsterdam: North-Holland, 1981.

Choo, H.C. et al. 'Estimates of Capital Stock in Korean Industries, 1966–77' *Research Report* Korea Development Institute, July 1982.

Cizaniskas, Albert C. 'The Changing Nature of Export Credit Finance and Its Implications for Developing Countries' World Bank Staff Working Paper No. 409, 1980.

Coats, Warren L. Jr and Khatkhate, Deena R. (eds) *Money and Monetary Policy in Less-Developed Countries: A Survey of Issues and Evidence* Oxford: Pergamon Press, 1980.

—— 'Monetary Policy in Less Developed Countries: Main Issues' Institute of Developing Economies mimeo, Tokyo: 1984.

Cole, David C. and Park, Yung-Chul *Financial Development in Korea, 1945–1978* Cambridge, Mass.: Harvard University Council on East Asian Studies, 1983.

—— 'Interest Rate Policy in Sri Lanka' Harvard Institute for International Development mimeo, November 1982.

Cooper, R. et al. *The International Monetary System under Flexible Exchange Rates: Global, National and Regional* Ballinger, 1982.

Dickie, Robert B. 'Development of Third World Securities Markets: An Analysis of General Principles and a Case Study of the Indonesian Market' *Law and Policy in International Business* Vol. 13, 1981.

Dilorenzo, Thomas J. 'The Myth of America's Manufacturing Sector' *The Heritage Foundation Backgrounder* No. 321, January 1984.

Dornbush, R. 'Equilibrium and Disequilibrium Exchange Rates' *Zeitschrift für Wirtschafts und Sozialwissen* Vol. 6, 1982.

—— and Frenkel, J. (eds) *International Economic Policy* Baltimore: Johns Hopkins University Press, 1979.

Drake, Peter J. *Financial Development in Malaysia and Singapore* Canberra: Australian National University Press, 1969.

—— *Money, Finance and Development* New York: John Wiley and Sons, 1980.

—— 'The New Issue Boom in Malaya and Singapore' *Economic Development and Cultural Change* 18, 1, October 1969.

—— 'Securities Markets in Developing Countries' *Journal of Development Studies* Vol. 13, January 1977.

Economic Planning Agency *World Econometric Model* Tokyo: March 1984.

Economist Intelligence Unit *Hong Kong: Economic Prospects to 1987* London: November 1983.

Eken, Sena 'Integration of Domestic and International Financial Markets: Japanese Experience' IMF paper, May 1984.

Emery, Robert F. *The Financial Institutions of Southeast Asia* New York: Praeger, 1970.

ESCAP Secretariat *ASEAN and Pacific Economic Cooperation* Development Papers No. 2, 1983.

Feldstein, M., The Dollar and Exchange Market Intervention, draft paper, April 1983.

Ferber, R. (ed.) *Determinants of Investment Behaviour* New York: NBER, 1967.

Fleming, M. 'Domestic Financial Policies under Fixed and Floating Exchange Rates' *IMF Staff Papers* November 1962.

Frenkel, Jeffrey, The 1984 Campaign for Liberalisation of Japanese Capital Markets, paper presented at the 'International Symposium on Current Issues in Changes in Socio-Economic Structure and Their International Implications' Tokyo, August 1984.

Friedman, Milton (ed.) *Studies in the Quantity Theory of Money* Chicago: University of Chicago Press, 1966.

Fry, Maxwell J. 'Money and Capital or Financial Deepening in Economic Development' *Journal of Money, Credit and Banking* 10, 4, 1978.

—— 'Models of Financially Repressed Developing Economies' *World Development* 10, 9, 1982.

—— 'Inflation and Economic Growth in Pacific Basin Developing Economies' in Federal Reserve Bank of San Francisco *Economic Review* Fall 1984.

—— 'Interest Rates in Asia' IMF mimeo, 1981.

—— 'Financial Structure, Monetary Policy and Economic Growth in Hong Kong, Singapore, Taiwan and Korea, 1960–1981' University of California (Irvine) mimeo, May 1983.

Galenson, Walter (ed.) *Economic Growth and Structural Change in Taiwan* Ithaca: Cornell University Press, 1979.

Garnaut, Ross (ed.) *ASEAN in a Changing Pacific and World Economy* Canberra: Australian National University Press, 1980.

Ghatak, Subrata *Monetary Economics in Developing Countries* New York: St Martin's Press, 1981.

Goldsmith, Raymond W. *Financial Structure and Development* New Haven: Yale University Press, 1969.

Grub, P.D. et al. *East Asia: Dimensions of International Business* Australia: Prentice-Hall, 1982.

Grubel, Herbert G. 'Towards a Theory of Free Economic Zones' *Weltwirtschaftliches Archiv* 118, 1, 1982.

—— 'The New International Banking' in Banca Nazionale del Lavoro *Quarterly Review* 1983.

Gurley, John G. and Shaw, Edward S. 'Financial Development and Economic Development' *Economic Development and Cultural Change* 15, 3, April 1967.

Hagiwara, Yoshiyaki (ed.) *Asia in the 1980s: Interdependence, Peace and Development* Institute of Developing Economies, Symposium Proceedings No. 7, Tokyo: 1982.

Haseyama, T. et al. *Two Decades of Asian Development and Outlook for the 1980s* Tokyo: Institute of Developing Economies, 1983.

Hewson, J. *Liquidity Creating and Distribution in the Eurocurrency Markets* Washington, D.C.: Heath Lexington Books, 1975.

—— and Sakakibara, E. *The Eurocurrency Markets and Their Implications—A 'New View' of International Monetary Problems and Monetary Reform* Washington, D.C.: Heath Lexington Books, 1975.

—— and Niehans, J. 'The Eurodollar Market and Monetary Theory' *Journal of Money, Credit and Banking* August 1976.

Hill, Hal 'Survey of Recent Developments' *Bulletin of Indonesian Economic Studies* 20, 2, 1984.

—— and Johns, Brian 'The Role of Direct Foreign Investment in Developing East Asian Countries' *Weltwirtschaftliches Archiv* 1984.

Hodjera, Zoran 'The Asian Currency Market: Singapore as a Regional Financial Centre' *IMF Staff Papers* June 1978.

Hong, Wontack *Trade, Distortions and Employment Growth in Korea* Seoul: Korea Development Institute, 1979.

Hong Kong, Department of Census and Statistics *Estimates of Gross Domestic Product, 1966–1983* Hong Kong: 1983.

—— *Hong Kong Monthly Digest of Statistics* (n.d.)

Hope, Nicholas C. and McMurray, David W., Loan Capital in Development Finance: The Role of Banks and Some Implications for Managing Debt, mimeo (n.p.), 1983.

Horiuchi, A., Economic Growth and Financial Allocation in Postwar Japan, University of Tokyo Working Paper, 1984.

Hosomi, Takashi 'A Draft Plan for the Establishment of an International Banking Facility in Tokyo' in the Institute for Financial Affairs *Newsletter: Money and Finance* Tokyo: February 1983.

Hufbauer, Gary and Adler, Michael *Overseas Manufacturing Investment and the US Balance of Payments* Washington, D.C.: US Treasury Department, 1968.

IMF 'Interest Rate Policies in Developing Countries' Occasional Paper No. 22, October 1983.

Jao, Y.C. *Banking and Currency in Hong Kong: A Study of Postwar Financial Development* London: Macmillan, 1974.

Johnson, Harry (ed.) *The New Mercantilism: Some Problems in International Trade, Money and Investment* Oxford: Basil Blackwell, 1974.

Jones, Leroy P. and Sakong Il *Government, Business and Entrepreneurship in Economic Development: The Korean Case* Cambridge, Mass.: Harvard University Council on East Asian Studies, 1980.

Jones, R. and Kenen, P. (eds) *Handbook in International Economics* Amsterdam: North Holland, 1984.

Kane, Edward J. 'Policy Implications of Structural Change in Financial Markets' *American Economic Review* No. 73, May 1983.

Kano, T. 'Interdependence in the ASEAN Region' Institute of Developing Economies Paper, Tokyo: 1980.

Katz, Jeffrey A. 'Capital Flows and Developing Country Debt' World Bank Staff Working Paper No. 352, 1979.

Khan, M. 'The Dynamics of Money and Prices and the Role of Monetary Policy in SEACEN Countries' The Southeast Asian Central Banks Research and Training Centre, Occasional Paper No. 1, 1980.

Kindelberger, Charles P. *The Formation of Financial Centres* Princeton: Princeton University Press, 1974.

King, Frank H.H. (ed.) *Eastern Banking: Essays in the History of the Hong Kong and Shanghai Banking Corporation* London: Athlone Press, 1983.

Kohsaka, Akira 'The High Interest Rate Policy in Economic Development' Institute of Developing Economies mimeo, Tokyo: March 1984.

Kouri, P. and Macedo, J. 'Exchange Rates and the International Adjustment Process' *Brookings Papers in Economic Activity* No. 1, 1978.

Kumar, Krishna, and McLeod, Maxwell G. (eds) *Multinationals from Developing Countries* Lexington: Lexington Books, 1981.

Kwack, Taewan 'Investment Allocation on a CGE Model for Korea' Korea Development Institute mimeo, October 1983.

Lecraw, Donald J. 'Comments on Wells' *Research in International Business and Finance* Vol. 4, Part A, 1984.

Lee, Dukhoon 'Recent Developments in Korea's Financial Sector' Economic Research Institute Discussion Paper No. 30, Economic Planning Agency, Tokyo: March, 1984.

Lee, Jungsoo 'The External Debt-Servicing Capacity of Asian Developing Countries' *Asian Development Review* 1, 2, 1983.

Lee Sheng-Yi 'Inflation and the Monetary and Banking System of Hong Kong' *Hong Kong Economic Report* 15 March, 1983.

—— 'Recent Developments in the Asian Currency Market and the Asian Bond Market' Institute of Economics and Business Studies Occasional Paper No. 32, Nanyang University, 1979.

Lee Sheng-Yi 'Foreign Exchange Management in Singapore' *Asia Pacific Journal of Management* August 1984.

—— and Jao, Y.C. *Financial Structures and Monetary Policies in Southeast Asia* New York: St Martin's Press, 1982.

Lin, Jian-Hai, Issues in Debt-Management: The China Perspective, mimeo (n.p.), 1984.

Long, M. 'Review of Financial Sector Work in the World Bank' World Bank mimeo, 1982.

Macedo, J., Exchange Rate Volatility in an Interdependent World Economy, draft paper, Princeton University, May 1983.

——, Small Countries in Monetary Unions: A Two-Tier Model, draft paper, Princeton University, April 1984.

—— 'Policy Interdependence under Flexible Exchange Rates: A Two-Country Model' Woodrow Wilson School, Discussion Paper in Economics No. 62, May 1983.

Machlup, F. et al. *Reflections on a Troubled World Economy—Essays in Honour of Herbert Giersch* London: Macmillan, 1982.

Maniotis, G.C. 'Reliability of the Equities Market to Finance Industrial Development in Greece' *Economic Development and Cultural Change* 19, 4, July 1971.

Marshall, A. *Money, Credit and Commerce* London: Macmillan, 1922.

McKinnon, Ronald I. *Money and Capital in Economic Development* Washington, D.C.: The Brookings Institution, 1973.

—— (ed.) *Money and Finance in Economic Growth and Development* New York: Marcel Dekker, 1976.

—— *An International Standard for Monetary Stabilisation* Washington, D.C.: Institute for International Economics, 1984.

—— and Beach, B. 'A Maximum Likelihood Procedure for Regression with Auto-Correlated Errors' *Econometrica* Vol. 46, 1978.

McLeod, Ross H., Finance and Entrepreneurship in the Small Business Sector in Indonesia, PhD Dissertation, Australian National University, 1982.

Monetary Authority of Singapore *Annual Report 1978–79* Singapore: 1979.

—— *Papers on Monetary Economics* Singapore: Singapore University Press, 1981.

Moxon, Richard W. et al. 'International Business and the Century of the Pacific' *Research in International Business and Finance* Vol. 4, Part A, 1984.

Mundell, R.A. *International Economics* New York: Macmillan, 1984.

Naya, Seiji 'Effects of External Shocks on the Balance of Payments, Policy Responses and Debt Problems of Asian Developing Countries' *Philippine Economic Journal* 23, 1, 1984.

NBER 'The Global Implications of the Trade Patterns of East and Southeast Asia' Conference Proceedings, Kuala Lumpur: January 1984.

OECD *Development Cooperation* Paris: OECD Publications, (n.d.).

—— *The Internationalisation of Banking—The Policy Issues* Paris: OECD Publications, 1983.

Oudiz, G. and Sachs, J. 'International Policy Coordination in Dynamic Macroeconomic Models' NBER Working Paper No. 1417, August 1984.

Pangetsu, Mari 'Japanese and Other Foreign Investment in the ASEAN Countries' Australia–Japan Research Centre Paper No. 73, 1980.

Park, Y.C. 'Export-Led Growth and Industrial Transformation in Korea, 1970–80' Institute of Economic Development Discussion Paper No. 7, Korea University, December 1983.

Patrick, Hugh T. 'Financial Development and Economic Growth in Underdeveloped Countries' *Economic Development and Cultural Change* 14, 2, January 1966.

—— 'Interest Rates and the Grey Financial Market in Japan' *Pacific Affairs* Winter 1965–66.

Rana, P.B. *ASEAN Exchange Rates: Policies and Trade Effects* Singapore: ASEAN Economics Research Unit, Institute of Southeast Asian Studies, 1981.

Ranis, Gustav et al. *Comparative Development Perspectives* Boulder: Westview Press, 1984.

—— and Ohkawa, Kazushi (eds) *Japan and the Developing Countries* Oxford: Basil Blackwell, 1984.

Reich, Robert B. *The Next American Frontier* New York: Times Books, 1983.

Reserve Bank of Australia 'Overseas Operations of Australian Banks' *Statistical Bulletin* February 1982.

Revelli, Jack 'International Financial Centres' University of Pavia Discussion paper, June 1983.

Sakakibara, E. and Kondoh, A. 'Study on the Internationalisation of Tokyo's Money Markets' in Japan Center for International Finance *Policy Study Series* No. 1, June 1984.

Samuels, J.M. and Yacout, N. 'Stock Exchanges in Developing Countries' *Savings and Development* Vol. 5, 1981.

Saw, Swee Hock and Hong, Hai (eds) *Growth and Direction of ASEAN Trade* Singapore: Singapore University Press, 1982.

Sekiguchi, Sueo (ed.) *ASEAN–Japan Relations: Investment* Singapore: Institute of Southeast Asian Studies, 1983.

Shaw, E.S. *Financial Deepening in Economic Development* London: Oxford University Press, 1973.

Shearer, Ronald A. et al. *The Economics of the Canadian Financial System· Theory, Policy and Institutions* 2nd edn, Ontario: Prentice-Hall, 1983.

Singapore Department of Statistics *Survey of Service Sector* Singapore: 1980.

Skully, Michael T. *ASEAN Regional Financial Cooperation: Developments in Banking and Finance* Singapore: Institute of Southeast Asian Studies, 1979.

—— *Merchant Banking in the Far East* London: Financial Times Business Publishing, 1980.

—— *Financial Institutions and Markets in Southeast Asia* London: Macmillan, forthcoming.

—— (ed.) *Financial Institutions and Markets in the Far East* London: Macmillan, 1982.

Stammer, D.W. 'Financial Development and Economic Growth in Underdeveloped Countries: Comment' *Economic Development and Cultural Change* 20, 2, January 1972.

Stiglitz, J.E. and Weiss, A. 'Credit Rationing in Markets with Imperfect Formation' *American Economic Review* June 1981.

Summers, R. and Heston, A. 'Improved International Comparisons of Real Product and Its Composition, 1950–1980' *Reveiw of Income and Welath* June 1984.

Supachai, P. 'Financial Structure: Segmentation and Development' in Bank of Thailand *Quarterly Bulletin* 21, 1, 1981.

Swoboda, A.K. 'Exchange Rate Regimes and U.S.–European Policy Interdependence' in *IMF Staff Papers* March 1983.

Tan, Kong-Yam, Flexible Exchange Rates and Interdependence: Empirical Implications for U.S. Monetary Policy, PhD Dissertation, Standford University, California, 1984.

Taylor, L. *Structuralist Macroeconomics: Applicable Models for the Third World* New York: Basic Books, 1983.

Thee, K.W. 'Japanese Direct Investment in Indonesian Manufacturing' *Bulletin of*

Indonesian Economic Studies 20, 2, August 1984.

United Nations *Economic Cooperation for ASEAN* New York: 1972.

—— *Transnational Corporations in World Development: Third Survey* New York: 1983.

Van Wijnbergen, S. 'Interest Rate Management in LDCs' Journal of Monetary Economics 12, 2, September 1983.

—— 'Short-Run Macroeconomic Adjustment Policies in South Korea: A Quantitative Analysis' World Bank Staff Working Paper No. 524, 1982.

Vernon, R. 'International Investment and International Trade in the Product Cycle' *Quarterly Journal of Economics* May 1966.

Vishkins, G.J. *Financial Deepening in ASEAN Countries* Honolulu: Pacific Forum, 1980.

Von Furstenberg, G. (ed.) *International Money and Credit: The Policy Roles* IMF, 1984.

Von Pischke, J.D. et al. *Rural Financial Markets in Developing Countries* Baltimore: Johns Hopkins University Press, 1983.

Wai, U Tun and Patrick, H.T. 'Stock and Bond Issues and Capital Markets in Less Developed Countries' *IMF Staff Papers* July 1973.

Wang, Y.K. 'Monetary Interdependence among ASEAN Countries' in United Nations *ASEAN and Pacific Economic Cooperation Development Papers* No. 2, 1983.

Wells, R.G.J. 'The Rural Credit Market in Peninsular Malaysia: A Focus on Informal Lenders' *Asian Economies* No. 31, December 1979.

Wells, Louis T. Jr. 'Multinationals from Asian Developing Countries' *Research in International Business and Finance* Vol. 4, Part A, 1984.

Williamson, J. (ed.) *Exchange Rate Rules* London: Macmillan, 1981.

Wong, John 'The Integration of China into the Western Pacific Basin Economy: Implications for ASEAN' Institute of Developing Economies Report, Tokyo: 1983.

—— 'ASEAN Economies: Growth and Adjustment' *Studies of Business and Industry* March 1984.

Wu, Yuan-li and Wu, Chun-hsi *Economic Development in Southeast Asia—The Chinese Dimension* Stanford: Hoover Institution Press, 1980.

Yoshitomi, M. 'The Insulation and Transmission Mechanisms of Floating Exchange Rates: Analysed by the EPA World Econometric Model' Economic Planning Agency mimeo, Tokyo: March 1984.

Youngson, A.J. (ed.) *China and Hong Kong: The Economic Nexus* Hong Kong: Oxford University Press, 1983.

Index

Italicised page numbers are for tables/figures. References to footnotes are to the page in the text in whcih they occur. A reference such as 203&n1 means that the footnote continues the discussion of the text. P.T. = Peseroan Terbatas (Indonesian limited company).